Photographic Returns

Photographic Returns

Racial Justice and the Time of Photography

Shawn Michelle Smith

Duke University Press *Durham and London* 2020

Printed in the United States of America on acid-free paper ∞
Designed by Drew Sisk
Typeset in Minion Pro, Italian Oldstyle MT, and Grotesque MT
by Tseng Information Systems, Inc.

Library of Congress Cataloging-in-Publication Data
Names: Smith, Shawn Michelle, [date] author.
Title: Photographic returns : racial justice and the time of photography / Shawn Michelle Smith.
Description: Durham : Duke University Press, 2020. | Includes bibliographical references and index.
Identifiers:
LCCN 2019015471 (print)
LCCN 2019980936 (ebook)
ISBN 9781478004684 (paperback)
ISBN 9781478004073 (hardcover)
ISBN 9781478005537 (ebook)
Subjects: LCSH: Photography in ethnology—United States—History. | Documentary photography—United States—History. | Art and photography—United States. | Photography in historiography. | Photography—Social aspects—United States—History. | Art and history—United States.
Classification: LCC GN347 .S658 2020 (print) | LCC GN 347 (ebook) | DDC 779/.93058—dc23
LC record available at https://lccn.loc.gov/2019015471
LC ebook record available at https://lccn.loc.gov/2019980936

Cover art: Rashid Johnson, *The New Negro Escapist Social and Athletic Club (Emmett)*, 2008. Lambda print, 48.5 × 73 inches. Courtesy of the artist and David Kordansky Gallery, Los Angeles.

Duke University Press gratefully acknowledges the support of the School of the Art Institute of Chicago, which provided funds toward the publication of this book.

CONTENTS

ACKNOWLEDGMENTS

I began to write this book under the auspices of a Georgia O'Keeffe Museum Research Center Fellowship in Santa Fe, New Mexico, in 2012–13, and I am forever grateful for the opportunity to spend a year in Santa Fe reading, writing, and thinking. A warm thank you to Carolyn Kastner and Eumie Imm-Stroukoff for making my year at the O'Keeffe so productive and engaging, and for their continued friendship. The fellows that year included Wanda Corn, Liam Considine, Emily Moore, and Nancy Mithlo, and it was a real pleasure to be in conversation with all of them. Cory Kratz and Kymberly Pinder provided homes away from home in the high desert.

The School of the Art Institute of Chicago has also been generous in supporting this project. I am thankful for a Shapiro Center Research Fellowship, which enabled me to work with a wonderful graduate research fellow, Erika Råberg, and a Roger Brown Residency, which gave me the time and space and peace of mind to work out a key portion of the text. I am also indebted once again to the dean of faculty at the time, Lisa Wainwright, who supported publication of the book with a subvention for the color plates.

Chapter 1 was first published in *Pictures and Power: Imaging and Imagining Frederick Douglass, 1818–2018*, edited by Celeste-Marie Bernier and Bill E. Lawson (Liverpool, UK: Liverpool University Press, 2017), 254–73. It is reprinted here with the permission of Liverpool University Press. Chapter 2 was originally published as "Photographic Remains: Sally Mann at Antietam," in *The Civil War in Art and Memory*, edited by Kirk Savage, Studies in the History of Art 81 (Washington, DC: National Gallery of Art, 2016), 103–24. It is reprinted here with the permission of the National Gallery of Art, Washington, DC, all rights reserved. A portion of chapter 5 was first published as "The Afterimages of Emmett Till," *American Art* 29, no. 1 (spring 2015): 22–27; and another portion of that chapter was published as "Archive of the Ordinary:

Jason Lazarus, *Too Hard to Keep*," *Journal of Visual Culture* 17, no. 2 (August 2018): 198–206, reprinted here by permission of SAGE Publications.

I presented portions of chapters in progress at a number of institutions, where thoughtful questions and comments from colleagues helped me to shape and focus my argument: Universität der Künste Berlin, Germany; University of the Western Cape, Cape Town, South Africa; Maison des Sciences de l'Homme, Saint Denis, Paris, France; European University, Saint Petersburg, Russia; Fotografika, Saint Petersburg, Russia; the University of Sydney, Australia; the National Gallery of Art, Washington, DC; Wayne State University; the University of Illinois, Urbana-Champaign; the University of Michigan, Ann Arbor; the Clark Art Institute; Williams College; the University of California, San Diego; Duke University; the University of California, Santa Cruz; Yale University; the University of California, Berkeley; the California College of the Arts; Washington University, St. Louis; Vanderbilt University; the Abraham Lincoln Presidential Library and Museum; Brown University; the Center for the Advanced Study in the Visual Arts, National Gallery of Art, Washington, DC; the Georgia O'Keeffe Museum Research Center; the University of New Mexico Art Museum; the Art Gallery of York University; the Newberry Library; and the American Studies Association annual meetings. My presentations in Saint Petersburg were supported by the US Embassy Moscow Speakers Office and the US Consulate General in Saint Petersburg. For their generous collegiality, I would especially like to thank Sebastian Köthe, Patricia Hayes, Magali Nachtergael, Maria Gourieva, Friedrich Tietjen, Donna West Brett, Natalya Lusty, Sarah Greenough, Sarah Kennel, Sara Blair, Kyle Frisina, Margaret Olin, Amos Morris-Reich, Mark Reinhardt, Lisa Cartwright, Elizabeth Wolfson, Priscilla Wald, Cheryl Spinner, Jennifer González, Jordan Reznick, Sarah Richter, Alyssa Bralower, Jessie Landau, Kate Phillips, Diana Rosenberger, Kelly Polasek, Renée Hoogland, Dora Apel, Lauren Kroiz, Leigh Raiford, Bryan Wagner, Tirza Latimer, Matthew Fox-Amato, Angela Miller, Jennifer Fay, Teresa Goddu, Lisa Guenther, Matthew Pratt Guterl, Ralph Rodriguez, Tricia Rose, Kymberly Pinder, Erika Doss, and Philip Monk.

For their brilliant insights, the example of their work, and many years of conversation, I am grateful to Laura Wexler, Priscilla Wald, Wendy Walters, Sara Blair, Leigh Raiford, Sharon Sliwinski, Elspeth Brown, Thy Phu, Sarah Parsons, Sarah Bassnett, Ruby Tapia, Erika Doss, Margaret Olin, Deborah Willis, Maurice Wallace, David Serlin, Ralph Rodriguez, Joseph Heathcott, Ashley Cruce, and Kelly McKaig.

I have also benefitted from the camaraderie of colleagues close to home, and I would like to thank the faculty and students of the Visual and Critical Studies Department at the School of the Art Institute of Chicago. I am especially indebted to Terri Kapsalis and Romi Crawford for their wisdom, generosity, and kindness. Through SAIC I am privileged to know dazzling thinkers and writers and makers, many of whom have been willing to lend this project an ear: Patrick Rivers, Kai Mah, Ellen Rothenberg, Dan Eisenberg, Mary Patten, Frederic Moffet, Oliver Sann, David Getsy, Margaret MacNamidhe, James Elkins, Rachel Weisz, Jefferson Pinder, and Sara Levine—thank you. There are wonderful scholars writing about African American art and visual culture in Chicago, and the work of Romi Crawford, Amy Mooney, Krista Thompson, Huey Copeland, and Darby English has influenced my thinking throughout this book.

Great thanks to all of the artists for their work, and for so generously sharing it with me: Rashid Johnson, Sally Mann, Deborah Luster, Lorna Simpson, Catherine Wagner, Jason Lazarus, Carrie Mae Weems, Taryn Simon, Stephen Spretnjack, and Dawoud Bey.

I am grateful to Ken Wissoker for his continued support and wise guidance, to Olivia Polk for staying with this project through all the details, and to Christine Riggio for going above and beyond with her help on the images. I would also like to thank the two anonymous readers for their insights and comments, which helped me to fine-tune the text throughout.

I cannot express my debt and gratitude to my family, but I can at least offer a profound thank you to Sandy, Jay, and Shannon Smith; Derek Hutchinson; and Haley and Dylan. My greatest thanks, as always and for everything, are to Joe Masco.

INTRODUCTION

Photographic Returns

Photographic Returns: Racial Justice and the Time of Photography is about contemporary photography that has one eye on the past. It studies art produced in the twenty-first century that draws into view historical moments of racial crisis and transformation in the United States that have also figured prominently in the history of photography. In concert with the work it addresses, the book calls attention to historical events that are known photographically, and in this way it is about the photography of history as much as the history of photography. It proposes that there is a temporal recursivity intrinsic to photography, a backward and forward movement inherent to the medium that invites such returns. The book highlights the fundamental oscillation of photographic time, as it also underscores the ways a number of artists deploy the temporal disruption of the photograph to expose the unfinished work of racial justice in the United States and the racialization of rights and privileges that persists today. As the book invites one to consider the time of photography, it also asks one to contemplate the well-past time of racial justice.

The photograph is emblematic of the way a past continues to inhabit and punctuate a present, and also one of the central vehicles through which that temporal collision takes place. As the artists studied here return to earlier moments they do so by returning to photographs, both heeding and initiating a chain of fluctuating temporalities. Their images refer to and call forth other images. They follow photographs to variously trace, bend, pierce, truncate, extend, and fold time, drawing viewers back and forth across mutable time lines.

When I began writing this book, I set out to consider the present, not the past. I wanted to focus my attention on contemporary art, rather than the nineteenth- and early twentieth-century photographs that had captured my imagination for so long. But in the course of my exploration, I found that the past persistently returned, and that contemporary photography brought conflicted pasts into view in unexpected ways. I discovered a striking coalescence of American artists working with photography in the first decade of the twenty-first century, artists of different generations, genders, races, and regions, who turned their attention back to historical moments of contest over the future of racial justice in the United States.

The artists studied here include Rashid Johnson, Sally Mann, Deborah Luster, Lorna Simpson, Jason Lazarus, Carrie Mae Weems, and Taryn Simon. They do not constitute a school or a movement, and in style and technique their work varies widely. Much of the work is political, but it is not uniformly so, and it often announces itself as such only obliquely. By curating the work of these artists together, I stage a conversation in which political import is animated by my readings and accrues across the separate case studies. I have identified a common current that runs through the work, a pattern of historical revelation and return, a unifying impulse to look to historical moments in order to negotiate the present, an inclination that is activated by photography's temporal dynamic. The specific returns examined here highlight legacies of antiblack racism and resistance, legacies that have situated the artists and their viewers in the present in significantly different ways. Indeed, the white artists do not carry the same burden as their African American peers in negotiating what Darby English has called "black representational space,"[1] but my reading of their work suggests that the history of antiblack racism in the United States has indelibly shaped the worlds they inhabit.[2]

The convergence of artists working on the temporal push and pull of historical moments of racial crisis and resistance suggests a shared impetus, a common motivation, a prevailing concern. Yet it is difficult to say what specific pressures animated these artists and compelled them to produce this work in the first decade of the twenty-first century, what hopes, ambitions, anxieties, and, more profoundly, what unconscious impulses, sent them back to earlier moments of conflict. A number of the artists have noted personal influences that will be detailed in the subsequent chapters, but I am more interested in their collective inclination to produce work with a backward look in this decade, and the way that shared impetus suggests that they were attuned to broader cultural influences and powerful, albeit inchoate, affective forces. What defined this decade in the United States? Among many registers of precarity one might cite the attacks of 9/11, the War on Terror, the revelation of torture at Abu Ghraib prison, the detentions at Guantanamo Bay, the exponentially increasing incarceration of men and women of color, Hurricane Katrina and its deadly aftermath, the financial crisis of 2008, and the increasingly felt effects of climate change. Some of the artists may have been spurred by a millennial reckoning, a desire to contemplate the century passing as a new century turned forward. Others perhaps, and one artist explicitly, were compelled to come to terms with what the presidency of Barack Obama meant in the long fight against antiblack racism in the United States. Certainly these events informed my own thinking during the first decade of the twenty-first century, and more recently, during the years I have been writing this book: the fatal shooting of Trayvon Martin; the police killings of Michael Brown, Eric Garner, Laquan McDonald, Philando Castile, and so many others; and the countervailing response of the Black Lives Matter movement initiated by Alicia Garza, Opal Tometi, and Patrisse Cullors have loomed large in my mind, bringing the work of the artists studied here, as well as the images to which they refer, into sharper focus as part of a history of antiblack violence as well as resistance to it. Indeed, one of the fundamental premises of this book is that how different pasts are activated and become visible is profoundly influenced by the present that one inhabits. Historical work is never only about a past; it is also about finding a way through a present and imagining a future.

In their reckonings with US history, the artists studied here also wrestle with photography, highlighting its extraordinary temporality, its materiality, its particularity as well as its expansiveness. Their work is about photography as much as it is about history and what any given photograph might be said to represent. In this light, it is striking how many of the artists have turned to analogue technologies and even nineteenth-century processes, such as wet-plate collodion. In the digital age they have chosen to work slowly, to encumber themselves with heavy cameras and messy chemistry and darkrooms, or they have collected and compiled paper prints, or they have sought to amplify the materiality of the ephemeral image by printing it on metal plates or felt panels. In the same decade in which many artists sought to understand the proliferation of images in the era of digital photography, smartphone cameras, and social media, to explore the new ways in which people make, share, access, encounter, and use images now, these artists have turned to analogue and antique forms.[3] In doing so, they create a moment of pause in the rush of the digital era, highlighting the ways in which photography can slow down as well as accelerate time.

Returning to earlier moments, these artists also return to periods in which the individual photograph had the potential to endure in a less crowded and fleeting visual terrain. Rashid Johnson, for example, styles himself after a portrait of Frederick Douglass, said to be the most photographed American of the nineteenth century, with 160 distinct images, an impressive number for the time that diminishes entirely in the era of the selfie.[4] A number of the other artists recall photographs and photographers included in *TIME*'s 2016 selection of "100 Photos"—"The Most Influential Images of All Time"—which range across three centuries, from Joseph Nicéphore Niépce's *View from the Window at Le Gras* (1826) to Nilüfer Demir's photograph of Alan Kurdi, a drowned Syrian refugee boy, taken in 2015.[5] Among them, Jason Lazarus evokes David Jackson's postmortem images of Emmett Till made in 1955, Sally Mann conjures Alexander Gardner's Civil War photographs made at Antietam in 1862, and Lorna Simpson recalls James VanDerZee's portraits of stylish African Americans made in the 1930s. Carrie Mae Weems works directly with three of the photographs on *TIME*'s list, including John Paul Filo's photograph of the Kent State University Massacre in 1970, as discussed in chapter 6. These contemporary artists return to iconic images, to photographs that have become stand-ins for expansive, mobile, and sometimes contradictory meanings. They bear witness to photographs and to photography itself at a moment in which it is difficult to predict whether any single image, or one hundred singular images, can and will have staying power in the years to come. As the curators for *TIME*'s "100 Photos" note, "In 2016 alone, hundreds of billions of images were made."[6]

Photographic Returns studies the time of photography, focusing on its fragmentation and multiplicity, its repetition and recurrence. The photograph encapsulates a temporal oscillation, always signifying in relation to a past and a present, and anticipating a future. It refers to the moment of its making as well as the many possible moments of its viewing. One might make similar claims for other kinds of representation, but the time of the photograph is distinguished by the relative instantaneity of its production and its famed indexicality. The photograph records the often imperceptible increment of time in which a camera shutter opens to expose a negative or sensor to reflected light, and in this way it seems to stop time, or to wrest a moment out of the flow of time. It makes visible a constellation of forces and things that came together in front of a camera's lens for a fraction of a second, drawing a moment into view in a way that it was never experienced. It functions as a trace of its subject, of light, and of time itself, and in this way it feels forever tethered to the moment of its making, intrinsically bound to the moment it records. But this stopping of time is also the starting of another time, the temporal trajectory of the photograph itself, and that time is multiple. Iconic images in particular accrue varied meanings for different generations, significations that are not fully effaced as they are transformed and passed on. In other words, the photograph does not return from a single past, the moment of its making, but accumulates the many pasts through which it passes, both synchronically and diachronically. The photograph is a record of a moment and its many possible receptions, and in this way it is always of pasts and presents and futures.

This book proposes that the temporality of photography informs historical understanding by exposing the openness of the present to the past. The photograph is an emblem of temporal disturbance that shows, quite literally, how a past inhabits a present.[7] For Roland Barthes, the photograph is a form of "temporal hallucination" that catapults a past moment into a viewer's present.[8] Despite a tenacious faith in the fixity of the image, the photograph does not preserve a past that is stable and accessible. It delivers a mutable and multiple past into a varied and shifting present. Indeed, the changing meaning of an image over time highlights the instability of the past, and the ways one comes to know a past differently in a mobile present. But this is not to say that the photograph is the standard of a kind of historical relativism, for even as an image is made legible within specific cultural discourses that shift and change its meaning over time, one of the photograph's striking characteristics remains its indexical status as a trace. The photograph presents a kind of brute fact, but one that is not necessarily meaningful. Bringing the visibility of photographic evidence into legibility is the work of artists and scholars, and fundamentally the task of this book. The photograph carries a tiny shard of reflected light into the moment of its viewing, offering a tiny flash of a past to a viewer who needs it.[9]

Among the artists discussed here, Rashid Johnson and Sally Mann look back to slavery and the Civil War, Lorna Simpson returns to the Harlem Renaissance, and Jason Lazarus and Carrie Mae Weems recall the civil rights movement. The periods and problems they explore have been central to the history of photography in the United States, just as photography has shaped the ways in which one understands their significance today. The Civil War, for example, was the first war in the United States to be covered by photographers, and illustrations made after photographs circulated widely for a national audience in *Harper's Weekly*. In the twentieth century, photographs from the civil rights movement became the most iconic images of antiblack racism and the African American struggle for civil rights in US history. For contemporary photographers and conceptual artists, such images provide touchstones for thinking about history's hold on the present, as well as historical amnesias and blind spots. While many of the artists studied here return to specific images and events, others recall widespread photographic practices invented and institutionalized in the nineteenth century. Deborah Luster and Taryn Simon turn their attention to police and prison photography, engaging disciplinary forms of visual inscription such as the mug shot and the crime scene photograph. My reading of their work points to systemic racism and the contemporary crisis of race and citizenship Michelle Alexander has called "The New Jim Crow."[10]

As *Photographic Returns* highlights the fluctuating temporality of photography, it also calls attention to the material history of the medium. Jason Lazarus collects snapshots that represent a range of popular twentieth-century analogue forms, while Sally Mann and Deborah Luster employ nineteenth-century photographic techniques. Mann, for example, uses an antique large-format view camera and wet-plate collodion, reenacting the photographic process of Alexander Gardner who photographed Civil War battlefields long before her. Mann's practice seems designed to accentuate the materiality of her images and the process of making them, and in this way it encourages one to employ what Elizabeth Edwards has called a "'material hermeneutic'" that moves "the analysis of photographs from questions of representation alone to questions of material practice."[11] In league with the artists studied here, this book invites one to take note of the material history of photography and its changing forms as well as its discursive parameters.

As photographers like Mann emphasize the making of their work, they highlight the performativity of photographic practice on both sides of the camera. Carrie Mae Weems's images are especially salient in this regard, as she and her collaborators have reenacted iconic civil rights era photographs, re-performing the poses and postures of people caught on film in moments of crisis. In some of the images she leaves video cameras on tracks visible in the frame, highlighting the performative staging of her scenes. Like Weems, Simpson and Johnson also underscore the performance of subjects for the camera, drawing out the collaborative work that takes place in the photographer's studio as people craft their images for later viewers.

Weems remakes documentary images in the realm of art, and the other artists studied here similarly transfer images from one institutional location to another, from the prison to the museum, the newspaper to the classroom to the gallery.[12] As they bring images from one era into another, they also move them from one discursive context to another. The artists mine a wide array of photographic genres, including police and prison photography; documentary, scientific, taxonomic, and ethnographic photography; portraiture, landscape, and the snapshot. They highlight, transform, and denaturalize the genres they engage. Focusing on photography per se, as well as specific modes of photography, they call attention to the medium itself and its many cultural forms. In this way, they refuse to allow the photograph to be conceived as transparent and foreground the work of photography in producing culturally legible subjects.[13]

The Photography of History

As Roland Barthes proclaimed, "The same century invented History and Photography."[14] And so perhaps it is not surprising that the two would be intimately intertwined. But for Barthes, the simultaneity of the two inventions in the nineteenth century presents "a paradox," because if history aims for narrative progression, photography offers temporal rupture.[15] In the almost two centuries since their advent, the relationship between history and photography remains perplexing, as well as generative, and it is this evocative correlation that provides the impetus for this book and the work that it studies.

The photograph heralded an age in which people were "no longer able to conceive *duration*," according to Barthes. "The age of the Photograph is also the age of revolutions, contestations, assassinations, explosions, in short, of impatiences, of everything which denies ripening."[16] Photography proffers what Walter Benjamin called the "dynamite of the split second," presenting flashes, fragments, and fleeting instants.[17] In this way it unsettled nineteenth-century understandings of history founded on advancement and unfolding, even as it was coterminous with them.[18] Photography inaugurated a new way of conceiving history, of apprehending a past in felt fragments.

Writing in the early twentieth century, almost a hundred years after the advent of photography, Benjamin embraced the photograph and its fleeting instants as the emblem of a new historical method. He understood that the photograph, like the historical materialist he celebrated, "blast[s] open the continuum of history."[19] In Eduardo Cadava's words, "The photographic image . . . interrupts history *and opens up another possibility of history*."[20]

Benjamin celebrated photography as a revolutionary art form, and he used photographic language to describe his radical historical method.[21] He sought to intervene in the narrative of history as progress, and he drew on the temporal disruption of the photographic image to make his case for historical materialism. In his aphoristic essay "On the Concept of History," he proclaims: "The true image of the past flits by. The past can be seized only as an image that flashes up at the moment of its recognizability, and is never seen again."[22] Such a moment of recognition strikes when one sees a past repeating in the present and refuses to acquiesce to history's narrative of progress.[23] Grasping "the constellation into which his own era has entered, along with a very specific earlier one,"[24] the historical materialist rejects the idea that the past remains discrete from the present by seizing upon the repetition and return of an image, by taking hold of it as it "flashes up" like a photograph in the present. Photography provided an apt language for Benjamin's historical method because it also disrupts a narrative of historical progression, offering up disjointed views of a past that seeks recognition in a present. As Benjamin called on photography to interrupt a narrative of history as progress, the artists studied here deploy photography to unsettle a narrative of social progress, using the photograph to bring to light the unfinished work of racial justice.

The Civil War was the most profound revolution in the nineteenth-century United States, and it exposed a rupture in the definition of the human inaugurated by slavery that would persist in its wake. As discussed in the first two chapters here, these radical transformations also figured photographically in images made at Civil War battlefields and in portraits of the newly emancipated making claims to freedom and self-possession. Rashid Johnson looks back to Frederick Douglass, who powerfully conjoins slavery, the Civil War, photography, and emancipation in his lecture "Pictures and Progress," discussed in chapter 1. For both Douglass and Johnson, separated by a century and a half, photography provided a fitting medium for registering the rupture of radical transformation as well as the burden of cultural inheritance.

Although photography challenges the conception of duration, the photograph itself endures, transporting a moment into unknown futures, and this is another aspect of its temporal disruption. The image persists, and as it does so, it opens onto new possibilities and enters into new configurations. As the image endures, its meaning changes. A photograph may snap into focus years after its production; it may be seen and understood in a new way at a new time, by a different viewer.[25] This unending aftereffect of the photograph is a dynamic central to the work studied in this book, in which artists engage images from a past and make them visible for new audiences in new ways at new times.

In many respects, the artists studied here engage the historical dynamic Benjamin celebrates. But they do not wait for historical revelations to reveal themselves in flashes. Instead they return to earlier moments and images with purpose, in order to invite consideration of a present in light of a past. Benjamin proposes that history contains images like photographic negatives that remain latent until future events conspire to make them recognizable. In his "Paralipomena" (or supplement) to "On the Concept of History," he states, "If one looks upon history as a text, then one can say of it what a recent author has said of literary texts—namely, that the past has left in them images comparable to those registered by a light-sensitive plate. 'The future alone possesses developers strong enough to reveal the image in all its details.'"[26] Benjamin employs the striking photographic imagery of light-sensitive plates and developers to describe the work of the historical materialist who brings images from the past into view in a new constellation in the present. The artists studied here, working with photography, become the developers of past images, engaging them in new patterns that open the photographs to new considerations, just as this book also draws the artworks and their referents into view in relation to specific constellations of past and present.

One of the places historians and artists find photographs is the archive. As I have argued elsewhere, archives stake a claim to history that is always contested and that many artists and scholars and activists have challenged by creating counterarchives that make visible alternative historical agents and narratives.[27] Further, for scholars such as Ann Stoler and Elizabeth Edwards, even those institutional archives most invested in colonial projects reveal tensions, contradictions, and conflicts in the practice of power.[28] For Edwards the photographic archive is "a place of potential" in which "meanings come in and out of focus, double back on themselves, adhere silently."[29] In other words, although the archive is often an institutional repository invested with authority and defined by material as well as conceptual constraints, it is not a static collection. Indeed, despite its institutional and ideological limitations, its absences and erasures, the archive preserves records that can be put into dynamic play in unanticipated ways. This is due in part to the nature of the photograph itself: "Photographs are very literally raw histories . . . their unprocessed quality, their randomness, their minute indexicality, are inherent to the medium . . . they are ultimately uncontainable."[30] Despite the structures that work to direct photographic meaning in the archive, the photograph is a contingent record, and from its random details artists and scholars can generate new historical visions.[31]

The artists studied here return to the archive as a site of potential, and they underscore the malleability of photographic evidence. All of them are heirs to the critique of photographic transparency that Allan Sekula, Martha Rosler, and John Tagg made so forcefully in the 1970s and 1980s.[32] As they engage and activate photographs as historical artifacts they also undermine them as stable records and authoritative evidence. But the work does not end there; indeed, in many ways that is where it begins, with the photograph as the unsettled and yet necessary link to a past that is also in play.

Not all photographs wait to be found. Some return uninvited. Indeed, as Ulrich Baer has argued, photography might be said to share the structure of trauma.[33] Like the traumatic flashback, the photograph perpetually replays a moment that seems to exist outside of time.[34] Traumatic histories flash up in the present across these chapters: slavery; the Civil War; the murder of Emmett Till; the assassinations of the civil rights era; police, prison, and crime scene photography; misidentification and wrongful conviction. Studying artworks that call forth photographs from these earlier moments, this book seizes on images that will not stay in place, and deploys the instability of the photograph to reconsider a past that is not fixed.

The photograph folds the past into the time of its viewing; it retains what is no longer present. This is the aspect of the photograph's temporality that so startled Barthes, its trenchant hold on a moment that is always already past, its embrace of a subject that is absent.[35] The photograph mirrors the dynamic of melancholia, in which the bereaved subject refuses to relinquish what has been lost. However, rather than understanding melancholia narrowly as a form of emotional arrest, following David L. Eng and David Kazanjian I consider melancholia a more expansive and generative temporal disturbance. In their reading of Freud, Eng and Kazanjian propose: "In melancholia the past remains steadfastly alive in the present." "Melancholia might be said to constitute . . . an ongoing and open relationship with the past—bringing its ghosts and specters, its flaring and fleeting images, into the present."[36] The photograph also carries "ghosts and specters," "flaring and fleeting images" of a past into a present. Its subject is both absent and close at hand, both then and now. Photography, like melancholia, opens a present to a past.

Despite its emphasis on history, the temporal direction of *Photographic Returns* is not only backward looking. The book also thinks with Benjamin about the way futures reside in photographs, waiting for the moment in which they can be recognized. As he outlines in a striking passage in "Little History of Photography," Benjamin saw such futures in "the tiny spark of contingency," the accidental detail, recorded in a photograph: "No matter how artful the photographer, no matter how carefully posed his subject, the beholder feels an irresistible urge to search such a picture for the tiny spark of contingency, of the here and now, with which reality has (so to speak) seared the subject, to find the inconspicuous spot where in the immediacy of that long-forgotten moment the future nests so eloquently that we, looking back, may rediscover it."[37] In the photograph one might find unexpected futures projected out of a past. Seemingly random details might hold the key to other worlds. As Baer has argued, "each photograph opens onto a future that, from *within* the image, is still radically undecided," and therefore photographic pasts might beckon still unanticipated futures.[38] In league with the temporal movement of the photograph itself, this book looks back to move forward.

This backward and forward momentum is most explicitly on display in the first chapter, which offers a reading of Frederick Douglass's early thoughts on photography inspired by Rashid Johnson's performative portrait after Douglass. Writing about photography in 1861 and 1865, Douglass had relatively little technological history to look back on, and indeed, his thoughts are mostly forward looking. Nevertheless, he also intuited that the persistence of the photograph might prove both a promise and a problem for later generations. By keeping a past alive in a present, the photograph could function as an impetus to change as well as a drag against transformation. Responding to Douglass a century and a half later, Johnson takes up both the potential and the burden of photography, highlighting the photograph's dual nature in a self-portrait that is both an homage to Douglass and an irreverent play on impasse.

Photographic Returns engages Benjamin's conception of history to explore the ways in which a past continues to inhabit a present in photographic fragments. The artists studied here put images of a past into play in their own present moments, and viewers understand their work in relation to still other temporal frames. The book invites readers to attend to this temporal dynamic without remaining locked in a historical loop. It encourages a conceptual telescoping of time that allows one to see an ever-shifting present in light of pasts that harbor their own alternative futures.

Photographic Returns focuses on contemporary artworks produced in the first decade of the twenty-first century, with the exception of one piece made in

1995, and another project that is ongoing. The works refer to photographs dating from the 1840s to the 1980s, and the chapters are organized in the chronological order of their historical touchstones. The case studies focus on discrete series and sometimes even a single photograph, situating the images in the historical constellations that flash up around them.

The first two chapters present the widest temporal gap between artwork and the images that inspired them, looking back from the twenty-first century to the mid-nineteenth century. In chapter 1, Rashid Johnson's *Self Portrait with My Hair Parted Like Frederick Douglass* recalls the many photographic portraits of the famous nineteenth-century orator and fugitive slave, as well as his thoughts about the social power and promise of photography. The first chapter is weighted toward Douglass, as if pulled by his gravitational force, but also because many of the considerations of the book unfold from Douglass's early and foundational questions about the effect of photographs on subsequent generations, the transformative power of what was for him a new technology. Looking back at Frederick Douglass's lecture "Pictures and Progress" through the lens of Johnson's work, the first chapter examines the abolitionist's surprising celebration of photography as an objectifying medium. Douglass found progressive power in the technology's capacity to alienate the self, a position one would not expect the formerly enslaved to embrace. As he highlighted photography's progressive potential, he also understood the persistence of photographs to be both a conserving and a conservative force, and Johnson's self-portrait after Douglass testifies to that doubled dynamic. The chapter explores Douglass's complicated embrace of photography as a medium of objectification as well as progress, as a link to the past and a call to the future viewer that Johnson would become.

The second chapter focuses on Sally Mann's Antietam photographs, made at the site of the bloodiest one-day battle of the Civil War, a battle that persuaded President Lincoln to announce the Emancipation Proclamation. Antietam was also the first US battlefield to be photographed before corpses were buried, and Alexander Gardner and James Gibson's gruesome images made in 1862 were circulated widely. Mann worked at Antietam much as her famous forebears did, with a large-format view camera and hand-coated wet collodion glass plates. But unlike those of Gardner and Gibson, Mann's photographs are dark and almost unintelligible. They draw attention to the opacity of the photograph and unsettle ideas about historical reclamation. Ultimately, Mann's Antietam photographs refer less to the site of the infamous battle and more to Gardner and Gibson's early views. Her work proposes that photography, rather than place, bears the weight of the past.

Like Sally Mann, Deborah Luster also uses nineteenth-century photographic technologies. Chapter 3 explores how her project *One Big Self: Prisoners of Louisiana* intervenes in the history of police and prison photography, as her portraits of incarcerated men and women challenge the legacy of visual inscription that frames "the criminal." Luster works both in and outside of the prison, recalling not only the visual history of the mug shot but also that of the crime scene photograph. In *Tooth for an Eye: A Chorography of Violence in Orleans Parish* she returns to crime scenes in New Orleans years after the fact to photograph empty, haunted sites. Her images subtly record a history of structural and systemic violence marked in the urban landscape.

Chapter 4 focuses on Lorna Simpson's enigmatic artwork *9 Props*. The piece is an oblique homage to Harlem Renaissance photographer James VanDerZee and the studio portraits of stylish African American men, women, and children he made in the 1920s, 1930s, and beyond. Working with gaffers at the Pilchuck Glass School in Stanwood, Washington, Simpson made reproductions of the vases that populate VanDerZee's studio in black glass. She then photographed the black vessels as surrogates standing in for VanDerZee's human subjects. Printing her images on felt, Simpson plays on the haptic qualities of the photograph and its status as a material trace. Displacing VanDerZee's central subjects, and highlighting the props in the studio, she underscores the production of an image, the performance of the subject for the camera, and the collaboration of photographer and subject in creating a forward-looking record of aspirations and dreams.

Jason Lazarus's photograph *Standing at the Grave of Emmett Till, Day of Exhumation, June 1st, 2005 (Alsip, Illinois)* launches chapter 5, a meditation on photography and melancholia. It proposes that Lazarus's equivocal photograph provides an emblem for the perpetual return of images of Emmett Till that first circulated in 1955. Those images communicated the horror of Till's murder to a segregated viewing audience, even as they also failed to capture the terrible crime itself. Lazarus's image evokes the paradox of spectacle and absence that characterized Till's murder and that continues to be marked by the repetition and return of Till's photographs over fifty years later. Elaborating on the link between memory and melancholia set forth by *Standing at the Grave*, the chapter also looks to Lazarus's ongoing project, *Too Hard to Keep*. Here the artist solicits submissions of images that people can no longer bear to keep and arranges them in installations of anonymous snapshots. The project engages the mutable nature of photographic meaning as images enter into new relations with other photographs and viewers.

Carrie Mae Weems's *Constructing History* (2008), the focus of chapter 6, exemplifies the most literal of photographic returns studied in this book, namely the reenactment of historical photographs. Weems looks back to iconic images from the civil rights era to reperform and reproduce them with her collaborators. She responds to the felt history of photography, and her reenactments amplify the embodied nature of the photograph's affective charge. As her images refer and defer to earlier photographs, she invites one to consider the role of photography in "constructing history" as well as memory. There is a striking recursivity in the work that comments not only on the relationship of photography to history but also on the nature of photography itself. Chapter 6 frames *Constructing History* as a form of photographic reenactment that calls attention to the disruptive time of photography.

The final chapter explores Taryn Simon's false returns. It studies *The Innocents*, a project in which Simon photographed wrongfully convicted subjects after their exoneration and release from prison. Like Luster's work, Simon's also comments on the historical use of photography in policing and the prison, highlighting specifically the problematic use of the mug shot in eyewitness identification procedures. *The Innocents* offers a critique of photographic evidence, but it is an ambiguous reconsideration that relies on the medium it troubles. Photographing some of her subjects at the scenes of the crimes for which they were convicted but did not commit, Simon folds time around incarceration, orchestrating a false return that situates her subjects on unstable photographic ground. By powerfully bringing into view the victims of mistaken identification, the project also unwittingly obscures other innocents, namely the victims of violent crime.

Photographic Returns concludes with a brief coda that reads Dawoud Bey's *The Birmingham Project* as emblematic of photography's temporal oscillations. Bey's work looks back, but also forward to a viewer whom it asks to take up the unfinished work of racial justice.

Photographic Returns is about the place of photography in history, and the place of history in photography. It explores historical moments of racial crisis that have come to be known photographically, and considers the ways in which a past travels and transforms via photographs. The artists studied here look back to charged moments in the history of the United States and the struggle for African American civil rights that have also figured prominently in the history of photography. There is an important politics to their returns, a vital dynamic that looks back in order to reflect on the present and imagine a way forward, a critical practice that this book engages and expands.

CHAPTER 1

Looking Forward and Looking Back

Rashid Johnson and Frederick Douglass on Photography

The man stares at the camera solemnly. He is turned slightly, but fixes his eyes on the lens, anticipating later viewers. He is dressed formally, in a black suit, white shirt, and striped copper tie. Light touches his features and draws them out of darkness. A soft beard dusts his cheek and chin. His hair, parted on the far left, hangs in shoulder-length locks along his face (plate 1).

This is Rashid Johnson's photograph of 2003, titled *Self Portrait with My Hair Parted Like Frederick Douglass*. In it, the artist has clearly made a careful study of Samuel J. Miller's striking daguerreotype portrait of Frederick Douglass, produced circa 1847–52 (plate 2). He sits at the same angle to the camera, and frames himself tightly, at midchest. He replicates the light that illuminates the orator's forehead, and mimics the serious look on his face. Johnson wears a modern suit, approximating in type if not in kind Douglass's elaborate formal attire. The two images appear as colored inversions of one another: as deep black offsets the golden tones of Johnson's face, the warm hues of a brass matt frame the gray shades of Douglass's image.

Johnson's self-portrait after Douglass elicits a number of questions about photography that are especially compelling in light of the predictions Douglass himself made about the medium. In 1861 and again in 1865, Douglass proclaimed that photography would have far-reaching effects on self-understanding. He proposed that photography made visible a model of the self as object, and somewhat surprisingly, he maintained that such objectification would serve as a foundation for social progress. But even as Douglass believed that photography forecast new futures, he also understood that photographs would uniquely keep the past alive in the present. In other words, photography would create forward momentum with a retrospective pull. Johnson's self-portrait after Douglass activates and responds to those propositions, offering his own self-representation with one eye on the past.

In some ways Douglass provides an unlikely place to begin a book about temporal disruption and photographic mutability, even as he offers an ideal opening for a discussion of photography, race, and social justice. His thoughts on photography in the 1860s are perhaps too resolute and intransigent for the former, even as they are appropriately steadfast for the latter. Douglass was trying to establish secure positions on unstable ground, and the stakes could not have been higher. Through his essays and lectures, and his performances for the camera, he endeavored to assert his very humanness in the face of slavery and the Civil War, and he recognized in photography a revolutionary technology he could harness to his cause. Writing in the 1860s, at a time of revolution, Douglass sought to underscore and also direct the social force and temporal disruption of the photograph, to harness its provocative power for social transformation. He was, therefore, perhaps too eager to moderate its temporal play, and temper its malleability. He strove to fix the photograph's representational significance as a counterforce to the redefinition of the human as property in slavery, and he posed photography as an alternative form of alienation that might prove a progressive tool for all.

Thinking about photography in the 1860s, Douglass faces forward, but he also intuits that photography will enable others to look back. Although the technology was only about two decades old, his performances for the camera were already numerous and would stretch over subsequent decades. He understood, as Roland Barthes would over a century later, how photography enables one "to see oneself (differently from in a mirror): on the scale of History."[1] Through his carefully orchestrated and repeated photographic performances, Douglass indelibly inscribed himself into history, forecasting a recursive look. Johnson returns to Douglass as an important foundation from which to consider photography's revolutionary potential. He pays homage to the persistence of the photograph and the power of Douglass's insights, even as he also unsettles the idea of fixity and highlights the photograph's temporal flux.

Johnson has worked with nineteenth-century photographic techniques, and therefore it is likely he would be attentive to the peculiarities of the daguerreotype, the first form of commercially viable photography in the 1840s and 1850s.[2] The daguerreotype was often likened to a mirror, and even called a "mirror with a memory," because it seemed to reflect the image it captured on its polished metal surface. Further, the daguerreotype's image, like a mirror image, was laterally reversed, a fact made visible in the reversed button placket of Douglass's shirt in Miller's portrait. Johnson's contemporary self-portrait, made with a large-format film camera, would not be reversed in the final print. Therefore, it is clear that Johnson modeled his portrait after Douglass's *image*, not his actual appearance sitting before the camera. In other words, presenting himself to the camera with his own hair parted on the left, Johnson reproduces Douglass's reflection, not his actual hairstyle. Indeed, in a painted portrait of Douglass, one sees that the abolitionist customarily parted his hair on the right, not on the left (fig. 1.1). Thus, Johnson performs a reversal in order to replicate the image.

This kind of slippage is not uncommon in Johnson's work, which Huey Copeland has characterized as marked by an "aesthetics of misdirection" in which "meaning, racial and otherwise, is . . . generated by specific visual phenomena that consistently gesture elsewhere for their charge."[3] Johnson's *Self Portrait with My Hair Parted Like Frederick Douglass* signals the orator through titling, and replicates one of his most famous portraits through pose and dress. But the work also misdirects, because in Johnson's self-portrait, besides the part (which is actually transposed), the hair is all wrong. Indeed, a much more accurate approximation of Douglass's hair is found in one of Johnson's later images, namely *The New Negro Escapist Social and Athletic Club (Emmett)* (2008) (fig. 1.2).

(Emmett) presents a doubled portrait, as if the subject is laterally reversed in a mirror, and it is impossible to discern which is the "original" exposure, and which is the reversed image, the reflection. Two versions of the man seem to face the camera, side by side, joined at the shoulder. The black background, suit, and deeply parted hair of *(Emmett)* resemble Johnson's self-portrait after Douglass, which of course resembles Miller's portrait of Douglass, but here, in the doubled image, it is as if the mechanics of the daguerreotype are laid bare, the lateral reversal revealed.

The titling and doubling of *(Emmett)* also gesture elsewhere. Indeed

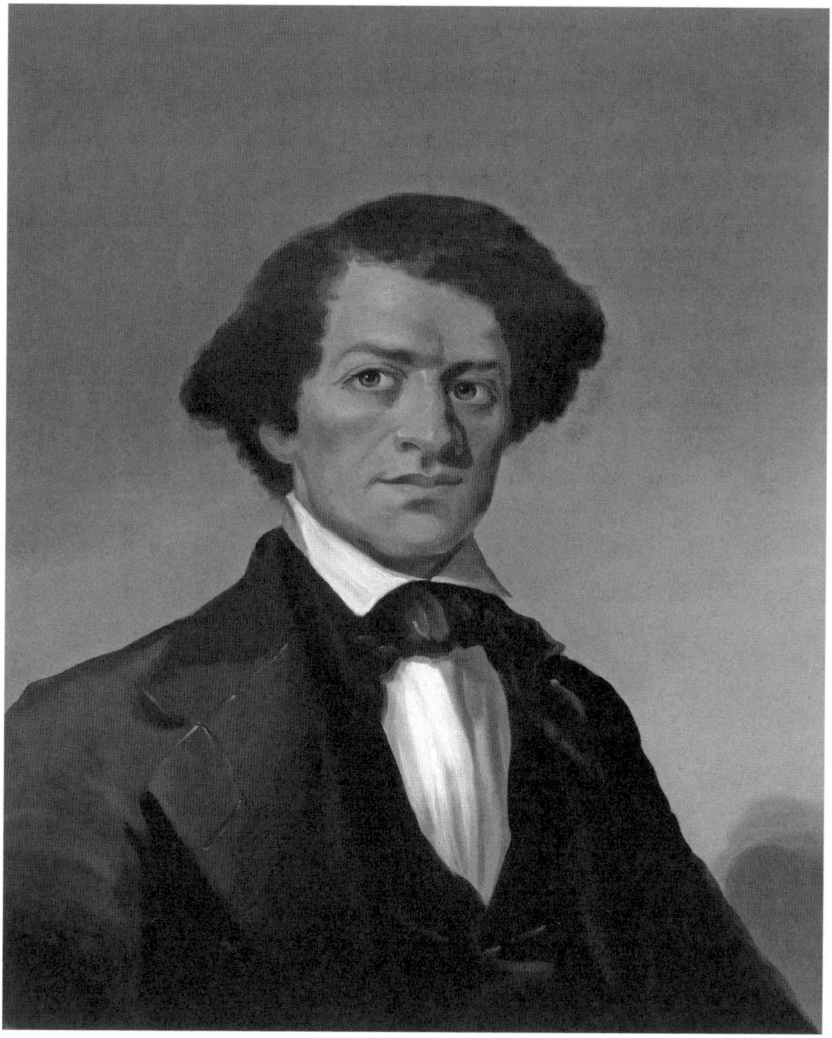

FIGURE 1.1 Frederick Douglass, unidentified artist, c. 1844. Oil on canvas, 27 5/8 × 22 5/8 inches (70.2 × 57.5 cm). National Portrait Gallery, Smithsonian Institution.

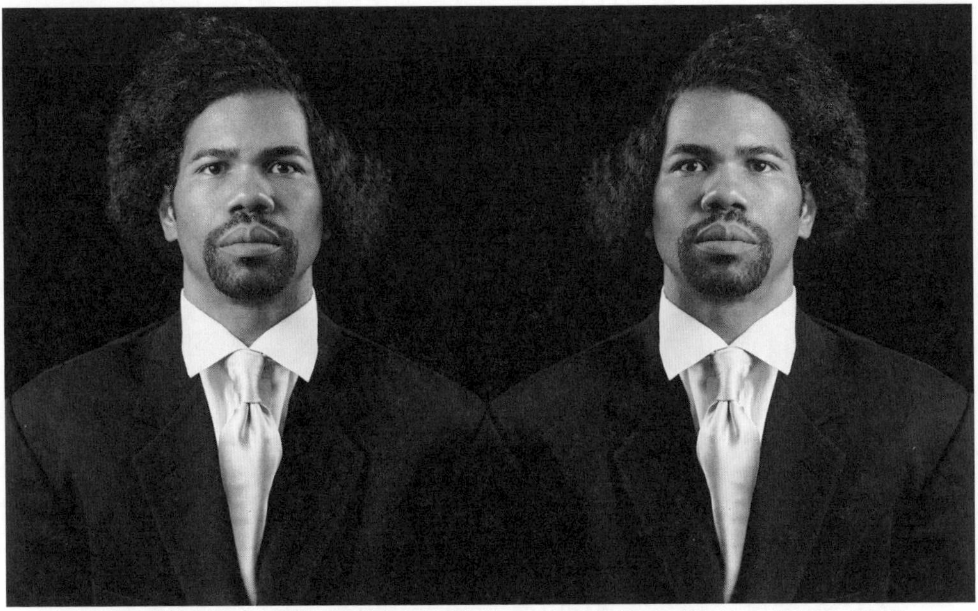

FIGURE 1.2 Rashid Johnson, *The New Negro Escapist Social and Athletic Club (Emmett)*, 2008. Lambda print, 48½ × 73 inches (123.2 × 185.4 cm). Copyright the artist. Courtesy of artist and Hauser & Wirth and David Kordansky Gallery.

they summon the infamous images of Emmett Till, a fourteen-year-old boy who was murdered in Mississippi in 1955. As discussed in chapter 5, devastating "before" and "after" photographs of Till circulated widely in the African American press: one image presented the dapper adolescent with his mother; the other showed his mutilated corpse. Johnson's *(Emmett)* offers paired photographs that recall Emmett Till, but here one is spared the image of the brutal murder; the artist has simply reproduced and flipped the image. Such redirected doubling recalls the mirrored images of the daguerreotype, and "Emmett" appears with Frederick Douglass hair.

Johnson's doubled image also evokes the doubled conception of self famously articulated by W. E. B. Du Bois in *The Souls of Black Folk* (1903). Du Bois defined "double consciousness" as "the sense of always looking at one's self through the eyes of others."[4] For Du Bois double consciousness was a racialized and racist dynamic in which "the eyes of others" were those of whites who looked at African Americans with contempt. In Johnson's work the doubled look becomes a distinctly *intraracial* gaze across time, in which Johnson looks at Douglass and Till, and imagines them looking back. As Copeland has said of this body of work, "taken together, these images fantasize an imagined space outside history where black men and those who love them might congregate."[5]

The persistence of the photograph enables such looks across time. Douglass recognized the photograph's durability and its status as an heirloom as preserving forces in the wake of slavery's social death. As early as 1861 he understood the power of the photograph's longevity, a fact that Barthes would make famous years later in *Camera Lucida* (1980). The photograph is destined to outlive its subject, and therefore one's image circulates beyond the bounds of one's life. In this way, for Barthes, the photograph signals the subject's death at every turn, but for Douglass the photograph's stability across generations is a conserving, if also conservative, force.

What Julie Rodrigues Widholm has said of Johnson's images is also true of Douglass's understanding of photographs: they "are located in an uncertain temporal space that looks both back in time and toward the future."[6] Johnson underscores the persistence of the photograph in his work, asking one to see in his homages to Douglass and Till the influence of previous generations. He mixes elements of images from different moments and merges them in new visions. In this way he highlights the transformative objectification and continued presence of the photograph that Douglass understood to be central to its progressive power, even as he also unsettles the image, highlighting its temporal oscillation and its capacity to morph and merge.[7]

Douglass formulated his thoughts on photography in "Pictures and Progress," a lecture he first delivered on December 3, 1861, at the Tremont Temple in Boston. The audience was surprised by his topic, and less than enthusiastic about his reflections on photography. In fact, one commentator called the lecture "nearly a total failure." As the Civil War waged, everyone expected Douglass, the formerly enslaved man and well-known antislavery activist, to give a rousing speech about slavery and abolition. Instead, on that winter evening, Douglass spoke about the revolutionary power of photography.[8] Although his ideas about the medium were not well received at the time, Douglass was one of the earliest and most innovative theorists of photography. For him, the technology not only offered a new means of representation but also inspired a new understanding of the self. Looking back to Douglass's lectures on photography today, one discovers in them a sophisticated theory of the medium and an emergent model of personhood founded in objectification.

When Douglass so publicly embraced photography, the new imaging technology was roughly twenty years old. As Miller's portrait of the orator makes clear, he was well acquainted with one of its earliest forms, the daguerreotype. By 1861, a new kind of image, the carte de visite, had recently been invented, and it greatly increased the availability of the photograph. Whereas the daguerreotype was a single positive image-object, this new form of photography created a negative from which any number of positive prints could be reproduced. The new technology was fast and inexpensive, and at the time of Douglass's lecture, photography could truly be said to be in the hands of almost everyone.

Curiously, in proclaiming his enthusiasm for photography in 1861, Douglass returns to the earlier technology, the daguerreotype. He intuits the recursive nature of photographic time and looks back, even though the history on which he reflects is only twenty years old. Douglass is interested in the advent of the medium as much as its contemporary manifestations because he sees in photography a new means of representation and even the dawn of a new era. To capture the potential of a radical new beginning vis-à-vis photography, he returns to the narrative of its invention: in "Pictures and Progress" he praises "the great father of our modern picture," Louis Daguerre, for "the multitude, variety, perfection and cheapness" of his pictures. Douglass proclaims:

> Daguerre, by simple but all abounding sunlight has converted the planet into a picture gallery. As munificent in the exalted arena of art, as in the radiation of light and heat, the God of day not only decks the earth with rich fruit and beautiful flowers—but studs the world with pictures. Daguerreotypes, Ambrotypes, Photographs and Electrotypes, good and bad, now adorn or disfigure all our dwellings. . . . Men of all conditions may see themselves as others see them. What was once the exclusive luxury of the rich and great is now within reach of all.[9]

Douglass emphasizes photography's democratizing powers, celebrating the accessibility of the medium for ordinary people.[10] He declares, "The humblest servant girl may now possess a picture of herself such as the wealth of kings could not purchase fifty years ago."[11] Leveling the social hierarchies of portraiture, photography offered a seemingly revolutionary and universal tool of self-representation.

The daguerreotype appealed to Douglass for a number of reasons, and the material qualities of the image may have been particularly meaningful to him. As many scholars have noted, the viewer of the daguerreotype sees herself reflected in the mirror-like image, and in this way, the daguerreotype seems to unite viewer and viewed in the same space of reflection, inviting and even requiring the viewer to see herself in relation to the photographed subject. The daguerreotype image is also unusual in that it flickers between negative and positive as it is held and tilted, making subjects appear both alive and dead, and both black and white. Marcy Dinius imagines that this aspect of the daguerreotype might have held particular importance for Douglass, representing "the dual racial identity that Douglass embodied and experienced as his slave mother's and white master's son."[12] Whether or not one takes the flickering of the daguerreotype as a racial metaphor, the instability of the image is indeed intriguing. As the genre of photography most fleeting and fragile, even as it is also solidly material, the daguerreotype serves as an appropriate medium for representing a fugitive freedom. As Celeste-Marie Bernier notes, "Just as Douglass was a 'fugitive slave,' so too did the daguerreotype record a 'fugitive' image, as elusive and ephemeral as it was palpable and real."[13] Indeed, according to Bernier, Douglass aimed to counter a history of "slave portraiture" with "fugitive portraiture," which represented the ways in which "slavery and freedom remained relative physical and psychological states of existence."[14] The daguerreotype offered Douglass a unique emblem of both photographic fixity and fugitivity, and in this way provided a compelling representation of slavery's contradictions.

The analogy between fleeting image and fugitive slave is more fundamental than one might suppose; indeed, in different ways, both trouble the distinctions between persons and property. The fugitive is, as Stephen Best explains, "two persons in one," "pilfered property and indebted person, object of property and subject of contract."[15] The fugitive slave, who is forced to "steal" himself, is legally defined as both subject and object, as both person and property. According to Cheryl Harris, there was always "some unease in slave law, reflective of the mixed status of slaves as humans and property," but "the critical nature of social relations under slavery was the commodification of human beings." "Slavery as a legal institution treated slaves as property that could be transferred, assigned, inherited, or posted as collateral."[16]

Photography enacted another kind of blurring of the distinctions between persons and property in the nineteenth century. As Best has argued, the introduction of "mechanically reproductive devices," such as the camera, encouraged people "to secure property rights in heretofore inalienable aspects of their personhood: *their visual image*, ideas, facial expressions, and even vocal style."[17] In other words, after the advent of mechanical reproduction, labor was no longer the only alienable property right; increasingly one could claim "intellectual property rights in one's countenance."[18] Remarkably, the problem of the fugitive as both subject and object parallels the changing definitions of legal personhood introduced by photography, namely the alienation of one's self as image, the production of one's self as object.

Douglass, once a fugitive slave himself, seized on photography's alienation of the subject, and saw its capacities for objectification as crucial to its social power. He celebrated photography as a new form of picture making, and one cannot overstate the importance Douglass accorded pictures. He argued that it was the "picture making faculty" that fundamentally determined what it meant to be human; "picture making" and "picture appreciating" distinguished men from animals: "The process by which man is able to invert his own subjective consciousness into the objective form, considered in all its range, is in truth the highest attribute of man's nature."[19] A person's ability to objectify herself through representation becomes for Douglass the essence of being human. Photography realizes a defining feature of humanity, and one that is surprisingly resonant with the status of the fugitive slave. In photography, then, Douglass finds an analogy to his own confounding legal status, one he deems the very indicator of the human.

The alienation and objectification of subjectivity enabled by the photograph is also a temporal disruption. If photography intervenes in one's conception of consciousness as interiorized, providing a distanced view of the self as object, it also unsettles the sense of consciousness as immanent presence and uninterrupted flow. It creates a sense of pause for contemplation and consideration of the self. In this way, picture making also serves, for Douglass, as the impetus for progress. Picture making and viewing provide a catalyst for social change because these practices uniquely encourage criticism. According to Douglass, "It is the picture of life contrasted with the fact of life, the ideal contrasted with the real, which makes criticism possible. Where there is no criticism there is no progress—for the want of progress is not felt where such want is not made visible by criticism." By making themselves objects of "observation and contemplation," people can begin to imagine better selves and better futures. For Douglass, portraits invite individuals to "see our interior selves as distinct personalities as though looking in a glass." Further, from this "power we possess of making ourselves objective to ourselves" arises the potential for "self-criticism out of which comes the highest attainments of human excellence."[20] Pictures allow people to see themselves as if from the outside, and, from this more distanced view, to contemplate and assess themselves. Encouraging self-critique in this way, pictures are the very foundation of progress, and photographic portraits can inspire social change.

To transform "subjective consciousness into the objective form" is a process of alienation, the very form of alienation sanctioned by intellectual property law. The objectification of one's image in photographs allowed one to claim property rights in that image, to own an aspect of one's self as property. In a much more fundamental way, the fugitive slave, who "stole" himself as object, was subject to and resisting a radical, violent alienation. Both forms of alienation troubled the boundaries of legal personhood, although of course they did so to dramatically different degrees. It is somewhat curious, then, that Douglass, once a fugitive slave, would embrace photography so enthusiastically, and perform the objectification of himself so extensively. Through photography Douglass realized a new model of personhood, a model in which the subject could be alienated as property, but through that objectification could also claim a new kind of self-ownership, and ultimately a new form of self-understanding.[21]

For Douglass the path to personal growth is through the critical contemplation of one's self as object, and photography provides all subjects an opportunity for improvement through objectification. Douglass is not alone in sensing the power of objectification through photography; what is unique about his view is that he understands such objectification as the defining feature of humanity and also as the path to progress. Writing more than a century later, Barthes also understood photography as a process of objectification. As he contemplated his own displeasure in being photographed, he mused, "The Photograph (the one I *intend*) represents that very subtle moment when, to tell the truth, I am neither subject nor object but a subject who feels he is becoming an object." Resisting objectification, Barthes proclaims, "It is my *political* right to be a subject which I must protect."[22] The very habit of composing one's self for the camera, of crafting one's image, was for Barthes a sundering of the self. The process through which Douglass proclaimed himself as subject was one in which Barthes only had political rights to lose. As Laura Wexler has argued, "Barthes experienced submission to photography in much the same way that Frederick Douglass experienced submission to slavery: as social death. But Barthes starts out alive and then dies into his picture, whereas the slave starts out as a social corpse and is animated through the photograph."[23] It is important not to overstate the analogy between slavery and photography, for clearly the dehumanization and devastation of slavery in no way compares to Barthes's discomfort before the camera. Nevertheless, it is also important to recognize that for both Douglass and Barthes photography activates a new way of objectifying the subject; it asks one to see one's self as an object, as others might.[24] For Barthes this marks the end of his sovereign subjectivity, but for Douglass it enables him to claim self-possession.

Samuel J. Miller's portrait of Douglass, made sometime between 1847 and 1852, in Akron, Ohio, the portrait that Johnson would reenact over a century and a half later, remains one of the most striking images of the orator (see plate 2). This daguerreotype was made at a moment of tremendous transition in Douglass's life, just after his legal emancipation, and during the years of his break with white abolitionist William Lloyd Garrison.[25] One can imagine, then, that Douglass crafted his portrait to convey his new independence, and his new status as a citizen-subject. How did Douglass greet the camera to represent such momentous transformation? Finely dressed and carefully coiffed, according to the conventions of middle-class portraiture. But beyond such trappings, the image does not adhere to middle-class standards; it does not mimic the space of the parlor, as do so many nineteenth-century photographs. Instead, Douglass sits at an angle to the camera, tightly framed and isolated in the image. The camera has come in close to focus on his head, shoulders, and chest, accentuating his face and solemn stare. As Bernier has proposed, his daguerreotype "adheres very closely to the conventions of heroic portraiture,"[26] and in Alan Trachtenberg's memorable words, Douglass is photographed as an "Illustrious American."[27]

Douglass's portrait announces his self-possession, but it remains shadowed by the contradictions of slavery. For Douglass's freedom was purchased, according to the dictates of slavery. In 1846 supporters in England paid for his emancipation, an act that pretended to secure his safety, even as it also reinforced the logic of slavery whereby subjects could be bought and sold as objects. As Douglass outlines in his *Narrative of the Life of Frederick Douglass* (1845), he had already emancipated himself through his learning, his fight with his purported master, Covey, and his escape. But his self-emancipation was not and would not be recognized by all; while slavery endured, legal freedom had to be secured according to the terms of the institution, through purchase. Douglass acquiesced so that he might continue his work of abolition without the constant threat of capture. Therefore, his portrait in freedom is perplexing, as it represents a legal freedom defined both against and according to the terms of the institution from which he escaped.

As a man someone once (and recently) claimed to own, could Douglass be confirmed in his self-possession? Would he ever be truly free while slavery persisted? Would anyone? And what about the afterlife of slavery in a postemancipation period? If the law could accommodate people alienated as property, wasn't the self-possession of all subjects put under pressure? In Miller's daguerreotype, Douglass asserts a self-possession he knows to be precarious. As Ginger Hill has argued, for Douglass the portrait "becomes a way to accumulate characteristics of self-possession. It does not reflect but *makes* a self."[28] The daguerreotype becomes a vehicle through which one can display the habitual "self-containment and control" central to self-possession.[29] As slavery unhinged the idea that self-possession was innate, racial discourses intervened to shore up self-possession as a category for whites only. As Matthew Frye Jacobson has argued, self-possession was a racially contested status in the nineteenth century: American citizens were presumed to have "*self-possession*—a condition already denied legally to Africans in slavery and figuratively to all 'nonwhite' or 'heathen' peoples in prevailing conceptions of human capacity."[30] If enslaved "Africans" were denied self-possession, what of fugitive slaves and free African Americans? Could they ever claim to be self-possessed citizens in the United States?

Douglass understood that legal emancipation was insufficient; he also had to secure his *image* as a free man, and he did so through repeated photographic performances. Indeed, as John Stauffer, Zoe Trodd, and Celeste-Marie Bernier have demonstrated, Douglass was the most photographed American of the nineteenth century.[31] He reenacted his freedom and self-possession by objectifying himself as image over and over again. According to Hill, "The circulation of these pictures helped create and guarantee his citizen status, visually proclaiming Douglass's 'natural right' to own property and thus be seen as equal, which is to say autonomous and free. Both the attention to detail within each act of self-presentation and the repetition of that act foreground Douglass's precarious claim to such social status of equality and also the fact that he understood such states of possession and recognition as systems of accumulation."[32] The repetition of his performance for the camera asserted his self-possession.

Douglass presents the promise and problem of the photograph as a fixed form. Its malleability and protean nature is not appealing to him. As Wexler has shown, across his many photographic portraits, Douglass performs a remarkable "consistency of the pose": he presents himself "with extraordinary consistency in many sittings over decades, beyond the requirements of the customary pose."[33] In some ways, his efforts to fix his image over time paradoxically underscore its potential changeability. Further, by keeping the pose stable, Douglass brings his own transformation, his physical aging, into view. Looking back at his photographic portraits from youth to old age, one watches his signature hair become streaked with gray and finally turn white (fig. 1.3). In this way, Douglass teaches one to read photographs diachronically as well as synchronically, forecasting the disruptive temporality later theorists such as Walter Benjamin and Barthes would seize upon, and later artists such as Johnson would put into play.

Although clearly optimistic about the promise of photography, Douglass was also highly attuned to the importance of the struggle over representation, and he knew photographs circulated in a contested visual culture. Describing it as a "mighty power," Douglass proclaimed, "This picture making faculty is flung out into the world—like all others—subject to a wild scramble between contending interests and forces."[34] He understood, as Sarah Blackwood has argued, that "the visual portrait . . . was an active site upon which the fight for African American political representation was taking place."[35] As the medium offered men and women an unprecedented opportunity for self-representation, it offered African Americans that opportunity as they were making claims on new legal, political, and socially recognized American identities in flux.

Douglass sought to challenge racist representations that cast African Americans as less than human. As early as 1849 he decried the difficulty of securing realistic portraits of African Americans at the hands of white artists, declaring in the *North Star*, "'It seems to us next to impossible for white men to take likenesses of black men, without most grossly exaggerating their distinctive features.'"[36] Even the daguerreotype, the revolutionary visual form Douglass lauded, could be manipulated to serve conceptual distortions. In 1850, Louis Agassiz commissioned Joseph T. Zealy to make a series of daguerreotypes of enslaved men and women to serve as evidence for his theory of polygenesis. Douglass condemned such scientific misrepresentations, taking aim a few years later at Samuel George Morton's *Crania Americana*.[37] He also made visual arguments against them. As Dinius has argued, a rare profile daguerreotype of Douglass made circa 1850 contests the racial

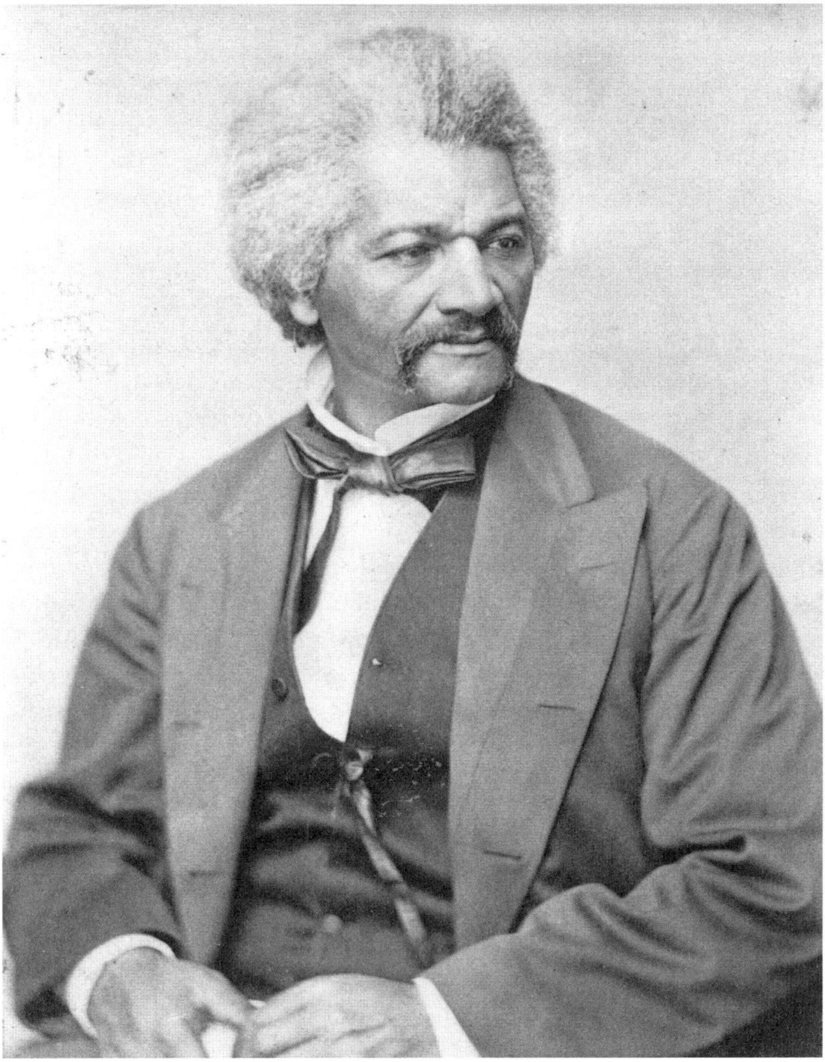

FIGURE 1.3 George Francis Schreiber, Frederick Douglass, 1870. Albumen print, 4 × 2½ inches. Library of Congress, Prints and Photographs Division, Washington, DC.

hierarchy proposed by Agassiz and Morton and the American school ethnologists by replicating scientific visual forms to propose different conclusions.[38] In these contested cultural contexts, photography might serve as a political tool to challenge racist hierarchies, but it would not do so automatically. One would have to use the technology to perform subjectivity and claim a place in public and political spheres.[39] It is no wonder, then, that Douglass tried so hard to fortify his own photographic portraits by performing a stable pose. Photography enabled him to present himself as the fully human object of his own gaze.

Douglass celebrated photography as a progressive tool, but he also declared pictures "decid[ed]ly conservative."[40] Once captured, one's image could be "considered a fixed fact, public property." Even as he tried to craft a consistent portrait, he also worried about becoming fixed as an image in the public eye. Although he repeated his pose with care, he also understood that one would have to fight conformity to one's image, endeavoring to use the photograph as a measure of self to be contemplated, not clung to. Further, as one would have to wrestle with the "public property" of the image, one would also have to consider the private property of the image and its traditional sentimentality. The enduring photograph promised to keep not only one's self but also one's family members riveted before one's eyes. Douglass proclaimed, "It is evident that the great cheapness, and universality of pictures, must exert a powerful though silent influence, upon the ideas and sentiment of present [and] future generations. The family is the fountain head of all mental and moral influence. And the presence there of the miniture [*sic*] forms and faces of our loved ones whether separated from us by time and space, or by the Silent countenents [*sic*] of Eternity—must act powerfully upon the minds of all."[41] In the proliferation and persistence of photographs Douglass saw a retrospective force that could shape the future. Photographs would preserve the ancestral ties obliterated by slavery, offering a visual lineage to confront social death.[42] But even in this most political power of sentiment, the photograph, providing an impetus toward progress, would also keep one looking back.

Douglass delivered his lecture "Pictures and Progress" one final time, in 1865. In the later version he acknowledged the "seeming transgression" of his desire to lecture on photography in light of the Civil War.[43] But he persisted with his topic because he believed "each new period, and each new condition seeks its needed and appropriate representation."[44] For Douglass, photography would provide an "appropriate representation" for the dynamic new period ahead.

The new era would be one of freedom, a status that Douglass struggled to represent.[45] According to Stauffer, Douglass intuited that "words could not represent the sensation of freedom."[46] As early as 1862, just as the Emancipation Proclamation was about to go into effect, as "a new age of legal freedom was at hand," "Douglass had doubts about prose being the appropriate form to describe the dawn of [this] new age."[47] He sensed that prose would fail to capture the radical revolution of freedom because, as Stauffer suggests, "a sharp break in linear chronology could not effectively be conveyed in prose."[48] But such a break could be represented in photography, and for Douglass, the age of freedom would also be the "age of pictures."[49]

Photography exemplifies a break in linear time, capturing, as Ulrich Baer has argued, the radical nonlinearity of time, rupturing narratives of historical progression. It brings a past and also a future into the present.[50] This temporal disruption is the contingency of photography that Benjamin described in the 1930s, the radical spark of futurity that reaches across time to claim its viewer. Once again, according to Benjamin, "No matter how artful the photographer, no matter how carefully posed his subject, the beholder feels an irresistible urge to search such a picture for the tiny spark of contingency, of the here and now, with which reality has (so to speak) seared the subject, to find the inconspicuous spot where in the immediacy of that long-forgotten moment the future nests so eloquently that we, looking back, may rediscover it."[51] Photography itself looks forward and back, anticipating a future viewer as it preserves a moment from the past.

In his tribute to Douglass, Johnson announces himself as the future viewer who has answered the hail of the photograph. He enters into the image to produce a new vision of self, composed of photographic fragments across time (see plate 1). In Douglass's daguerreotype, Johnson sees an image to preserve, but also one to transform. Calling attention, with his transposed part, to the image of Douglass rather than the man himself, he both venerates and dodges the conserving and conservative pull of the photograph. Repeating the image with a difference, Johnson heeds the call of the past but is not contained by it.[52]

Johnson's self-portrait after Douglass enacts a doubled temporal disruption. He reperforms Douglass's pose for the camera, even as Douglass

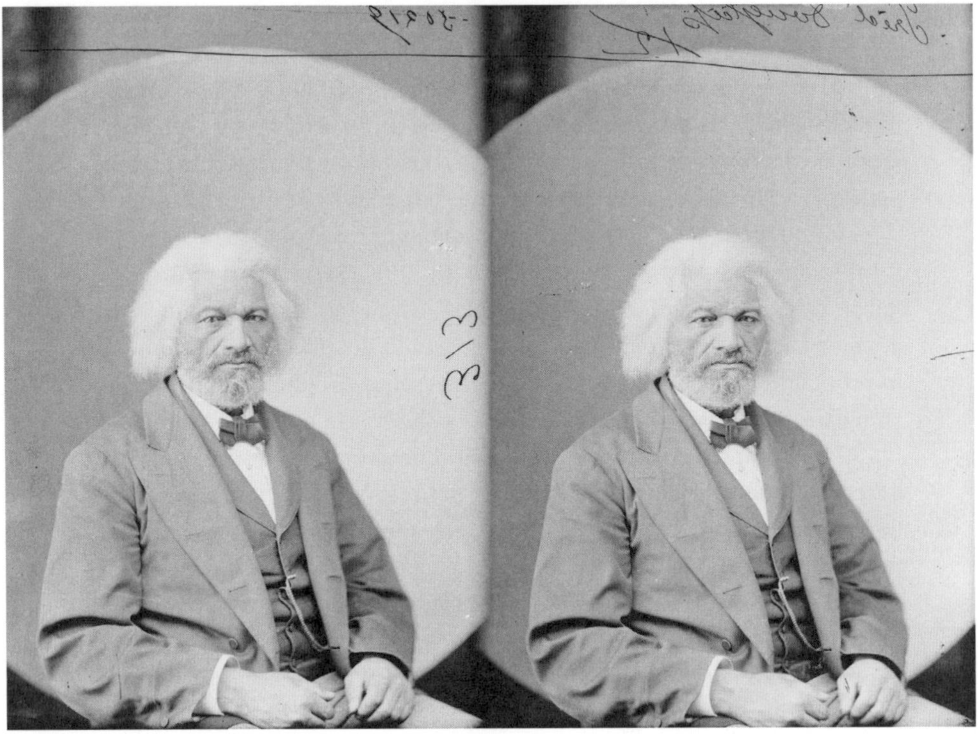

FIGURE 1.4 Mathew B. Brady, Frederick Douglass, ca. 1865–80. Glass negative. Library of Congress, Prints and Photographs Division, Washington, DC.

crafted his own pose according to the dictates of middle-class and heroic portraiture in the nineteenth century (figure 1.4).[53] As Rebecca Schneider has argued, "The pose is a kind of hail cast into a future moment of its invited recognition."[54] As the pose reiterates a past gesture and seeks future recognition, so does the photograph both record a past moment and seek a future viewer. Johnson's performance highlights the photograph's temporal play, seeking a future viewer by reenacting Douglass's pose from the past. Underscoring the ways the photograph belongs to a past and a future in the present, Johnson's self-portrait after Douglass performs the fugitive time of photography.

Ultimately, Johnson's self-portrait takes one back to Douglass and to Miller's famous daguerreotype of the orator (see plate 2). In that image one might glimpse a spark of the profound social shifts Douglass anticipated with the end of slavery and the proliferation of photography. His portrait circa 1847–52 catapults one to a past moment in which the future was uncertain, in which it was fugitive. The daguerreotype registers an important moment in Douglass's self-understanding, for it marks a moment when he could legally claim self-ownership and chose to announce that new status through the objectification of the photograph. The transformation of subject into object is embodied by the once fugitive slave who fashioned himself photographically. Douglass saw in the objectification of the photograph an opportunity for a new kind of self-understanding, one founded in self-observation and self-possession. Finally, then, one might see flickering in the unstable daguerreotype not only a new form of representation but also a new form of personhood. This is the legacy of photography that Douglass understood looking forward, and Johnson understands looking back.

CHAPTER 2

Photographic Remains

Sally Mann at Antietam

The photograph is almost impossible to see. A dark mass rises to what one imagines is a dark sky. Tiny white flecks suggest stars. A smaller mass coheres into a squatty, conical tree, probably an evergreen, at the far right edge of the frame. One can just barely discern that this is a landscape, or, perhaps better said, an empty terrain with occasional trees. The space does not coalesce into a recognizable place. It does not invite one in, and hardly even allows one to look (fig. 2.1).

In the spring of 2001, Sally Mann began to photograph Civil War battlefields. She started her work at Antietam in Sharpsburg, Maryland, producing *Battlefields, Antietam (Bubba Hill)* (2001) among other images, and over the course of the next two years extended her work to sites in Virginia, including Manassas, Fredericksburg, Chancellorsville, Wilderness, and Appomattox. Focusing specifically on Mann's Antietam photographs, this chapter examines the ways in which her latter-day Civil War images reframe a site that holds a significant place in both the history of the United States and the history of photography. Her images recall Alexander Gardner's famous photographs made at the same site in 1862, images that radically transformed the stakes of the war for noncombatant viewers in the nineteenth century, showing its gruesome toll in the bodies of the dead.[1] But if Gardner's photographs made the war startlingly clear in new ways, Mann's photographs make it only ever more obscure. Mann reenacts Gardner's process, photographing at Antietam

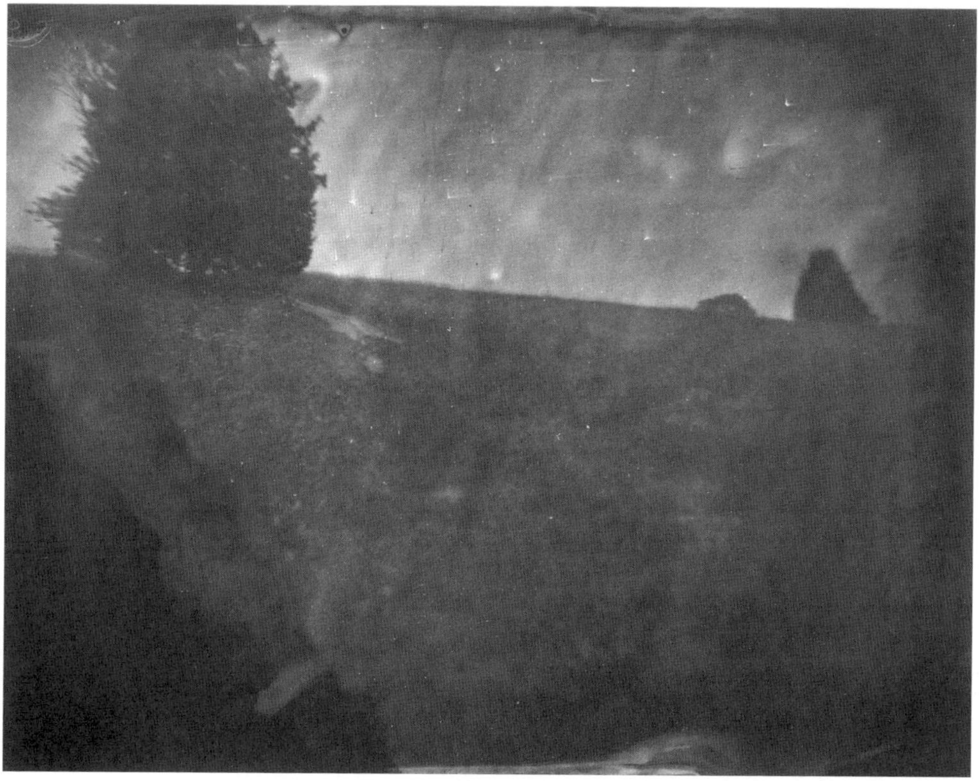

FIGURE 2.1 Sally Mann, *Battlefields, Antietam (Bubba Hill)*, 2001. Gelatin silver print, varnished, 40 × 50 inches (101.6 × 127 cm). © Sally Mann. Courtesy Gagosian.

with a large-format view camera and wet collodion chemistry. She returns to a site laden with historical importance, in a seeming attempt at a reparative project that fails. With her dark, opaque images of the battlefield, she deflects and redirects the view. Her work suggests that it is not the site of Antietam that bears the import of the past, or conveys the traumatic rent in the nation initiated by slavery and fought over so savagely during the Civil War. It is not the place that bears the weight of the past but photography. Mann returns to Antietam, but her images defer to other photographs. In their seeming non-referentiality, her smudged and smeared images call attention to photography itself and to the present time and place from which one considers a past that persists in struggles over the racial contours of the nation today.

The battle of Antietam was the bloodiest one-day battle in American history. It began at daybreak on September 17, 1862, in the countryside near Sharpsburg, Maryland, along the banks of Antietam Creek, and by nightfall, thousands of men were dead.[2] Although infamous for the number killed, the battle of Antietam was indecisive from a military point of view, for although the Union troops nominally won, the battle did not turn the tide of the war. It did, however, effect an important change in the *meaning* of the war. As Richard Slotkin has argued, "The indecisive battle" produced "a decisive political result": "Antietam was victory enough to allow Lincoln to issue the Emancipation Proclamation."[3] Just five days after the battle, on September 22, 1862, President Lincoln presented the final draft of the preliminary proclamation to the cabinet. The document greatly expanded presidential powers in wartime, giving the president the authority to confiscate property in rebel territories without judicial or criminal proceedings, and it suggested that enslaved African Americans could use violence in self-defense, and that free African Americans, North and South, could join the forces of the US military.[4] The proclamation definitively linked the war and the restoration of the Union to the end of slavery.[5]

The Emancipation Proclamation was an ultimatum the president knew the South would reject. It declared that such measures would not go into effect if Southern leaders ended the rebellion by January 1, 1863, a mere three months away.[6] Lincoln understood that his revised and more radical proclamation would prove controversial, and he couched his decision and determination in religious terms, telling the cabinet that he had "'made a vow, a covenant, that if God gave us the victory in the approaching battle [Antietam], he would consider it an indication of divine will and that it was his duty to move forward in the matter of emancipation. . . . God had decided this question in favor of the slaves.'"[7] The president thus harnessed the battle of Antietam to the project of emancipation.

Mann's photographs of Antietam are "unrelentingly dark," as Anne Wilkes Tucker has argued.[8] In *Battlefields, Antietam (Spindly Trees)* (2001), a long horizon line runs across the top third of the frame, separating a dark expanse from a slightly lighter sky (plate 3). As one stumbles around in the dark, tiny triangular shapes come into focus as trees. The emulsion shrinks back from the corners of the image, its once liquid form evident in the viscous fingers that pull away from darkness in the bottom left corner. It appears as though the image itself has been poured onto the plate.

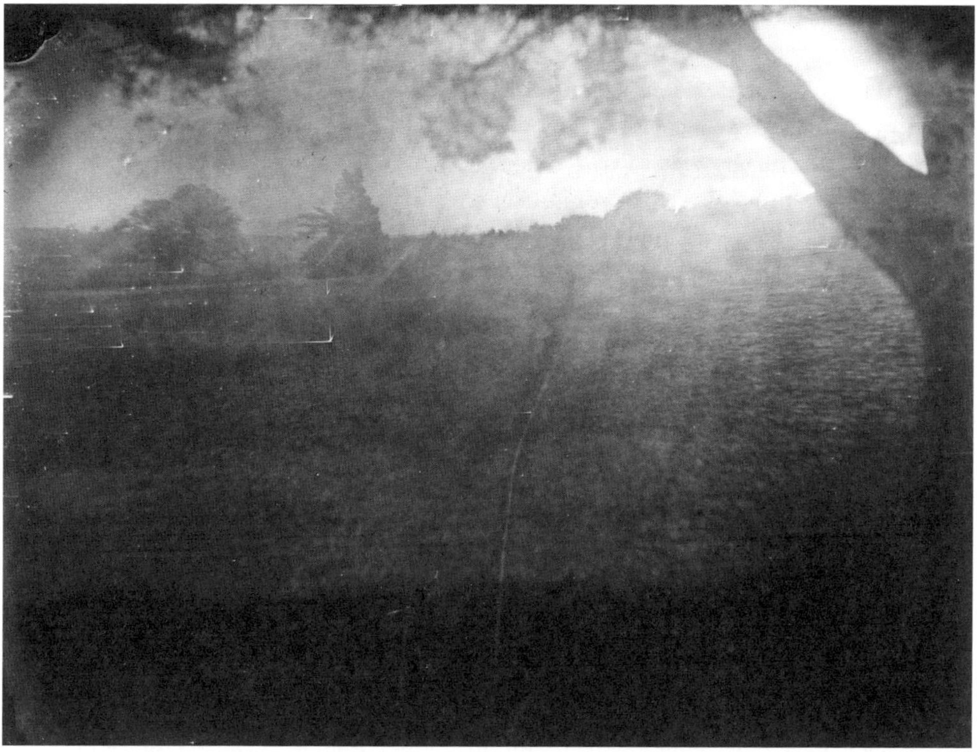

FIGURE 2.2 Sally Mann, *Battlefields, Antietam (Blast)*, 2001. Gelatin silver print, varnished, 40 × 50 inches (101.6 × 127 cm). © Sally Mann. Courtesy Gagosian.

In *Battlefields, Antietam (Blast)* (2001), one of Mann's brightest images from Antietam, and one that also affords the viewer a momentary illusion of depth, the trunk of a tree close to the camera runs up the right side of the frame, anchoring the viewer in this almost-place (fig. 2.2). The large limbs of the tree reach out into a light sky, and lacy branches dip back down into the upper center of the frame. The bottom quarter of the photograph has been obscured, but light picks out the blurred details of grass stretching back across a sloping plane to more trees. A white vertical scratch divides the image down the middle, and tiny L-shaped marks suggest encounters with sharp edges. A large circular portion of the frame is textured, as with canvas or with skin.

Mann's photographs of Antietam largely exclude the viewer, practically denying access to the scenes. These "landscapes" collapse into flat abstractions, an effect enhanced by the surface disruptions of Mann's haphazard collodion process. They are antithetical to ideas about historical retrieval as well as photographic evidence. One knows these are sites laden with national importance, but she recognizes this only because Mann has named them "Antietam." The images themselves fail to document much of anything, except perhaps the impossibility of comprehending the past.[9] Indeed, Ulrich Baer's assessment of contemporary photographs of Holocaust sites also pertains to Mann's photographs of Civil War battlefields: "It is the unavailability of referential markers, and not information that could be embedded in historical contexts, that is captured in these images as the truth of history."[10] Mann's dense and dark images present information that is not directly referential, pointing as much to the materiality of photography as to anything the photographs might be said to represent. The dark, viscous textures of the images are their most salient subjects.

Mann worked like a Civil War photographer at Antietam. She used a large view camera to make eight-by-ten-inch wet-plate collodion negatives from which she then made forty-by-fifty-inch silver gelatin prints. The collodion wet-plate process is a uniquely tactile operation in which the photographer coats a large glass plate with liquid collodion and then silver nitrate, places it in a light-tight negative holder, loads it into a view camera, exposes the plate and develops it with a solution of guncotton dissolved in ether, and finally washes, fixes, and washes the plate again, all while the initially applied collodion and silver nitrate remain wet.[11]

Photographers working with the wet-plate method in the field must bring a portable darkroom with them, and Sally Mann uses the back of her truck for this purpose. There is plenty of room for error in the process: the collodion and silver emulsion fails to cover the plate completely or it peels back from the glass; dust and contaminants stick to the gummy plate; light leaks into the darkroom, the plate holder, or the camera itself. Mann embraces, and it would seem deliberately seeks, errors that call attention to the tactility of the practice and the deterioration intrinsic to it.[12] She coats and textures her prints as well, highlighting the opacity of the photograph rather than its celebrated transparency, attending to surface rather than depth. Her process underscores some of the elements that are intrinsic to photography but largely ignored as one looks at, and imagines she looks through, photographs.[13]

With their surface opacity and dense atmosphere, Mann's photographs refer to photography itself. Made with nineteenth-century processes, they evoke historical photographs more than historical events, and a viewer of

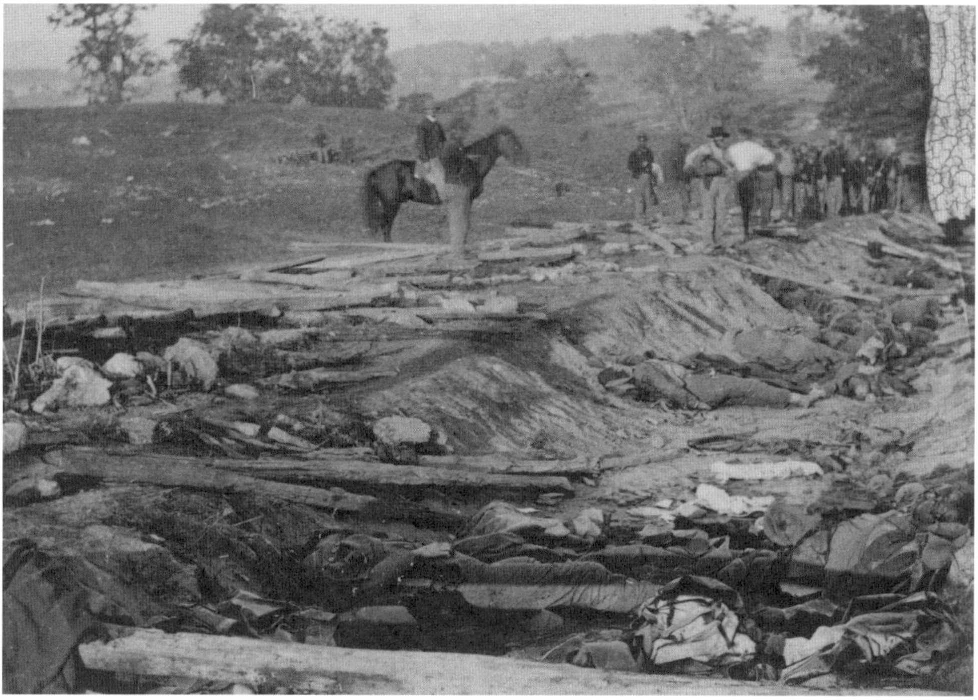

FIGURE 2.3 Alexander Gardner, *View of ditch, which had been used as a rifle-pit at the Battle of Antietam*, 1862. Albumen print on card mount, 11.5 × 15 cm (mount). Brady's Album Gallery no. 565. Library of Congress, Prints and Photographs Division, Washington, DC.

Mann's Antietam photographs might recall the most famous photographs of this site, those made just days after the battle, by Alexander Gardner and his assistant James Gibson. Indeed, it is as if Mann is performing a kind of re-enactment at Antietam, a reenactment of Civil War photography.

Gardner and Gibson photographed at Antietam from September 19 to September 22, 1862, beginning two days after the battle.[14] As William Frassanito has emphasized, "Antietam was the first battlefield in American history to be covered by cameramen before the dead had been buried."[15] Over the course of four days, Gardner and Gibson made 105 photographs of the aftermath, including seventy-eight stereo negatives, among which were twenty images of dead soldiers, such as *View of ditch, which had been used as a rifle-pit at the Battle of Antietam* (1862) (fig. 2.3).[16]

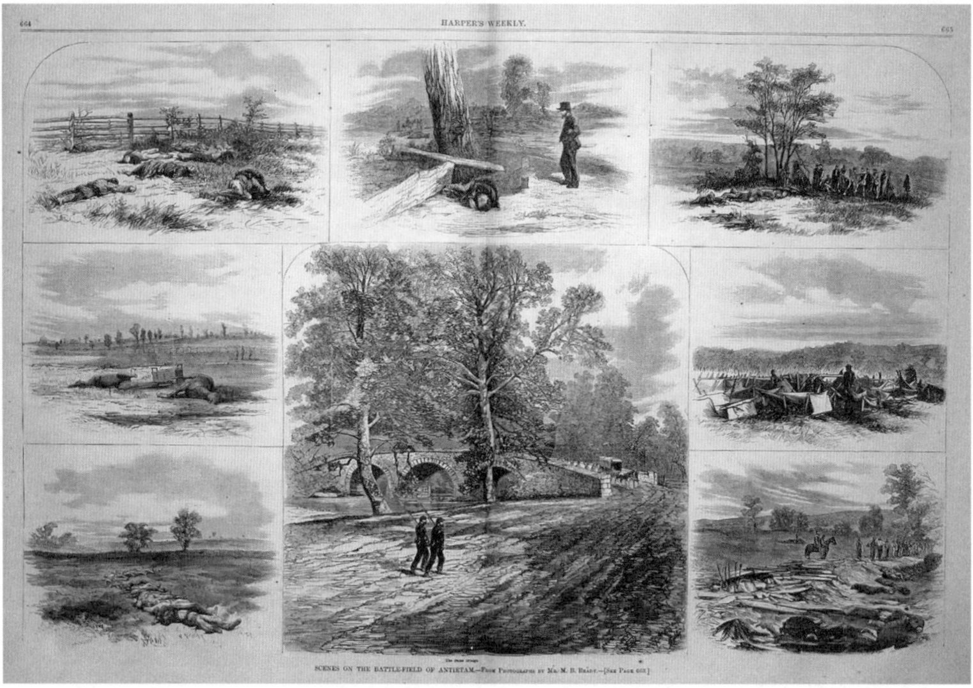

FIGURE 2.4 *Scenes on the Battlefield of Antietam*, *Harper's Weekly*, October 18, 1862.

Gardner and Gibson's scenes of death and destruction at Antietam were the most famous and widely discussed photographs of the Civil War, and they also helped shape subsequent views of the war, providing an example for other entrepreneurial photographers to follow.[17] Displayed in Mathew Brady's studio on Broadway in New York, the photographs were seen by crowds of curious viewers, and some were reproduced and circulated widely as engravings in the October 18, 1862, issue of *Harper's Weekly* (fig. 2.4).[18] Remarkably, the battle itself had been a viewing spectacle, with a crowd of nearly five thousand watching from a hill nearby,[19] and the aftermath of the battle became a national scene through the display and reproduction of photographs of the dead.

After visiting Brady's exhibition of Gardner's photographs, titled *The Dead of Antietam*, a writer for the *New York Times* marveled at the precision of the photographs, even as he also noted their limitations. He remarked on the "weird copies of carnage": "It seems somewhat singular that the same sun that looked down on the faces of the slain, blistering them, blotting out from the bodies all semblance to humanity, and hastening corruption, should have thus caught their features upon canvas, and given them perpetuity forever." The very sun that would transform and deform the corpses, accelerating their decay, would also enable them to be preserved in photographs, or "sun pictures." The same writer declared, "Mr. Brady has done something to bring home to us the terrible reality and earnestness of war. If he has not brought bodies and laid them in our dooryards, and along the streets, he has done something very like it." "These pictures have a terrible distinctness. By the aid of the magnifying glass, the very features of the slain may be distinguished." And yet, even as the photographs brought the war dead home so vividly, they also failed to capture the emotional wreckage of the war wrought on orphans, widows, and desolate homes. The writer who heralded the power of the Antietam photographs also acknowledged their shortcomings: "All of this desolation imagination must paint—broken hearts cannot be photographed."[20]

The empty fields so prevalent in Mann's images call forth the dead bodies that once filled them, and Gardner's dramatic photographs of battlefields littered with corpses. One of Gardner's most famous photographs, *View on Battlefield of Antietam* (1862), shows four corpses sprawled in disarray along a wooden fence (fig. 2.5). He made the image on September 19, 1862, two days after the battle, along the Hagerstown Pike, and it shows the bodies of young men from brigadier general William E. Starke's Louisiana troops contorted in death.[21] The men likely died in a mere fifteen minutes, between 6:45 and 7:00 a.m. on September 17, 1862, and their commander, General Starke, was mortally wounded with them.[22] The corpse on the far left seems to rest the remains of its head on the lowest rung of the fence. The body on the right is twisted in its death thrall; rigor mortis has frozen a bent knee and an arm raised high above the figure, the hand puffy with bloat. Perpendicular to this corpse, which careens away from the viewer, another lies flat, back pressed into the grass, left arm and leg, closest to the viewer, extended, right hand laying on stomach, right knee bent toward the sky. The pose, which might suggest a breezy afternoon of cloud gazing, is radically disrupted by the figure's face, which is distorted and discolored. Disconcertingly, the man's pants are unbuttoned and his pelvis is exposed below the hips. (Perhaps a survivor or a scavenger has taken his belt.) Another body lies perpendicular to this one, its head tucked underneath the fence, covered with a thick cloth or sack. Perhaps the photographers sought to hide some impossible disfigurement, visu-

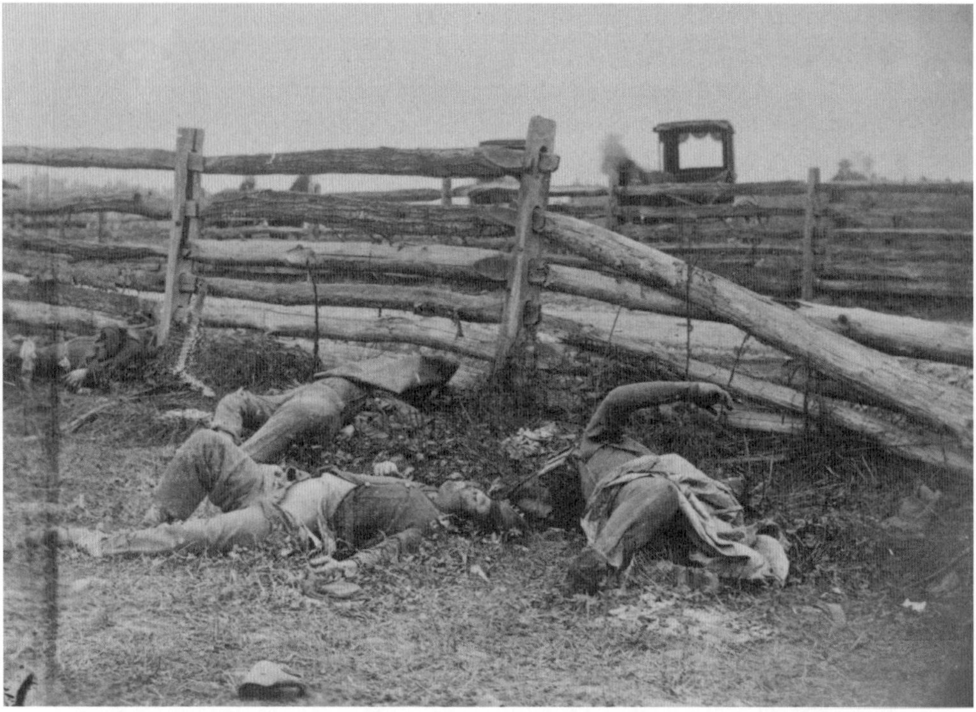

FIGURE 2.5 Alexander Gardner, *View on Battlefield of Antietam*, 1862. Albumen print on card mount, 11.5 × 15 cm (mount). Brady's Album Gallery no. 567. Library of Congress, Prints and Photographs Division, Washington, DC.

ally editing what nevertheless remains a gruesome scene. Horses are visible through the slats of two layers of fence on the left, and on the right a horse-drawn buggy recalls the hearse of death come to collect the corpses.[23] The horse that pulls the buggy has moved during the long exposure, making most of its head disappear, further heightening the otherworldly atmosphere of the space beyond the fences.

Gardner's photographs of the dead dismayed and compelled viewers with their "terrible distinctness." They also disheartened them by showing the suddenness of death in battle, for the "Good Death" was nowhere visible in these scenes of mangled bodies that would be buried together in mass graves. As Drew Gilpin Faust has outlined, in the mid-nineteenth century, before the Civil War, dying still took place primarily in the intimate confines of the home, where the terminally ill were surrounded by loved ones who helped them through, and witnessed, the ritualized process of the "Good Death." A death was deemed "good" if one could demonstrate that he or she was prepared to die, accepted God's will, and could pass on to loved ones the irrefutable wisdom of words from the deathbed. A good death assured loved ones that they would eventually be reunited in the afterlife.[24] What Gardner's photographs of Antietam showed were men caught quickly and violently by death, without the comfort or consolation of loved ones near to witness their passing. The photographs showed extensive death, and bad death, and finally death that would not be consecrated or humanized by individual burials.[25]

As photography brought scenes of the battlefield to those at home, it also brought home to the battlefield, allowing some soldiers to be with family by proxy in their final moments. A number of soldiers, mortally wounded, but with a few moments to spare and their wits about them, used photographs to recall the loved ones who should have been physically present at their passing. As Faust reports, "Descriptions of battle's aftermath often remark on the photographs found alongside soldiers' corpses. . . . Denied the presence of actual kin, many dying men removed pictures from pockets or knapsacks and spent their last moments communicating with these representations of absent loved ones."[26]

Gardner's photograph, so full of the evidence of death, and of the remains of battle, reinforces the emptiness of Mann's images of Antietam but also fills them. Mann's work hails a viewer who can recall the earlier image, just as Gardner himself depended on a visual culture saturated with images and narratives of the war to make legible his singular photographs.[27] In the 1860s, Gardner was learning to frame a view; indeed, he was learning to frame *the* view of the Civil War. Mann's photographs refer and even defer to Gardner's, but as Anthony W. Lee has argued, Gardner's photographs were also belated, as they could not capture the war but only discrete scenes stilled after the fact. In other words, the absence so pronounced in Mann's photographs of Antietam was also present in nineteenth-century Civil War photographs, if to a different degree. According to Lee, Gardner's famous photographs of Antietam were "prodigious attempts to signal an action nowhere present": "The camera pictured not events but instead only the sites and remains of events already passed . . . it everywhere betrayed its own belatedness."[28] Gardner and Gibson crept to the brink of war with their images of death and destruction, registering bodies and buildings and terrain touched by violence, but they could not capture the events of war. Their landscapes without corpses are even more

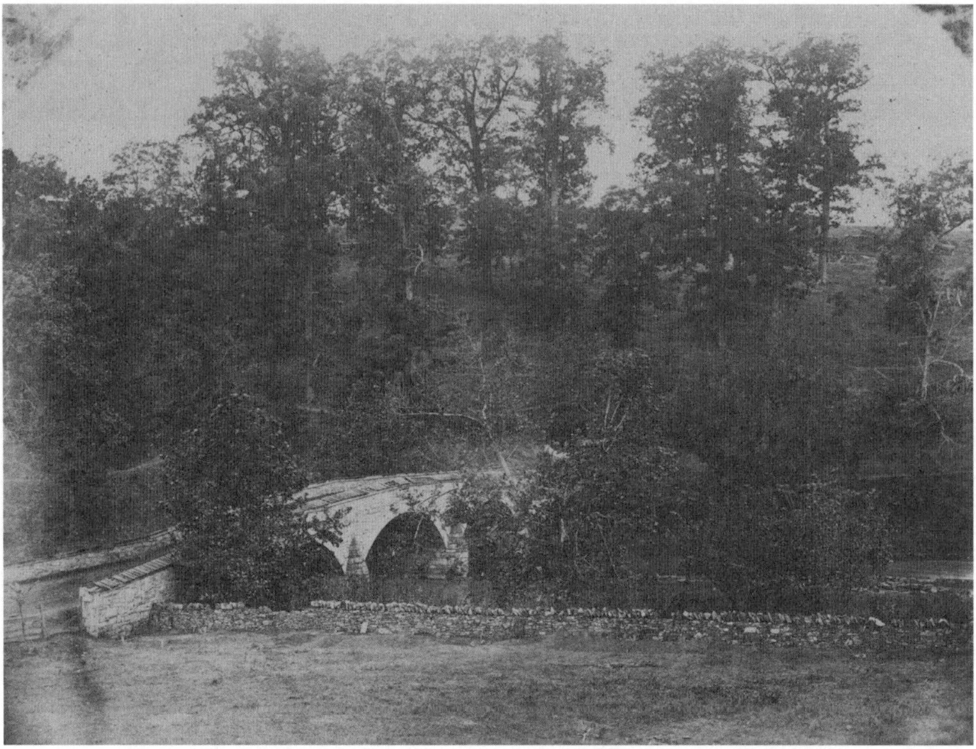

FIGURE 2.6 Alexander Gardner, *Burnside Bridge, across Antietam Creek, Maryland*, 1862. Albumen print. From Gardner's *Photographic Sketch Book of the Civil War*, no. 20. Library of Congress, Prints and Photographs Division, Washington, DC.

pronounced in their belatedness. For example, Gardner (or perhaps Gibson) took a number of empty, tranquil pictures of Burnside Bridge, noting, "'It was at this point that some of the most desperate fighting of the battle of Antietam occurred'" (fig. 2.6).[29] With these quiet, elegiac images they underscore the passing of time, inviting future viewers to imagine the "desperate fighting" nowhere visible in their photographs. Even for the "original" Civil War photographers, then, the photographic referent persisted out of view; something was captured before the camera's lens, but never the war itself. As afterimages, Mann's dark and thick and marred photographs keep one focused on photography, and its limits, showing one the impossibility of historical reclamation and the profound mediation of the past. Mann's reenactments capture first and foremost the material remains of photography itself.

Mann's Antietam photographs recall the long-standing relationship between photography and death. Dark and empty, the images seem to grope back in time for Gardner's Civil War photographs so replete with corpses. But not all of Mann's photographs are devoid of the dead, and in this context the work she undertook just before Antietam brings a new lens to bear on her Civil War battlefield photographs. In 2001, Mann photographed corpses at the University of Tennessee Forensic Anthropology Center, where bodies donated to science are exposed to the elements, left in the woods to decompose, and forensic scientists study the manner and rate of their decomposition.[30] Mann presented this work with her Antietam images in *What Remains*, an exhibition at the Corcoran Gallery of Art from June 12 to September 6, 2004, and they might be said to fill, or at least inform, the empty frames of Mann's battlefield photographs. The forensic images might also account for the resistance some viewers expressed with regard to Mann's Antietam photographs, as the two series were seen and evaluated together, and their effect and meaning infused one another. In her review of the exhibition for the *New York Times*, Sarah Boxer criticized what she saw as "two kinds of violation" in the show, both the "violation of the privacy and the decency of the dead" and "the dreadful things Ms. Mann has done to the surfaces of her photographs."[31]

Boxer's critique misses the way Mann's "dreadful surfaces" call attention to both the materiality of photography and Mann's exaggerated presence in making these marred images. However, her discussion of the "violation of the privacy and decency of the dead" is more complicated, and calls to mind nineteenth-century anxieties about Civil War soldiers killed in battle, whose bodies lay bloating in the sun for days before they could be buried in shallow graves.[32] These bodies created anguish for survivors who could not bear the thought of such unsentimental, and unmarked, disposal of loved ones. As Faust observes, "Tens of thousands of men were interred without either identities or ritual observances," and survivors "found undocumented, unconfirmed, and unrecognized loss intolerable."[33] Not knowing when, or where, or how, or even if a loved one's body was buried created profound anxieties for nineteenth-century survivors unable to care for the dying and the dead.

The Forensic Anthropology Center at the University of Tennessee is, for many, a disturbing place by definition. John Ravenal explains the work of the laboratory: “In order to test and document the decomposition of human flesh under a wide range of simulated natural, accidental, and criminal circumstances, the bodies are buried in shallow graves, deposited in the open air, hidden in wooded areas, covered with plastic wrap, submerged in pools of water, or placed in rusting cars. Some are clothed but more often they are naked; occasionally they are subjected to fire, chemicals, and other artificial effects.”[34] The intersecting vectors at the site are widely divergent: there is the forensic science of decay and decomposition, the stuff of observation, sampling, and chemical analysis; there are the nightmares evoked by bodies left and found in the woods, the stuff of horror films, serial murders, police investigations, and national scandals; there is nature in all of its complexity, as well as vast and varied cultural responses to death.

Mann’s black-and-white images of decomposing bodies are carefully lit, with rich dark tones and smoky brights. Light filtering through the trees dapples bodies paired together, making some of the scenes look almost romantic, despite mummified skin and empty eye sockets. Close-ups of mottled epidermis and the dark shriveled toes of a foot become literal still lifes. The images are at once repellent and compelling. In one image a grassy hill scattered with leaves rises up from the bottom to the center of the frame (fig. 2.7). The photograph suggests that the viewer is entering a clearing in the woods, enclosed on the left and across the top by dense trees and shrubs. The scene is dark, as if at dusk, and on the left the leaves of a bush shine unnaturally in the darkness. Just above the center of the frame, a white form lying on the grass stands out incongruously in contrast to the dim wooded space. It appears to be a large plastic bag, tied at either end, enclosing something long and hefty. The bag occupies the point of sharpest focus in the image, and a vignetting of the camera lens elongates and blurs the leaves in the foreground, which seem to rush visually toward the white form in the center of the frame. The image recalls a scene from Michelangelo Antonioni’s *Blow Up*, a scene that one never quite sees—that of a murdered body left under a bush in a park at dusk.

Oddly enough, the images of the more deteriorated corpses are easier to look at because the fleshy, recently dead bodies still resemble the forms of people one might know. A female body curled on its side, bottom sagging slightly, is familiar, with knees bent, the lower leg pressing into the slack skin of the leg above. The feet of the corpse lie side by side in an ordinary gesture, but the bottom foot is distended. Bands with tags encircle swollen ankles.

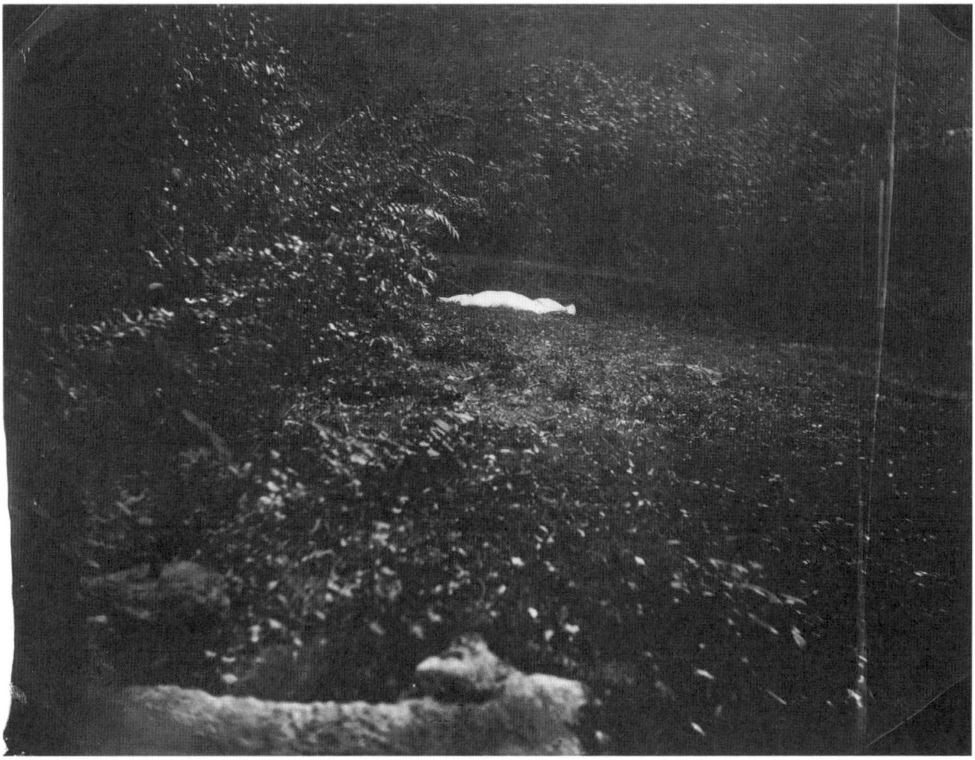

FIGURE 2.7 Sally Mann, *Untitled*, 2000. Gelatin silver print, 30 × 38 inches (76.2 × 96.5 cm). © Sally Mann. Courtesy Gagosian.

It is hard to read this body simply as biological material; it is difficult not to care for it.

A head melts into the ground. The tightly framed face has liquefied and oozes and melds into pine needles and leaves and earth.[35] It is recognizable as a head mostly because of the abundant white hair that remains attached to it, and the hint of an ear in the middle of the form. Some part of the skin seems to have peeled back from the shoulder, revealing a deeper layer textured like orange rind (fig. 2.8). Mann photographed this decaying corpse a number of times: she captured it full length beneath the arching bows of leafy vines, and then apparently months later, after the leaves had fallen and the corpse had shrunk down to the form of its skeleton, the remaining skin mummified.

Many of Mann's corpses are still fleshy, decaying hosts for a variety of

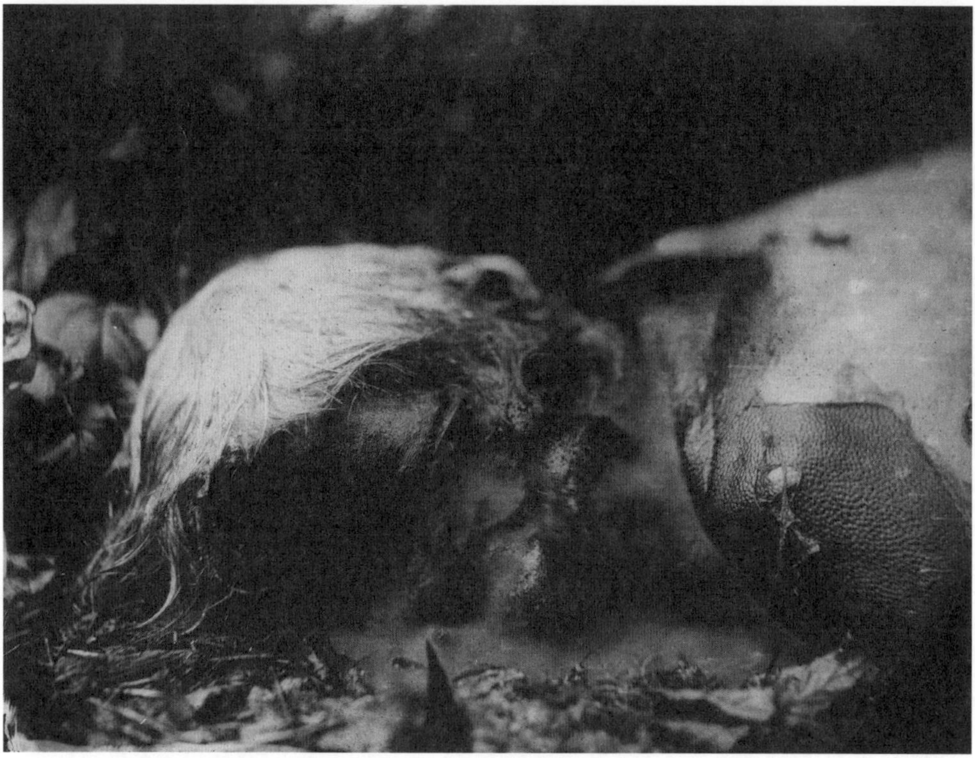

FIGURE 2.8 Sally Mann, *Untitled*, 2000. Gelatin silver print, 30 × 38 inches (76.2 × 96.5 cm). © Sally Mann. Courtesy Gagosian.

carnivorous creatures, bodies with a long way to go before they dissolve into the cold clarity of bones. As Rebecca Schneider has argued, the flesh is a kind of remains not easily reconciled to Western ways of knowing; unlike bones, flesh cannot be archived, but persists as messy, fleeting excess that unsettles systems of documentation.[36] If the bones record forces that have impacted a body "like a palimpsest,"[37] the flesh continues to shift and transform, taking its record with it. At the Forensic Anthropology Center at the University of Tennessee, scientists are trying to learn how to read the flesh, decode its secrets, and script its narratives.

Mann used the collodion wet-plate process to photograph at the forensic laboratory, and here her shrinking and shriveling emulsions echo the skin that tightens and slackens in her images. Sometimes the photographic skin is in worse shape than the decomposing flesh of her subjects. In the photograph of the recently deceased corpse, for example, the collodion of the glass plate is terribly marred and torn, as though the emulsion was scraped back from the negative, perhaps as Mann loaded it into the light-tight carrier. Once again, although one might at first guess that Mann is careless, it is more likely that she was careful in achieving this effect. In the final step of her process, Mann treats her prints with Soluvar matte varnish mixed with diatomaceous earth, the white powder of algae fossils, ensuring that her photographic surfaces are touched by soil. Mann marks her images with the stuff of photography, of earth, and of the body.

Like Sally Mann, writer Mary Roach visited the forensic laboratory at the University of Tennessee in order to learn more about the process of physical deterioration after death. She went to the site as part of her research on what might be called the afterlife of human corpses, asking, "When you let nature take its course, just exactly what course does it take?"[38] She learned that the first stage of human decay is marked by "autolysis, or self-digestion": enzymes eat through cell walls, allowing the liquid inside them to ooze out. That liquid separates the layers of skin, and the top coat begins to slough off. Flies lay eggs at the body's entry points, and freshly hatched larvae feast on fat. Deeper inside the body bacteria eat the liquid released from cells, and as bacteria eat and excrete they produce gas that causes the body to bloat. After about a week, something in the body gives way, releasing the gas, and putrefaction begins in earnest. "Putrefaction refers to the breaking down and gradual liquefaction of tissue by bacteria." The digestive organs and lungs deteriorate first, as they have the largest number of bacteria, and the brain also dissolves quickly. After three weeks the organs have melted and blended together. Carnivorous beetles devour muscles, and if the skin is not eaten, and the conditions are right, it dries out and mummifies.[39]

In her trip to the site, Roach was most struck by the smell of decaying bodies. Trying to describe it, she says, "It is difficult to put words to the smell of decomposing human. It is dense and cloying, sweet but not flower-sweet. Halfway between rotting fruit and rotting meat."[40] As one of her colleagues noted, "The smell just stays with you."[41] Indeed, Roach confides, "The soles of my boots, despite washing and soaking in Clorox, would smell of corpse for months after my visit."[42] Roach's description of the forensic laboratory enables one to return to Mann's photographs with what Mark Smith calls an "intersensorial" perspective.[43] In recent years, scholars have begun to unsettle the primacy of vision so salient in regard to photographs, encouraging viewers to attend to the sound of the photograph and to its touch and feel.[44] Extending further the sensory reach of the image, Sally Mann's views of corpses invite one to heed the smell of the photograph.[45]

Photographs of dead bodies hint at olfaction,[46] and when combined with narratives about the experience of smell, like Roach's, photographs further animate and expand the range of one's sensory understanding of specific sites. A "World correspondent" describing the "Horrors of the Battlefield" at Antietam in the October 11, 1862, *Harper's Weekly* declared, "The stench which arose from the bodies decomposing in the sun was almost unendurable."[47] In his own assessment of Civil War photographs of human and horse corpses, historian Mark Smith turns to the letters and diaries of the residents of Gettysburg at the time, which recount the horrible heaviness and thickness of the atmosphere days after the famous July battle. A young volunteer nurse describes the stench as follows: "The air grew heavier and fouler until it seemed to possess a palpable horrible density that could be seen and felt and cut with a knife."[48] In other words, the air smelled so bad you could see and feel it. As smell transmogrifies into sight, viewing might also become olfactory and photographs might be said to reek.

Sally Mann's photographs are thick with an atmosphere that one might understand to be dense with smell. As she clouds her photographs, she also calls attention to the air itself, "the medium for olfaction."[49] In one of her photographs of a large body lying face down, long white vertical bands and scratches form a kind of curtain that shrouds the body from the viewer. On the left the bands clump together into a semitransparent, textured white mist, and in the very center of the image a dark smoky spot seems to rise out of the corpse. The scratches remind one of the photographer's (clumsy) touch and the noxious fumes of her wet collodion; the murky whiteness, punctuated by the small dark blot, suggests a heavy air, one that might be laden with the smell of decay emanating from the body or of chemistry dripping off the photographic plate. Another image is so permeated by white smoke that it is almost hard to see the decaying body sprawled on the leafy ground (fig. 2.9). This image underscores the thick atmosphere, calling attention to what one must see *through* in order to see, suggesting an intense "intersensoriality" in which one can hardly see the scene for the smell. The image bears other traces of intersensoriality as well; it is marked prominently by Mann's touch—her chemically stained fingers have left dark prints in the upper left corner of the image.

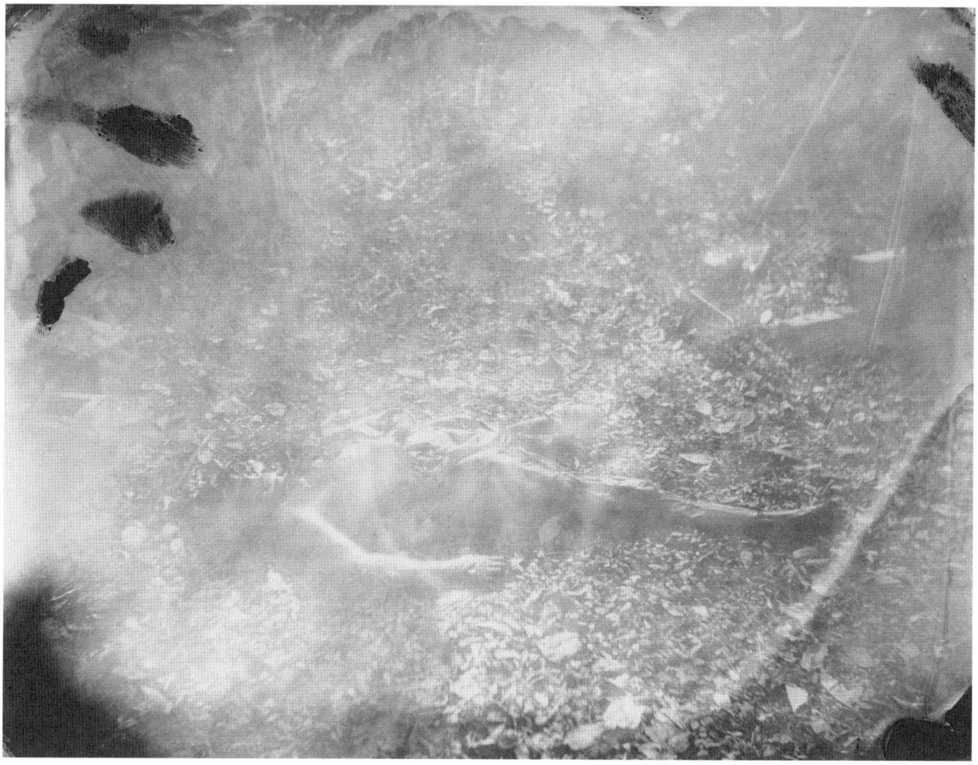

FIGURE 2.9 Sally Mann, *Untitled*, 2000. Gelatin silver print, 30 × 38 inches (76.2 × 96.5 cm). © Sally Mann. Courtesy Gagosian.

With their evidence of touch and suggestion of smell, Mann's photographs unsettle the optical primacy of the photograph as well as its pristine surfaces.[50] They also invite an unexpected intimacy, as smell registers particles of foreign material taken into the body and ingested, blurring the boundaries of interiority and exteriority.[51] As Mann worked in the forested forensic laboratory, particles from the bodies she photographed entered her own body, and the corpses became part of her living being. In the seepage of light and dust and air intrinsic to her process, odiferous particles borne through the air fixed in her nasal cavities even as they also adhered to her wet collodion plates. As she made close-up views, the legs of the tripod supporting her large-format camera dug into soil saturated with the liquid ooze of decaying bodies. In one instance, she put the camera itself on the ground, and stretched out flat behind it.[52] Did she, like Roach, wash everything that touched the ground with Clorox? Or did she accept, even invite, this pungent residue? Part of what one sees in Mann's photographs, which announce her process so loudly in their marks and marring and smoky atmospheres, is the smell of photography.

Photography bore intimate relations to death throughout the nineteenth century, and the practice was incorporated into new rituals of mourning. As Gardner made startling views of soldiers killed on the battlefield, other photographers invented new forms for memorializing the civilian dead, advertising their services in postmortem photography to the bereaved, and in special cases, proclaiming skills in spirit photography. Postmortem portraits were photographs made to function precisely as portraits, those preeminent representations of (living) subjects, and such an image, especially of a young child, was sometimes the only photograph a family could secure, standing as the only visual representation of a life lived. Therefore, photographers often posed their deceased subjects as if living, basking in a peaceful sleep, and today many viewers find these images somewhat disturbing, even if compelling, because they seem to confuse and blur the boundaries that separate life from death. As Kelly Christian has demonstrated, postmortem photographers worked under extremely constrained conditions, hoping to make it to the body before rigor mortis set in, negotiating bereaved family members, dealing with the excretions of the newly dead, and manipulating the body in various ways to make it appear alive. In one startling account relayed by Christian, a photographer gives fellow practitioners advice on how to close the eyes of the deceased, rubbing them with photographic chemistry to set the face in place before it is captured in a photograph.[53] In this instance, the relationship between photography and death, between photography and the corpse, could not be more intimate or direct, as the dead body is literally fixed photographically.

Postmortem portraits were part of an elaborate culture of mourning in the nineteenth-century United States. Just as the "good death" was defined by a set of protocols, so were proper mourning practices. As Faust has outlined, the mourning rituals of dress included colors to be worn for specific lengths of time, through periods of deep mourning and half mourning that ranged in length from six months to two and a half years. Only black was appropriate for deep mourning, but after a set period of time, women might begin to incorporate gray and lavender into their dress as they observed half mourning.[54]

As women displayed their grief and status as mourners publicly, they also produced private photo-objects to memorialize the dead, combining photographs with even more indexical traces of the departed, such as locks of hair or snippets of garments, and extending the temporal frame of the photograph with the labor of needlework and collage.[55]

Spirit photographs also brought photography to bear on changing responses to death in the nineteenth century. Such images, popularized by William Mumler in the United States during the Civil War, used photographic techniques of double exposure to combine a regular studio portrait with the shadowy image of a "spirit extra."[56] Supported by the rise of Spiritualism, a popular movement that sought to prove scientifically the existence of ghosts, spirit photographs claimed to record extrasensory presences. Early Spiritualist experiments with mediums emphasized auditory communication with spirits, but by the 1870s, as Molly McGarry has argued, a "second wave of Spiritualism" brought "a shift from sound to vision . . . paralleling new developments in photography."[57] Mumler led the way in this new photographic practice, making spirit photographs in Boston as early as 1861. He proposed that, with the help of his clairvoyant wife, Hannah, his camera could function as a kind of medium, recording the presence of a spirit in the studio. Although the sitter would not see the spirit in the room, the camera would register its presence, and the image of the ghost would be recorded in a photograph.

To twenty-first-century eyes, the manipulation of double exposure in spirit photographs is readily apparent. Although the "spirits" in the photographs appear predictably ethereal and transparent, they also appear very much as they did when alive. For this reason many nineteenth-century viewers declared the images to be a hoax, and some Spiritualists sought to explain this canny resemblance by proposing that spirits might take on their once embodied images to communicate with the living in recognizable form. Mumler himself was famously put on trial for fraud in 1869, and photographers, Spiritualists, and even P. T. Barnum, an "expert" in trickery, testified at the trial. Although the judge declared that he believed spirit photography to be a deception, he ruled in favor of Mumler, stating that the prosecution failed to make a convincing case to disprove the practice.[58]

Read against this history of ritual and Spiritualist belief, the starkness of Mann's forensic photographs comes into full focus. Her images are not memorials, and although they are produced with nineteenth-century technologies, they do not participate in the practices of mourning that animated postmortem portraits and spirit photographs. Indeed, Mann's photographs are not about mourning but about "matter." In her book *What Remains* (2003), she introduces the section *Matter Lent* with text from a seventeenth-century sermon on death by Jacques-Bénigne Bossuet (1627–1704):

> All things summon us to death;
> Nature, almost envious of the good she has given us,
> Tells us often and gives us notice that she cannot
> For long allow us that scrap of matter she has lent . . .
> She has need of it for other forms,
> She claims it back for other works.[59]

Mann's photographs focus on the ways the earth reclaims the physical material of the body, and as John Ravenal states, "*Matter Lent* shows the earth to be a greedy and impatient host, absorbing its denizens quickly into its own body once their spirits have departed."[60] Mann's work strips the dead of the comforting rituals that reaffirm the community of the living, and in this way it is not surprising that the images provoke anxiety for many viewers (fig. 2.10). But perhaps those who have criticized her work for violating the privacy of the dead are actually responding to the utter, "indecent" disregard of beetles and maggots for the bodies of once living beings. The photographs ask one to look at scenes that are largely obscured for twenty-first-century viewers, scenes of death familiar to nineteenth-century viewers, and scenes of decay that became shockingly familiar during the Civil War.

Anxieties about death were intertwined with anxieties about race and the social death of slavery during the Civil War. Once again, Antietam was the catalyst that incited Lincoln to issue the Emancipation Proclamation, definitively linking the Civil War to the end of slavery. As discussed in chapter 1, slavery fundamentally troubled the terms of self-possession and personhood on which citizenship was founded: the enslaved, the fugitive slave, and the so-called contraband were all persons legally considered property.[61] After the Emancipation Proclamation, how were the formerly enslaved and self-emancipated to be incorporated into a white supremacist nation?

Another Gardner photograph brings such questions into view. *A Burial Party, Cold Harbor, Virginia* (1865), shows five African American soldiers burying corpses from the battle of Cold Harbor (fig. 2.11). In that battle, which had taken place ten months earlier, seven thousand Union soldiers died in a single morning. It was the custom of the time for local residents to bury the

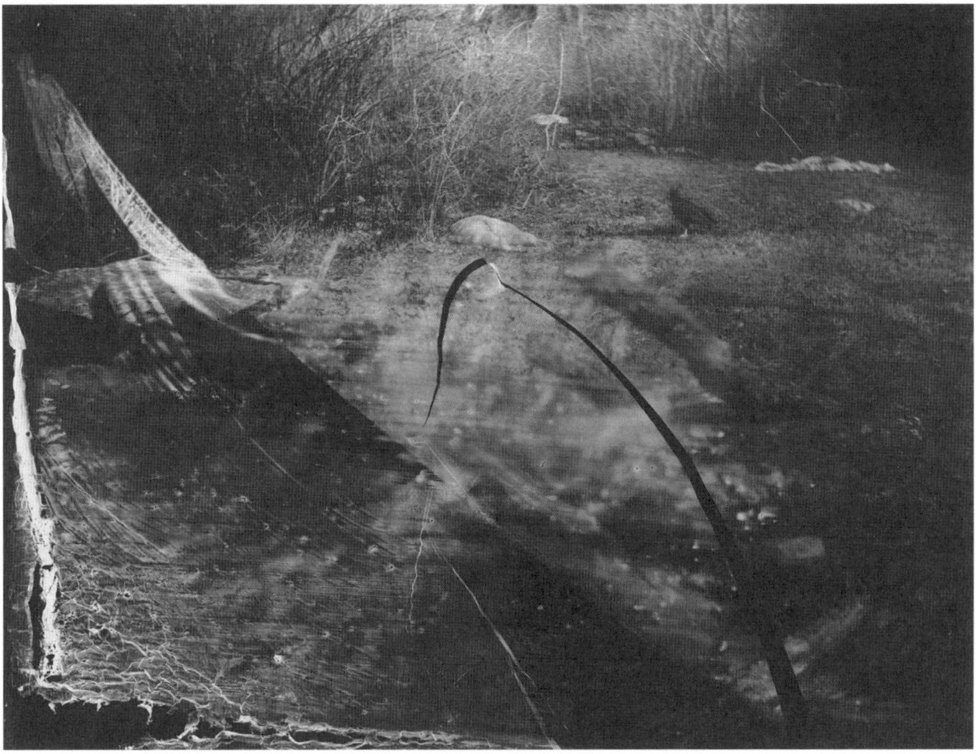

FIGURE 2.10 Sally Mann, *Untitled*, 2000. Gelatin silver print, 30 × 38 inches (76.2 × 96.5 cm). © Sally Mann. Courtesy Gagosian.

bodies of the dead, regardless of their loyalties, but the people of Cold Harbor defied this practice and left the corpses to decompose uninterred.[62] When Union soldiers returned to the scene ten months later, the bodies were in a state of advanced decay.

In Gardner's photograph, an African American soldier sits behind a stretcher stacked with a disconcerting jumble of bones.[63] Surely the disarray of skeletal remains would have disturbed nineteenth-century viewers for its display of bad death and disregard for the remains of the dead. But the African American soldier tending to the remains might also have troubled white viewers' conceptions of selfhood and citizenship. In the photograph, his head falls uncannily in line with the skulls on the cart, begging for them to be likened to one another. Both the man and the skull closest to him seem to

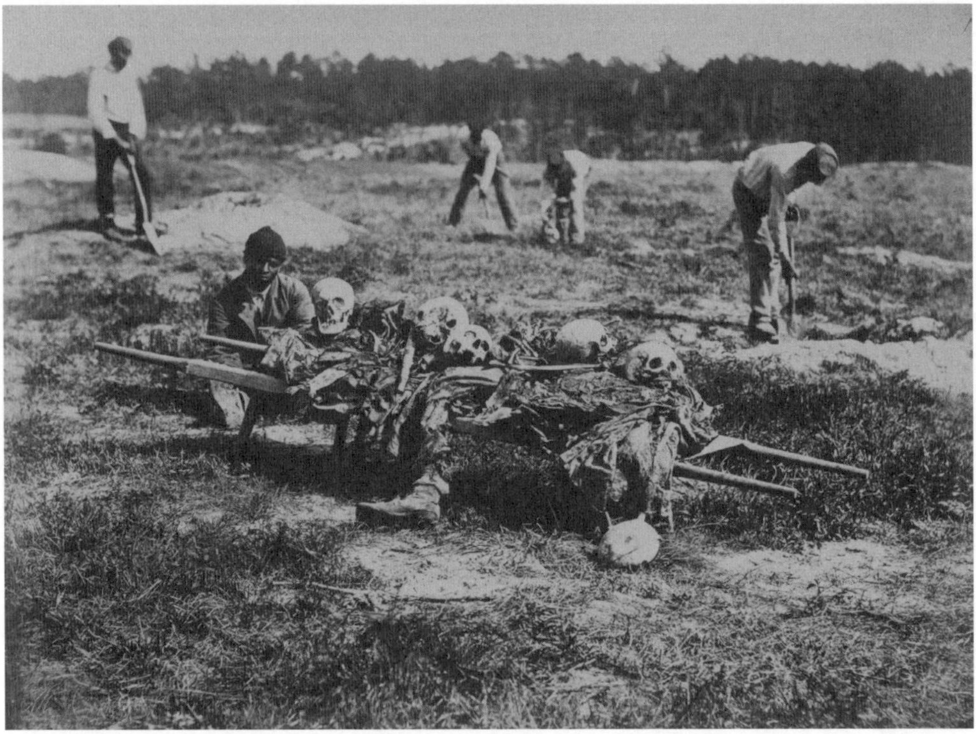

FIGURE 2.11 John Reekie and Alexander Gardner, *A Burial Party, Cold Harbor, Virginia*, 1865. Albumen print. From Gardner's *Photographic Sketch Book of the Civil War*, no. 94. Library of Congress, Prints and Photographs Division, Washington, DC.

stare back at viewers.[64] Made two years after the Emancipation Proclamation, the photograph attests to African American soldiers in the Union army. But it also shows, in Saidiya Hartman's words, how "in the aftermath of emancipation the place of blacks within the body politic was still uncertain."[65] In the wake of the war, the claims of African Americans to full citizenship and even humanity would continue to test the racialized bounds of the nation.

Indeed, even the African American soldier, welcomed to Union troops by Lincoln, had to be visually inscribed into manhood. As Maurice O. Wallace has argued, "The first possibility of an imagined national black manhood was constructed by the technological and commercial means of Civil War photography. . . . Very powerfully, photography made visible . . . black male bodies no longer outside of the law as ciphers to its civil and human rights but directly beneath its custodial thumb."[66] According to Wallace, photography helped people to see how the slave was made into a man, in Frederick Douglass's famous words, drawing black masculinity into view in the photograph of the black soldier. But as it did so, it also contained black masculinity within hierarchies of spectacle and display, as well as legal forms of servitude in the post-Reconstruction era. Wallace proposes that the state's surveillance of black manhood was intertwined with the reinvention of black servitude in the prison camp, a legal form of post–Civil War slavery enabled by the Thirteenth Amendment, as discussed in the following chapter. Mann's photographs, therefore, are haunted not only by the physical death of soldiers but also by the social death of slavery and its reinvention in the prison industrial complex.[67] They conjure questions brought into focus during the Civil War that remain unresolved today—questions about the racially differential terms of citizenship.

———

Today it is almost impossible to think about photography and death without returning, as so many scholars have done, to Roland Barthes's *Camera Lucida*, a book about photography that is saturated with death. Contemplating the striking portrait of a young prisoner condemned to death, Barthes states, "I observe with horror an anterior future of which death is the stake. . . . The photograph tells me death in the future." "Whether or not the subject is already dead, every photograph is this catastrophe."[68]

Barthes's thoughts on the "catastrophe" of photography are inspired by a Civil War photograph made by Alexander Gardner, but surprisingly not one of his grisly battlefield scenes. Instead, it is a portrait of Lewis Powell (also known as Lewis Payne), participant in the plot to assassinate President Lincoln, vice president Andrew Johnson, and secretary of state William H. Seward (figure 2.12).[69] The man condemned for conspiracy and attempted murder hovers briefly on the threshold between life and death, and it is the certainty of his impending death that alarms Barthes, allowing him to see in the photograph an extreme or heightened version of what is also the case for every photographic portrait—the photograph will outlive its subject, and viewers will look back, like Barthes, and understand that "he is dead and he is going to die."

For Barthes, all photographic subjects approach death, but perhaps this photograph uniquely tells him death in the future because it also evokes

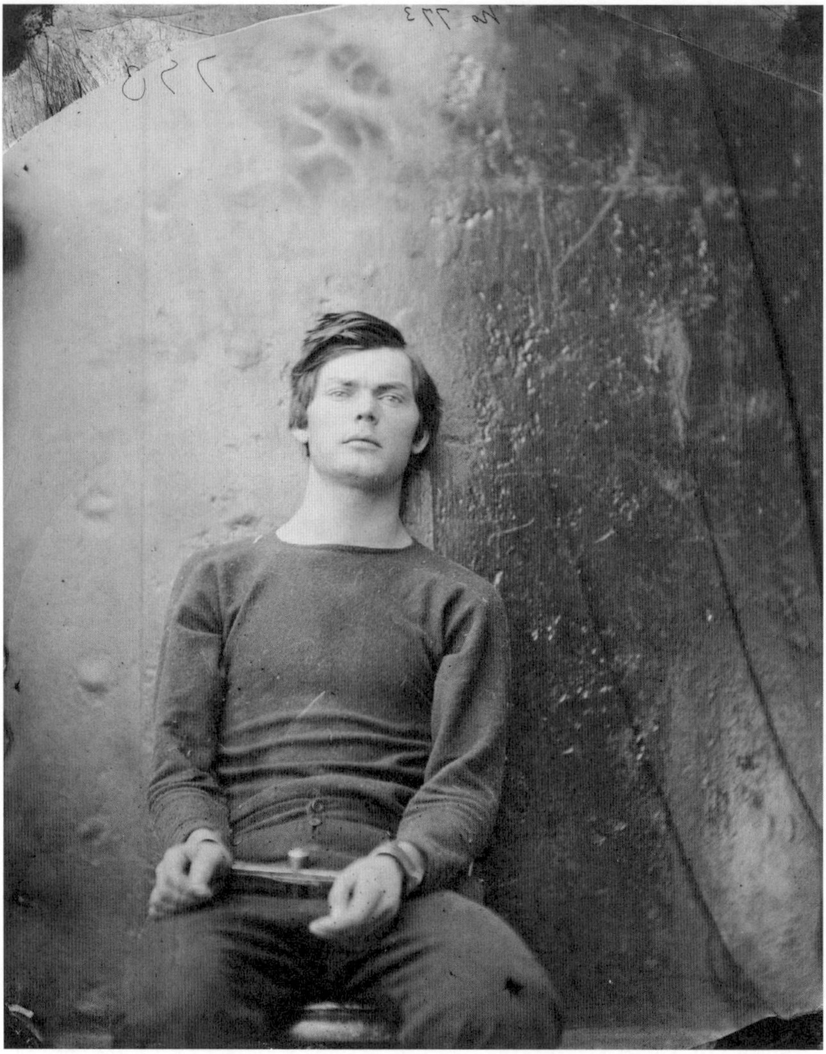

FIGURE 2.12 Alexander Gardner, *Lewis Payne [Lewis Powell]*, 1865. Glass negative. Library of Congress, Prints and Photographs Division, Washington, DC.

so much death in the past. The Civil War haunts Gardner's photograph of Powell, and as one looks at the image of Powell it is hard not to recall Gardner's photographs of all the bodies left dead. One looks at the photograph of Powell and understands that Lincoln is dead and he is going to die. One looks and understands that the soldiers of the battle of Antietam, and the soldiers of the battle of Cold Harbor, African American and white, are dead and they are going to die.

Mann's photographs of Antietam are also about death and photography. In their emptiness and opacity they point to the photograph's limits and absences, but also to its substance. Her vacant images evoke the bodies that populate earlier photographs of these same battlefields, scenes that even at the time marked the belatedness of photographers to the events of war. But as Mann's Antietam photographs seem devoid of subjects, they are unusually marked by the photographer herself. Mann highlights her presence almost obsessively in the images, in the traces of stained fingers, in the haphazard application of collodion, in scratches and smudges, and the smoky light leaks of ill-fitting lenses—in the matter of photography itself. Such blemishes draw attention to the surface of the photographic plate, to the chemical and material elements of the photograph, and to the photographer's hand in making it.[70] Mann refuses to disappear from her images, and her presence pulls death into life, past into present, activating the oscillating time of the photograph.[71]

Mann's irregular images, consistently imprinted with her touch, recall Barthes's musings on the tactile nature of the photograph. Barthes famously proposed that photographed subjects touch their viewers with an uncanny caress: "The photograph is literally an emanation of the referent. From a real body, which was there, proceed radiations which ultimately touch me, who am here."[72] The only body actually photographed in Mann's Antietam images is her own. She reinserts the photographer back into the dynamic from which Barthes would remove her, announcing her presence as mediator of a photographic past. Leaving residues of her own flesh in the photographs, Mann gestures toward her own anterior future, preserving in her touch a photographic trace of herself beyond death.

Mann's presence in the photographs also pulls the viewer into focus. These opaque images, like *Battlefields, Antietam (Starry Night)* (2001) (plate 4), provide a kind of dark mirror. Asking one to see photography, they also invite one to see oneself seeing, to recognize the time and place from which one views an image and considers a past. Mann's Antietam photographs recall Gardner's images of the dead, but what else do they bring into view? What might one see in them today as the terms of full citizenship continue to be racially circumscribed? As the lives and deaths of African Americans continue to be devalued by the state?

Photographs evoked by other photographs return in unusual ways. They come into focus differently at new moments for distinct viewers. Mann's images refuse to allow one to see through them; instead, they encourage one to reflect on the legacy of photography at the sites they fail to represent. They bring one back to Gardner's photographs of Antietam, to the images that first made death in war visible and tapped into anxieties about race, slavery, and the future of the nation. Today, in the wake of police violence and protest, Mann's photographs might also remind one of the ways in which race continues to determine who can claim full citizenship in the United States, as well as whose deaths—and whose lives—matter.

CHAPTER 3

The Scene of the Crime

Deborah Luster

The man is young and appears slight, despite his muscular forearms. He raises his fists toward his face, assuming a pose that seems both defensive and ready to fight. Cocking his head slightly, he stares directly at the camera with dark, wide-set eyes. His T-shirt announces "Angola Boxing," and he wears a large champion belt that accentuates his thin waist. The man is James Wells, born in Franklin, Louisiana, on July 30, 1976. He is a member of the "Cobras" boxing team, and won the Light-Middleweight Crown at the 2001 Boxing Extravaganza. He is serving a twenty-five-year sentence at Angola prison in Louisiana (fig. 3.1).

This is Deborah Luster's portrait of Wells, part of *One Big Self: Prisoners of Louisiana* (1998–2002), a project in which she photographed men and women incarcerated in her home state over the course of three and a half years. *One Big Self* documents inmates at three sites: Transylvania Prison Farm, Louisiana Correctional Institute for Women, and Louisiana State Penitentiary at Angola. Respectively, these are minimum-security, full-range, and maximum-security facilities. Angola is the largest, housing 5,000 men on 18,000 acres.[1] Together these institutions imprison approximately 6,200 men and women, the majority of whom are African American. Most of the men at Transylvania serve terms of less than five years, while most of those at Angola will die there. As Luster and her collaborator, poet C. D. Wright, note, the United States imprisons more of its citizens than any other country,

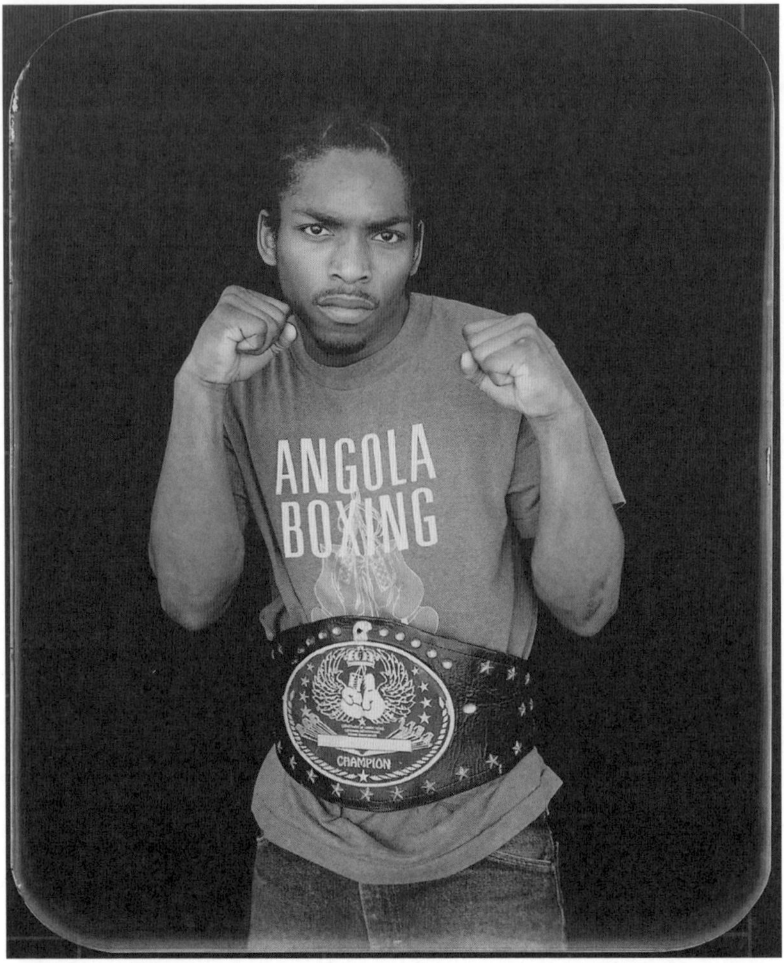

FIGURE 3.1 Deborah Luster, *One Big Self*, James Wells, Angola, Louisiana. Department of Corrections no. 345585. Date of birth: 7.30.76. Place of birth: Franklin. Entered Louisiana State Penitentiary 1996. Sentence: 25 years. Angola "Cobras" boxing team member. Boxing Extravaganza 2001 Light-Middleweight Crown. Photograph made at Louisiana State Penitentiary 4.22.99. Silver emulsion on prepared aluminum. Courtesy the artist and Jack Shainman Gallery.

and "Louisiana imprisons more of its population than any other state in the union."[2]

Looking closely at *One Big Self* and another of Luster's major projects, *Tooth for an Eye: A Chorography of Violence in Orleans Parish* (2008–10), this chapter explores several different kinds of photographic returns. Like Sally Mann, Luster looks back to nineteenth-century photographic processes, using wet-plate collodion or mimicking its forms with contemporary materials. Her work evokes the advent of specific systems of photography in the nineteenth century, exploring the convergence of policing and incarceration with disciplinary practices of photography in the mug shot, the prisoner identification image, and the crime scene photograph. She also physically returns to crime scenes to photograph them years after the violence occurred, and her latter-day images, with their long exposures, provide an oblique form of photographic evidence that points to slow, structural violence.[3]

Luster's images heed time. Her portraits of inmates mark time, noting dates of birth, dates of imprisonment, lengths of sentences, and dates of photographing. Her photographs of crime scenes register the recurrence of violence at specific sites in New Orleans, overlaying the dates of multiple murders on top of one another. The inmates Luster photographs are "doing time"; they are bound to disciplinary carceral routines that measure homogeneous chronological time meted out in sentences. Their worlds are asynchronous with life outside. In photographs that mimic nineteenth-century tintypes, Luster captures the out-of-time, other-time quality of prison life. Her prison portraits double up on the idea that a photograph snatches a moment out of time, showing how photography not only accelerates but also slows time, refusing to concede to an institutional conception of time as the incremental progression of equivalent moments. In this way, her photographic portraits also challenge the standardized disciplinary time of the prison, allowing inmates to choose to make a moment matter and expand and connect to life outside.

Luster's *One Big Self* resists the restrictive parameters of the mug shot and prisoner identification picture and their visual circumscription of inmates. In such institutional portraits the subjects "have no interest in the photographs being made": "They will never receive copies of them and will in most cases never see them."[4] Unlike the police and prison personnel who make such disciplinary images, Luster collaborates with her subjects to the degree that it is possible within the confines and vastly disparate power relations of the prison, and she shares copies of the portraits with the men and women she photographs, giving each of them ten to fifteen wallet-sized images, and allowing them to circulate their photographs both within and outside of the prison. Working within this highly delimited context, Luster aims to enable incarcerated men and women to renegotiate their one-sided relationship to photography and to assert a degree of control over their images. But Luster's work is not only a kind of artist activism; she also circulates the images in art galleries. The photographic encounters she stages are thus complex and multivalent, as ownership of the images and the right to look shift as the photographs, and the photographer, move in and out of the prison.[5]

To produce the images, Luster had to work quickly, as prison personnel would allow her to photograph only one or two days at a time. She taped up a simple black velvet background, and photographed anyone who wanted to be pictured, sometimes forty or fifty people a day. She took ten to fifteen photographs of each of her subjects, and tried not to direct them, asking instead how they would like to be represented.[6] In her portrait of an unnamed white man at Angola, one sees the haphazard manner in which Luster's black velvet cloth is taped to the cinder-block prison walls (fig. 3.2). The backdrop extends the full length of the wall and across the floor toward the viewer, its ends marred and dusty from the stream of subjects. The man stands, turned partly sideways, looking warily at the camera. He wears the dark hat, jeans, and wide-striped shirt of his rodeo gear. His event is bulldoggin'.[7]

Luster's *One Big Self* overtly recalls nineteenth-century institutional systems of policing and carceral identification. Indeed, the images she exhibits approximate nineteenth-century tintypes. She coats four-by-five-inch sheets of aluminum with liquid silver emulsion, making photographs that are durable and weighty, yet also intimate and small, as much objects as images. The "tintypes" include recto image and verso text, and in this way they conjure the codifications of nineteenth-century identification systems that paired photographic likenesses with descriptive text. Further, she displays her image-objects in a custom black steel cabinet reminiscent of nineteenth-century filing systems.[8] Echoing these early forms, Luster encourages viewers to understand her work within the long history of police and prison photography.

Luster's evocation of the visual culture of nineteenth-century criminology also subtly draws into view other linkages between the nineteenth century and the prison industrial complex today. Indeed, the echoes of slavery,

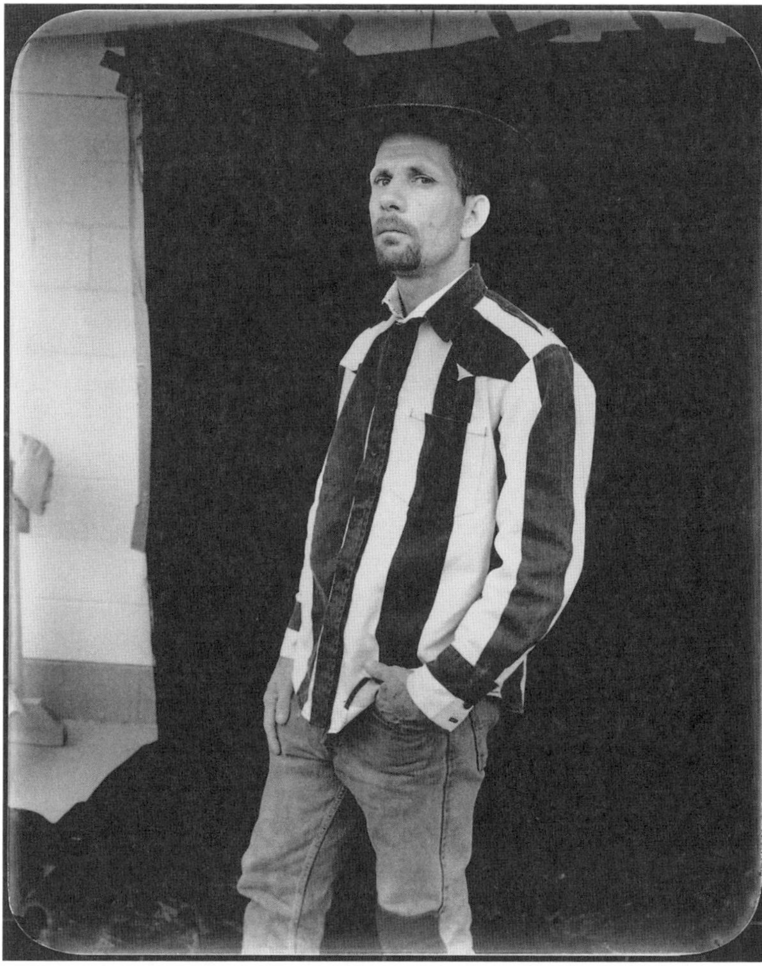

FIGURE 3.2 Deborah Luster, *One Big Self*, Angola, Louisiana. Department of Corrections no. 93665. Date of birth: 6.29.63. Place of birth: Florida. Entered Louisiana State Penitentiary 1982. Sentence: 41 years 9 months. Work: Metal fabrication. Rodeo event: Bulldoggin'. Photograph made at Louisiana State Penitentiary 10.31.99. Silver emulsion on prepared aluminum. Courtesy the artist and Jack Shainman Gallery.

brought to the fore in the previous two chapters, also resound here, through the infamous clause in the Thirteenth Amendment to the US Constitution that officially abolished slavery even as it preserved the system in new form, through imprisonment. The Thirteenth Amendment declares: "Neither slavery nor involuntary servitude, except as punishment for crime whereof the party shall have been duly convicted, shall exist within the United States, or any place subject to their jurisdiction."[9] As Dennis Childs and Michelle Alexander have argued, the amendment that was to quell slavery reinstated it anew through criminal conviction.[10] The legacy of slavery that lives on in the US prison industrial complex is readily brought into view at Angola, which has functioned as a prison *plantation* since the antebellum period, and where, to this day, incarcerated men, overwhelmingly African American, pick cotton.[11] Luster's portrait of Matthew Haynes at Angola, one of a few images she made outside, shows him standing in a field, rows of leafy plants stretching back to the horizon behind him (fig. 3.3). He holds a straw hat to his chest and stairs pensively at the camera. He works Line 1, in Camp C.

Police departments in the United States began photographing suspects as early as the 1850s.[12] The Saint Louis Police Department's photograph collection, for example, includes dozens of ambrotypes and tintypes that date from the 1850s and 1860s.[13] But it was not until later in the nineteenth century, as negative-positive paper printing processes made photographs easy and inexpensive to reproduce, that police stations in the United States and Europe standardized the institutional practice of photography. They used the mug shot, a pair of tightly framed photographs, one with the subject posed in profile, the other looking directly at the camera, to record, catalogue, and identify suspects.

French anthropologist Alphonse Bertillon invented the mug shot as part of an elaborate biometric system—"Bertillonage"—that was widely adopted throughout the United States in the late nineteenth century. He supplemented the paired photographic images with records of nine different physical measurements, including breadth of the arm span, diameter of the head, length of the foot, and even size of the ear. Bertillon's "portrait parle," or talking portrait, also added detailed supporting text to the mug shot, including descriptions of the color of the eyes and hair, as well as written depictions of the face and profile presented in the photographs (fig. 3.4). Indeed, the text on the front of the card occupied as much space as the images, and the back of the card was devoted entirely to written comments, with room to observe any scars or particular marks on the body that might help to identify the indi-

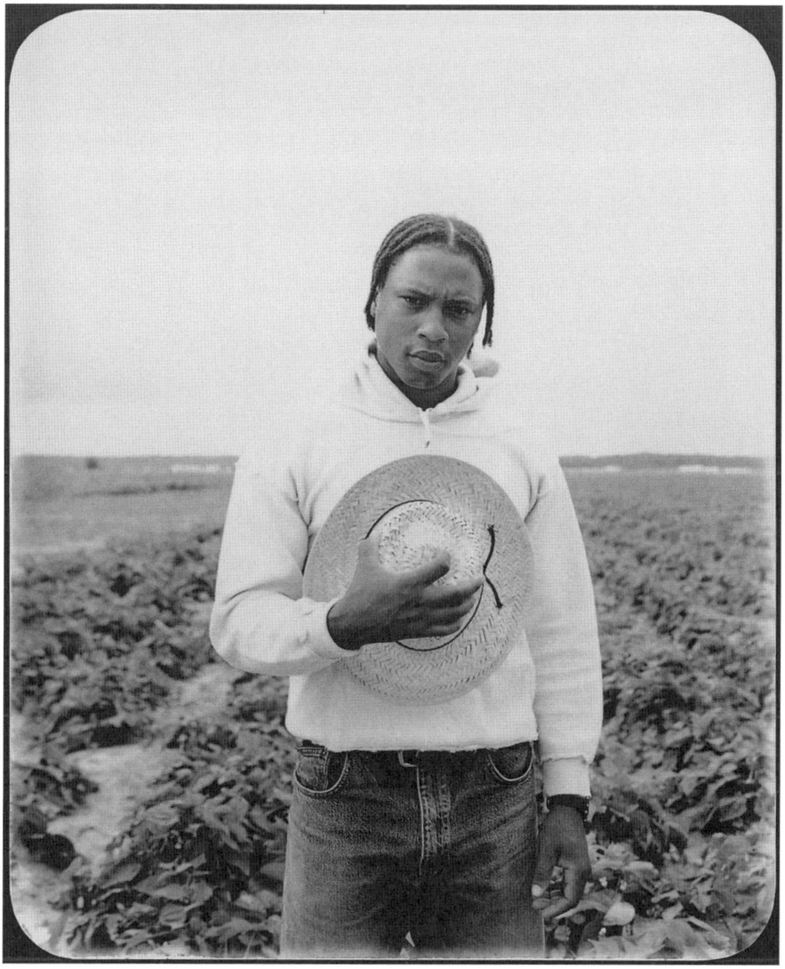

FIGURE 3.3 Deborah Luster, *One Big Self*, Matthew Haynes, Angola, Louisiana. Department of Corrections no. 312754. Date of birth: 1.29.71. Place of birth: New Orleans. Entered Louisiana State Penitentiary 1994. Sentence: Life. Work: Camp C. Line 1. Photograph made at Louisiana State Penitentiary 6.11.99. Silver emulsion on prepared aluminum. Courtesy the artist and Jack Shainman Gallery.

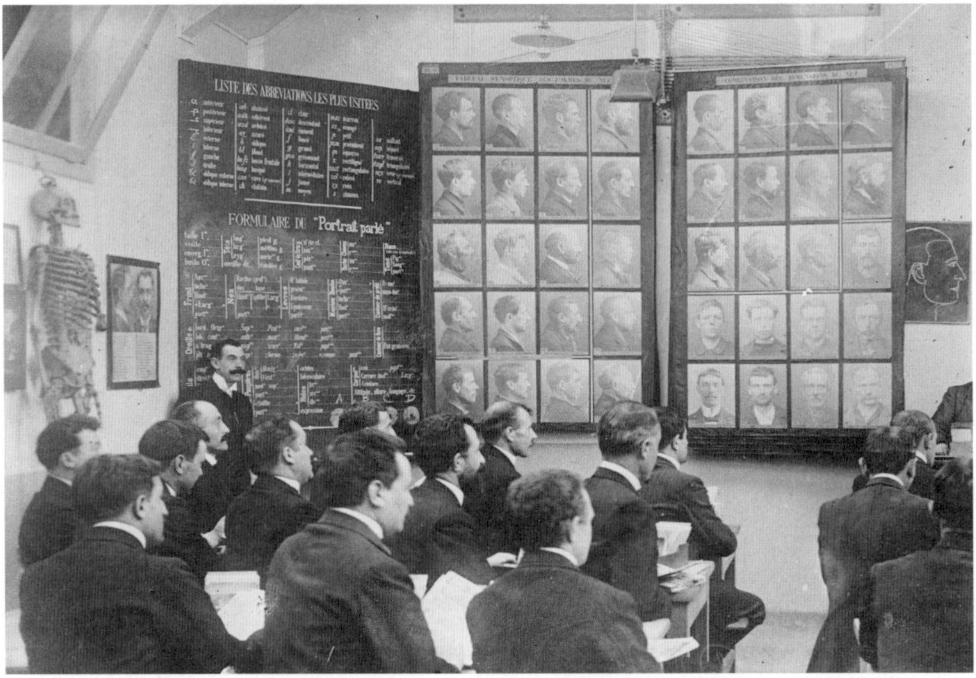

FIGURE 3.4 Portrait Parle class, France, ca. 1910–15. Glass negative. Library of Congress, Prints and Photographs Division, Washington, DC.

vidual, as well as name, address, relatives, and profession. Bertillon designed the system to catch "passers," masters of disguise who committed crimes under different aliases. He proposed that although a repeat offender might camouflage himself, one would be able to discover him if his physical measurements matched those of "another" offender already recorded.

Bertillonage is the exemplar of a professionalized way of seeing, measuring, and recording the body.[14] As such detailed documentation flourished in US police stations in the late nineteenth century, a parallel form of popular, public viewing was also encouraged by the rogues' gallery. As Rachel Hall argues, in the 1860s,

> the rogues' gallery served as a transitional space between community and professional policing. Ordinary Americans visited detective offices, where they consumed outlaw displays curated by the professional police.

> But their practices of looking were variously understood as a popular form of amusement and as an invitation to practice the art of detection as a personal safety strategy. These uses of the rogues' gallery thrived, despite the fact that the initial rationale for its establishment focused on the gallery's instrumental function.[15]

By 1866 such public viewing places had become so popular that the New York City Police Department was forced to close its own rogues' gallery to the public "due to the overwhelming crowds of visitors."[16] Nevertheless police departments worldwide continued to collect photographs of suspects along with biographical information, and in 1886, Thomas Byrnes, chief detective of the New York City Police Department, made such images available to the public in his book *Professional Criminals of America*.[17]

Other visual forms continued to encourage what Hall has called popular "vigilante viewing" throughout the twentieth century: in the 1930s true crime magazines came into vogue, and in 1949 the *Washington Daily News* began to publicize the FBI's "most wanted" lists.[18] In 1988 the FBI's Public Affairs Office collaborated with Fox Network to coproduce the weekly hour-long television show "America's Most Wanted," which showcases "dramatic reenactments of fugitive escapes and prison breaks" to promote "an active audience of armchair crime fighters." By 1994 the show elicited three thousand calls per episode from viewers offering clues and information related to the cases dramatized.[19]

Today the mug shot, first standardized by Bertillon, and popularized in rogues' galleries and the FBI's "most wanted" campaigns, remains an iconic (paired) image, the visual sign that an individual has caught the attention of the police and entered a new kind of visibility, one that threatens removal from public view. The mug shot marks the first step in the visual inscription of the body within policing parameters. It is a liminal point, a threshold, in which the future of the subject represented is still undetermined, in which he or she is caught, by the police and in the flash of a camera, yet still not bound. The subject is neither guilty nor innocent, but her brush with the law has shaded her toward criminality. She is now "suspect," and the mug shot shows it.

If the mug shot represents a liminal state before its subject's fate has been sealed, the prison identification photograph comes after legal determinations and marks an individual as the property of the prison. As Bruce Jackson explains, arrest mug shots "evince the transient condition of a person just taken into custody"; their subjects "face an uncertain future." But in prisoner identification portraits, "all possibility is foreclosed": "The individuals sitting for those photographs have already been in jail, through trial, and unambiguously removed from ordinary life."[20] The prison identification record signals that its subject has been withdrawn, physically and visually, from the so-called free world, and is now bound by new forms of institutional surveillance even as he or she is made largely invisible to the outside world.

Luster enters the prison to make portraits, negotiating and disrupting institutional uses of photography. Her photographs reinstate individuals in social relations through the portrait form, refusing the disciplinary inscription of the mug shot and the prisoner identification photograph. As Allan Sekula has argued, the portrait is bound to discourses of respectability and social acknowledgment, framing individuals as valued citizens; it is always in conversation with its inverse, the mug shot, but the portrait holds its shadow identifications at bay.[21] Even as Luster's recto-verso images, organized in their custom cabinet, call attention to the restrictive institutional spaces and codified systems that her photographs engage, her portraits nevertheless refuse to define and confine their subjects solely within the time and place of the prison.

Luster's images are not the stark frontal and hard profile pairs required by the penal system; instead, they announce themselves as posed portraits, choreographed by both subject and photographer. Further, the information Luster gathers is not intended exclusively to identify her subjects as incarcerated but instead to establish them in relationships beyond the prison walls. Michelle Hill, for example, is the mother of two (plate 5). An inmate at Louisiana Correctional Institute for Women, she presents herself in the crisp white coat and puffy hat of a chef that stand out in bold relief against Luster's black velvet backdrop. She poses slightly turned away from the camera, and her face, framed by the white bonnet, is calm and beautiful, on the verge of a smile. On the back of the tintype Luster has written notations in white ink, drawing a visual parallel to the white-against-black pattern of the portrait. She notes the institution in which Hill resides with the initials "L.C.I.W.," and then records her name and Department of Corrections number, the date and place of her birth, and length of her sentence. Luster also indicates that Hill has two children and works in the culinary arts, and finally she writes the date on which the photograph was made, April 30, 1999. Luster juxtaposes Hill's institutional identity, her Department of Corrections number, with her status as a mother and her creative work, refusing to reduce Hill to her position within the prison. Such notations are a standard element in Luster's project, with slight variations due to information men and women choose to share. Those with shorter sentences occasionally comment on their postprison plans, which often include, simply, "work."[22] The information Luster records on the backside of portraits denotes lives and futures that extend beyond the spatial confines of the prison and the temporal bounds of the prison sentence.

The men and women Luster photographs send their portraits to family members outside, as well as to loved ones residing in other prisons. The photographs thus circulate within the subjects' own communities, helping to reinforce bonds of affection and memory within and outside the prison walls.[23] In his portrait, Keith Gabriel holds a small white board on which he has written, "Missing you" (fig. 3.5). Presumably, Gabriel had a specific recipient of his portrait in mind when he and Luster made this image, and today, perhaps, that person keeps a wallet-sized print close at hand. Luster has stated, "The act of photographing and returning prints to these incarcerated persons and their eventual distribution of the portraits to friends and family are as important to this project, and compelling to me, as any formal exhibition or publication of the images." She has said she would like to have a map of the paths these photographs take as they circulate near and far, linking individuals in a larger social web.[24]

As incarcerated people send Luster's photographs to establish and reinforce social bonds, the photographer also circulates the images within her own social and professional networks. With her subjects' permission, she presents them for anonymous viewers in "formal exhibition [and] publication." One might encounter Gabriel's image as I first did, as a small metallic object in an art gallery. In such a setting the "missing you" message feels like a direct address, and one is invited to imagine that she is Gabriel's intimate. But in these contexts, this address is also an uncomfortable invitation to voyeurism that asks one to attend to the situation of viewing, and the intended viewer (that one is not).

The cabinet in which Luster presents her portraits also subtly invites a voyeuristic gaze, for it recalls not only the police file but also the cabinet of curiosities. Some of the men and women she photographs pose in elaborate and striking costumes. Some appear decidedly "curious," almost freakish. At the minimum-security L.C.I.W., the inmates celebrate both Halloween and Mardi Gras, and several of the women presented themselves for their portraits in costume. Yolanda Banks sits before the camera in a half mask and elabo-

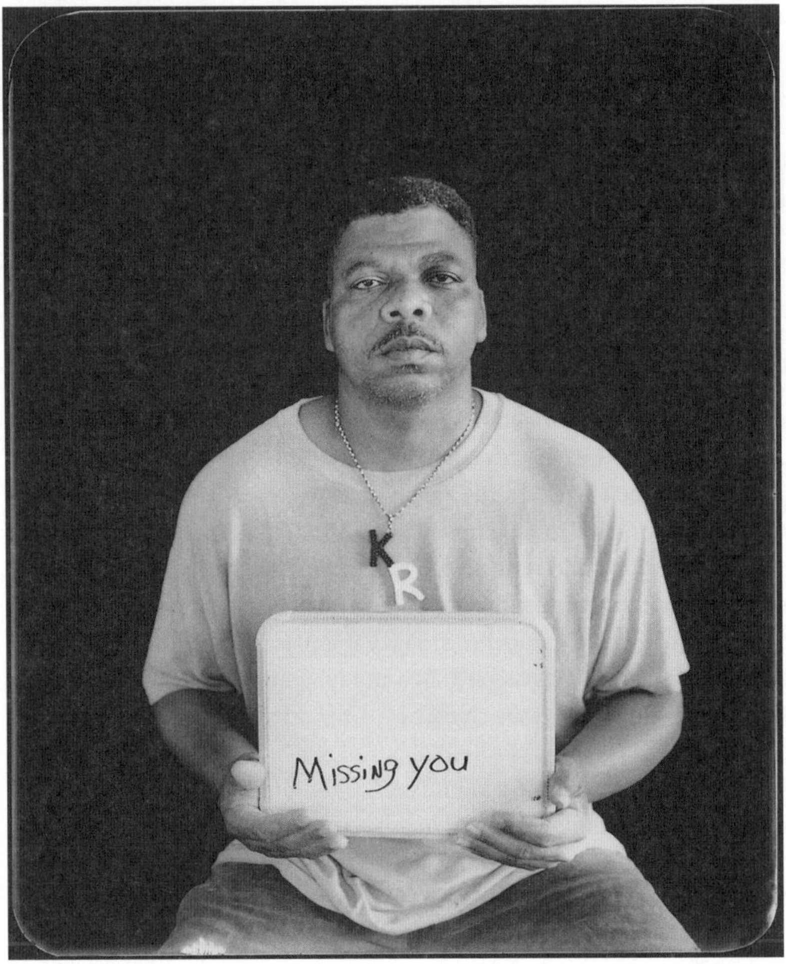

FIGURE 3.5 Deborah Luster, *One Big Self*, Keith Gabriel, Transylvania, Louisiana. Department of Corrections no. 110182. Date of birth: 7.8.61. Place of birth: Independence. Sentence: 33 months. Four children. Future plans: Work. Photograph made at East Carroll Parish Prison Farm on 7.15.00. Silver emulsion on prepared aluminum. Courtesy the artist and Jack Shainman Gallery.

rate robe (plate 6). She curls inward and tilts her head to look at the camera. Her eyes are framed by the small round holes in her dark mask, which blends into the turban that covers the top of her head and hair. The bottom half of her face is left visible and a slight smile is forming on her lips. The full sleeves of her light robe end in dark satin, and a satin circle outlines her shoulder. She hides her hands in the billowy robe. Notations suggest that she is dressed in her Halloween Haunted House costume, which appears to be that of a wizard or clairvoyant.

Maureen Oubre also wears her Halloween Haunted House costume for her portrait (fig. 3.6). She sits facing the camera in a wide-striped T-shirt, her hands in her lap. On closer inspection, one sees a thin band or belt wrapped around her wrists, binding them together. Her face is somber, her mouth down-turned. Her short hair is spiky and stiff, as if overgelled; it stands up like a bird's nest on top of her head. In her costume she is the "Electrocuted Inmate," a joke that calls attention to and macabrely undercuts the authority of the world she inhabits, inverting its terms by embracing its ultimate threat. The joke is funny until one reconsiders Oubre's vacant expression.

It is hard to discern precisely the viewing position imagined and inscribed for these image-objects. Encountering them in the custom cabinet in a gallery, one is invited to pick them up and arrange them according to one's own associations and interests. One is authorized to look and read and sort. Does this align the viewer with the look of a prison warden, or a curious bystander, or a loved one? The nineteenth-century institutional archives that Sekula describes and to which Luster's work gestures worked to distinguish property-owning bourgeois subjects from criminal offenders according to the logic of possessive individualism. Further, according to Childs, the spectacle of prison life as entertainment for viewers also serves to cohere white supremacy outside the prison.[25] Does Luster's archive unwittingly do the same? What are the limits of "empathetic" looking and the "humanizing" work of portraiture? Whose comfort does such looking serve? Viewers might identify with photographed subjects through an intimate encounter with these tactile images, or they might differentiate themselves in terms of class or race from the men and women they see pictured. The shadow archive accommodates both possibilities.

One Big Self also takes the form of an oversized art book, and here Luster's images are framed by text written by poet C. D. Wright, who accompanied the

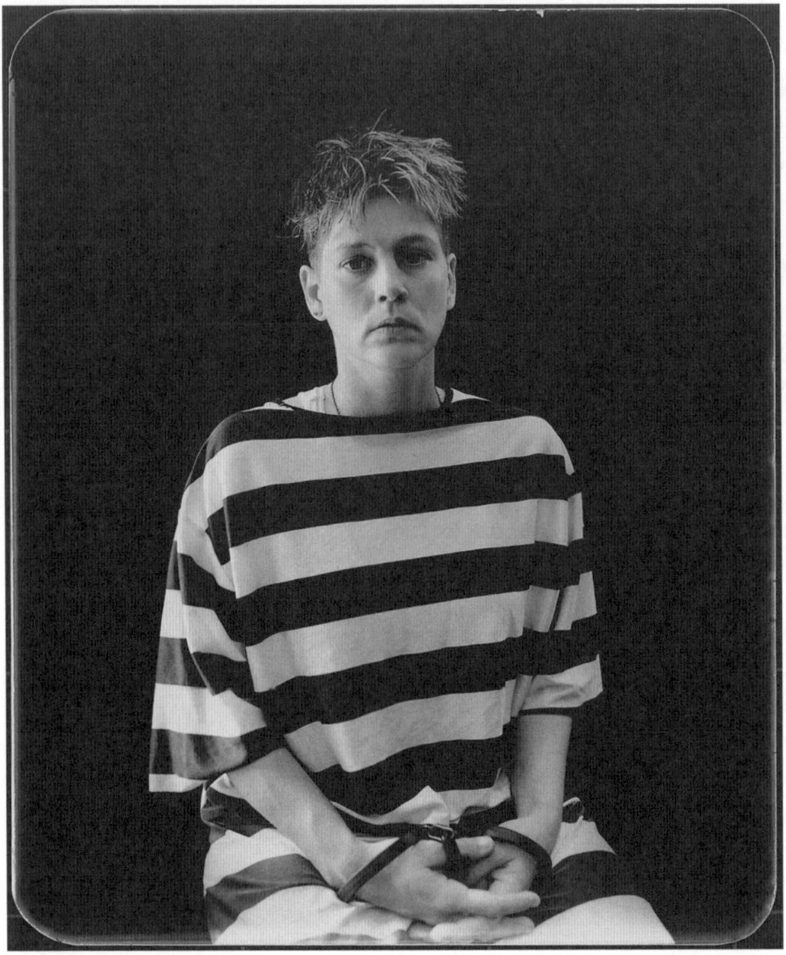

FIGURE 3.6 Deborah Luster, *One Big Self*, Maureen Oubre, Saint Gabriel, Louisiana. Department of Corrections no. 388646. Date of birth: 3.15.68. Place of birth: Marrero. Sentence: 5 years. One child. Work: Vocational-tech sewing. Halloween Haunted House, "Electrocuted" Inmate. Photograph made at Louisiana Correctional Institute for Women 10.27.00. Silver emulsion on prepared aluminum. Courtesy the artist and Jack Shainman Gallery.

photographer on a number of trips to the prisons. Wright spent the day talking with inmates waiting to be photographed, and she observed the numbing routines of prison life and the repetitive homogeneity of prison time. Working with this material, she then produced a poetic text out of fragments of conversations, daily drills, and images. Weaving disparate statements together, she presents much of the text in the voices of inmates themselves, some of whom are quoted by first name, such as Willie, Zabonia, Franklin, Juanita, and George. Speakers talk of things they miss—screen porches, clematis, bathtubs, driving, dogs, families.

In its fragmentary form, the text rejects a single, omniscient, third-person narrative, and does not pretend it can adequately depict the experiences of the incarcerated. Certain lines repeat, such as the list of an inmate's possessions: "Soapdish, vaseline, comb, hairpick, paperback." One is told, "Don't ask"; "That's hard. I don't go there." Anonymous institutional commands punctuate the text: "0 exceptions." Some phrases subtly shift; for example, "If you were a felon you'd be home now" becomes "If I were a felon I'd be home now."

Wright's text offers a glimpse of women as they wait to be photographed, making visible what happens behind the scenes of Luster's camera:

> The women pass around a handmirror and a tube of lipstick
> they sit on the slab walk, smoke and talk
> They pass a stuffed bunny from hand to hand
> For their turn in front of the camera

This look at photography also includes commentary on photography. One woman declares, "My mug shot totally turned me against being photographed." She must have understood the way the police photographs inscribed her as suspect, as object, as subject to the state. One wonders if she waited with others to be photographed by Luster, if she saw Luster's practice as categorically distinct from the institutional practices that defined her as "criminal."

One Big Self draws attention to the vast numbers of women and mothers incarcerated in the United States. According to Ruby Tapia, "Women's imprisonment in the United States has increased by over 757 percent since 1977," and "most women in prison are mothers." As in the larger prison population, women of color figure disproportionately in this group: "Nearly 70 percent of women in prison are African American or Latina," and "most women in prison were accused or convicted of nonviolent offenses or low-level drug offenses."[26]

Luster's photographs of mothers are steeped in sentimentality. Pamela Winfield poses in an Easter Bunny costume for Children's Visiting Day at the L.C.I.W. (fig. 3.7). She is entirely covered in terry cloth, and holds a small sign with her name to identify herself. An unnamed woman stands before the camera dressed in white; she has lifted her T-shirt to show her pregnant belly. Another woman poses with her child at the L.C.I.W. Children's Day Christmas Party (fig. 3.8). She sits on a stool, embracing her daughter from behind, as the child, captured in the blur of motion, tilts her head back and up to give her mother a kiss. Tapia encourages one not to discount or condemn the sentimentality of such representations. Indeed, she proposes, "the idioms of representation theories . . . are ill matched to the stakes of rendering the experiences of incarcerated women. . . . What we think we know about dangerous investments in realism and the tenderly violent project of sentimentality, for example, has to be revisited. The photograph is an illustrative place to start."[27] Sentimentality and its "tender violence," in Laura Wexler's words, might signify differently when family ties, and the privileges of seeing or not seeing sanctioned by domesticity, are radically disrupted by the prison.[28]

One Big Self relies not only on discourses of sentimentality but also, and more fundamentally, on photographic logics of exposure. It assumes that for anonymous viewers the camera can rehumanize those it has helped to objectify, enabling them to see inmates as people with names and families and skills. It proposes that visibility humanizes. But such an objective also begs important questions precisely about visibility and invisibility: to whom are the incarcerated invisible, and for whom are they being made visible? Certainly, family members do not need reminders that relatives are incarcerated.[29] And for other viewers, visibility also has limitations, as seeing does not necessarily translate into recognition. As Ta-Nehisi Coates has argued, "The mettle that it takes to look away from the horror of our prison system, from police forces transformed into armies, from the long war against the black body, is not forged overnight. This is the practiced habit of jabbing out one's eyes and forgetting the work of one's hands."[30] Luster's work will not alleviate that structural blindness, but it might help to illuminate it. *One Big Self* brings into view the institutional forces of inscription and erasure through which the incarcerated are removed from public sight and the temporal patterns of daily life outside. The work encourages outside viewers to see beyond the circumscription of the mug shot and prison identification photograph, to see impris-

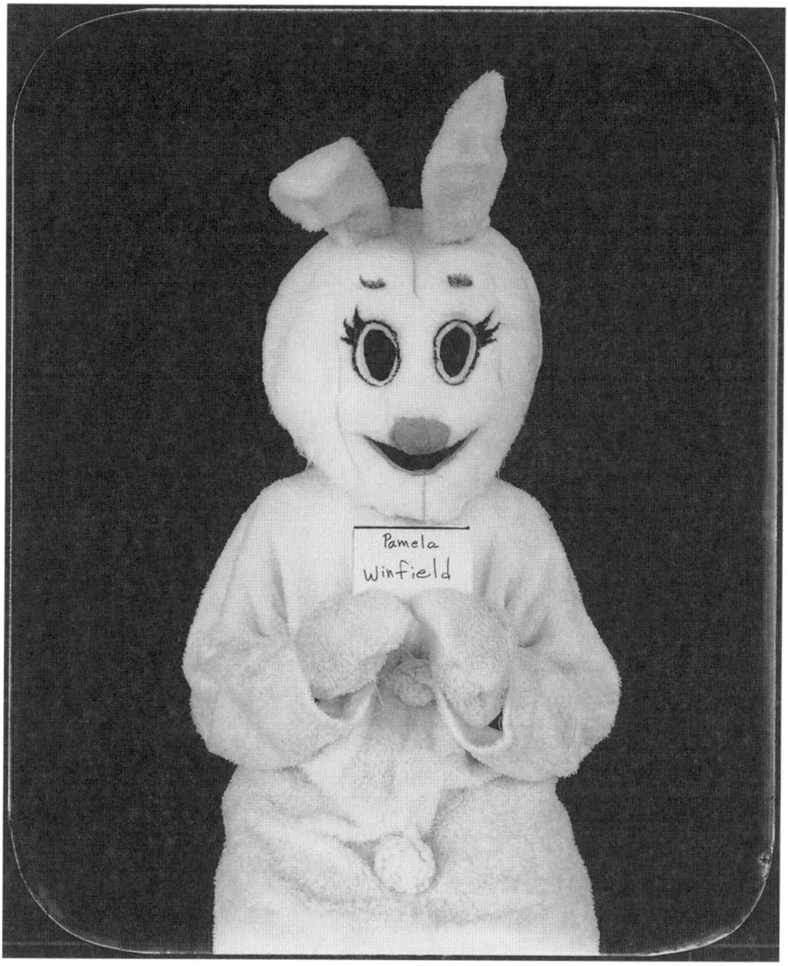

FIGURE 3.7 Deborah Luster, *One Big Self*, Pamela Winfield, Saint Gabriel, Louisiana. Department of Corrections no. 312197. Date of birth: 11.25.64. Place of birth: N. Kingston, RI. Sentence: 5 years. Work: Floor worker. Easter Bunny, Children's Visiting Day. Photograph made at Louisiana Correctional Institute for Women 4.14.00. Silver emulsion on prepared aluminum. Courtesy the artist and Jack Shainman Gallery.

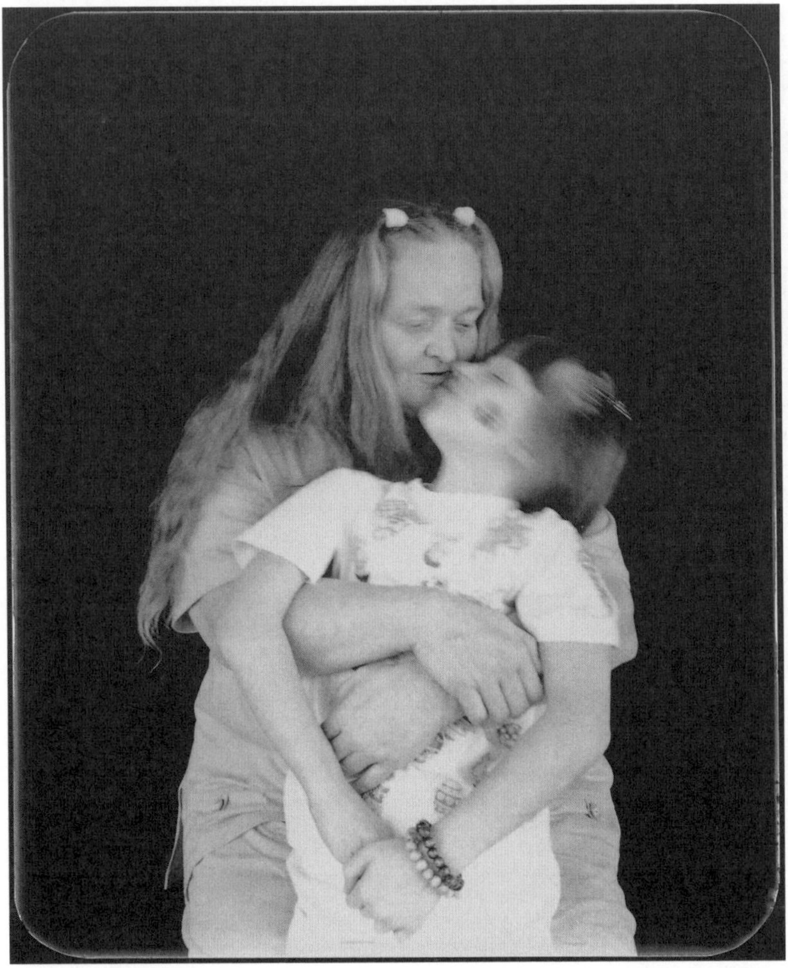

FIGURE 3.8 Deborah Luster, *One Big Self*, Saint Gabriel, Louisiana. Department of Corrections no. 402710. Date of birth: 2.13.53. Place of birth: Florida. Sentence: 15 years. One child. Work: Library. Children's Day, Christmas Party. Photograph made at Louisiana Correctional Institute for Women 12.9.00. Silver emulsion on prepared aluminum. Courtesy the artist and Jack Shainman Gallery.

oned men and women resisting institutional definition and reclaiming their photographic subjectivities.

The Scene of the Crime

Luster has continued to probe the complexities of visibility and invisibility in relation to photography and policing. In *Tooth for an Eye: A Chorography of Violence in Orleans Parish* (2008–10), she photographed hundreds of scenes of crime in New Orleans. Mining police reports and newspaper stories, she plotted sites on Google maps, and searched out the places of murders, photographing them long after the violent events occurred.[31] Her photographs record the places but not the moments in which individual time lines were brutally cut short, and in this way the images are out of sync with the violence they evoke. They are devoid of the subjects who died in these places, as well as the survivors who mourn them. Instead, the photographs focus on deserted street corners, vacant lots, and abandoned buildings, offering a morbid map of the city as haunted space.

The title of this work, *Tooth for an Eye*, recalls Old Testament, biblical justice—an eye for an eye, a tooth for a tooth. But Luster has mixed registers, offering a tooth for an eye, highlighting the incommensurability of murder and "justice" meted out by the law or through revenge and retaliation. The photographer also notes that at one time people believed that removing an eyetooth might cure a person of blindness, and in this way, a tooth might be offered for an eye, to make a blind orb see. Luster has said that her project is about trying to photograph a population made literally invisible by murder, and once again the work begs further questions: Who is invited to see, and what exactly are they invited to consider? Focusing on deserted murder sites, Luster's photographs draw larger structural inequities into view.

Luster's crime scene photography has historical as well as theoretical antecedents. Indeed, Walter Benjamin celebrated a modern era in photography by likening Eugène Atget's images to "scenes of a crime." In his influential essay, "The Work of Art in the Age of Its Technological Reproducibility" (1936), Benjamin praises Atget's photographs for their deserted quality, which reminds him of crime scenes. For Benjamin, Atget is the photographer whose work at the turn of the twentieth century most clearly marked a shift from the ritual value of art, steeped in aura, to the exhibition value that might open the work to political purposes. After a long period of decline in the late nineteenth century, after decades in which photography was industrialized and commercialized and dominated by the conventional portrait, Atget was the first to "disinfect" the practice by initiating "the emancipation of object from aura."[32] Benjamin proclaims:

> To have given this development its local habitation constitutes the unique significance of Atget, who, around 1900, took photographs of deserted Paris streets. It has justly been said that he photographed them like scenes of crimes. A crime scene, too, is deserted; it is photographed for the purpose of establishing evidence. With Atget, photographic records begin to be evidence in the historical trial [*Prozess*]. This constitutes their hidden political significance.[33]

Benjamin believed that for photography to attain the status of historical evidence, it would have to detach itself from the lingering aura of ritual surrounding art, and the human subject, so prevalent in popular, commercial portraiture throughout the nineteenth century, would have to be removed. That is in large part why he found Atget's depopulated images so appealing. "They demand a specific kind of reception. Free-floating contemplation is no longer appropriate to them. They unsettle the viewer; he feels challenged to find a particular way to approach them."[34] If the auratic portrait called for an affective response from the viewer, Atget's unpopulated images unsettled that dynamic and required a new mode of inquiry. Certainly they did not have evidentiary status in policing or criminological terms, but for Benjamin they provided historical evidence of capitalism's transformation of Parisian life.

Luster's photographs of literal, if latter-day, crime scenes are art works, and as such they reverse Benjamin's political hopes for photographs of deserted places. Indeed, the images are extra-auratic, made with nineteenth-century technologies that privilege the artist's touch. And yet Luster's photographs might also serve as a kind of historical evidence not unlike Atget's photographs. Because people are absent from these scenes, the images encourage viewers to focus on the places in which violent crimes recur. They invite viewers to observe signs of systemic racism and poverty visible in the built, and deteriorating, urban environment.

Historically most actual crime scene photographs are not deserted; indeed, they focus on the corpse. Luc Sante's *Evidence*, first published in 1992, provides a salient example. It is a compilation of images from the New York Police Department photograph collection, dating from 1914 to 1918, once housed in the New York City Municipal Archives. As Sante tells the story, in the early 1980s,

Centre Street police headquarters was sold, and in the process of clearing out the building, workers removed roomfuls of files and dumped them into the East River. But they overlooked a small room under a staircase, in which filing cabinets containing 1,400 glass plate negatives were stored in manila envelopes.[35] Ten years later, from the collection preserved in that tucked away corner, Sante selected photographs to be reproduced in *Evidence*.

It is impossible to say how many photographic prints and glass plate negatives were dumped into the East River on that moving day in the 1980s. The glass may still be settling at the bottom of the river, but the photographic emulsions must have floated up and away from the plates like jellyfish. One wonders why these archives were destroyed. It might have been due to laziness or irresponsibility, or simply to a lack of storage space at the new site. Perhaps the New York Police Department needed a clean slate. The evidence of too many unsolved crimes might have been a burden the department wanted to leave behind, to weight and sink into the river like so many dead bodies.

The photographs that were preserved present a solemn archive of murder scenes documented by New York police photographers over the course of five years in the early twentieth century (again 1914–18). The images were made by a number of different photographers, including John Golden, Clement Christensen, Arthur DeVoe, Frederick Zwire, Charles Abrams, and Charles Carsbrer, but they are marked by a similar visual style, likely shaped by the directives of the police department itself. All show bodies as they lay dead, men and women killed by bullets and razors, in public places, in apartment buildings, in streets, and in houses. Sometimes a larger crowd is visible at the edges of the frame. Almost all were taken at night or indoors, requiring the harsh illumination of a flash. Many present a disorienting perspective, as if one is viewing the body of a victim laying at the bottom of a long shaft, and in such images, the legs of the tripod and the occasional foot of the photographer help one to establish the point of view.

A photograph of a woman crumpled in death showcases this disorienting perspective (fig. 3.9). The body is viewed from above, as if from the ceiling of a cramped wooden structure. A stove in the bottom right corner suggests that this is a domestic scene, a kitchen. The victim, Marion Hart, a thirty-nine-year-old white woman, is folded gracefully over a table lined with a woven mat. Her throat has been cut and a puddle of blood flows from her body across the table. Despite this horror, one notes her slender form and tied back hair, the way she has rolled up her sleeves as if to prepare for cooking before she was violently interrupted. In the top right corner of the photograph,

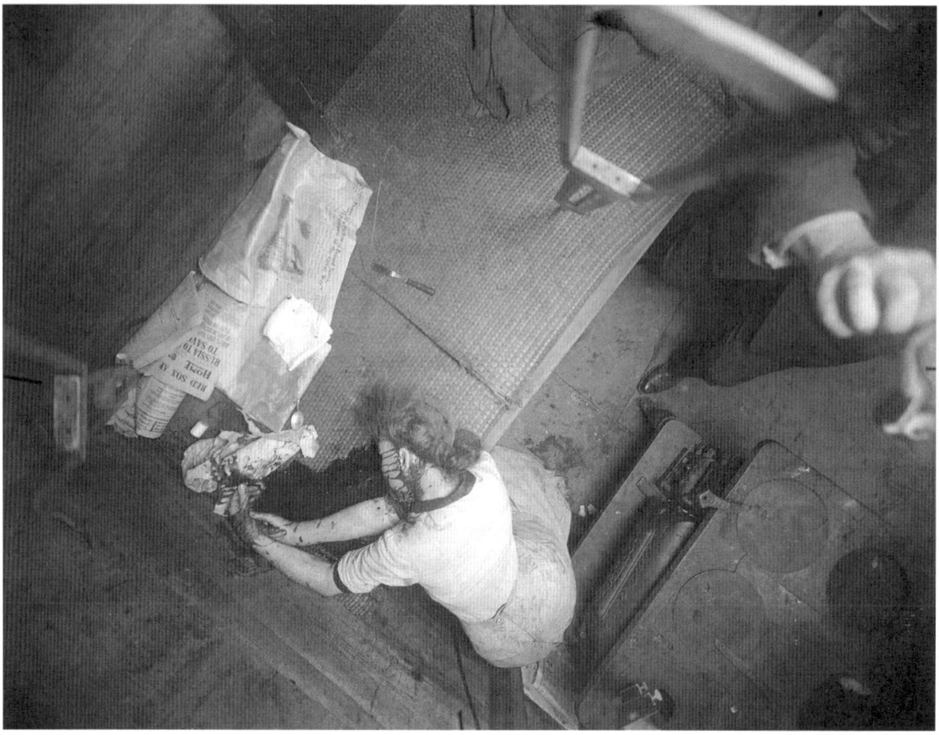

FIGURE 3.9 Marion Hart, murdered in dwelling at Old Stone Road and Bullshead Golden, 1915. Courtesy NYC Municipal Archives.

a structure that looks like a wooden crutch descends down into the space of the image, its end resting on the table. A similar structure punctures the left side of the image space, its furthest point nestled in the newspapers pushed to the edge of the table, against the wooden wall. Finally one discerns that these are two legs of a tripod, and that the third peeks into the bottom of the frame, resting on top of the stove. The camera has been suspended above the victim, its body parallel to hers, so that one is looking down, not quite with a God's-eye view of this scene, but certainly with an elevated one. At the right side of the image, a man's white hand, disproportionately large and out of focus, reaches up toward the camera. His body is placed parallel to the most visible leg of the tripod, and extends down further into the space of the image, ending in a shiny dark shoe made to look impossibly small by the wide angle of the camera lens. Presumably this is the photographer who has inadvertently caught himself in the image. The photograph is illuminated with a flash that creates a bright center spot, glinting off a lonely fork on the table, and the tip of the photographer's polished shoe.

In *Evidence* Sante curates and compiles photographs made by police photographers, authorized images, largely standardized, that focus on bodies as they fell. Unlike Luster's photographs of sites made years after the fact, these images were presumably meant to serve as evidence or at least as records of murders and perhaps as documents attesting to the police department's rapid response to crimes. The fact that so many images like them were allowed to sink to the bottom of the East River, however, demonstrates how irrelevant the images might have been as legal evidence. Or perhaps en masse they provided unwanted evidence of another kind, recording too many unsolved murders and the ineffectiveness of the police.[36]

Luster's views of murder sites in New Orleans are almost completely unpopulated. In striking contrast to the photographs Sante has compiled, there is no body to see, no trail of blood, no gun, no crowds of curious onlookers. As in Sally Mann's Antietam images, the bodies that fell on the sites that Luster photographs are nowhere to be seen in her images, and in their absence, one might conjure the bodies visible in other crime scene photographs, such as those collected by Sante. Yet Luster's *Tooth for an Eye* also invites other considerations. The images present other things to view; they don't push one to consider the surface of the photographs in the way that Mann's images do, nor do they refer and defer to other photographs so definitively. Luster's latter-day images may evoke other crime scene images, but unlike Mann's Antietam images, their primary referents are not other photographs. If Mann's work is in part a refusal of photographic evidence, Luster's work offers evidence of a different kind. Looking at the images as Benjamin looked at Atget's photographs, one is invited to focus on the urban landscape in a state of disrepair rather than its inhabitants. Luster's photographs of murder sites do not present images of violent crime but instead subtly offer evidence of systemic disinvestment—not the abrupt brutality of homicide but the slow violence of racism, poverty, and climate change.[37]

Tooth for an Eye presents a catalogue of black-and-white photographs of deserted places. The minimal text Luster offers as a key is essential to understanding the images as records of former crime scenes. For each image, she outlines the victim(s)'s name and age, the police ledger number, the murder location, and the date(s) of the crime(s). Together the accumulating images and texts provide a dark taxonomy of places inscribed by violence. Their haunted air is enhanced by the ill-fitting antique lens Luster uses with her eight-by-ten-inch view camera, which renders each photograph circular within a rectangular frame, and also by a slow ASA, which registers bushes blown by the breeze, and anything else moving in front of the camera, as animated blur. Like Sally Mann, she uses the wet-plate collodion process of nineteenth-century photographers, and has made a darkroom in her car so that she can coat plates on site. But her process, unlike Mann's, is pristine. Luster has said she appreciates the laborious wet-plate collodion process because it slows her down and keeps her in the places she photographs for some time.[38] Wet-plate collodion heightens the indexical presence of photographed subjects by anchoring not only exposure but also development to places pictured.

In some ways, *Tooth for an Eye* is a project of memorialization. The homicides Luster records did not rise to the level of national attention and outrage. Why? Perhaps because the victims were not killed en masse. Or perhaps because the majority of them were not white. Or perhaps because their sudden deaths were not seen as shocking to privileged viewers, but an expected element of urban life in a "bad neighborhood." As Luster notes in the epilogue to *Tooth for an Eye*, New Orleans has "a homicide rate nearly eight times the national average." The photographer refuses the invisibility of these deaths beyond the families of mourners, recognizing them as tragedies. As empty memorials, her images show in inverse, in Erika Doss's words, "who and what is deemed memorable in American history, and in terms of an imagined national future."[39] The memorial nature of the work was heightened in the exhibition of *Tooth for an Eye* at Louisiana State University, where an image wall was created for family members to leave photographs of the deceased, making a shrine within the gallery to mark their losses.[40]

Luster displays the photographs in a number of different ways. She exhibits the images as large prints made for the gallery wall (twenty by thirty inches or forty-nine by sixty-one inches), and in bound ledgers placed on viewing tables. In galleries, the photographs are often arranged in a large grid of twenty-four images, with text at the side, which highlights the taxonomic register of the work. The photographs are also presented in an oversized book published by specialty photography press Twin Palms Publishers in 2011, which measures fourteen-by-seventeen inches, and includes twenty-

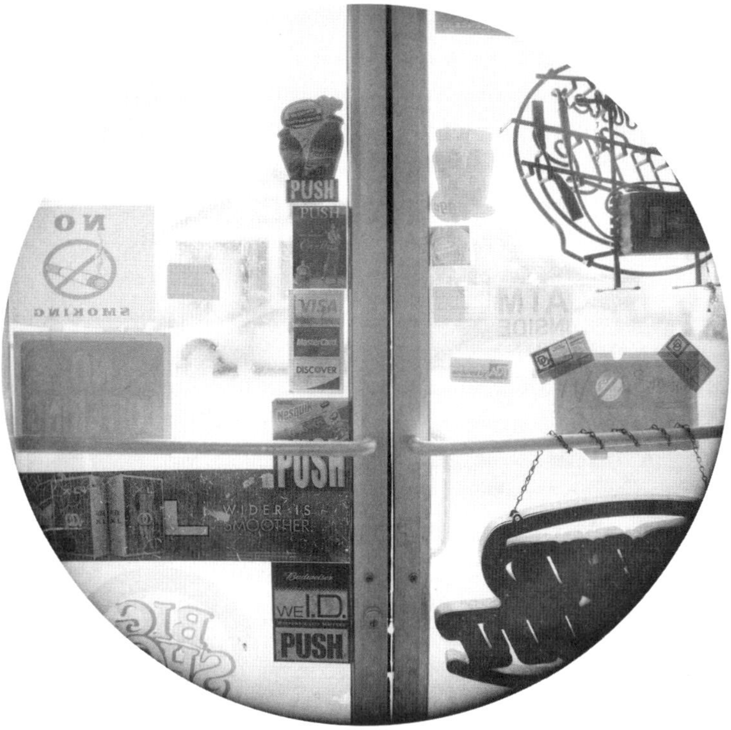

FIGURE 3.10 Deborah Luster, *Tooth for an Eye*. Disarchive no. 04-23. Location: Olive Meat Market, 8841 Olive Street (Hollygrove). Date: January 8, 2002, 9:25 p.m. Name: Brandon Aggison (17). Notes: Drive-by shooting. A stranger used Aggison as a human shield. Courtesy the artist and Jack Shainman Gallery.

nine images with text on facing pages. The endpapers of the book reproduce photographs of the victims donated by family members, images in which the living beam back at the camera, posing in graduation robes and formal attire, surrounded by loved ones. The endpapers echo the memorial images included in the exhibition at Louisiana State University, and Luster dedicates the book to the victims of homicides and their families.

The first photograph in the book *Tooth for an Eye* situates the viewer in a familiar if not precisely known place (fig. 3.10). One stands inside a convenience store, looking at glass doors. Through the glare of the scratched and smudged glass, the shape of a modest house with a car parked in front is just visible across the street. The circular frame of the photograph is divided, nearly in the center, by the metal doorframe. Stickers run along the frame, telling the viewer to "push" the door open, and advertising the credit cards accepted by the establishment. At the far left of the image, one can read, in reverse, signs placed on the front of the door, proclaiming "no smoking" and "no loitering" to those outside. On the right side of the image the interior scaffoldings of neon signs, likely advertising beer for sale, are attached to the inside of the door. One is situated in a small neighborhood convenience store where she can withdraw cash from the ATM, or buy Kool cigarettes and beer with a VISA card. The text on the facing page tells one that this is the Olive Meat Market at 8841 Olive Street in Hollygrove, and that at 9:25 p.m. on January 8, 2002, Brandon Aggison, age seventeen, was killed here in a drive-by shooting. A stranger used Aggison as a human shield.

The photograph of Olive Meat Market sets the scene for the rest of the volume. It is a threshold image that asks one to push through the door to enter New Orleans, to walk into the city through a murder site. The second image is also a kind of passage, a narrow alley between two buildings, divided down the center by a chain-link fence (fig. 3.11). The path on the left is overgrown with vines, the one on the right burdened with a row of metal window-unit air conditioning boxes. Both sides of the alley are gated, but the one on the right is open, "inviting" the viewer to traverse a long, tight passageway. This, one learns, is the site of two murders in the Tremé neighborhood, separated by twelve years. On September 16, 1989, Johnson Davis (twenty-six) was beaten with a bat; on January 5, 2001, Richard Schroeder (thirty-two) was shot.

Tooth for an Eye presents the city as a dark palimpsest of murder overlaid on murder. By the third image one has run into a wall, a dark wood-paneled blockade that tells her to keep moving—"no loitering" (fig. 3.12). The trash cans to the far left suggest that one is in a back alley, and Luster's text identifies the building as Big Time Tips Bar and Lounge. This too is a multiple murder scene; two young men were shot at the bar at 9:00 p.m. on November 30, 2003, and almost six years later, on July 31, 2009, an unidentified man was shot on the sidewalk. That man, perhaps, was the "Ralph" commanded to R. I. P. (rest in peace) by the spray-painted text on the concrete ground of the alley.

Most of Luster's photographs are made outside, at the edges of buildings, fields, and railroad tracks. Some show abandoned buildings, boarded-up houses, cracked sidewalks, and empty lots, as if the city is falling into ruins. One image made in the 7th Ward depicts a lot overgrown with grass and two

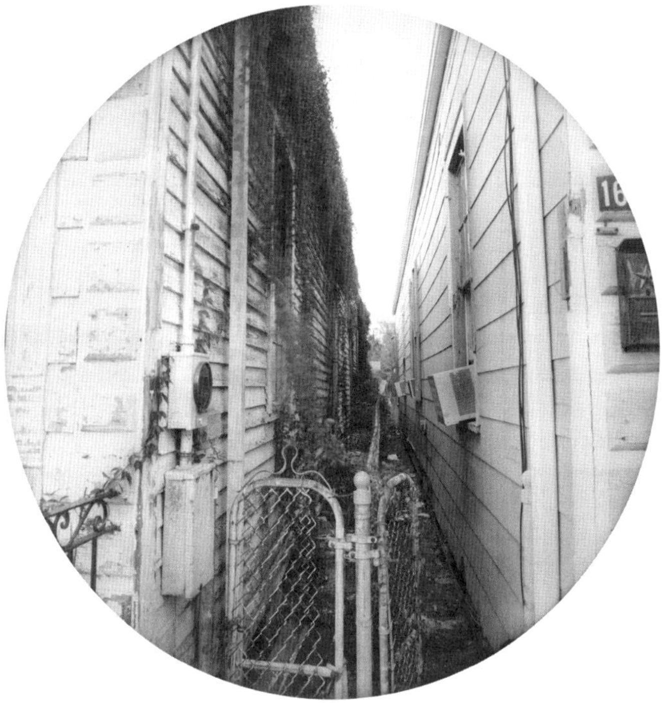

FIGURE 3.11 Deborah Luster, *Tooth for an Eye*. Disarchive no. 05-09. Location: Saint Philip near North Claiborne Ave. (Treme). Dates: September 16, 1989; January 5, 2001. Names: Johnson Davis (26); Richard Schroeder (32). Notes: Davis—Beaten with a ball bat. Schroeder—Gunshot. Courtesy the artist and Jack Shainman Gallery.

concrete staircases that face each other, leading nowhere (fig. 3.13). They are likely the remnants of a building that once occupied the flat field that stretches behind them. Many of the images are framed as if the viewer is peering out from a slightly protected distance, looking through a gate, or from under a highway, or atop a bridge. In a photograph of the site where four young men were killed over a span of sixteen years in Saint Roch, the viewer is placed on a once grand, now decrepit balcony (fig. 3.14). White chipped wooden pillars split the visual field. Through them one sees a house with its windows and door blown out, and the still-standing façade of a neighboring house strewn with vines. To the right, another small house with boarded-up windows, freshly

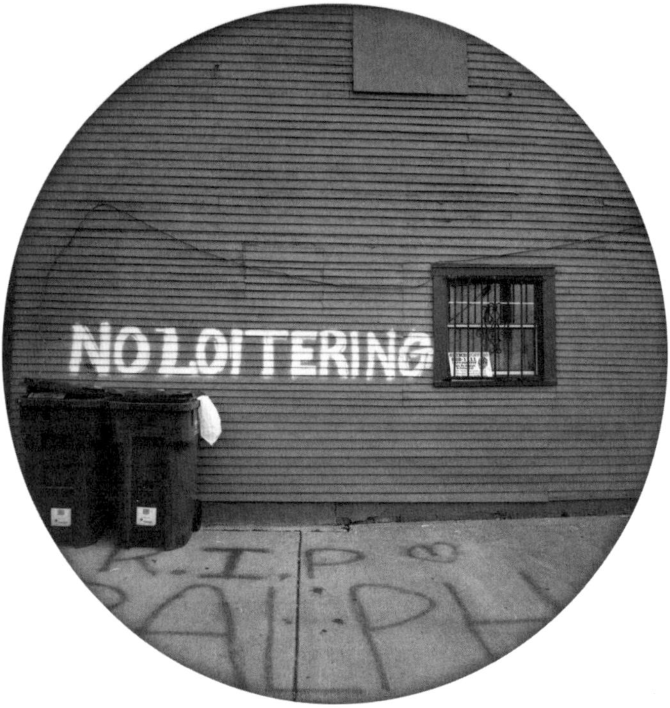

FIGURE 3.12 Deborah Luster, *Tooth for an Eye*. Disarchive no. 06-22. Location: 8801 Edinburg at Eagle—Big Time Tips Bar and Lounge. Dates: November 30, 2002, 9:00 p.m; July 31, 2009. Names: Jeffery McLeod (24) and Ivory White (27); unidentified man. Notes: Gunshot—at bar; Gunshot—on sidewalk. Courtesy the artist and Jack Shainman Gallery.

FIGURE 3.13 (FACING PAGE, TOP) Deborah Luster, *Tooth for an Eye*. Disarchive no. 04-01. Location: 1800 Derbigny Street (7th Ward); Date: June 30, 2004. Name: Marlon "Marty" Edwards (30). Notes: Gunshot. On July 3rd, Coven Grady (26) was fatally shot while attending Edwards's memorial party. Police later announced that Edwards was responsible for the 2002 murder of popular youth baseball coach Vauchon "Cujoe" Cojoe (33) in front of his young ball team. Courtesy the artist and Jack Shainman Gallery.

FIGURE 3.14 (FACING PAGE, BOTTOM) Deborah Luster, *Tooth for an Eye*. Disarchive no. 06-16. Location: 2400 North Villere Street (Saint Roch). Dates: January 10, 1993; January 18, 1993; June 13, 2009, 1:00 a.m.; November 17, 2008. Names: Jermaine White (20); Brother Emerson (17); Leroy Harris (19); Kendrick Thomas (22). Courtesy the artist and Jack Shainman Gallery.

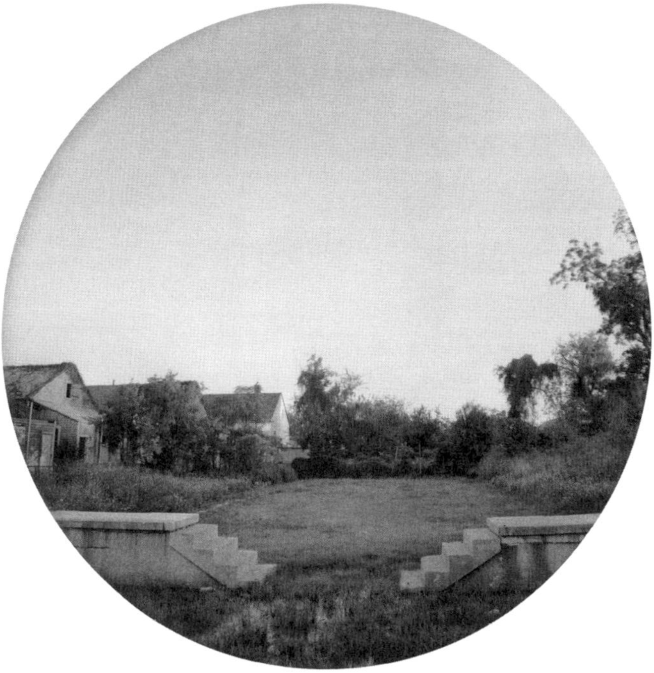

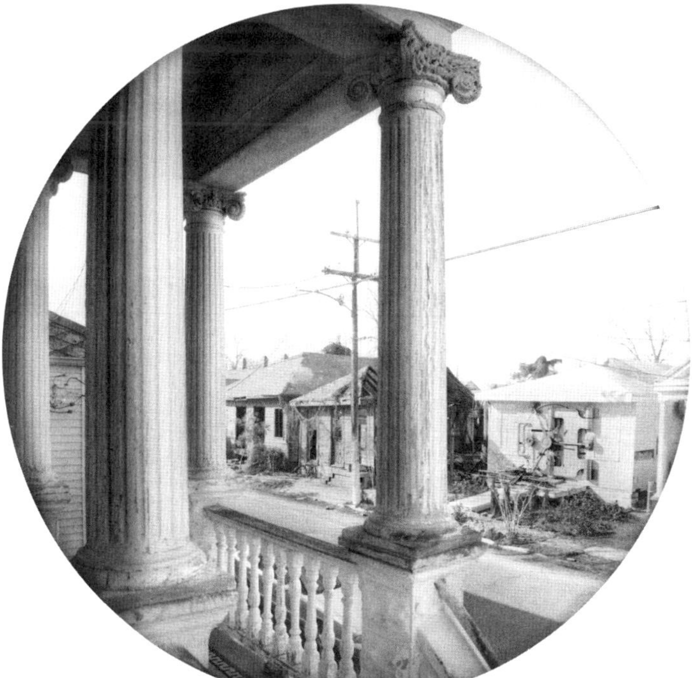

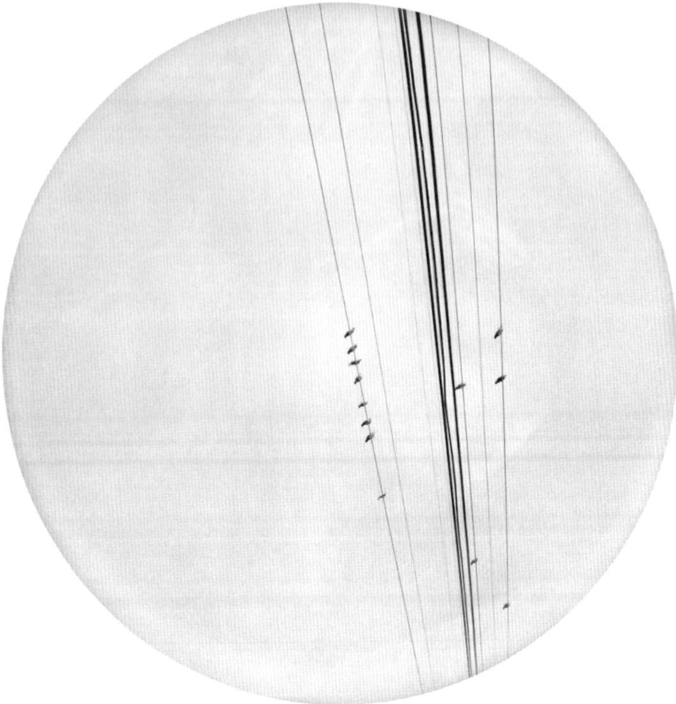

FIGURE 3.15 Deborah Luster, *Tooth for an Eye*. Disarchive no. 01-26. Location: 1800 Leonidas Street (Carrollton). Date: July 14, 2009, 7:55 a.m. Name: Brian Christopher Smith (22). Notes: Face up. Multiple gunshot wounds. Courtesy the artist and Jack Shainman Gallery.

painted white, is dominated by a mechanical apparatus that suggests major reconstruction. As Luster notes in her afterword to the book: "*Tooth for an Eye* not only documents sites where violence has occurred, it also finds itself documenting the city's physical loss as her unique material culture crumbles and transforms following generations of political failure. Many buildings that served as backgrounds for violent death have disappeared since they were photographed for this project." If *Tooth for an Eye* is a palimpsest, then it reveals not only murder accruing murder but also many different kinds of violence layered on top of one another—the violence of poverty, natural disaster, and national disregard.

A number of Luster's photographs capture residues of the 2005 Hurricane Katrina disaster and its aftermath (see, for example, fig. 3.14). Over 80 percent of the city flooded after the hurricane, and some of Luster's deserted scenes might once have been filled with dead bodies floating in high water. According to Henry Giroux, "The bodies of the Katrina victims laid bare the racial and class fault lines that mark an increasingly damaged and withering democracy and revealed the emergence of a new kind of politics, one in which entire populations are now considered disposable, an unnecessary burden on state coffers, and consigned to fend for themselves."[41] Giroux reminds one that before the flood New Orleans had the third-highest rate of child poverty in the United States, a 40 percent illiteracy rate, and a drastically underfunded public school system. New Orleans was the twelfth-poorest city in the nation, and its impoverished citizens were concentrated in segregated neighborhoods.[42] The shadow of Katrina marked by dilapidated buildings and empty lots in Luster's photographs underscores the deterioration of the built environment, the devastating effects of systemic racism and segregation, and the vulnerability of impoverished neighborhoods. Luster subtly makes such structural inequities visible across her photographic projects, highlighting in *Tooth for an Eye* and *One Big Self* the precarity of those people and places deemed disposable by the state.

The final image in *Tooth for an Eye* is a large, nearly white circle, cut on the diagonal by dark power lines (fig. 3.15). Thirteen pigeons perch on the cables, as if notes in a musical score. Here, at 1800 Leonidas Street in Carrollton, one is offered the point of view of the victim, namely Brian Christopher Smith, aged twenty-two, shot multiple times on July 14, 2009, at 7:55 a.m. He died face up, perhaps looking at the power lines above.[43] According to Luster, the last thing you see when you die remains on the cornea for some time.[44] By framing her image looking up at the sky, she puts her viewer in the place of Smith's body. Therefore, if one enters the landscape mapped by *Tooth for an Eye* as a bystander to the drive-by shooting that killed Brandon Aggison, one exits as a corpse. One cannot traverse this terrain unscathed.

Tooth for an Eye is as much about what cannot be seen as it is about what is seen. Images are divided down the middle by barriers that disrupt and direct sightlines. Tightly framed walls, boarded-up doors, or dense vines block otherwise open sites. Some images deflect the viewer with aggressive text—"no loitering" in large letters, or "fuck you." The view is often obstructed in the very moment that it is offered, drawing one's attention to failed seeing. But even as it seems to hinder sight, the project also brings photography itself into view. The unusual framing of circular images within rectangles calls attention to photography as a particular way of seeing that is technologically, as well as institutionally and culturally, produced.[45] Luster draws the historical relation between photography and policing into relief, but her crime scene photographs offer an oblique view that directs attention away from the spectacle of murder and toward other kinds of slow and systemic violence.

Luster works like a modern-day Atget, directing her camera toward deserted places of urban transformation. With one exception there are no people here—no victims, perpetrators, or detectives, no neighbors or family members, no bystanders or shopkeepers. It is an almost apocalyptic landscape, in which traces of people are registered only by seemingly abandoned houses and cars, train tracks and highway overpasses, spray-painted directives, political posters and commercial signs, stoplights and electrical wires. Plants are beginning to repossess the urban terrain: grass grows through cracks in sidewalks, shrubs cover over building foundations, vines threaten to smother houses. Luster's images point, like Benjamin's angel of history, to "the pile of debris," and "wreckage upon wreckage" that accumulates in the wake of what capitalism and the neoliberal state deem "progress."[46]

In *Tooth for an Eye* image and text together provide a kind of oblique evidence. But this evidence, produced long after the crimes it documents, is not for the purpose of policing, and Luster does not imagine these photographs will help to convict or exonerate anyone. Instead, the photographs provide an accumulation of historical evidence. Luster's images of deteriorating urban landscapes encourage viewers to see the structures of racism and disinvestment that have marked particular neighborhoods in New Orleans, and to consider the effects of poverty and political neglect that result in violent crime. Reading across Luster's *Tooth for an Eye* and *One Big Self*, one finds a deserted and politically abandoned urban landscape on the one hand and overpopulated prisons on the other. Together the two series underscore which places and people are valued by the state and which remain chronically vulnerable to catastrophe.

CHAPTER 4

Photographic Referrals

Lorna Simpson's *9 Props*

Lorna Simpson's *9 Props* (1995) is an homage to James VanDerZee and the studio portraits of fashionable African American men and women he made in Harlem in the 1920s, 1930s, and beyond.[1] But it is a strange kind of tribute, an enigmatic celebration that both refers to and obscures its subjects. The project began with VanDerZee's photographs and ended with Simpson's own. Along the way, Simpson employed several processes of translation and transformation that redirect reference, making *9 Props* paradoxically a close study of VanDerZee's photographs at a remove. In this seemingly minimalist work, Simpson opens up a web of associations that probe the material nature of photography and the politics and complexities of black representational space (plate 7). She offers an oblique return to VanDerZee that underscores the fragile futures the photographer and his subjects dreamed together in his studio. VanDerZee and his subjects looked forward to a time in which the aspirations they marked and performed in front of the camera could be inhabited reliably in the worlds outside the studio. With *9 Props* Simpson "gives props" to VanDerZee and to his visions of black futurity.

9 Props is a self-contained work, seemingly a one-off, but it shares material and conceptual elements with some of Simpson's other projects from the mid-1990s. As in *Wigs* (1994) and *Wigs II* (1994), the human figure is removed from the frame and replaced by a surrogate. Like those works and the large *Public Sex* pieces Simpson made in 1995, *9 Props* is also a grid of images reproduced on felt. As in some of her more recent projects, such as *1957–2009* (2009) and *Chess* (2013), the work directly references specific "found" photographs, but *9 Props* both evokes and obscures its inspirations in a way that the later works do not.[2]

Simpson began this work during a residency at the Pilchuck Glass School in Stanwood, Washington. As she tells the story, she accepted an invitation to Pilchuck in order to try something completely new and push her thinking and work outside her comfort zone. And the residency did just that. Finding herself captivated but disoriented by the theater of glass blowing, she took a break and made a trip to Seattle. There, browsing in a bookstore, she found a volume she knew well—Deborah Willis-Braithwaite and Rodger Birt's *VanDerZee: Photographer*. She brought the book back to Pilchuck and studied the images, attending to the glasses, bottles, and vases that framed VanDerZee's figures. Conceptually isolating and extracting the vessels from the images, she asked gaffers to blow replicas of the objects in black glass. When the residency ended, she shipped the glass pieces back to her studio in New York, where she photographed them. Finally, she printed the images on felt using a heat transfer process.[3]

The nine felt panels that constitute *9 Props* are relatively small, measuring 14⅛ by 10⅛ inches, and the images are smaller, just 8¼ by 6½ inches. The work is quiet and unassuming, but the vessels have a surprising presence: the blacks are rich and the cream of the wool felt is warm. When it is displayed in a museum or gallery, Simpson prefers the panels to be pinned directly to the wall, but if curators choose to they may also frame the images together in a single grid, ordering the images as they see fit. Simpson produced the work in an edition of thirty, and each set is stored in a custom-made clamshell box.[4]

In *9 Props*, each vessel corresponds to a specific VanDerZee photograph, and each felt panel indicates its photographic referent. Just below each image is text that offers a title, the date of the photograph that inspired the piece, VanDerZee's name, and Simpson's description of the image. For example, a panel showing a bulbous black bowl has the following extended caption: "*Woman with a goldfish bowl*, 1923, James Van Der Zee. A woman wearing pearls stands behind a bouquet of flowers and goldfish bowl. Her right hand rests on the rim of the bowl, as she gazes at a painted image of a butterfly in flight." Simpson's description of the VanDerZee photograph is striking in its discordant relationship to her own image (plate 8). The viewer is invited to look at a bowl, which presumably refers to the goldfish bowl Simpson notes, but one's attention is directed to "a woman wearing pearls" whom one cannot see. Simpson's panel conjures the woman even as it displaces her with the prop (which is itself a replica).

Titling the work "*9 Props*," Simpson draws attention to the symbolic function of the vessels she replicates. The props in a photographer's studio support the subject, literally and figuratively. A chair holds a seated person, and a table may provide a surface on which to lean, even as furniture also signals class status or aspiration, according to its style, its display of what Pierre Bourdieu has called "taste."[5] Objects function both practically and symbolically, opening the space of the studio onto broader realms, metonymically referencing larger systems of signification.[6]

Simpson has chosen specific objects: five vases, a cocktail glass, a fish bowl, a milk bottle, and teacups. She has not reproduced the telephones, books, lamps, and clocks that also populate VanDerZee's photographs. Her decisions were likely influenced by her residency at Pilchuck, by an orientation to things made of glass, but other symbolic concerns may also have informed her choices. Vases are decorative, holding cut flowers, bringing a trained and harnessed nature into the crafted space of the artist's studio. Flowers are "cultivated" and add a cultured sensibility to the scene. Cocktail glasses, like teacups, are objects of social use, associated with gatherings of people, as well as social networks. Such vessels are also easily broken, fragile bearers of social relations and status.

The props that Simpson focuses on signal a new moment in VanDerZee's career as a photographer. According to Rodger Birt, in VanDerZee's early work "the emphasis is on the sitter," and "the use of props is minimal." The portraits he made between 1920 and 1945, however, are "remarkably different," "employing a variety of studio props and elaborate painted backdrops." In the years of his greatest popularity, "VanDerZee posed his subjects in dramatic *tableaux vivants*, placing more emphasis on the setting." The photographer also famously provided his clients with articles of fine dress. As Birt has noted, "In addition to maintaining a variety of backdrops, a room of furniture, and ersatz architectural elements (columns, gates, and so forth), VanDerZee kept available a selection of fashionable clothes for both men and women. Whether dressed in one's own finery or in the habiliment provided by VanDerZee, in the studio the client was offered the opportunity to construct alternative realities to the social roles determined by the exigencies of class and race."[7] VanDerZee encouraged his subjects to imagine themselves into a visual and material culture; using clothing and props he helped sitters to mimic "certain media-provoked images."[8] In his photography studio VanDerZee invited subjects to engage, in Leigh Raiford's words (which echo Birt's), "a confrontation with, a staging of, alternative futures."[9]

Simpson's *9 Props* is about those alternative futures, an homage to the worlds that VanDerZee and his subjects conjured. Through its references and displacements, it acknowledges the cultural constraints that limited mobility and circumscribed self-representation, but also celebrates the possibilities performed in front of VanDerZee's camera. Simpson's work highlights the collaborative work of aspiration undertaken by VanDerZee and his subjects, inviting one to see his photographs as records of a fragile world of potential.

---

9 Props invites one to consider VanDerZee's photographs in a new light, and it also encourages one to contemplate more broadly the nature of photography itself. Simpson highlights the opacity and materiality of the photograph, its haptic qualities as an object, even as she also calls upon the photograph as an indexical trace of an absent subject. Condensed in this quiet piece are several different ideas, long debated, about what, exactly, photography is.

In the process of making this work, Simpson extracted and transformed photographic detail, making it material and unique through craft production. The vessels, produced at the Pilchuck studio, are reproductions of the objects that populate VanDerZee's photographs, but with a couple of differences. The shapes reference but do not exactly replicate VanDerZee's props because what were likely industrially manufactured things, recorded and mechanically reproduced in photographs, are rendered for Simpson by glass blowers. *9 Props* highlights the artist's touch, presenting objects that, even though they are copies, are also original and unique, in a way that the photograph is not. In the years following the advent of the medium, early photographers struggled to define their practice as art precisely because photography, as a mechanical medium, seemed to deny the importance of the artist's hand.[10] Although Simpson's glass objects do not register the imprint of the artist's touch in their hard surfaces, they are nevertheless handmade, and further, as small items of domestic use, they are also things to be handled.

Simpson has made her vessels strikingly opaque. She has represented a multihued array of objects—light, patterned, and ornamented—in black glass. Their monochromatic appearance abstracts the objects, making them seem the ideal forms of vases and bowls, and the uniformity of material suggests that they are members of a series or set. The clear fish bowl, milk bottles, and cocktail glasses in VanDerZee's photographs become mysterious and impenetrable in *9 Props*. The black glass renders them reflective but not transparent; they are given density and gravitas, and seem heavy despite their fragility. Making once-clear objects opaque, Simpson subtly comments on photography. Her multiple transformations call attention to the opacity of the photograph, clouding the trenchant translucency that viewers often continue to associate with it, despite decades of scholarship to the contrary.[11] Like black glass, a photograph is not transparent; it is an object that one does not see through.

In *9 Props* Simpson extracts and materializes the photographic detail, realizing three-dimensional objects flattened and miniaturized in photographs, only to turn them back into images again. What happens to the tactility of the vessels when Simpson photographs them? One might imagine that this translation would strip the objects of their materiality, in the way that Mary Bergstein describes photographs of sculpture: "Drained of physical presence, [the object's] density, mass, and textural qualities are replaced with representations of those qualities in the cool play of light on sensitized paper."[12] Printing her images on felt, however, Simpson compensates for the compression of the three-dimensional object, keeping touch accentuated in texture, and drawing attention to the tangible quality of the photograph itself.[13] The photograph is an object, as Elizabeth Edwards and others have argued, and Simpson emphasizes the materiality of the photograph in the heft and plush surface of her final felt panels.

Simpson's multilayered translations of VanDerZee's photographs underscore the haptic in relation to viewing.[14] In her hands the optical primacy of the photograph is disrupted first by the solid materiality of glass and then by the soft textures of felt. Indeed, the smooth, shiny black glass objects rendered as images on felt put into play the varied nature of texture. According to Eve Sedgwick, even the glossy surface that "signifies the willed erasure of its history" has texture, for "however high the gloss, there is no such thing as textural lack."[15] Light reflects off the gleaming black surfaces of Simpson's vessels, and as Krista Thompson has argued, "artists have used shine, the visual production of light reflecting off polished surfaces . . . to emphasize the materiality and haptic quality of objects."[16] Highlighting the materiality of her objects in this way, Simpson then brings the tactile nature of texture further into focus by printing her images of shiny black vessels on felt. As Sedgwick proposes, texture "tends to be liminally registered 'on the border of properties of touch and vision.'"[17] Texture, in other words, is multifaceted; it is registered by multiple senses, and blurs the detachment of vision with the immediacy of touch.[18] If Simpson distances VanDerZee's subjects by displacing them, she then brings them into proximity through the brush of texture.

9 Props points toward the photograph's opacity, but also highlights the touch of its indexical sign. The work underscores that the photograph is not transparent, but nevertheless plays on the idea of it as a tactile trace, a direct link between signifier and signified. Straining in opposite directions, it severs the image from its referent, while also keeping that referent close at hand.

Although it continues to be debated, the photograph's status as an indexical sign that attests to the presence of its referent has captivated many of the medium's thinkers. And as Margaret Olin has argued, "Theories of the index at least covertly seem to depend on the reality of touch."[19] Famously, for Roland Barthes, viewers *feel* the presence of the photograph's indexical referent. Looking at a photograph, he muses, "From a real body, which was there, proceed radiations which ultimately touch me, who am here . . . light, though impalpable, is here a carnal medium, a skin I share with anyone who has been photographed."[20] If one heeds Barthes, the photograph itself is haptic, and it is haptic in an extraordinary way, as the light that facilitates the making of the image touches the viewer, like a shared skin.

Touch registers intimacy, both spatially and affectively. One touches and is touched by things, physically, due to proximity, and also figuratively, emotionally.[21] Indeed, for Tina Campt, the *tactile* qualities of the photograph as a material object become *haptic* only when an image is affectively charged. "Haptic images are objects whose effects are structured by a tripartite sense of touch—an indexical touch, a physical touch, and an affective touch."[22] Simpson's felt prints are clearly tactile, and they are also haptic in Campt's sense of the term. Perhaps paradoxically, as Bergstein proposes, photographs of objects are often "more emotionally charged than the original" due to a "decontextualized close view,"[23] and *9 Props* presents close views of undeniably decontextualized objects. Simpson isolates the things in VanDerZee's photographs, literally taking them out of his studio and, through a series of transformations, into her own. Singled out in prints on felt, the objects acquire a renewed tactility, as well as a new affective charge. As fragments distilled from a larger view, they have a solemnity and strange presence about them, as if they are relics from another time. Amplifying the haptic through her translations of the objects, Simpson opens viewers to the touch of VanDerZee's photographs.

Even as *9 Props* radically transforms VanDerZee's photographs, it nevertheless keeps those images close at hand. Once again, printed beneath each vessel is text that outlines the title and date of the photograph that inspired it, along with a description of the image. As Simpson has stated, the text describes the photograph from her point of view, and she is interested in "the way VanDerZee composed these images to say something about aspirations or wealth or meaningful objects that should constitute a narrative about the person's life."[24] For example, she describes the scene in *Dinner Party with Boxer Harry Wills*, 1926, in this way: "Harry Wills aka 'The Black Panther,' boxer, businessman—sits with seven other men and women, mostly women with cocktail glasses raised as a woman on his left makes a toast in his honor. There are three bottles of champagne, a crystal decanter, a bottle of port, an arrangement of flowers and fruit, and before each guest an untouched china plate setting." This is an efficient description of VanDerZee's photograph focused on the objects, but it hardly sets the scene. The image from 1926 shows an elaborate dining room with paneled walls (fig. 4.1). A long table, covered in a white tablecloth, fills the room and the photograph, and a fringed modern chandelier hangs above the floral arrangement, its presence large in the frame. The men seated at the table, three in all, wear suits, and the five women wear fine clothes and jewelry, and all of the latter have cut their hair in fashionable short bobs. The unoccupied place setting closest to the viewer suggests that the woman at the head of the table has moved to the back of the room to raise a toast to her esteemed guest (or perhaps her husband), Harry Wills. The camera squares off front and center before the group, and the composition is symmetrical within the photographic frame. A strong light or flash from the side casts shadows to the left.

Another caption to the VanDerZee photograph tells one that Wills and his wife lived on Strivers' Row in Harlem. In *VanDerZee: Photographer*, Willis-Braithwaite and Birt describe Strivers' Row as follows: "A group of 106 houses on tree-lined 138th and 139th streets between Seventh Avenue and Eighth Avenue built for wealthy whites by a developer in 1891. By the end of WWI, African American lawyers, doctors, writers, musicians, and businessmen and their families had begun to move into the stately houses, earning for them the name bestowed by less well-to-do Harlemites."[25] The text that Willis-Braithwaite and Birt provide for this image points toward the growth of an African Ameri-

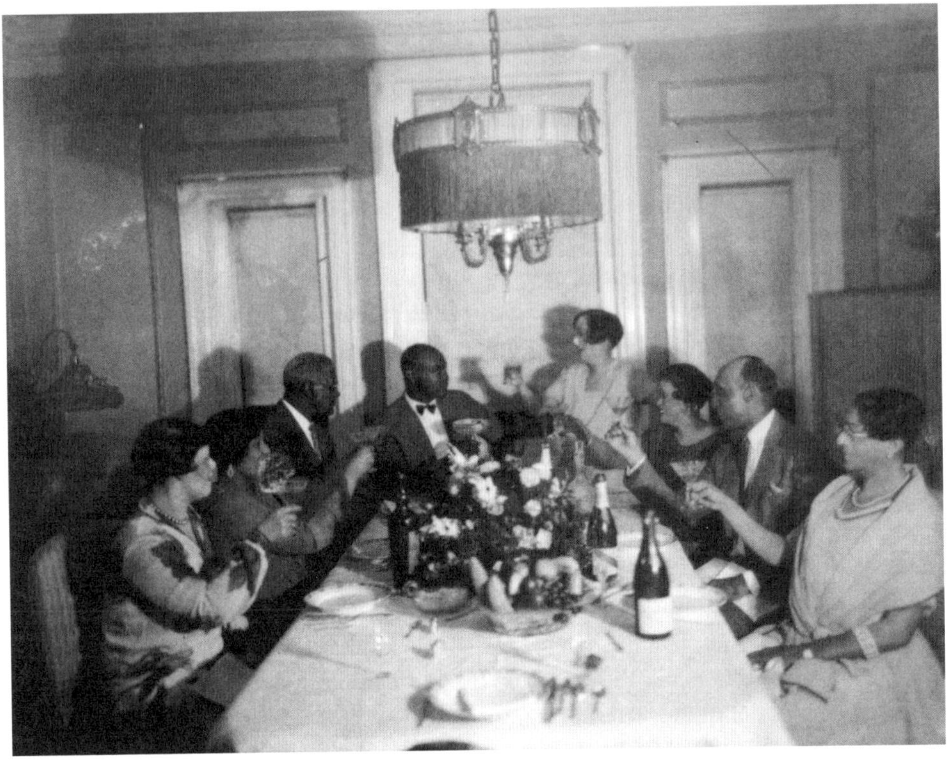

FIGURE 4.1 James VanDerZee, *Dinner Party with Boxer Harry Wills*, 1926. Copyright Donna Mussenden VanDerZee.

can upper class. It also tells a story of shifting urban demographics, the mobile boundaries of the color line, and the transformation of segregated spaces. Wills was the world colored heavyweight champion three times, but he was never allowed to compete for the heavyweight championship title against white boxer Jack Dempsey. The color line cut short his aspirations.

This complicated cultural history is signaled in Simpson's work by simple, descriptive text and a single black cocktail glass (plate 9). The image, in contrast to its inspiration, is provocative in its simplicity. It appears groundless, table and wall blurring into one another, as if the glass floats in a medium gray surround. Simpson has said that her "work is and always has been about deleting information,"[26] and such simplification is readily apparent here. The entire scene of VanDerZee's image, the social world of "strivers" as well as the color line, has been condensed into the solitary metonym of a black glass. The cocktail glass becomes a symbolic marker of the complex past that it, like VanDerZee's photograph, does not fully reveal.

Simpson's strategy of reduction is fascinating in light of Siegfried Kracauer's thoughts on photography, set forth in 1927, in a different context, but coincident with VanDerZee's most successful years. Kracauer was disturbed by the proliferation of images he saw in the early twentieth century, but, more importantly, by the proliferation of details recorded in any given image. According to the theorist, the photograph's extraneous information, its overwhelming detail, hinders the production of memory-images, which are affectively selective. Unlike the memory-image, "photography appears as a jumble that consists partly of garbage."[27] The photograph is overloaded with distracting visual information that does not allow one's memory to take hold of the essential elements of a subject.

As distillations, the images in *9 Props* might be likened to memory-images, but they are askew, each one focused on a detail. Simpson deletes extraneous, and one might even say important, information (such as the figure) from VanDerZee's images, while raising seemingly superfluous details to the center of observation. *9 Props* presents condensed memory-images not of specific people but of props. By focusing on objects, Simpson encourages one to consider the parade of people that passed into and out of the studio in relation to them. She deflects attention away from individual subjects, directing it toward the larger community crafted in VanDerZee's photographs. Rather than limiting one's attachments to the people represented in specific images, the work opens onto a larger community and its patterns of representation, broadening the compass of the photograph's affective invitation.[28]

Many of the images in *9 Props* are displaced portraits. As Sara Blair has argued, "Simpson invites the viewer to engage with a play of displacements"; the text references "a visual object and a portrait subject that remain unavailable."[29] In Simpson's translation of VanDerZee's studio portraits, objects stand in for subjects, and yet they provide what Okwui Enwezor has called a "rumor of the body."[30] Indeed, the stem of the cocktail glass is elegant, curvy, and almost anthropomorphic; it has a "certain sensuality" about it.[31] Through its displacements *9 Props* interrogates the photographic portrait, asking, as Kristen Eckrich has, "To what extent can portraiture be understood and still regarded as such without its usual signifiers?"[32] The work pushes portraiture to its limits, and given its removal of the figure, one might understand *9 Props* as Enwezor and Huey Copeland have described other works by Simpson, as "anti-portraits."[33] *9 Props* presents metaportraits that comment on the portrait tradition VanDerZee employed to help his sitters perform their aspirations.

Props support the choreography of self produced in portraiture. By focusing on VanDerZee's props, Simpson highlights the self-fashioning of the subject according to cultural codes and individual fantasies, drawing attention to the performative aspects of the portrait. Many of VanDerZee's subjects aimed to envision a class mobility that lay out of reach, and they figured their aspirations not only by donning fine clothes but also by enacting normative gender roles. As Kevin Gaines and others have demonstrated, African American progress was often circumscribed along the lines of gender propriety in the early twentieth century; indeed, the middle class was defined, in part, by its adherence to normative codes of gender.[34] Many of VanDerZee's photographs are "overtly, aggressively middle class,"[35] as Miriam Thaggert has argued, and in what Deborah Willis has called their "overt celebration of black middle-class life, and particularly family life,"[36] they accord with the tenets of African American prescriptive literature at the time. VanDerZee's "countless wedding portraits" celebrated the orderly marital relations that authors of conduct literature held up as measures of African American progress.[37] According to Michele Mitchell, social reformers depicted "patriarchy and moral motherhood as transformative, regenerative forces" and "both women and men reified motherhood as the primary catalyst for black progress."[38] The readers of such prescriptive texts were likely to overlap with VanDerZee's clientele, including what Mitchell describes as "aspiring-class and relatively elite women and men: self-schooled strivers." In his studio, VanDerZee arranged objects to simulate elegant domestic spaces, producing a visual register of an aspiring community coded in terms of class and gender.[39]

But not all of VanDerZee's subjects were so normatively inclined, and the literature of racial reform proliferated precisely as the mobility of the Great Migration generated anxieties about sexuality and new forms of social interaction in urban spaces. As Harlem was home to "strivers," it was also a center of artistic production, cultural experimentation, political protest, racial mixing, and nonnormative gender presentation. VanDerZee's photographs mark a range of desires including middle-class respectability, as well as political mobilization, and various forms of gender performance. Simpson takes her objects from photographs that highlight the multiplicity and complexity of this singular moment in African American self-representation, giving one a more nuanced view of VanDerZee and of Harlem.[40]

One of the vessels in Simpson's *9 Props* is a tall vase that recurs in a number of VanDerZee's portraits, including *Couple* (1924), *Portrait of a woman* (1924), *Identical twins* (1924), *Three girls, probably sisters* (1926), *Family portrait* (1928), and *Brothers and sisters* (1928). Some of these photographs are among VanDerZee's most famous, such as *Identical twins*, and others are among his most heteronormative, portraying couples and children, the gendered bourgeois pillars of African American "uplift." The vase also figures prominently in *Beau of the Ball* (1926), VanDerZee's portrait of a young cross-dresser who sits, turned partway toward the camera, displaying the sweeping skirt and sleeves of an elegant dress lined with fur (fig. 4.2).

Simpson identifies her vase with VanDerZee's *Beau of the Ball* (1926), and describes the image in her work as follows: "S/he is dressed in a skirt and small jacket with bell sleeves. The neck, sleeves and bottom of the skirt is [*sic*] trimmed in fur, and her/his silk stocking legs and with and satin shoes are crossed at the ankle. She/he is seated and rests her/his left elbow on the table, and her/his right hand on her/his hip. A painted backdrop of a window and a landscape appears behind her/him. A vase with flowers and a phone are on the table." Simpson's clunky description marks the way the subject's gender performance disrupts the either/or binary of normative language, but the less obvious slippage in the text—"and with and satin"—suggests a both/and indeterminacy that accords with her gender play. Simpson might have chosen any one of a number of photographs of gender normativity as referent for her vase, but she focused on *Beau of the Ball*, highlighting gender performance outside the bounds of bourgeois conformity in VanDerZee's Harlem studio (plate 10).[41] In this way, Simpson's *9 Props* calls one back to look at VanDerZee's Harlem anew, using his images to recall a vision of Harlem that is not strictly bound to the class and gender dictates of "striving."

As *9 Props* probes the aspirational politics of early twentieth-century Harlemites and the performance of portraiture, it also points toward the broader representation of Harlem itself. Indeed, this seemingly simple work becomes more multifaceted the further one considers it. Simpson takes her objects from photographs made in the heyday of VanDerZee's popularity in the 1920s and 1930s, but also from his later portraits of prominent African Americans made in the 1970s and 1980s. A teardrop-shaped vase, for example, was in-

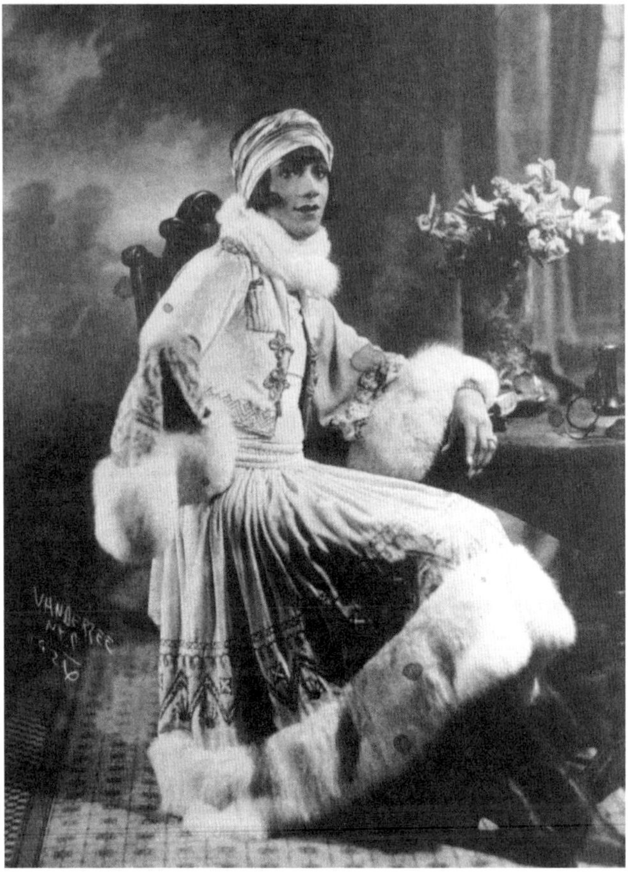

FIGURE 4.2 James VanDerZee, *Beau of the Ball*, 1926. Copyright Donna Mussenden VanDerZee.

spired by VanDerZee's 1976 portrait of the painter Benny Andrews (plate 11 and fig. 4.3). Among the things for which he is well known, Andrews was a founding member of the Black Emergency Cultural Coalition (BECC), a group organized to protest the Metropolitan Museum of Art's 1969 exhibition *Harlem on My Mind*.[42]

VanDerZee's portrait of Andrews is charged in a number of ways. It represents the photographer's return to portraiture after a long period of decline, a return that was inspired, in part, by the fame he garnered from his participation in *Harlem on My Mind*, the exhibition that Andrews so passion-

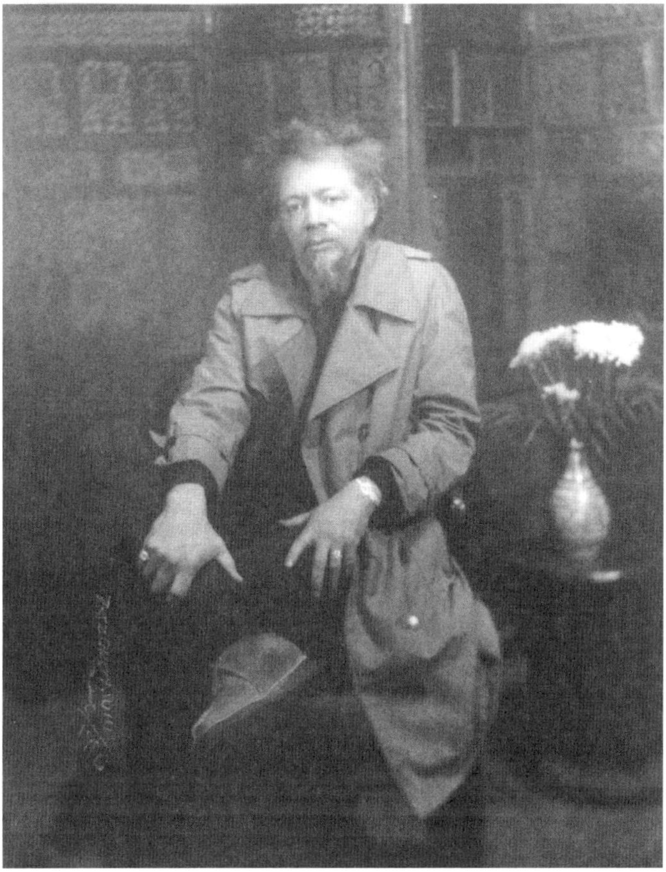

FIGURE 4.3 James VanDerZee, *Benny Andrews*, 1976. Copyright Donna Mussenden VanDerZee.

ately challenged. As Bridget Cooks has argued, for VanDerZee, "*Harlem on My Mind* was the pivotal event of his career."[43] After World War II, in another shift in urban demographics, the middle class had begun to leave Harlem, and VanDerZee's clientele had diminished precipitously. Further, VanDerZee refused to change his aesthetic with the times.[44] According to Birt, "The painted backdrops, the architectural details, and the glamorous poses that made a VanDerZee photograph a prized possession to the preceding generation now marked the photographer's images as quaint relics from another era."[45] His props were no longer working. By 1967, VanDerZee and his wife were destitute, and his business desperately needed a boost. Therefore, when Reginald McGhee entered his studio looking for photographs for the Metropolitan's Harlem exhibition, VanDerZee was happy to contribute.[46]

The controversy surrounding *Harlem on My Mind* centered on the exclusion of African American artists from the show, and the centrality of photography, which many saw as antithetical to art at the time. When it came to thinking about Harlem, the Metropolitan, a renowned art institution, produced an exhibition that was deemed "socio-documentary" and even perceived as "ethnographic."[47] The exhibition featured over two thousand photographs, including many by VanDerZee, some printed as large wall murals.[48] The BECC "accused the museum of giving up art for social science,"[49] and it took particular issue with the preponderance of photographs in the exhibition. One of the group's picket signs read, "Visit the Metropolitan Museum of Photography," and according to Birt, "it was carried by Benny Andrews, a painter, who must have considered his sign's message the ultimate insult."[50] In this context, VanDerZee's portrait of Andrews calls forth a contest over the status of photography as art, a debate that plagued its nineteenth-century practitioners, and could be waged as late as 1969.

By bringing one back to VanDerZee, and through his photographs, to Andrews and the BECC, Simpson subtly situates her own work in relation to these debates about photography and art. Simpson is prominent among a generation of artists for whom photography has been a central component of artwork, and like Martha Rosler and others, she has undermined the strategies of sociodocumentary photography, which depends on the purported transparency of written and visual texts to communicate its message. As Coco Fusco has said of Simpson's work, it "points to the inadequacies of language, written and photographic," to represent African American experience, and it often uses image and text to unseat the authority of both.[51] Documentary photographs typically have explanatory text or captions that direct the reading of images and attempt to control their meaning. Simpson's *9 Props* calls attention to the relationship of text to image by creating a disjunction between the two. Once again, her captions describe absent images. Simpson engages a long-standing conversation about the absence of the photographic subject (despite its seeming presence), but in *9 Props* absence reverberates because her images and text refer to unavailable photographs that in turn refer to missing subjects. With her work, one might say that Simpson definitively settled the debate about whether or not photography could be considered art in the decades following the controversy over *Harlem on My Mind*. Indeed, *9 Props* is housed in the permanent collection of the Metropolitan Museum of Art, along with several other works by Simpson.

Simpson's work proclaims photography for art, but it also draws on the forms of social science, and given the historical critiques surrounding *Harlem on My Mind*, it is striking how *9 Props* engages the photographic registers of science and early anthropology. In the sparseness of the images, and the repetition of framing and form, *9 Props* mimics a scientific taxonomy, and Simpson has often displayed the felt panels in a grid, heightening the sense of systematization.[52] The work recalls Bernd and Hilla Becher's taxonomic grids of architectural forms, as well as Catherine Wagner's studies of scientific systems. Indeed, Wagner's *Sequential Molecules* of 1995 is almost a visual inverse of Simpson's *9 Props*, presenting nine clear bulbous vessels lined with white residue, photographed against a black background (fig. 4.4).

Practices of photographic taxonomy have a marked racial history. As many scholars have outlined, photography was central to the visual production of "race" in the nineteenth and early twentieth centuries. Polygenesists, biological racialists, anthropologists, and eugenicists wielded photography in efforts to visually codify bodies as distinct racial types.[53] Among the earliest and most famous, the scientist Louis Agassiz commissioned Joseph T. Zealy to photograph enslaved men and women in South Carolina in 1850 in order to support his idea of polygenesis, the theory that the different races were created at distinct times as different species. The daguerreotypes show men and women violently stripped before the camera, photographed from the front and side.[54]

Simpson's *9 Props* subtly gestures toward such racialized taxonomies.[55] Her anthropomorphic black vessels might evoke "black" bodies, and she has kept her backgrounds simple, plain, and placeless. Indeed, her photographs are almost ethnographic in their measured documentation, and what Enwezor has said of another project is also true of *9 Props*: "In her work the marriage of text and image reappropriates one of the signal tropes of anthropology, an invidious taxonomy which sorts, grades and classifies objects in stark arrangements with terse commentary attached."[56] *9 Props* repurposes ethnographic photography, which often linked people to objects in efforts to define a culture, as in Edward Curtis's *The North American Indian* (1907–30).

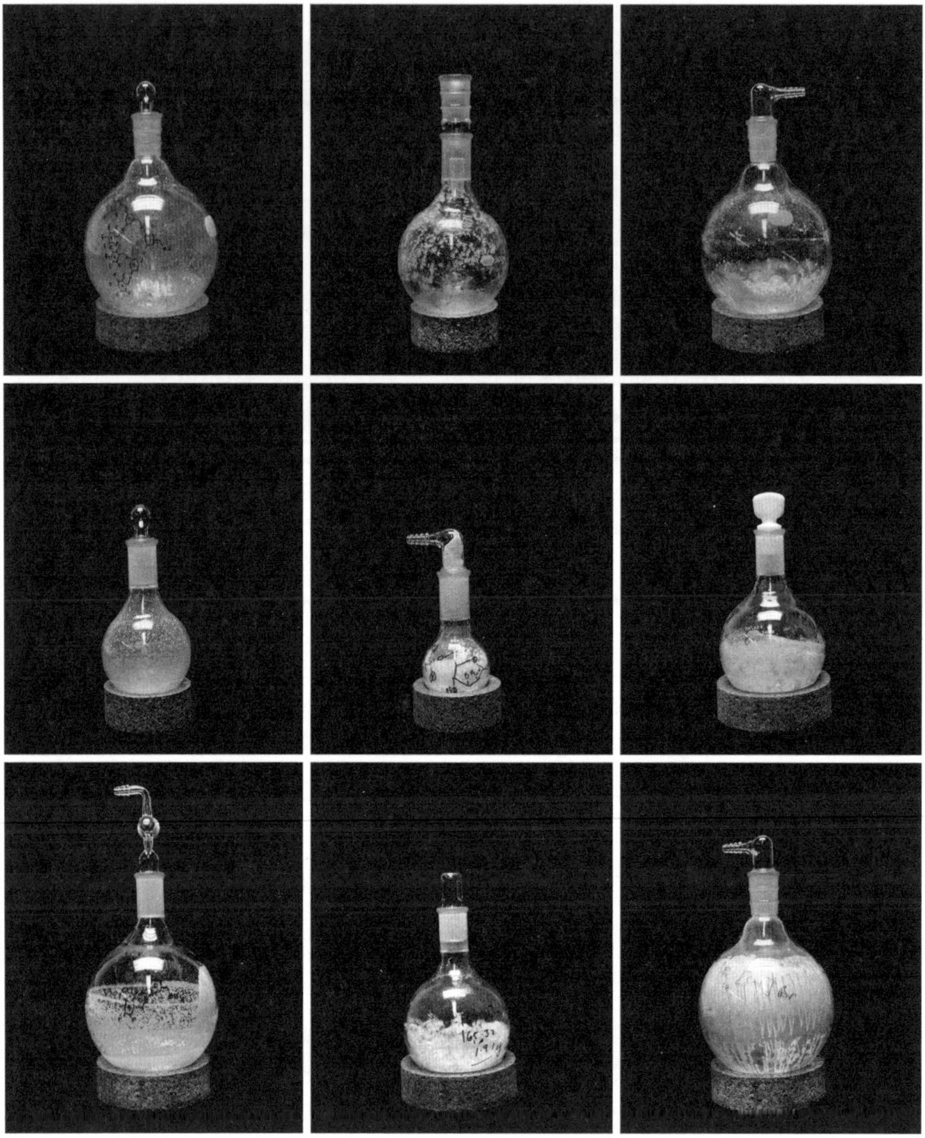

FIGURE 4.4 Catherine Wagner, *Sequential Molecules*, 1995. Nine-panel typology, gelatin silver prints, each 24 × 20 inches. From *Art and Science: Investigating Matter*. Courtesy the artist.

In Curtis's photograph of "water carriers," made outdoors at Zuni pueblo, two women stand, directly facing the camera, wrapped in folded dark blankets, balancing large painted pots on their heads (fig. 4.5). Clearly staged and stilled, the photograph is a portrait that is also meant to depict how women use the decorated vessels. But even when Curtis makes a more traditional portrait of a Zuni woman, situated against a plain background, framed tightly from the chest up, he photographs her with an ornately painted pot balanced on her head (fig. 4.6). It is as if the woman and the vessel are conflated in his view of the Zuni, a people made equivalent to the objects of their production and use.

Simpson evokes ethnographic photography even as she redirects it. She shows the sleight of hand whereby people are objectified and objects obscure people in an ethnographic taxonomy. And yet her work also recalls Frederick Douglass's surprising investment in the objectification of the photograph. Replacing people with props, Simpson heightens the photographic production of self as object that Douglass envisioned as a vehicle of social progress. In *9 Props*, she underscores the fabrication of both scientific and portrait scenes, using ethnographic strategies to conjure the dreams and visions beckoned in VanDerZee's photographs.[57] Displacing people with props, she directs one's attention away from VanDerZee's most obvious subjects, the individuals posed in front of his camera, and brings into focus the desires that animate his images. Her black glass vessels stand as surrogate witnesses to dreams summoned. Abstracting and idealizing VanDerZee's props, isolating them in a placeless surround, Simpson creates a fanciful ethnography of aspiration.

9 Props both recalls and refuses racial categorization. Simpson renders her vessels in black glass, exaggerating the idea of blackness and making it literal, rather than cultural or racial. As the work condenses the cultural complexities surrounding Harry Wills or Benny Andrews into a single, surrogate vessel, it also condenses the cultural weight of "blackness" in black glass. *9 Props* celebrates the African American community that comes into focus in VanDerZee's photographs, even as it also questions the meaning of "blackness" and "black art." Taking one back to the debates about African American art and culture inspired by *Harlem on My Mind*, Simpson calls into view the discourses, such as social science, that circumscribe African American aesthetic production and require it to signify as "cultural." With her black vessels and felt prints, Simpson emphasizes, in Darby English's words, the "aesthetic life of the object," not simply its "predetermined social" life.[58]

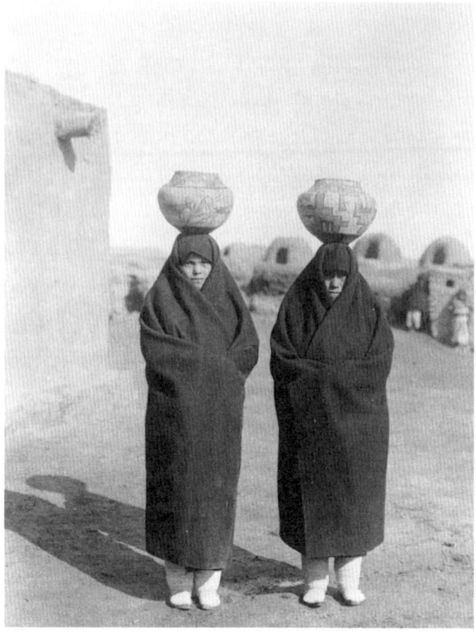

FIGURE 4.5 Edward S. Curtis, *Zuni water carriers*, c. 1903. Library of Congress, Prints and Photographs Division, Washington, DC.

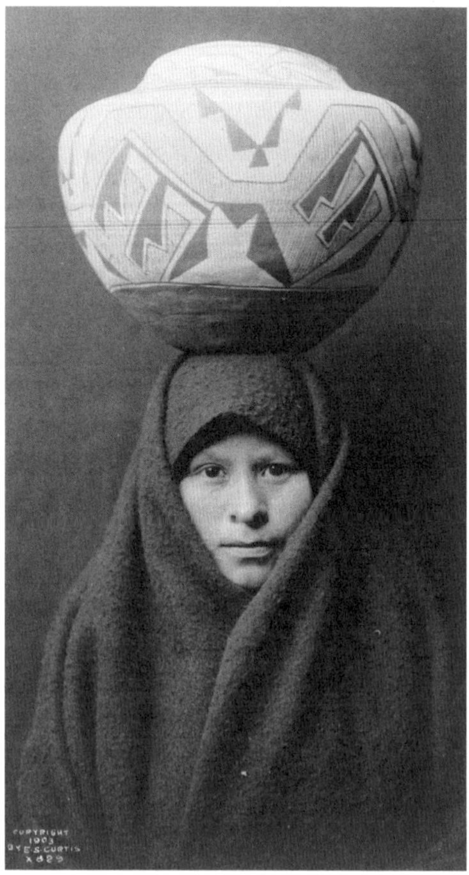

FIGURE 4.6 Edward S. Curtis, *Zuni girl with jar*, c. 1903. Library of Congress, Prints and Photographs Division, Washington, DC.

In the early twentieth century, VanDerZee provided an important, self-affirming counterpoint to the racist taxonomies of a prior era, creating tableaus of desire and promise with his subjects. Through a series of displacements and redirections, Simpson elicits not only VanDerZee's photographs but also the visions of futurity VanDerZee's images aimed to represent. Recalling VanDerZee's props, even as she transforms them, she creates an ethnography of aspiration that evokes and evades the photographic frames of race.

CHAPTER 5

Afterimages

Jason Lazarus

At first the photograph seems ordinary: a wide grassy park, spring trees, a pale blue sky brushed with thin white clouds. Bright bits here and there dot the green. In the foreground, on the right, thin sheets of wood mar the lawn. Around the boards the grass looks ashen (plate 12).

The caption changes everything. This is Jason Lazarus's photograph titled *Standing at the Grave of Emmett Till, Day of Exhumation, June 1st, 2005 (Alsip, Illinois)*. The bright spots on the lawn are bouquets of flowers. A strip of light brown earth in the distance marks a new grave. The boards in the foreground cover a deep hole in the ground where Emmett Till's body had lain for fifty years.

The captioned photograph raises questions. If it is the day of exhumation, where are the camera crews, the protesters, the family members, the curious? Why is the grave left unattended, and why was the photographer allowed to get so close? Why was the body disinterred in the first place, and what else lies buried in that cemetery? Despite the palpable emptiness of the photograph, Lazarus marks his presence just outside the scene. The photograph is not "The Grave of Emmett Till," but "*Standing* at the Grave of Emmett Till," being there, witnessing, trying to make sense of it. The framing and naming of the image places viewers with Lazarus—everyone is "standing at the grave of Emmett Till."

Photographs that depend so entirely on titles for their effect are generally less compelling. The harnessing of image to word is almost always an attempt to contain and constrain the many possible meanings a photograph might generate, to curtail its essential excess. A long line of critical thinkers have sought to make the photograph useful for political work by adhering the image to a caption that directs its import, as Mark Reinhardt has outlined.[1] Lazarus's text changes the meaning of the photograph, but instead of closing it down, it ruptures the image, opening it up in all its messy ambiguity, unlocking its excess of meaning, allowing its many pasts to return.

Emmett Till's body will not stay buried. US culture is haunted by his ghost, and haunted by the covering over too. Americans can't seem to lay Till's body to rest, and how *could* they? The corpse was exhumed so that a medical examiner could identify it as the body it was already known to be—"the body in Emmett's grave"[2]—the body identified by his mother fifty years ago, the body she refused to cover over. Those who claimed not to recognize it then, those who doubted, really just denied.

The body of Till returns in photographs. Images of his mutilated corpse refuse to stay in the past; they come back, like the repressed, to disturb the present. The lynching of a fourteen-year-old boy in 1955 constituted a national trauma of savage white supremacy and antiblack violence that could not, and still cannot, fully be comprehended. Photographs are the conduit through which that horrific past touches the present, and Lazarus's latter-day image of Till's open grave recalls the body of the boy that reappears in photographs.

Till's body was unearthed to confirm a story twice told. In the summer of 1955, Till, a fourteen-year-old African American boy, left his home in Chicago to spend some time in Money, Mississippi, with his great uncle, Mose Wright. On August 24, Till and his friends visited Bryant's Grocery and Meat Market, where Till had some kind of an interaction with Carolyn Bryant, a white woman and the market owner's wife.

Early in the morning of August 28, Carolyn's husband, Roy Bryant, and his half brother, J. W. Milam, and at least one other person abducted Till from his uncle's home. They beat him, shot him in the head, fastened a large metal cotton gin fan to his neck with barbed wire, and sank his body in the Tallahatchie River. On August 31, Till's naked body was found floating in the river, the large metal fan still attached to his neck. Till's mother, Mamie Bradley, made the extraordinary decision to leave the casket open at her son's funeral because she wanted the world to see the brutality of the crime perpetrated against him. For four days, tens of thousands of people came to view Till's body in a Chicago church. JET magazine and the *Chicago Defender* published photographs of his maimed face, and the murder became international news that highlighted the violent racism of the Jim Crow South. The trial of Bryant and Milam was held in September in a Mississippi state court, and the all-male, all-white jury acquitted the men, who later bragged about their crime.[3]

This is the story of Till's murder in its most condensed and common form. But as Jacqueline Goldsby has noted, two crucial moments in the story continue to be contested and unknown. The exchange at the grocery store between Till and Bryant "remains now hopelessly in dispute."[4] Even after Bryant admitted to historian Timothy B. Tyson, decades after the murder and trial, that she lied in court about being physically assaulted, Tyson suggests that what took place between Bryant and Till "will never be revealed to a certainty, probably not even to her."[5] As Bryant told Tyson, "'You tell these stories for so long that they seem true.'"[6] Exactly what happened in the early morning of August 28 when Till was murdered also remains uncertain. Although Tyson has added detail to the horrible story of Till's torture and murder through his careful research, his account remains peppered with speculation about "likely" events. Therefore both the encounter that initiated a devastating sequence of events and some details about the murder itself remain unknown.

What is certain is that Bryant and Milam admitted to kidnapping Till from Wright's home, and they were arrested and charged with murder. During the trial, witnesses for the defendants used the illegibility of Till's body to question the identity of the corpse. Sheriff H. C. Strider proposed that the body pulled from the Tallahatchie River could not be Till's because it was too decomposed, too destroyed, and a local physician and an undertaker reinforced Strider's position. On the fourth day of the trial, after a mere sixty-seven minutes of deliberation, the jury delivered a not guilty verdict, proclaiming that "the state failed to prove that the recovered body was Emmett Till's." Months after the trial, Bryant and Milam admitted to a journalist for *Look* magazine that they had murdered Till to defend a white Southern patriarchy.[7]

In current national memory, the crisis and catalyst of Till's murder figure photographically. There is an image of a beaming young man with his mother, and there is a photograph of a horribly distorted, mutilated face. Today one cannot see the first image without conjuring the second; they are forever joined by a brutal murder and by the decision of a mother to expose its gruesome face to the world.[8] Mamie Bradley wanted to "make the whole world see" the white supremacist violence perpetrated against her son, and "African Americans who lived during the time of Till's murder . . . often speak of a photograph that jolted them into recognizing the historic importance of lynching's cultural logic."[9]

David Jackson made that photograph on September 2, 1955, at A. A. Rayner and Sons Funeral Home on the south side of Chicago. According to historian Brenna Wynn Greer, Jackson, a photographer for Johnson Publishing, with his colleague Simeon Booker, a correspondent, staked out the funeral home, waiting through the early morning hours for Till's body to arrive. With Bradley's permission, he photographed the corpse of her son. The photographs, including the infamous image of Till's mutilated face, were published in *JET* magazine on September 15, 1955.[10]

Jackson's photographs of Till's corpse incited outrage among African Americans and helped to catalyze the growing civil rights movement in the United States. They provided a kind of visual shorthand that aroused and inspired African Americans to action. As Leigh Raiford reminds one, "Photography does not do the work of community-building and consciousness-raising alone." It can, however, encourage these processes, and "the 1955 circulation of the Till postmortem photographs offered a refocusing of the liberatory and galvanizing potential of visual technology for black political communities."[11] In other words, African American viewers saw in the Till photographs not only the brutality of white racism but also the efficacy of photography and the mass media as tools in political campaigns.

Till's murder occurred in a moment when Southern whites were vehemently resisting African American protests against segregation, and Till's lynching marks a high note of white anxiety about the dissolution of racial boundaries, expressed as fear over the crossing of sexual boundaries, as Fred Moten has argued. As late as 1955, the sexual discourses that fueled lynching in the United States were evoked to explain the torture and murder of a fourteen-year-old boy. Till was certainly not the first and not even the last in this lineage of nightmares. Nevertheless, according to Moten, "The fact that whatever force Till's death exerted was not originary does not mean, however, that that force wasn't real. For even if his death marks panic and even if that panic had already led to the deaths of so many so that that death was already haunted, its force only the animating spirit of a train of horrors, something happened."[12] The "something" that happened started with people looking at Till's battered body reproduced in photographs. The photographs helped to generate, in Sharon Sliwinski's terms, a shared judgment among far-flung spectators who refused the degradation of the boy's body, of the boy himself, to "mere matter."[13] The person most heartbroken by the view of Till's mutilated body, his mother, made others look. She proclaimed, "'They had to see what I had seen. The whole nation had to bear witness to this.'"[14] Bradley made others look with her and judge, and in Jackson's photograph of Till's almost inhuman face, they could see the long legacy of lynching.

The mass media of the nation was heavily segregated in 1955, and it was primarily African Americans who looked with Bradley and judged. As Martin A. Berger has carefully outlined, the white press did not print photographs of Till's funeral as black newspapers and magazines across the country did. Both the white-owned *Chicago Tribune* and the *Chicago Sun-Times* sent photographers to cover the funeral, but they did not run their photographs, even as the prominent black press in Chicago led the charge in circulating images of Till's funeral in the *Chicago Defender* and Till's corpse in *JET*. White interest in the case grew during the trial of Bryant and Milam, and the *New York Times*' coverage of the trial more than tripled as the focus turned to southern white men and away from the murder itself.[15] As Berger argues, "The corpse photographs that exerted a powerful effect on blacks were absent from national television reports and from white newspapers and magazines. According to one photographic historian, not until the 1987 airing of the first episode of the civil rights television documentary *Eyes on the Prize* did significant numbers of white Americans see a photograph of Till's mutilated corpse."[16] The images made iconic in the black press in 1955 were finally seen by white viewers more than three decades later, and today they can be said to haunt a less segregated national memory.

Moten has recently taught one to see the photographs of Till anew, and to see them through sound, as images ruptured by the sound of Mamie Bradley's grief.[17] Moten suggests that one cannot see the images without hearing Bradley's cry, without hearing, in the words of Cathy Caruth, the "wound that cries out, that addresses us in an attempt to tell us of a reality or truth that is not otherwise available."[18] The postmortem photographs of Till, their reproduction and repetition and return, function as indices of trauma, for here, as in the experience of trauma, the "delayed appearance" and "belated address" of the photographs repeat what could not and can never be fully fathomed.[19] Bradley had the images of her murdered son reproduced so that others could see what she had, but as she describes her motivations, she also reveals the ultimate unintelligibility of the photographs: "If other people could see it with their *own* eyes, then together we might find a way to express what we had seen."[20] Bradley invited others to view the photographs, even as she also underscored their inability to adequately represent the events they purport to record.

Some of what took place on the early morning of August 28, 1955, is known through the injuries recorded on Till's body—clipped ear, broken bones, gouged-out eye[21]—but most is forever irretrievable. Ulrich Baer has argued that "photography can provide special access to experiences that have remained unremembered yet cannot be forgotten."[22] In the case of Till's murder, however, the photographs tell one only of a before and after of trauma. As Goldsby writes,

> It was (and still is) impossible to "perceive the photographic signifier" in the instance of Emmett Till's murder, because there was no visual record of either the moment of his exchange with Carolyn Bryant or the struggle with his attackers that ended his life. Nor could there be. In the photographic void created by those acts, the images that do exist do so in their stead, as compensation for what cannot be rendered as visible evidence of the cause of the event.[23]

The photographs of Till are like traumatic memories, images that return again and again but refuse to give one access to the events they signal.

The paired pictures of Till are partial and insufficient; they miss their referent, his murder, entirely.[24] The violence remains unseen, forever caught somewhere between the two photographs. The portrait of the smiling boy has been radically altered by its pairing, as the doubling leads one to read it now as a "before" image that marks an incalculable loss.[25] But Till's photographs are not unique in this regard. According to Georges Didi-Huberman, all photographs are only ever partial, and one must be careful not to ask too much of them: "Ask too much of it [the photograph]—'the whole truth' for example—and we will quickly be disappointed: the images are merely stolen shreds, bits of film. They are therefore *inadequate*." Nevertheless, photographs remain essential, "inadequate but necessary, inexact but true," important barriers against the erasure of history and knowledge.[26] Just as photographs do not themselves create political action, neither do they create history and knowledge—that is the task of viewers, activists, and scholars, who must interpret the images and provide the contexts in which they come to have meaning.

The postmortem photographs of Till refuse to tell the story of the violence that left his body so terribly damaged, and, once again, during the murder trial in 1955, witnesses for the defendants suggested that the defaced body might not be Till's at all. Speaking of the exhumation and examination of the remains fifty years later, in 2005, FBI spokesman Frank Bochte stated, "'The first and foremost thing we're trying to do is to put to rest any theories that the body inside there is not Emmett Till. We would like to settle that issue once and for all.'"[27] Thus, forensic scientists read the bones for traces of life lived and death violently delivered. As Thomas Keenan and Eyal Weizman have argued, "The bones of a skeleton are exposed to life in a similar way that photographic film is exposed to light"; bones are "like a palimpsest or a photograph with multiple exposures."[28] Like photographs, the marks left on bones must be interpreted. Forensic scientists make their calculations and judgments based on probability, and therefore their conclusions are never certain but, rather, are matters of "presentation and representation."[29] Forensic evidence is called on to trump faulty photographic evidence, but it, too, is a recorded trace that must be deciphered.

Lazarus's latter-day photograph asks one to see this long history of image making and of repetition and return. In his picture, the boards lying flat in the foreground disrupt the quiet normalcy of a spring scene of green grass and bright blue sky. What cannot be seen in the photograph, the hole the boards cover over, is physically deep and psychically deeper. It reminds the viewer of what was never seen, never photographed, never known at the time of Till's murder. This still photograph opens on to a deep wound, bearing witness to the trauma of Emmett Till's death and calling forth a mourning of fifty years, a melancholia. Once again, as David L. Eng and David Kazanjian have argued, "Melancholia might be said to constitute . . . an ongoing and open relationship with the past—bringing its ghosts and specters, its flaring and fleeting images, into the present."[30] Till's grave has been literally cut open, and through that rupture his ghost flashes in the present. Looking at Lazarus's photograph, one senses a collective inability to move past this death, a traumatic return of the repressed that is also a measure of melancholia. The image, in its emptiness, its return, and its incomprehensibility, would seem to refer to trauma per se. Till was murdered, his battered body was displayed and photographed, and then it was buried. His murderers were tried, and acquitted, and then they boasted about their crime. Fifty years later Till's body was exhumed in an attempt to lay it all to rest. A cycle of denial and repression and revelation continues to call forth Emmett Till—his body, his ghost, his photographs. This is what Lazarus asks one to see in all its complexity, standing at the grave of Emmett Till on the day of exhumation.

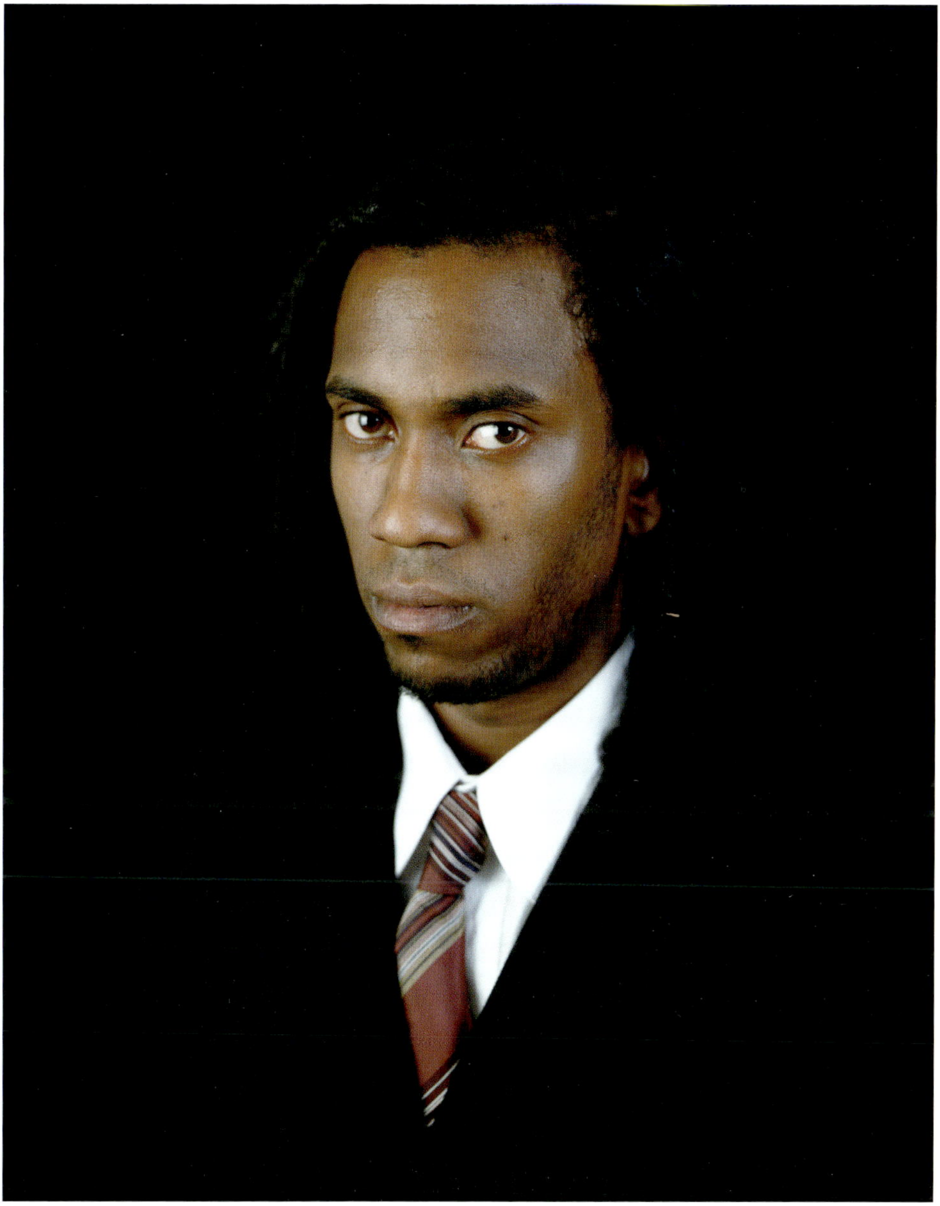

PLATE 1

Rashid Johnson, *Self Portrait with My Hair Parted Like Frederick Douglass*, 2003. Lambda print, 54½ × 42⅛ inches (138.5 × 107 cm). Copyright the artist. Courtesy of artist and Hauser & Wirth and David Kordansky Gallery.

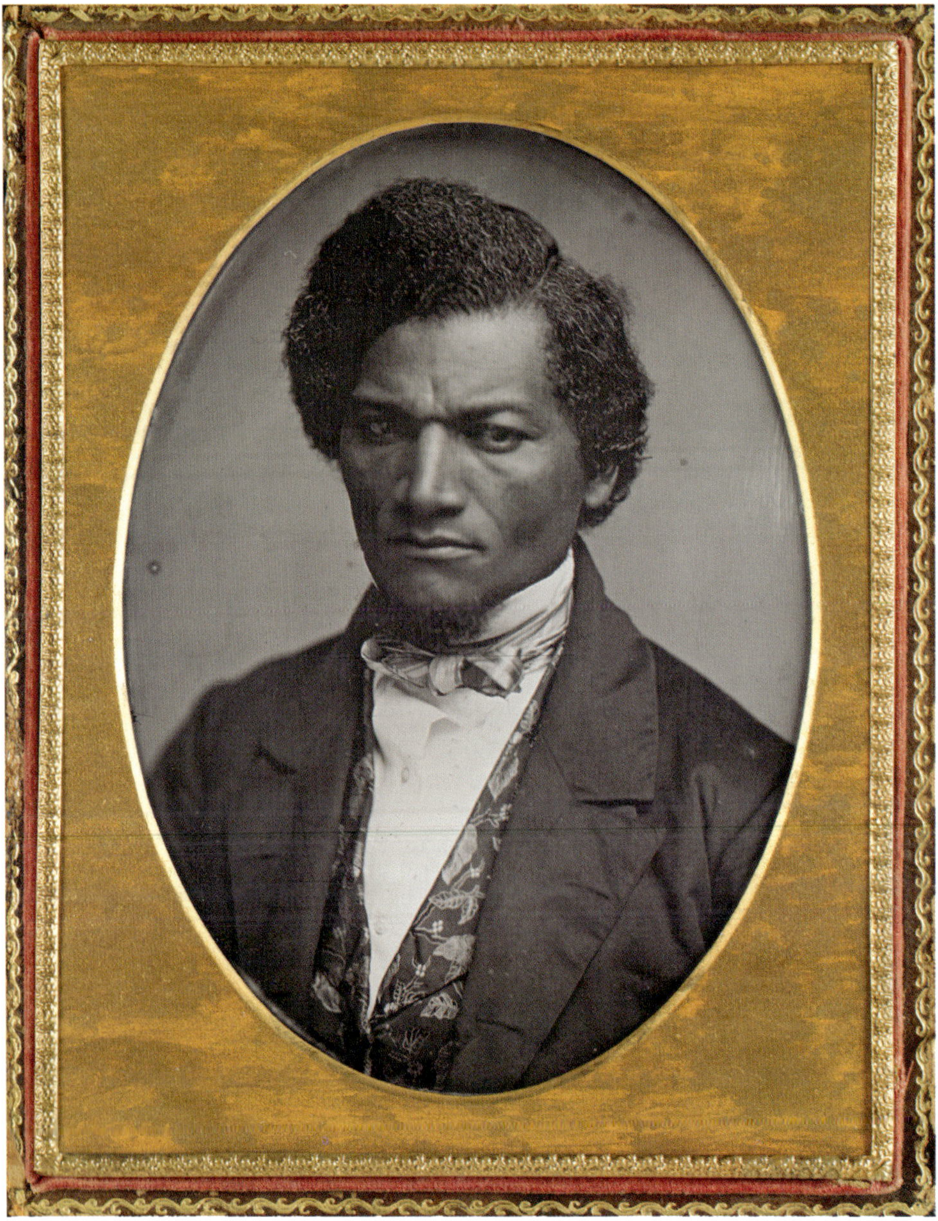

PLATE 2

Samuel J. Miller, *Frederick Douglass*, 1847–52. Cased half-plate daguerreotype, 5½ × 4⅛ inches (14 × 10.6 cm). Major Acquisitions Centennial Endowment 1996.433. The Art Institute of Chicago/Art Resource, NY.

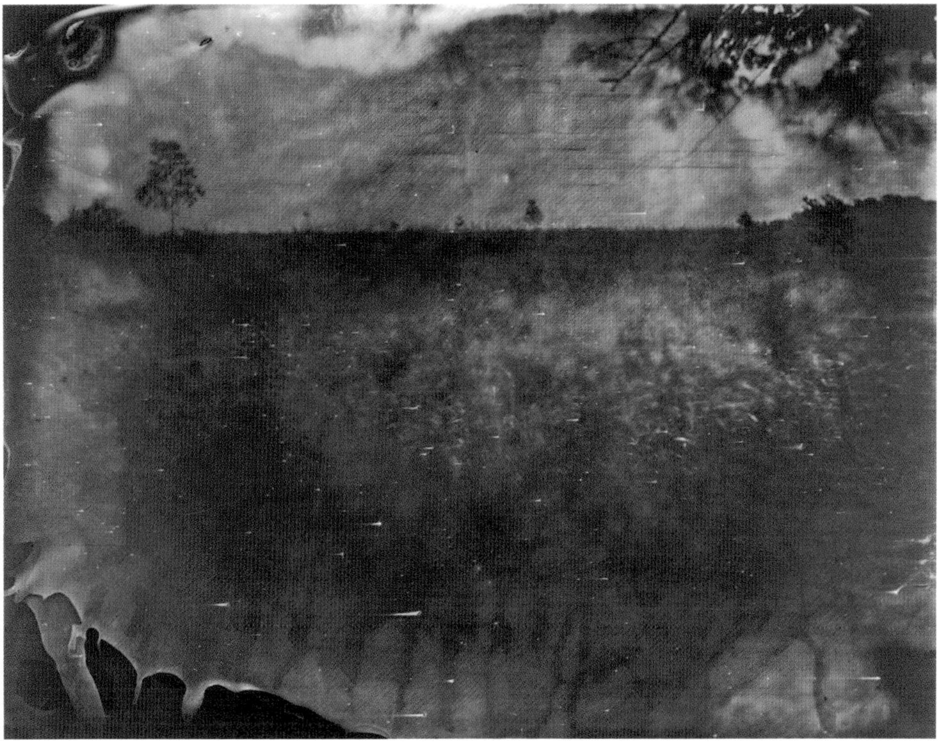

PLATE 3 Sally Mann, *Battlefields, Antietam (Spindly Trees)*, 2001.
Gelatin silver print, varnished, 40 × 50 inches (101.6 × 127 cm).

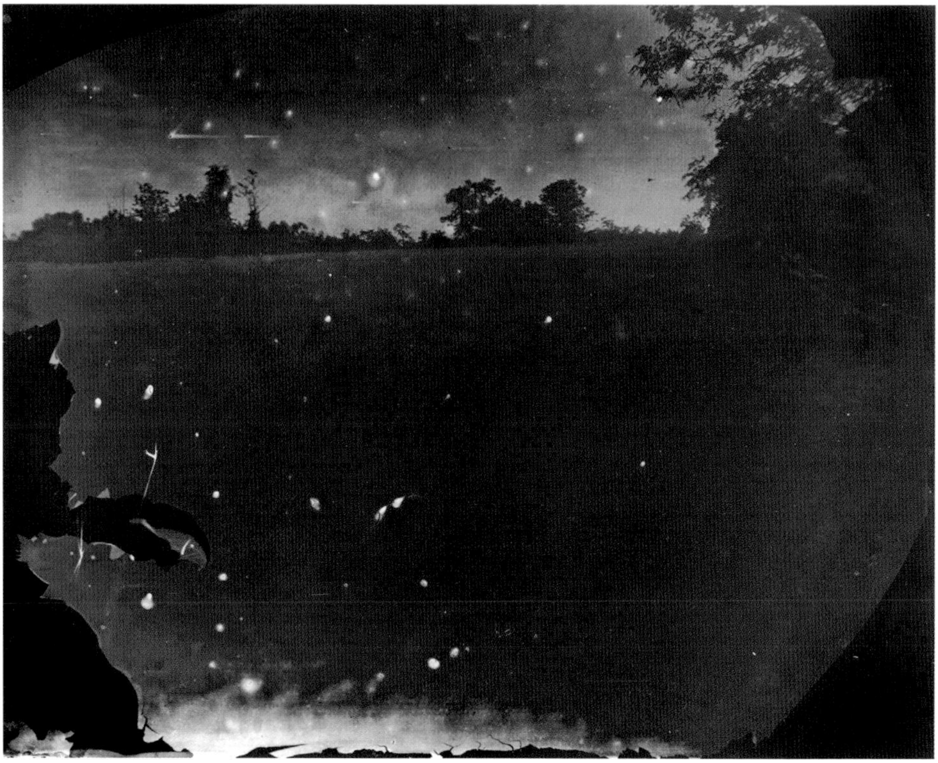

PLATE 4 Sally Mann, *Battlefields, Antietam (Starry Night)*, 2001.
Gelatin silver print, varnished, 40 × 50 inches (101.6 × 127 cm).

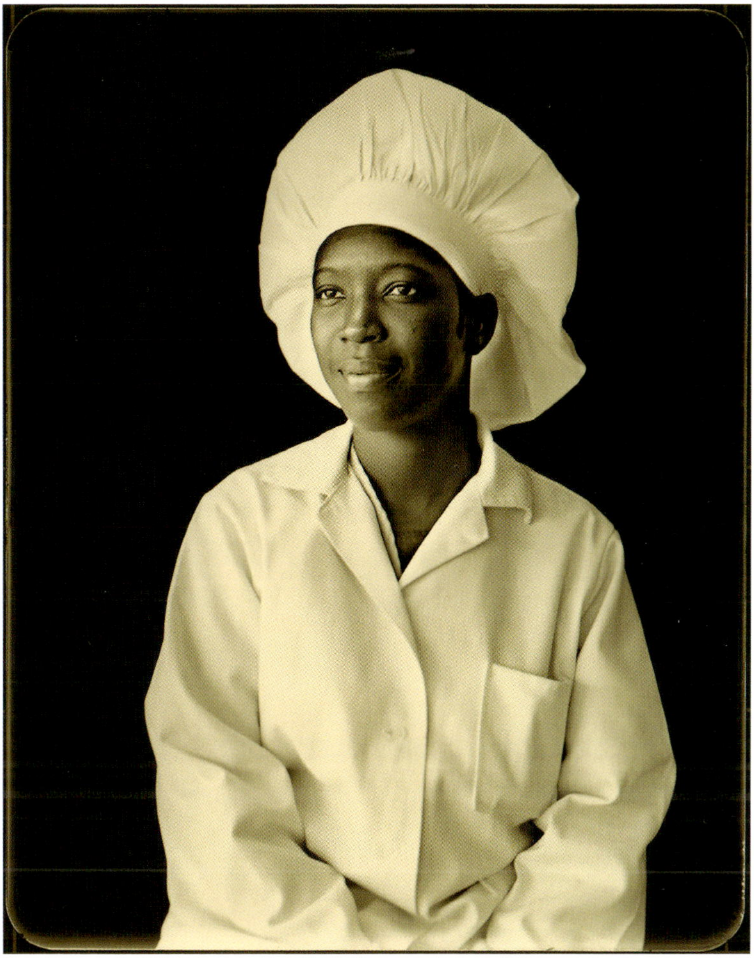

PLATE 5 Deborah Luster, *One Big Self*, Michelle Hill, Saint Gabriel, Louisiana. Department of Corrections no. 391637. Date of birth: 12.27.67. Place of birth: New Orleans. Sentence: 2½ years. Two children. Work: Culinary arts. Photograph made at Louisiana Correctional Institute for Women 4.30.99. Silver emulsion on prepared aluminum. Courtesy the artist and Jack Shainman Gallery.

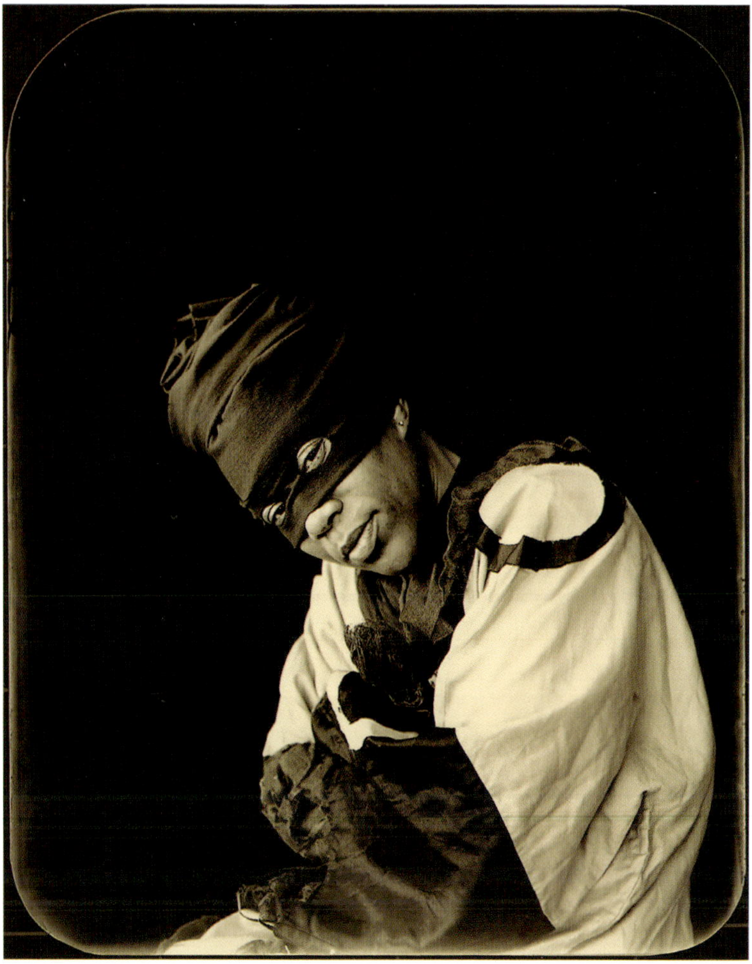

PLATE 6

Deborah Luster, *One Big Self*, Yolanda Banks, Saint Gabriel, Louisiana. Department of Corrections no. 128877. Date of birth: 10.2.58. Place of birth: New Orleans. Sentence: 5 years. Two children. Work: Kitchen. Halloween Haunted House. Photograph made at Louisiana Correctional Institute for Women 10.27.00. Silver emulsion on prepared aluminum. Courtesy the artist and Jack Shainman Gallery.

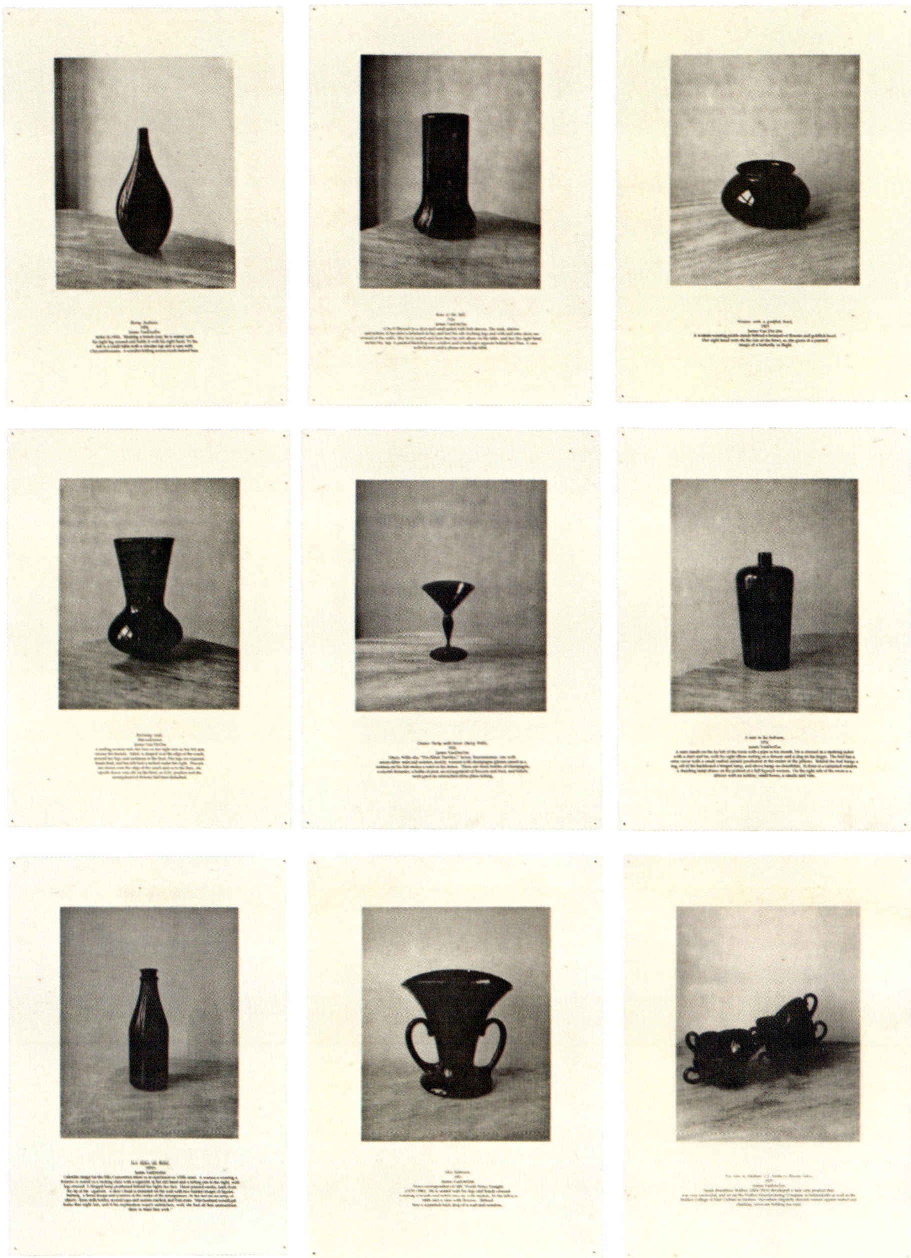

PLATE 7

Lorna Simpson, *9 Props*, 1995. Nine heat-transferred felt panels, each 14⅛ × 10⅛ inches (36.8 × 26 cm). Copyright Lorna Simpson. Courtesy the artist and Hauser & Wirth.

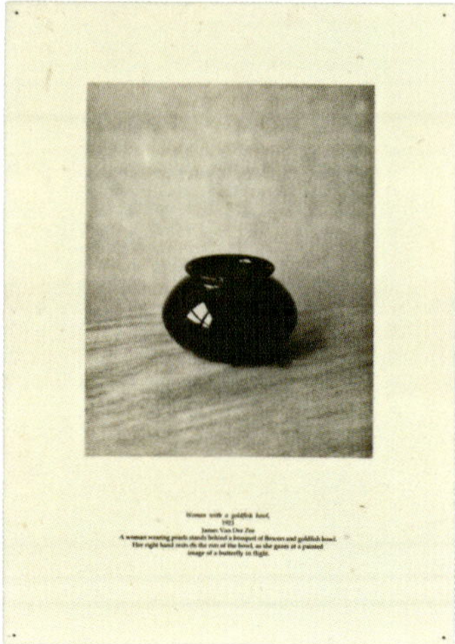

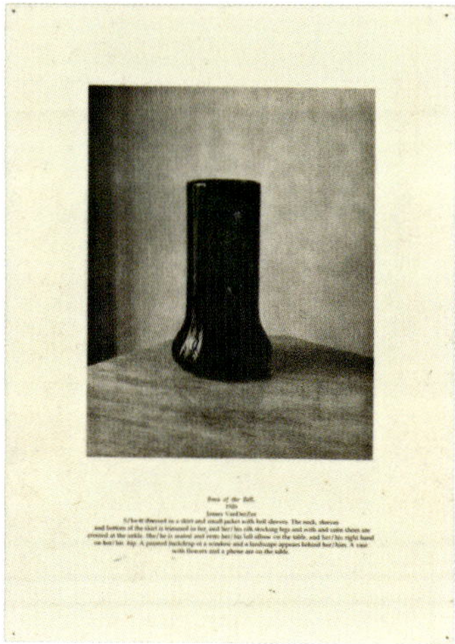

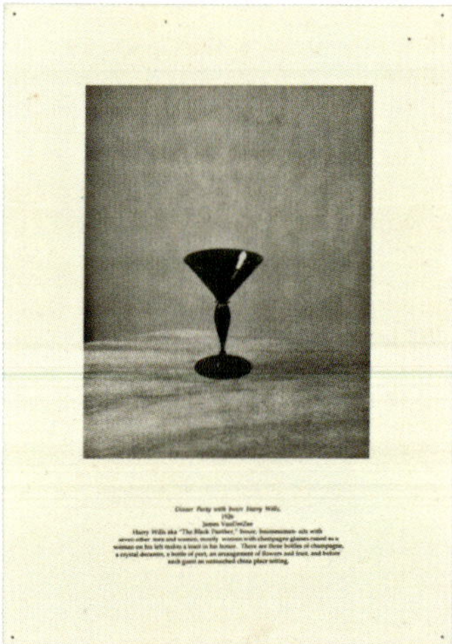

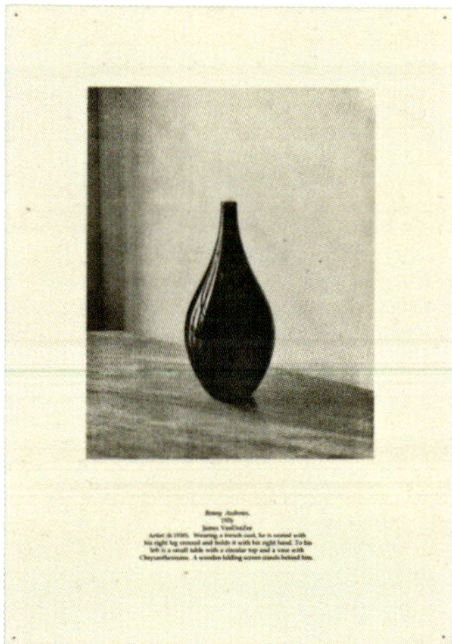

PLATE 8 (TOP LEFT) Lorna Simpson, *Woman with a goldfish bowl*, from *9 Props*, 1995. Heat-transferred felt panel, 14⅛ × 10⅛ inches (36.8 × 26 cm). Copyright Lorna Simpson. Courtesy the artist and Hauser & Wirth.

PLATE 9 (BOTTOM LEFT) Lorna Simpson, *Dinner Party with boxer Harry Wills*, from *9 Props*, 1995. Heat-transferred felt panel, 14⅛ × 10⅛ inches (36.8 × 26 cm). Copyright Lorna Simpson. Courtesy the artist and Hauser & Wirth.

PLATE 10 (TOP RIGHT) Lorna Simpson, *Beau of the Ball*, from *9 Props*, 1995. Heat-transferred felt panel, 14⅛ × 10⅛ inches (36.8 × 26 cm). Copyright Lorna Simpson. Courtesy the artist and Hauser & Wirth.

PLATE 11 (BOTTOM RIGHT) Lorna Simpson, *Benny Andrews*, from *9 Props*, 1995. Heat-transferred felt panel, 14⅛ × 10⅛ inches (36.8 × 26 cm). Copyright Lorna Simpson. Courtesy the artist and Hauser & Wirth.

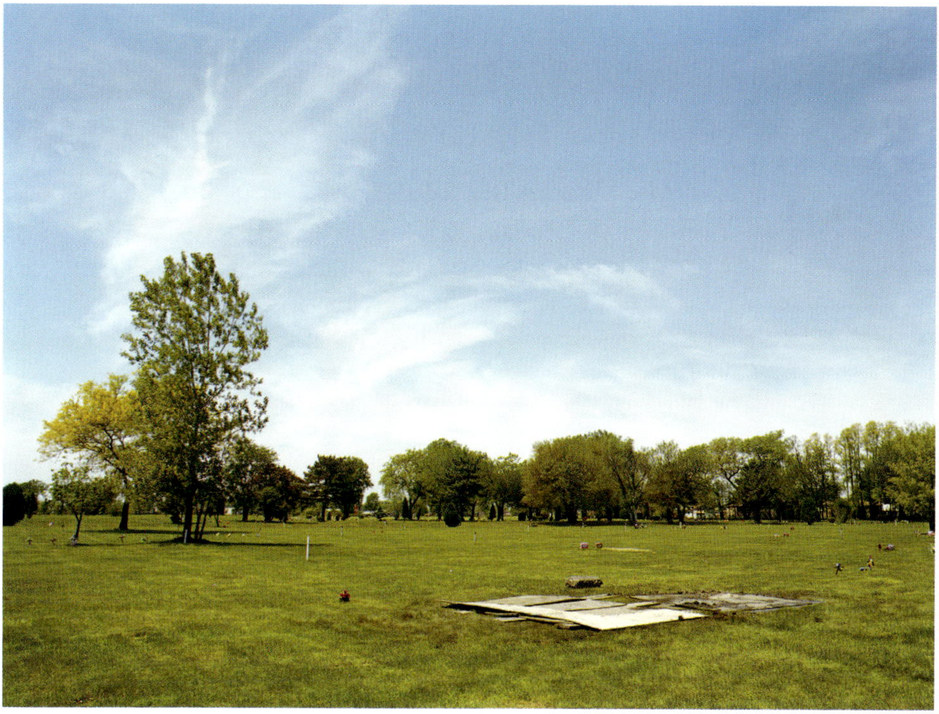

PLATE 12 Jason Lazarus, *Standing at the Grave of Emmett Till, Day of Exhumation, June 1st, 2005 (Alsip, Illinois)*, 2005. Archival pigment print, 43 × 56 inches. Courtesy the artist and Andrew Rafacz Gallery.

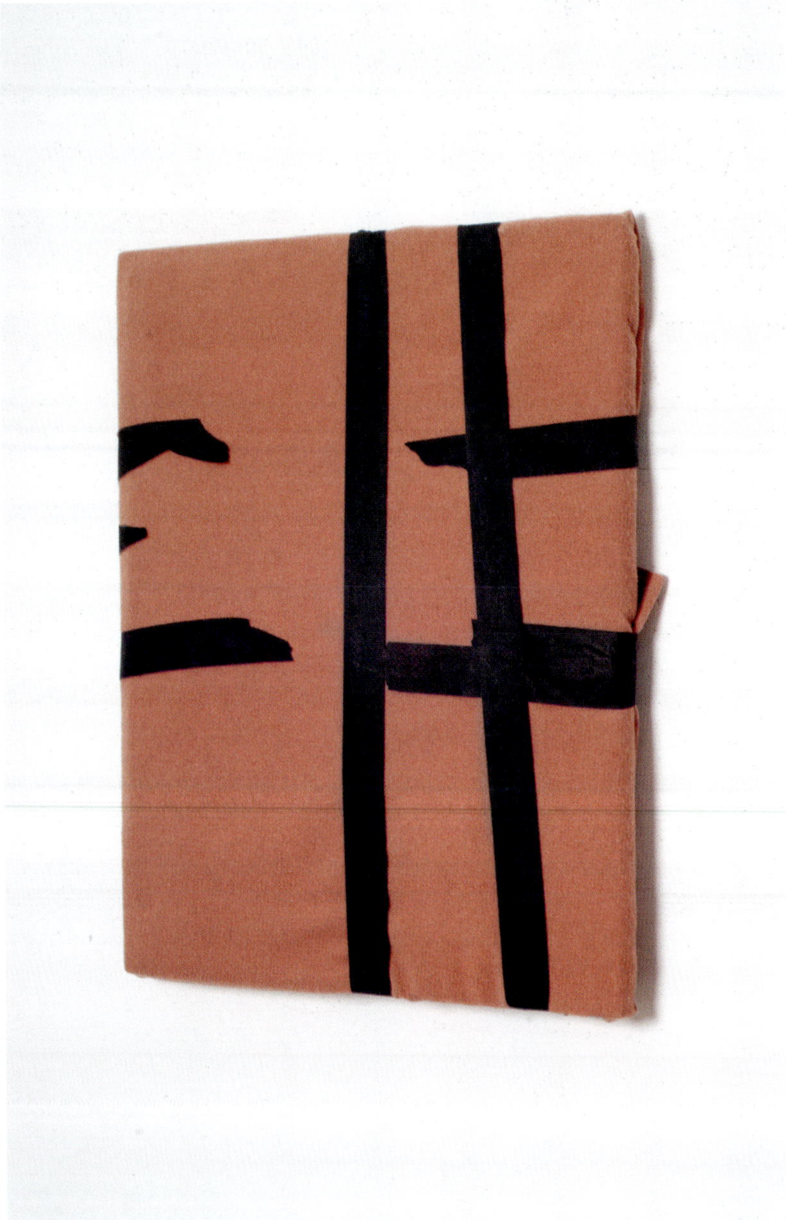

PLATE 13 Jason Lazarus, *Untitled*, 2011. Found photos, board, blanket, gaffer's tape, mounting hardware, 33 × 29 inches. Courtesy the artist.

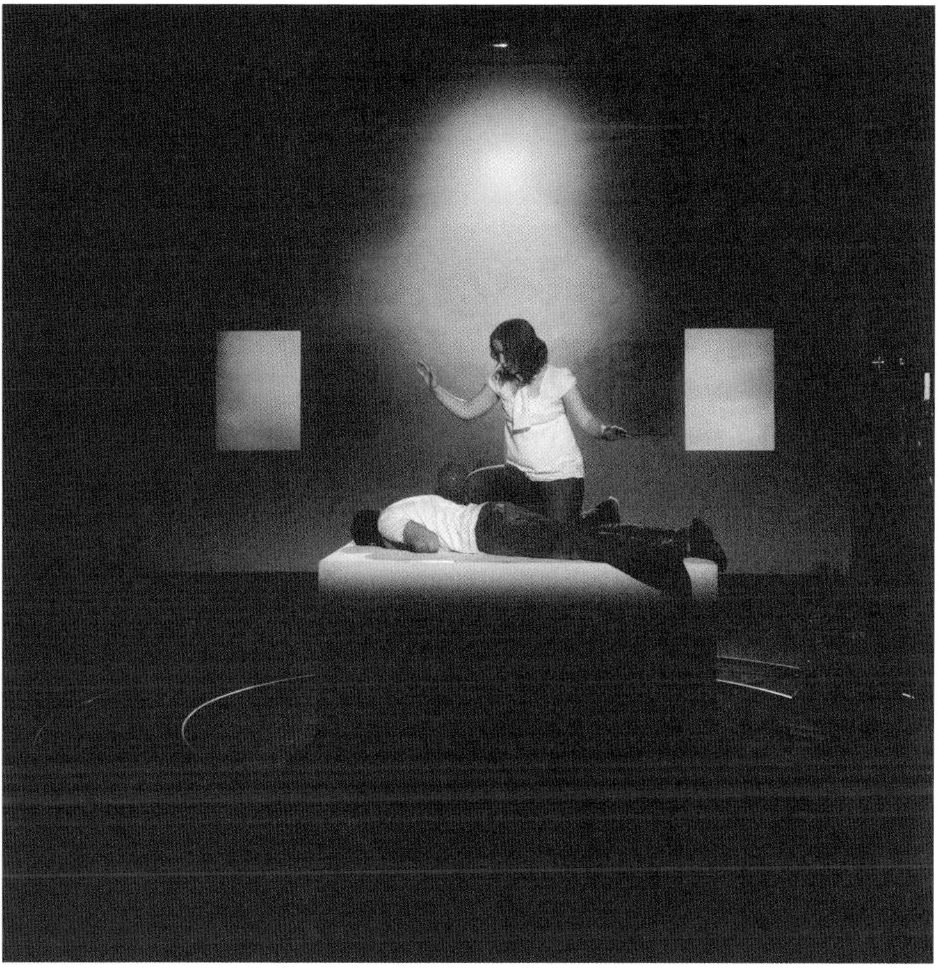

PLATE 14 Carrie Mae Weems, *Suspended Belief*, 2008. Archival pigment print, 24 × 20 inches. Copyright Carrie Mae Weems. Courtesy of the artist and Jack Shainman Gallery, New York.

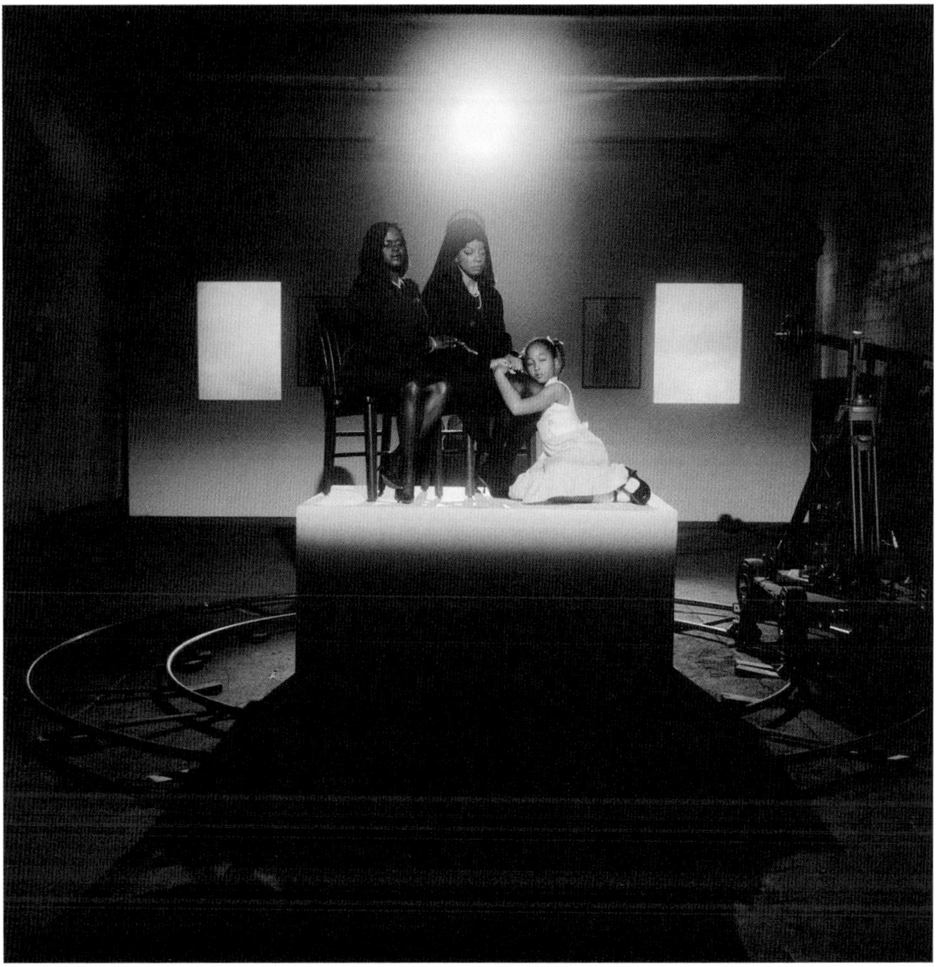

PLATE 15 Carrie Mae Weems, *Mourning*, 2008. Archival pigment print, 61 × 51 inches framed. Copyright Carrie Mae Weems. Courtesy of the artist and Jack Shainman Gallery, New York.

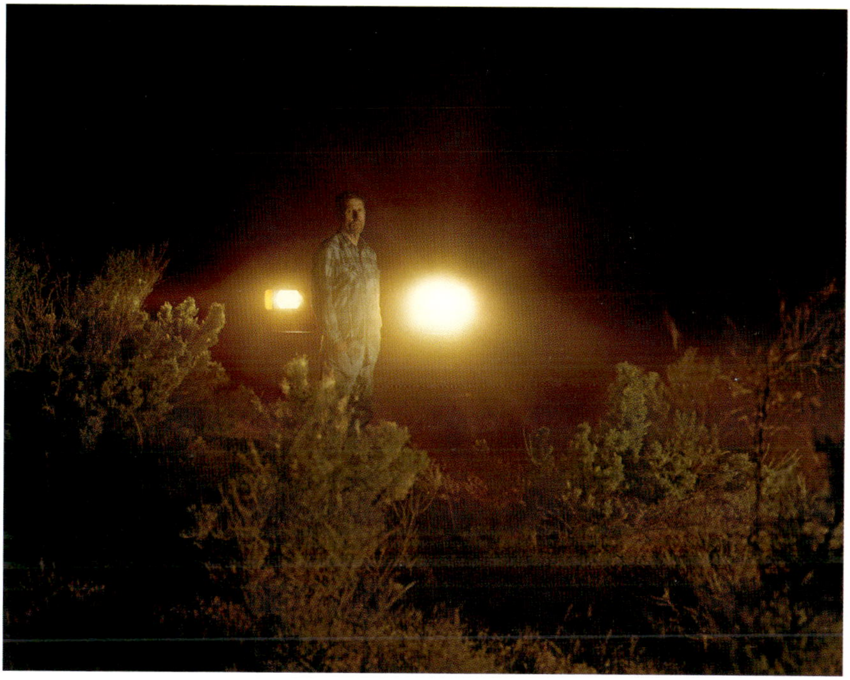

PLATE 16 Taryn Simon, from *The Innocents*, 2002

Charles Irvin Fain

Scene of the crime, the Snake River, Melba, Idaho
Served 18 years of a Death sentence for Murder, Rape and Kidnapping

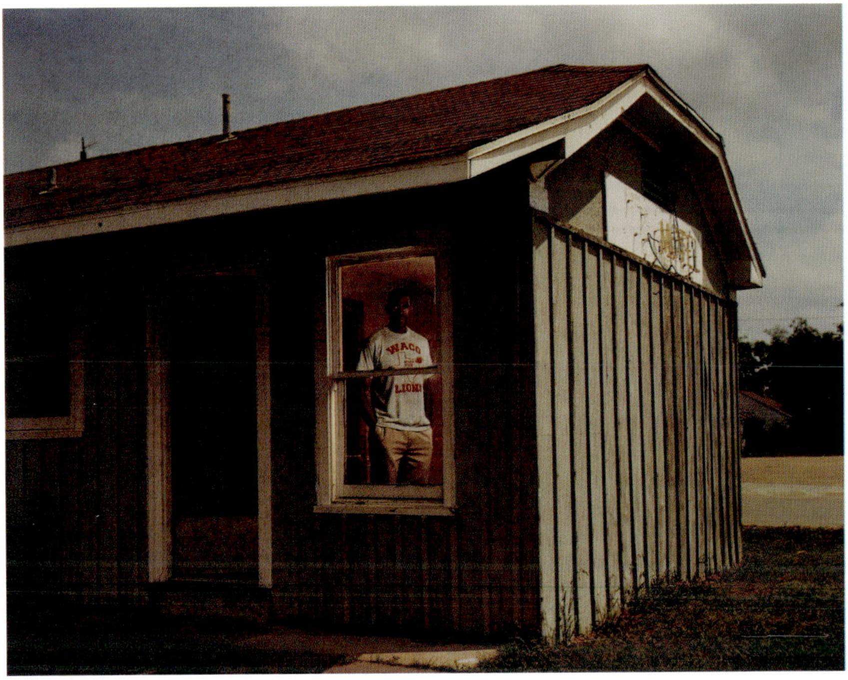

PLATE 17 Taryn Simon, from *The Innocents*, 2002

Calvin Washington

C&E Motel, Room No. 24, Waco, Texas
Where an informant claimed to have heard Washington confess
Served 13 years of a Life sentence for Murder

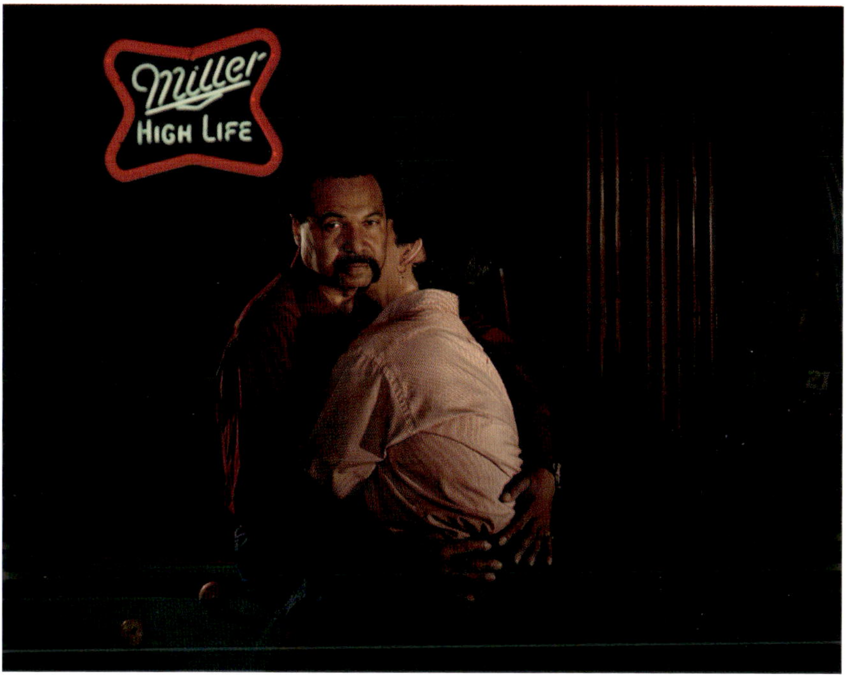

PLATE 18 Taryn Simon, from *The Innocents*, 2002

William Gregory

Wick's Parlor, Louisville, Kentucky
With fiancée Vicki Kidwell, whom he dated prior to conviction
Gregory was pool champion in prison
Served 7 years of a 70 year sentence for Rape and Burglary

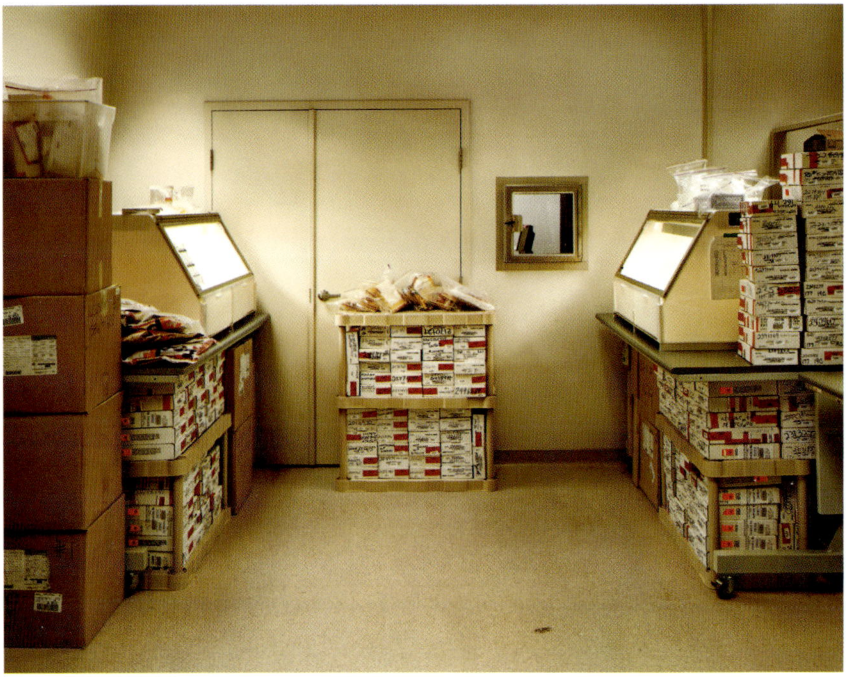

PLATE 19 Taryn Simon, from *An American Index of the Hidden and Unfamiliar*, 2007

Sexual Assault Kits Awaiting DNA Analysis, Bode Technology Group, Inc., Springfield, Virginia

Bode Technologies is the largest private forensic DNA laboratory in the United States. It assists local, state and federal agencies in processing the large number of backlogged sexual assault evidence kits. It was recently estimated that there are as many as half a million sexual assault kits in the U.S. awaiting analysis.

A sexual assault kit, also known as a rape kit, is a sealed white box that contains physical and biological evidence collected from the victim during a medical examination. Sexual assault kits are administered by nurses to assist in identifying and prosecuting the crime's perpetrator. Forensic evidence stored in the kit can include: blood, clothing, fingernail scrapings, hair and semen.

All images courtesy of the artist

Too Hard to Keep

In many ways, *Standing at the Grave* is about the burden of photographs that refuse to stay in the past. It is about the relationship of photographs to memory and melancholia, both individual and collective. Such questions continue to inform Lazarus's work, but he has recently taken another tack, offering people a way to distance themselves from difficult images. In 2010 he began an ongoing project, *Too Hard to Keep*, a collection of photographs that cause people distress. He solicits submissions of images that are too hard for people to keep but too painful to destroy. Specifically, these are images "that are too difficult for their original owners to continue to live with because of a painful memory associated with them."[31] *Too Hard to Keep* is a repository of snapshots sent to Lazarus to be stored and displayed among other affectively charged images. It is an unusual archive—"an archive of feelings"—in Ann Cvetkovich's words.[32] The project is a novel engagement with the promises and limitations of photography, the mediation of private and public relationships, the affective import of ordinary images, and the shifting nature of photographic meaning as images travel across time and enter into new constellations for new viewers.

In Lazarus's archive and installations of donated photographs, images are no longer linked to the specific feelings of the individuals who made them but released into the diffuse, inchoate, and shared registers of affect.[33] Because so much is unknown about the images, the installations allow viewers to think beyond their visible referents. As the particularities of signification fade, recognizable genres, as well as historical prints and technologies, come into view as shared social forms. The anonymity of the images invites viewers to consider what is unconsciously known and experienced through rituals of photographic practice. As specific feelings fade, viewers begin to sense collective affect.

To date, Lazarus has collected approximately five thousand images. They are mostly vernacular photographs—snapshots printed on paper—the remains of a dying form.[34] Storing them in boxes and drawers in his home, Lazarus marks his own space with the traces of other people's lives. The project is a generous endeavor, and the artist has said that there is "a lot of empathy in the work." When asked how he came to the idea, he said, "I would use the archive if it wasn't mine," and he has, in fact, included one of his own images in the collection.[35]

Too Hard to Keep is part of a larger shift in the artist's work, in which he has moved away from making photographs to collecting, archiving, and curating already existing images. As Lazarus has said, he is less and less interested in producing images, because there are already so many photographs.[36] *Recordings* (2009), for example, is a series of found photographs with writing on the back. Lazarus installs the images face to the wall, so that viewers see only the text on the back, and are left to infer what the images might depict. The writing becomes an elliptical narrative, inviting speculation. Some of the notes provide seemingly simple identifiers—names and dates and places—while others are more mysterious—"January 1967, Big Storm, Mom." The text points to the ways in which people use photographs to tell stories and to build communities, offering oblique insights into the relationships between images and writers, and images and viewers. In this way, *Recordings* might help one to understand Margaret Olin's proposition that "in the area of interpersonal relationships, photographs act rather than represent," they "actively participate in building communities and relationships" "beyond their representational roles."[37] In other words, what photographs picture may be subordinate to the relationships they perform.

Another project in which Lazarus has worked with already extant photographs is *Sarasota Photomat (Lindsey, teenage-goth one-hour photo technician, 1997–2000)* (2011), which consists of photographs illicitly culled by an employee of a Florida Photomat in the 1990s. Lazarus curates selections from Lindsey's clandestine collection to produce large wall installations, and the work participates in a complicated dynamic of privacy and surveillance.[38] Out of other people's snapshots, Lindsey created her own archive—her own body of evidence, curio collection, fantasy dreamscape, or extended family album. A decade later, Lazarus makes his installations using images from Lindsey's idiosyncratic time capsule.[39]

Lazarus frames the images as the covert collection of a photo technician. One wonders, in Elspeth Brown and Thy Phu's words, "What desires animate [this] archive?"[40] What was Lindsey, the "teenage-goth," up to? Was her collection a rejection of middle-class norms, like her black clothes and dark lipstick? Did she cull the images as gags to amuse her friends, or as evidence for future blackmail? Was she looking for images she could identify with, building her own imagined visual community? Or did she simply copy what caught her eye on any given day in Sarasota?

The project implicates the viewer as voyeur, and reminds one how often her private life is subject to public scrutiny. A viewer might become indignant about Lindsey's surreptitious theft of these images, or Lazarus's display of them, and happily bid farewell to analogue photographic forms that required her to turn over negatives to photo technicians. However, in the digital age, one might also consider the NSA's ability to tap phones and monitor email, or the police's mobile "Stingray" towers that extract data from cellphones, and look back at Lindsey's invasions of privacy with nostalgia.

In *Too Hard to Keep* a form of collaboration guides the collecting. Lazarus both solicits images and offers a service, and people knowingly contribute photographs to this archive. These images then, are not exactly found, for they were never lost.[41] They are given, released, purged, and sent to Lazarus with the knowledge that he may display them in one of his installations. Contributors to the collection can also designate images "private," in which case Lazarus will only display them face to the wall.

One of the most notable aspects of the photographs that comprise *Too Hard to Keep* is their banality. In general the images appear entirely ordinary, even though one knows they have become extraordinary for their donors. Many are vacation snapshots, graduation pictures, and holiday photographs that one has seen over and over again. And this is not surprising, for as Catherine Zuromskis has argued, despite one's personal investment in them, snapshots remain the most conventional of images, photographs made according to "prescriptive cultural ritual."[42] This is why one recognizes so many of the images in Lazarus's archive, even though one cannot precisely identify them. The project highlights the dual nature of the photographic snapshot—simultaneously banal and emotionally charged, tedious and intensely affecting, private and public, a site of cultural normativity as well as resistance. The archive underscores how the original import of individual snapshots might be known only to a small circle of viewers, and perhaps even to an audience of one. But the repetition of snapshot forms, including the material formats of images and the performative registers of poses, links a vast, anonymous group of viewers in an affective community of familiar photographic practice.

The archive contains square Polaroids with bright white frames and washed-out highlights, color photographs starting to turn orange, black-and-white pictures cut roughly with scissors, half an image torn in two. One finds young women caught in flashes smoking and drinking, sunsets snapped out of car windows, couples mugging for the camera. Among the most curious images are empty landscapes—a photograph of the sea with a tilted horizon.

A couple of the images point directly to violence—a blackened eye; a bloody nose. A few overtly suggest loss: a corpse laid out in a coffin; an elderly woman in a hospital bed. Some ask viewers to guess at horrors, and the photographs of children in this context are especially disturbing. But most tell one next to nothing about the narratives they mark for the people who once owned them.

How did these images become "too hard to keep"? It is impossible to say. As Lazarus has argued, "The darkest part of something is not in the photograph." Further, few of the photographs in the collection were made to record a disturbing event; most, as Lazarus notes, were "taken with enthusiasm, love, abandon."[43] The meaning of the images has shifted over the course of their existence: They have had a before and after life. Despite the fixed appearance of the images, they have, perhaps, called forth radically different feelings for their original viewers.

Too Hard to Keep is about such shifts in photographic meaning, about the malleability of the photographic message. The import and function of the images changes again as they enter Lazarus's archive, as they join and mix with other ambiguous records, becoming markers of anonymous memories among others. This diffusion and dilution of their specific emotional triggers is part of the pleasure and relief of sending the images to Lazarus, part of the process whereby the original owner can begin to detach herself from a moment of distress, from the painful redirection of a once happy story.

The project is called *Too Hard to Keep*, but it is also about images that are too hard *not* to keep, that are too hard to destroy.[44] If an image is disturbing, why not simply throw it away? Why send it to Lazarus to preserve? His archive is a strange kind of in-between place, where one can relocate something without having to ruin it, a repository that will shelter one's melancholia even as one tries to move beyond it. In Freud's description of mourning and melancholia, mourning is a process in which the bereaved gradually relinquishes a lost object, and is "healed" by learning to live without it. Melancholia, on the other hand, is a state in which the bereaved refuses to let go, holding onto the lost object, identifying with it. Melancholia is mourning gone awry, grief that refuses to release what has been lost. In this way, as Sliwinski has argued, melancholia resembles photography itself: "The melancholic turns away from the reality of the loss and holds onto the beloved in a hallucinatory manner—in effigy, in the truest sense of the word."[45] And, as she notes, this is precisely how Roland Barthes describes the photograph in the final pages of *Camera Lucida*.[46] The photograph, like the melancholic, will not release its object.

By sending an image to the *Too Hard to Keep* archive, the mourner can loosen her grip on the photograph, and thereby relax the hold of melancholia, without fully letting go. It offers donors a way to mourn but to maintain a

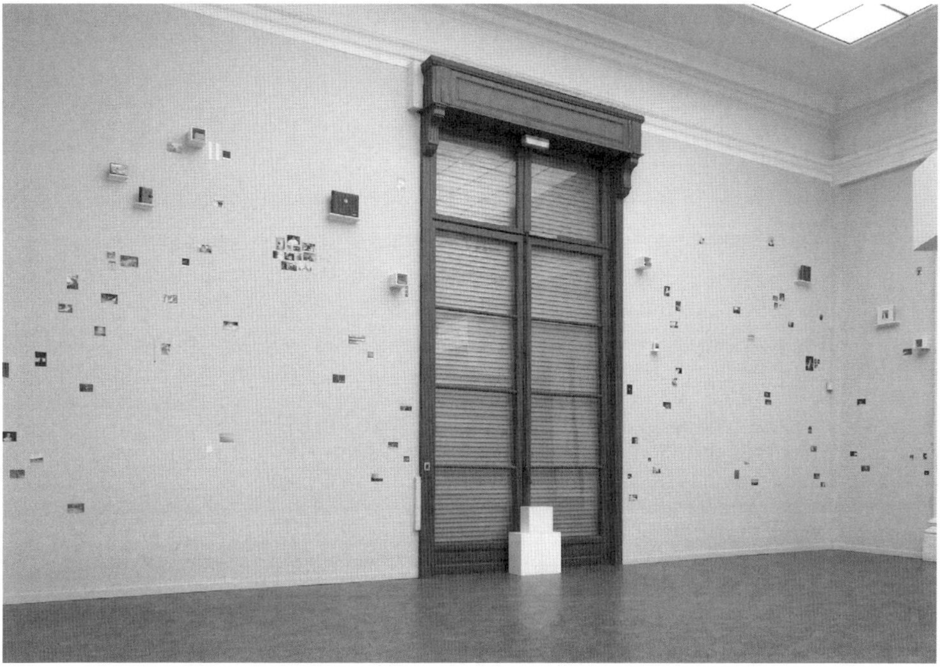

FIGURE 5.1 Jason Lazarus, *Too Hard to Keep*, Liege, Belgium, 2012. Courtesy the artist.

bit of melancholy too. What one has given away is not lost, just kept by someone else, preserved in a drawer along with other fragments that are too hard to keep, and too hard not to.

The meaning of the images shifts yet again as they are displayed for anonymous viewers in Lazarus's installations in galleries and museums. To produce the installations the artist inhabits a given place for two or three days, creating site-specific works that respond to the proportions, flow, and feel of a space. The exhibitions are generally sparse, small constellations of images gathered on walls. In Liege, Belgium, the installation occupied a shallow alcove divided by long glass windows (fig. 5.1). Lazarus scattered snapshots across the light-gray walls, arranging images almost down to the floor and up to the edge of the recessed ceiling. Many were placed too high or too low to have been seen comfortably by viewers standing in the gallery. In the exhibition tiny shelves support framed images and albums. Small white boxes hold neat stacks of prints. A few of the images are mounted face to the wall.

Eleven images are clustered together, suggesting a connection between them. Others float alone on the wall, or in pairs, or in looser associations, as if a kind of gravitational force is beginning to pull them together.

A poetic sensibility guides the arrangement of the images. Although Lazarus calls the collection an "archive," he does not gesture toward institutional forms in his displays. There is no attempt to catalogue the images or record metadata. The organizing principle of this collection is a felt one. The photographs are presented just as they are, usually small, sometimes worn, adhered to the wall without borders or frames or labels. This presentation highlights both their material and ephemeral qualities. Historians of photography, as well as most Americans over the age of forty, will recognize shifting photographic technologies and forms in the installations: the black-and-white snapshot, the four-by-six-inch glossy color print, the square Polaroid, the long narrow photo booth strip, the Sears portrait, the school picture, the small green metal canister of undeveloped film.[47] The materiality of the images marks historical time periods but tells one nothing of the stories that once animated individual snapshots. Indeed, Lazarus has said he prefers not to know the narratives donors attach to the images. That is because the archive is not about preserving individual records but instead about providing a kind of historical testimony to cultural practices, to the community-building impulse that informs the making and circulation of snapshots, to the ubiquity, and ultimately the opacity, of such images.

In the installations, the negative spaces, the wide white expanses left around the images, underscore how much one does *not* know about the photographs, how much they refuse to tell, how inadequate and partial they are as traces (fig. 5.2).[48] The sparseness also highlights how *much* one asks of photographs, regardless of how misguided one's faith in them might be. People depend on these tiny fragments to hold import they cannot contain. And yet, Lazarus's display also has a light touch. The installations do not overwhelm. One senses a generosity in the anonymous sharing of images, and in the artist's willingness to preserve these delicate traces for others.

Not knowing is also underscored by the images facing the wall, and these photographs demonstrate how little the visual content of the images actually matters (fig. 5.3). They are not invisible exactly, but opaque. They are rectangular scraps of paper that signal photographs but do not serve their purpose, photographs that no longer function as images. As blank ciphers, the photographs facing the wall invite viewers to project their own images onto them. But actually, these off-white squares and rectangles are not quite blank. As

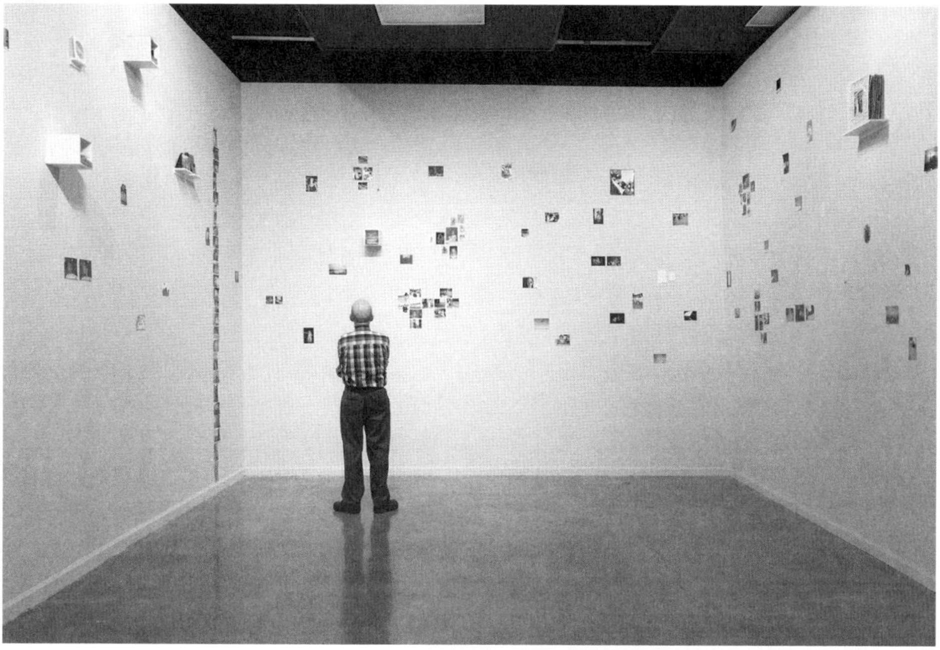

FIGURE 5.2 Jason Lazarus, *Too Hard to Keep*, Illinois State University, Bloomington-Normal, 2011. Courtesy the artist.

Kendra Paitz has argued, "Though emptied of a photographic visuality, the private submissions are replete with the visuality of the photographic process."[49] They are mechanically printed with dates and the company names of photographic papers, and some have handmade marks on the back—dates, places, and other notations. In many ways the photographs that turn their backs to viewers emblematize all of the images in the collection—they are signs that remain largely indecipherable in their specificity, but call attention to the mechanical and material history of snapshot photography and its circulation and exchange.

Too Hard To Keep makes apparent how much of photographic meaning is located *not* in images but in viewers.[50] An image that seems utterly boring to one person might signal joy or anguish for another, because, as Zuromskis has argued, "the amateur snapshot photograph is the site of both banal conformity and deep affective response."[51] Despite the ritualized nature of snapshot practice, one rarely responds to one's own snapshots as part of a genre. Holi-

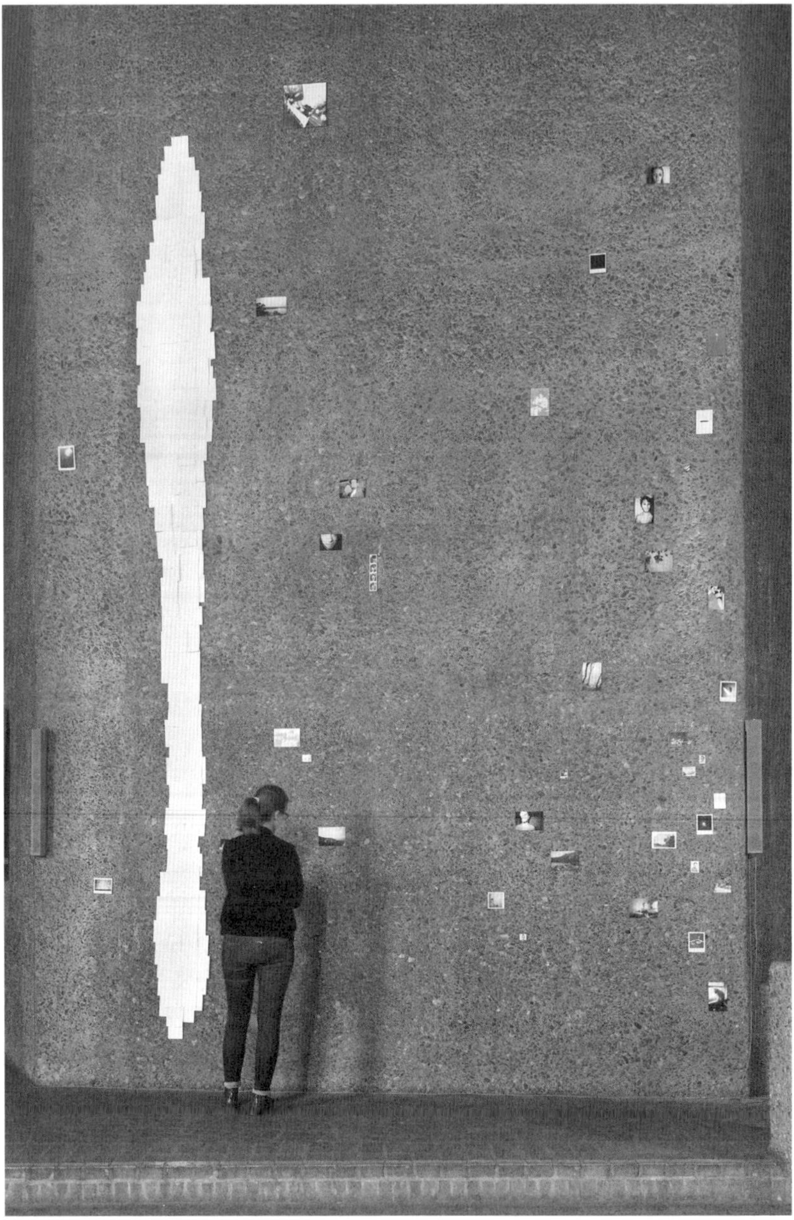

FIGURE 5.3 Jason Lazarus, *Too Hard to Keep*, Cologne, Germany, 2016, showing a large group of images facing the wall. Courtesy the artist.

day photographs are generic, but one might prize one's own. Lazarus's installations illuminate Olin's proposition that "how photographs look may be less central to their habitus than how people look at them."[52] The photograph is a prompt that solicits an unspecified response. What Cvetkovich has said of objects in general pertains to photographs as well: "Value resides in our attachments to things, not in the things themselves."[53] Affect activates photographs, readying them to focus the disparate feelings of viewers.

For Lazarus the project is not about loss but about collectivity. He has said he would like it to have "lots of sentiment, without being sentimental."[54] In part, the very banality of the photographs helps to build a sense of imagined community because one understands these vernacular images as shared cultural forms. There is a sense of play in recognizing genres and artifacts one has seen, experienced, or made. In this way the installations demonstrate how groups of photographs can "create a community or the illusion of one."[55] The images do not ask viewers to "feel someone else's pain"; indeed, they obscure the stories they mark. Instead, the installations ask viewers to acknowledge unknown but perhaps familiar struggles through the recognizable and shared cultural forms of snapshot photographs.

As the photographs enter Lazarus's archive and then are displayed in installations for anonymous viewers, the particularity of the feelings they evoke fades. Indeed, the very lack of specificity, its diffusion, helps to inspire a collective impulse in viewers. Individual events are not legible in their distinctiveness. The photographs are both specific and general, inaccessible to anonymous viewers in their precise forms, but recognizable as common cultural objects. *Not knowing* what any specific image signifies in a narrow sense allows viewers to acknowledge and project shared experiences of loss, disappointment, happiness, elation, embarrassment, anger, and transformation. The recognition of shared practice taps into the affective potential of photographs that may or may not trigger specific feelings in viewers.

The legibility of images that remain indecipherable in specific terms is the effect of a collective repetition that informs the practice of snapshot photography. Many people compulsively repeat the gesture of photography at socially scripted moments, at holidays, birthdays, weddings, and graduations. These are symbolic cultural moments in which the specific event is subsumed by the more important cultural repetition, and snapshots made at such celebrations work in the same way to make the personal conform to social practice.[56] Just as one repeats these rituals, one repeats their photographic documentation; indeed, as a number of scholars have noted, the act of photographing becomes an essential part of the ritual itself. As Pierre Bourdieu proposed, popular photography serves community cohesion, making the group visible to itself as a group.[57] One photographs moments of transition to mark the group and also to reinforce its coherence in the midst of change.

The repetition of ritualized acts of photography also marks the photograph's inadequacy. One's photographing is never complete, never enough. One repeats these performances to stave off future loss. It is a repetition compulsion that precedes an anticipated trauma.

Photographs also exceed the grasp of their subjects and makers in the extended reaches of what Ariella Azoulay has called "the event of photography." Although Azoulay considers images made (or not made) under radically different political circumstances, her insight that the event of photography supersedes the photograph itself might also be brought to an understanding of ordinary snapshot photography.[58] Lazarus's installations call attention to the endless character of what one might call "the snapshot event," to the ways in which the meaning of an image changes over time and under different conditions, and always depends on who is looking. Further, his work extends an understanding of the meaning and effects of images beyond the shifting registers of circulation to include the inchoate and unconscious registers of affect. Lazarus's work brings the snapshot event into view as collective photographic practice animated by affect.

The images collected in *Too Hard to Keep* are the residues of altered narratives. If the one who understands the transformation a snapshot measures can no longer bear it, she can send it to Lazarus. In doing so, she detaches the image from a past narrative and opens it up to future possibilities. She allows the image to take on a new life and new resonance, brushing up against the fragments of other people's stories and calling upon a new audience of unknown viewers who may recognize the image in different ways. If the snapshot is about inscribing one's particular experience into larger cultural narratives, Lazarus's installations allow donors and viewers to understand themselves as part of a larger, anonymous community founded in the practice of photography, its shared material forms and affective potentialities.

The Whiteness of the Archive

There is privilege as well as pain reflected in the *Too Hard to Keep* archive. Judging by the snapshots included in the collection, the anonymous community it hails is largely white.[59] Lazarus has reflected on the racial parameters of the archive. He is attuned to questions of race and representation, and a number of his projects have dealt explicitly with African American history and black visuality, including, of course, *Standing at the Grave*. When asked about the relative whiteness of *Too Hard to Keep*, he surmised that the contexts in which he shows and solicits images—galleries, museums, art schools, universities—necessarily shape the contours of the archive and its contributors. This might also explain the look of the images, which seem to have grown self-consciously "arty" over the years.

But the worlds of art and higher education are not exclusively white, even if they remain bastions of white privilege. What other factors might contribute to the whiteness of this and other archives of snapshots in the United States? On the one hand, it is a privilege to have images, and on the other, it is a privilege to let them go. It is also a privilege to claim access to narratives of normalcy gone awry. One of the assumptions that implicitly informs *Too Hard to Keep* is that the stories one attaches to photographs are ordinarily celebratory, that things usually go well. Ruptures that interrupt those narratives and shift the meaning of images are not only hard—they are *too* hard. In the end, perhaps, images are only too hard to keep when people can imagine letting them go. The desire to release an image suggests that one does not need it—that one can assume access to representation when one wants it.

As many scholars have argued, black representational space is freighted by both invisibility and hypervisibility. Images of black banality have been largely absent from the public sphere, whereas images of the violated black body recur. Under these circumstances, ordinary snapshots can create an important counterarchive for African American viewers.[60] As bell hooks has said of photography during the era of Jim Crow segregation, "The camera was the central instrument by which blacks could disprove representations of us created by white folks."[61] And as Leigh Raiford has argued more recently, "The significance of photography as a liberatory tool of black self-representation cannot be overstated."[62] The importance of photography in African American communities might underscore a reluctance to let go of images, no matter how hard they are to keep. Or it might indicate a historically founded concern over controlling one's images, a fear of what might happen to them in someone else's hands.

In this light, the snapshots produced as part of Lazarus's *Michael Jackson Memorial Procession* (2010) are significant. To mark the one-year anniversary of Michael Jackson's death, Lazarus organized a procession of cars that made its way from Gary, Indiana, the site of Jackson's birth, to Chicago, Illinois. Drivers decorated their cars with flags, signs, and photographs in

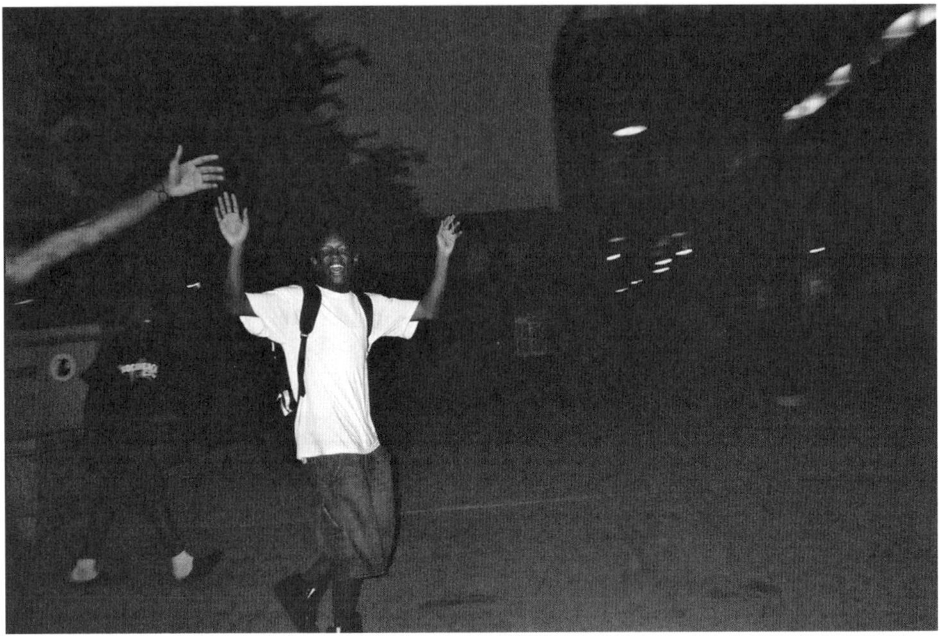

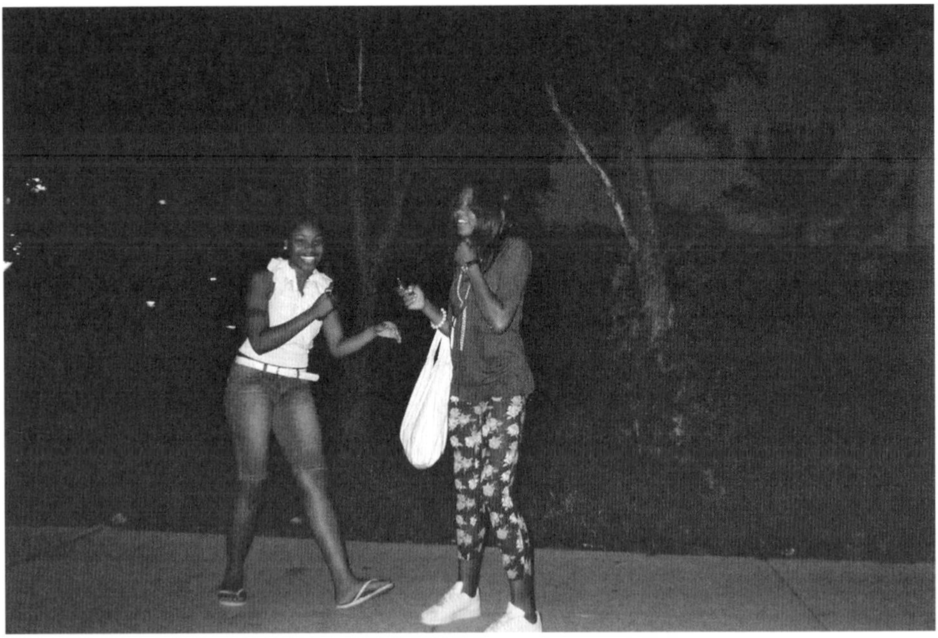

honor of the King of Pop and blasted a synced Michael Jackson playlist as they wound their way through predominantly African American neighborhoods, reproducing what for Lazarus was the effect of hearing Jackson's music everywhere on the streets of Chicago in the wake of his passing. Participants were also given cameras and encouraged to document their experience of the event. Several took snapshots of people responding to the sonic memorial, waving and photographing back from cars, laughing and dancing on sidewalks (figs. 5.4 and 5.5). These photographs of mostly African American men, women, and children were taken with "enthusiasm, love, abandon." They are ordinary and therefore, in the public realm of black visuality, extraordinary.

One final work by Lazarus brings questions about black visuality into focus in a different way. *Untitled* (2011) is about "retiring" images—taking them out of circulation and out of view (plate 13). In 2011, on a visit to New Orleans, Lazarus found in a thrift store a board of scavenged family photographs marred and stained by Hurricane Katrina. The owner of the store explained that the damaged snapshots of African Americans were often rented out to film crews eager to capture an auratic trace of the disaster. Because family photographs are among the treasures most often named as the first to be rescued by victims fleeing a disaster, one might imagine that the owners of these images did not survive the hurricane. Lazarus purchased the board and the thrift store owner wrapped it for travel in a deep mauve blanket secured with black gaffer's tape. Today Lazarus displays the board as it was wrapped, a repository of images taken out of view.

With *Untitled* Lazarus invites one to reflect on the spectacle of black suffering without reproducing it. *Untitled* asks one to contemplate both an over- and underattachment to certain images of the black body in US culture. Read in relation to *Too Hard to Keep*, *Untitled* begins to draw into focus some of the privileges of whiteness and white archival practices. Whiteness is seen and not seen, ubiquitous but taken as a norm and therefore not recognized as white-

---

FIGURE 5.4 (PREVIOUS PAGE, TOP) Jason Lazarus, from *Michael Jackson Memorial Procession*, 2010. Courtesy the artist.

FIGURE 5.5 (PREVIOUS PAGE, BOTTOM) Jason Lazarus, from *Michael Jackson Memorial Procession*, 2010. Courtesy the artist.

ness per se. In this sense, the generic and indecipherable quality of the snapshots in *Too Hard to Keep* reinforces the whiteness of the subjects represented in so many of the images. Looking back at the archive from this perspective, one might contemplate further *what* is too hard, and *for whom*, to keep?

Finally, going back to the legacy of Emmett Till, to his murder and the photographs that mark but do not represent it, one might also consider further images that refuse to be given up, photographs that persistently infuse the present with a past. *Standing at the Grave* reminds one that the return of some photographs is a measure of just how hard they are to keep.

CHAPTER 6

Photographic Reenactments

Carrie Mae Weems's *Constructing History*

Thirteen women stand, pressing close together. They are dressed in black and clasp their hands as if in prayer. The women face the camera but only one or two look directly at the lens. The others cast their eyes downward or stare off to the side. Their poses and performance suggest a funeral or memorial, but they are situated in a theatrical space that highlights the artifice of the scene. The women are illuminated against a black background and rendered in black and white in a square-format photograph. Their feet have been cut out of the frame somewhat awkwardly at the bottom, and their heads rise only to the midpoint of the photograph. The darkness of the background engulfs the top half of the image and looms over them like an ominous sky (fig. 6.1).

This is Carrie Mae Weems's *Looking Forward/Looking Back* (2008), a photograph included in the series *Constructing History*. The image was produced in 2008, when Weems was a distinguished visiting faculty member at the Atlanta campus of the Savannah College of Art and Design.[1] There she created with students a body of work about the social and political discord of the 1960s and 1970s, including a series of twenty-one black-and-white photographs and a twenty-four-minute video, *Constructing History: A Requiem to Mark the Moment* (2008). Although the photographs are closely tied to the video, they are not stills captured from moving images but companion pieces

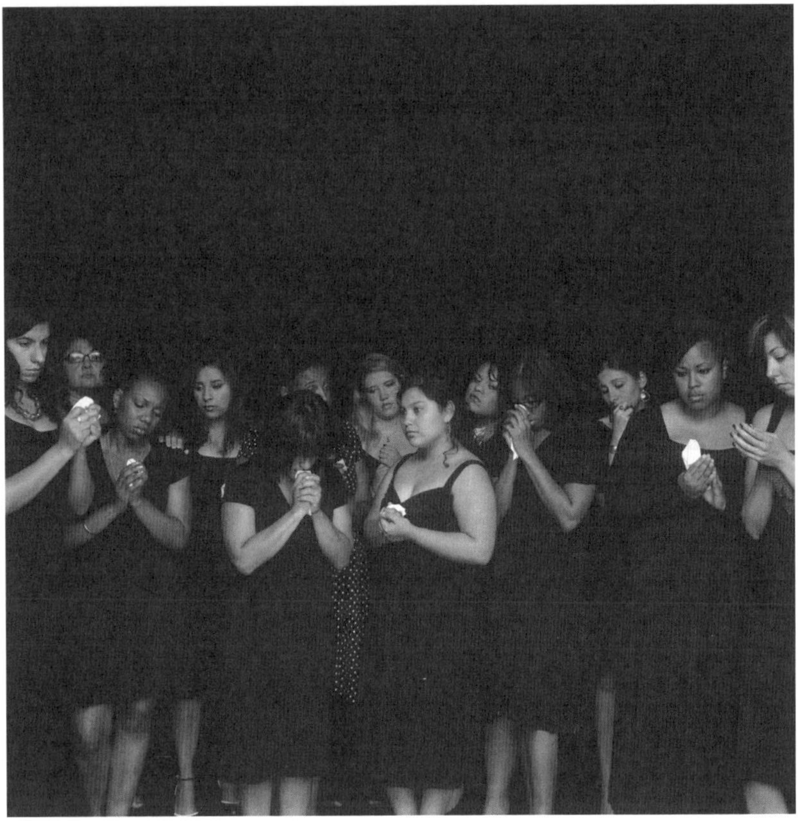

FIGURE 6.1 Carrie Mae Weems, *Looking Forward/Looking Back*, 2008. Archival pigment print, 61 × 51 inches framed. Copyright Carrie Mae Weems. Courtesy of the artist and Jack Shainman Gallery, New York.

made on set and designed to stand on their own. This chapter focuses primarily on the photographs, but it also draws important narrative framing for the images from the video. (To distinguish between the two interconnected bodies of work, the video will always be referred to by its full title, *Constructing History: A Requiem to Mark the Moment*, and the photographs by the shorter title, *Constructing History*.)

In many of the photographs in *Constructing History*, Weems and her collaborators have re-created iconic images from the 1960s and 1970s. But the artist has made significant choices about which images to reproduce: these are not the striking photographs from Birmingham, Selma, or Little Rock that show African American activists demonstrating, marching, and protesting in the face of white supremacism. They are not photographs of protestors standing up to white policemen and attack dogs or white firemen and high-pressure hoses. Instead of highlighting confrontation and resistance, Weems has focused on images of sacrifice, assassination, and mourning. A number of her photographs allude to the infamous murders of civil rights leaders, politicians, and activists, including the Reverend Martin Luther King Jr., Malcolm X, Medgar Evers, president John F. Kennedy, and senator Robert F. Kennedy. Others are more allegorical, like *Looking Forward/Looking Back*, and they depict women and angels watching, mourning, witnessing. *Constructing History* is elegiac and ambivalent. The photographs enact a form of melancholia that suggests an affective openness to the past and a political project that remains unfinished.

Importantly, *Constructing History* largely records the performances of students *after* photographs. These are not only reconstructions but also *re-enactments* of photographs. There is a striking recursivity in the work that comments not only on the relationship of photography to experience and memory but also on the relationship of photography to history. By restaging iconic images, the work invites one to consider the role of photography in "constructing history," and through *photographic reenactments* it draws attention to the time of photography and the felt history of the photograph's affective charge.

Weems presents *Constructing History* as a history lesson. Most of the photographs were made in a makeshift classroom that comes into focus clearly in *A Class Ponders the Future* (fig. 6.2). In this image, ten young men and women sit at desks in a darkened room, facing forward, their backs to the camera. They wear white T-shirts and black berets, a uniform reminiscent of the Black Panther Party.[2] The seated "students" look toward the wall, which features an institutional clock mounted high in the center, two rectangular projections that mimic windows, and two framed images, a man on the left and a woman on the right. Under the clock a cabinet supports books and three round globes. A figure stands at each of the windows, back to the camera, looking out. It is clear that the classroom is a kind of theatrical set: the scene has been created in the larger, rougher space of a painted-brick and concrete loft by erecting a single white wall. Many of the subsequent images in the series are

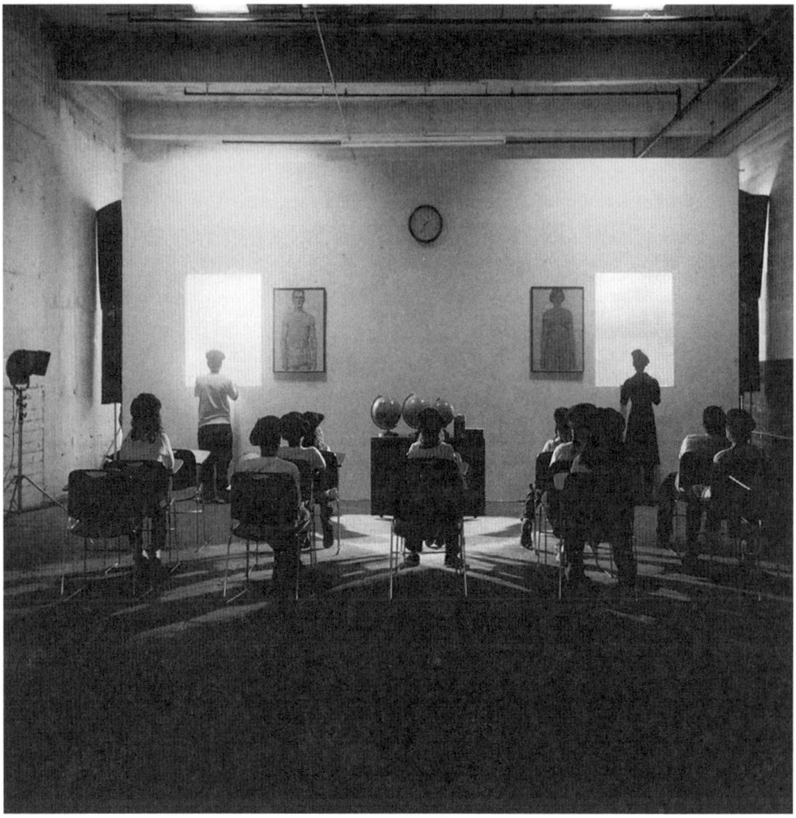

FIGURE 6.2 Carrie Mae Weems, *A Class Ponders the Future*, 2008. Archival pigment print, 61 × 51 inches framed. Copyright Carrie Mae Weems. Courtesy of the artist and Jack Shainman Gallery, New York.

produced in the same room, with desks and students removed, but clock and screens and framed images visible on the back wall. In these latter images a large white platform has been installed in the center of the classroom. There, Weems's collaborators perform iconic photographs for the camera, and these staged scenes constitute the history lessons students are encouraged to learn as they "ponder the future."[3]

A Class Ponders the Future reflects the terms of its making. The image provides a window onto the production of the photograph series overall, as well as the video. Once again, Weems made this work with students in a class she taught at the Atlanta campus of the Savannah College of Art and Design. As she explains in the narration for the video, "This is a story within a story. How to enter this history. What to show, what to say, what to feel. It was a creation myth. How things came to be as they are. In this constructed place, our classroom, we revisit the past. The students examine the facts and will participate in the construction of history. A history that has been told to them by others. But now, with their own bodies, they engage their own dark dream, their own winter" (5:16+). *Constructing History: A Requiem to Mark the Moment* is a history of the present, of "how things came to be as they are." It is a story about the making of history, and also about the teaching and transfer of generational knowledge, about how to tell a history. As narrator, Weems notes the divide that separates her from the students, as she wonders how to communicate and explain the events that shaped the world of her youth to a new generation—"what to show, what to say, what to feel." She assumes the role of the historian, who, as Keith Jenkins has argued, is the "interpreter who stands between past events and our readings of them."[4] Indeed, history is always constructed; "it is always for someone."[5] But in fashioning a history, Weems's work also aims to bring student actors and later viewers closer to a position of witnessing and experiencing a past. Such relations are also mediated, of course, but Weems suggests that through photographic reenactment one can both construct a history and feel a past.

The relationship of memory to history, and memory as it is photographically mediated, is central to this work. As Weems sets out to understand her own experience of the 1960s and 1970s as history, to see herself "on the scale of History" in Roland Barthes's terms,[6] she also endeavors to help her students comprehend a historical narrative intimately via the lived experience of performance. In part the problem of memory and history is a problem of proximity and distance. Weems stands apart from the students, a closer witness to the events they encounter only remotely, through texts, and photographs, and classrooms, even as her own relation to and memory of a past has also been mediated by images. Through a process of performance and re-creation, she hopes to help her students bridge the chasm between themselves and the events of the civil rights era, and between themselves and her. Through photographic reenactment, she endeavors to help them "remember" the history of the 1960s and 1970s, and to physically embody "a history that has been told to them by others." *Constructing History* asks, on the one hand, how does what one has lived through, what one is living through, become history? And conversely, how can one understand a past through which one has not lived?

The photographs and video offer a history of the present, and both are permeated by a sense of burden and ambivalence. The video tells a somber story; it is "a requiem to mark the moment," and the moment is 2008, on the eve of the Democratic presidential nomination. Hillary Clinton and Barack Obama are the candidates, and the video begins with extreme black-and-white close-ups of their faces. The simple fact that a white woman and an African American man could vie for presidential nomination in the United States is a legacy of the civil rights movement, but Weems refuses to celebrate this as a victory. She does not present a triumphal narrative of the events leading to this moment, but instead offers a requiem, a token of remembrance for the dead. Indeed, the work focuses on political assassinations and mourning, on the onus Clinton and Obama carry as the heirs to so much sacrifice and murder. As the video draws to a close, Obama has won the primary election, but the narrator remains ambivalent, and even deeply skeptical, about the future. She wonders about this turn of events, asking if it is "evidence that the President is a mere figurehead; evidence that America is changing; evidence of conspiracy; . . . evidence of the declining significance of race; . . . evidence that democracy was winning; evidence that tyranny was winning?" Looking back as if on political heirlooms of the past, the video suggests that the future remains uncertain.

Constructing History holds forth not only the promise but also the encumbrance of what Leigh Raiford has called "critical black memory": "black memory also describes and carries within it the failures of the past: the failure to produce the desired political transformations, the failure to create or sustain a culture of mourning or to successfully work through that mourning. Black memory has also been a burden, turning experiences into icons, forcing racial and gender conformity and eliciting prescribed responses to racial events."[7] Weems's staged, still photographs seem to call forth these failures. They ask one to feel the weight of an unfinished project of racial justice.

Tableaux vivants emerge at different moments in the video, as students perform scenes recalled from images on the elevated stage in the classroom. These are the performances that will be translated back into still images in Weems's photographs, and a number of them reproduce iconic images. *Suspended Belief*, for example, is a reconstruction of John Filo's photograph of the Kent State University Massacre from May 4, 1970, an image that has become visual shorthand to evoke the student protests against the War in Vietnam. In Weems's re-creation of this photograph, two student actors, a man and a woman, take to the stage in the constructed classroom (plate 14). They

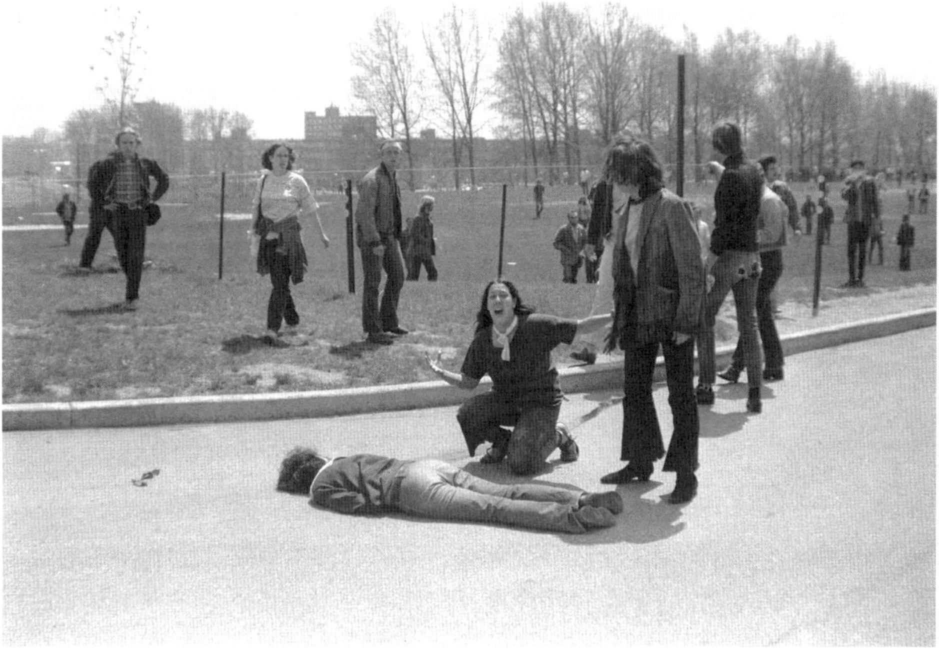

FIGURE 6.3 John Filo, *Kent State Protest*, 1970. Getty Images.

are alone together, elevated on a pedestal, and lit from above. The two figures seem to float in the dark room, lifted off the ground by light. The man lies prone, his face turned away from the camera; the woman kneels beside him, her body open to the lens, gaze fixed on the man, raising her hands as if to bless him. A bright cloud, perhaps of smoke, hovers above and behind the pair.

Weems's re-creation of Filo's Kent State photograph is one of the most faithful reproductions in *Constructing History*. Nevertheless, the artist has made some significant changes to the image. In Filo's famous photograph, the kneeling woman's upturned face and open mouth, as well as her outstretched arms, focus the energy of the photograph outward and direct its emotional effect (fig. 6.3). The woman seems to call out to viewers, asking them to bear witness to this inexplicable crime, to attend to the death as well as to her grief and outrage. Amid men and women scattered from background to foreground, she appears to be the only person concerned with the corpse in the scene, the only one dismayed and enraged by the murder of the man. As Robert Hariman and John Louis Lucaites have argued in their careful reading of this image, the woman's "intense expressiveness is heightened by contrast with those around her, none of whom are acting in a manner that would draw notice on any city street."[8] According to Hariman and Lucaites, this simultaneous display and containment of emotion is central to the image's power: the woman's "emotional display is counterbalanced" by the seeming calm of others. Further, the corpse over which she gestures is also remarkably intact—"the body is not mangled, no wound shows, the face is averted, the blood drained away; it is a body 'at rest.'"[9] The tension in the image between anguish and disregard, between murder and calm, helps account for its iconic status, for, as Hariman and Lucaites explain, "the icon is a complex representation of both rupture and continuity, transgression and order, emotional expression and management, dissent and moderation . . . ambivalence is inseparable from its influence."[10]

In her photographic reenactment of this iconic image, Weems has isolated the central figures in the scene, removing the people milling about in Filo's photograph in order to focus on the prone man and kneeling woman. In doing so, she has also tempered the friction in the image. In Weems's rendition, the woman kneeling beside the prone figure does not shout toward the viewer, calling for an emotional response; instead, she turns her gaze downward to the body before her. Her reaction seems suspended: she may be dismayed, but she also seems tranquil, a kind of angelic witness. Weems's translation and transformation of the image resembles a pietà scene of the Virgin Mary holding the dead body of Christ, and as Ruby Tapia has argued, such "American Pietàs" conjoin "the threat of death and the promise of resurrection."[11] Weems collapses the contradictions in the image, as if transforming it into a reliquary that protects a sacred artifact from another time.

Suspended Belief encapsulates the sense of stasis that characterizes many of the images in *Constructing History*. The photographs seem to capture moments already stilled, as if the performers are frozen in amber. And in one sense, of course, they are. As images modeled on other images, as photographs performed and produced after other photographs, they reproduce instants already transformed, fractions of seconds already framed, a past already mediated. Twice removed, Weems's photographs appear to be both in and outside of time.

There is a kind of reduction and distillation in *Suspended Belief* as in all of Weems's re-creations of iconic photographs. Here and elsewhere she has focused in on the central characters, on the victims and mourners, erasing all of the detail and specificity from the images. The extraneous information recorded in the photographs has been edited out so that Weems's photographs evoke what Siegfried Kracauer called "memory-images." According to Kracauer, "Memories are retained because of their significance for that person. Thus they are organized according to a principle that is essentially different from the organizing principle of photography. Photography grasps what is given as a spatial (or temporal) continuum; memory-images retain what is given only insofar as it has significance. Since what is significant is not reducible to either merely spatial or merely temporal terms, memory-images are at odds with photographic representation."[12] Kracauer saw photography as antithetical to memory because the photograph is not selective. It records whatever is present before the camera lens at a particular time and place, regardless of its relative importance to a viewer. Memory, on the other hand, focuses on what matters to an individual, selecting what has moved the viewer affectively. As Kracauer explains, "Compared to photography[,] memory's records are full of gaps," but "from the perspective of memory, photography appears as a jumble that consists partly of garbage."[13] In her photographs, Weems resists the deluge of details that thwarts memory. She reduces the photograph's excess of arbitrary particulars, filtering its noise to approximate a memory-image.

If memory is antithetical to photography, it is also at odds with a modern conception of history founded on the march of homogeneous chronological time. For Kracauer, an individual's memory remains out of sync with chronological time because it is attached with intensity to particular events that form a subjective time curve.[14] Indeed, no one ever really experiences or remembers the homogenous chronological time of modern historical narratives. The past is "an incoherent mixture" of asynchronous time cycles, rather than a sequence of equivalent moments.[15] Weems invites students to *remember* events that for them might exist only as incremental dates and facts on a timeline. Through reenactment, she encourages students to imbue an abstract and detached chronology with a subjective time curve in which the struggles for civil rights are not relegated to a homogenous past but continue in a heterogeneous, asynchronous present.

Weems further complicates the relationship between photography and memory and memory and history because she constructs a history through memory-images based on photographs. The work demonstrates how memories transform events and can even warp seemingly stable photographic referents. Barthes was attuned, both knowingly and unwittingly, to the power of memory to effect one's perception of images. In *Camera Lucida* he provocatively proclaimed, "I may know better a photograph I remember than a photograph I am looking at."[16] Here "knowing" a photograph is not about recalling its specific details but transforming it into a memory-image that selects and even displaces those details. In his now well-known discussion of James VanDerZee's *Family Portrait* (1926), what becomes important in Barthes's memory of the image is a detail that isn't actually there (he displaces a pearl necklace in the photograph with "a slender ribbon of braided gold").[17] This slippage demonstrates, as Margaret Olin has argued, that the affective importance of the photograph, registered in the *punctum* and inscribed in memory, does not necessarily adhere to its indexicality.[18] Just as photographs can shape one's memory, memory can also transfigure the photograph, directing what one sees and remembers seeing in an image.

Weems's *Constructing History* calls attention to the morphing and malleability of memory vis-à-vis the photograph. *The Tragedy of Hiroshima*, for example, recalls W. Eugene Smith's photograph *Tomoko Uemura in Her Bath* (1971) but redirects its meaning. Weems's collaborators reproduce the gestures recorded in Smith's image but ultimately shift the referent (fig. 6.4). Smith documented the devastating physical effects of Minamata disease caused by severe mercury poisoning in Japan, the result of the Chisso Corporation's release of methyl mercury in its industrial wastewater from 1932 to 1968.[19] In his photograph, Tomoko Uemura's mother, Ryoko, cradles her daughter in a tub. The image is dark, but light from above catches the girl's upturned face, torso, and limbs.[20] Weems's *Tragedy of Hiroshima* evokes not mercury poisoning but the bombing of Hiroshima. Re-creating another striking pietà image, she reproduces the gesture of a mother holding her daughter in the bath, but reverses the embrace from left to right, and inverts the darks to whites. The image is recognizable, if askew; it reminds one of Smith's photograph, but redirects the referent. Weems's photograph recalls the devastation of the atomic bombing of Japan by the United States, rather than the chemical poisoning of people by a Japanese corporation. In this way, *Tragedy of Hiroshima* underscores the ways in which memory can loosen photographs, even iconic images, from their specific referents and imbue them with alternative

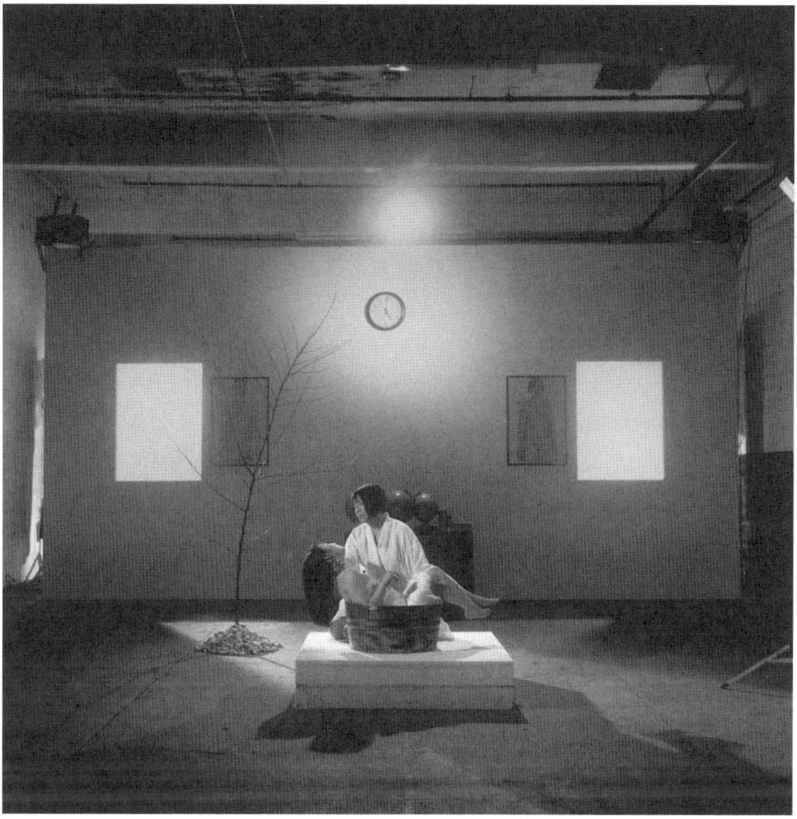

FIGURE 6.4 Carrie Mae Weems, *The Tragedy of Hiroshima*, 2008. Archival pigment print, 24 × 20 inches. Copyright Carrie Mae Weems. Courtesy of the artist and Jack Shainman Gallery, New York.

meanings. In Weems's constructed history, a subjective time curve bends photographic reference.

In *Constructing History*, Weems presents photographs of *performed* memory-images, inspired by photographs. She has made no attempt to hide the constructedness of the scenes; indeed, she puts their fabricated nature on display—the stage is revealed and the seams are showing. In this sense, the photographs are not particularly unusual, as artists have highlighted the theatrical nature of the photograph for decades.[21] But the images in *Constructing History* are not simply fabricated; they are *reenacted*. They start with photographs, which are then performed, in order to be photographed again.[22]

A number of the performances are notably awkward. Indeed, what Philip Auslander has said of the video also applies to the photographs: "Since the characters are students, it is not surprising that their enactments tend to be amateurish." For Auslander, "Their incredibility detracts from the video's force by periodically jarring the viewer out of a meditative mood."[23] I would like to propose, contrary to Auslander, that the amateurish acting plays a more productive role, especially in the photographs, one that reinforces their artifice in meaningful ways. It is in large part the near-miss of the images, the slippages in their approximation of iconic referents, that energizes them. The almost, but not-quite nature of these performances for the camera refuses the imagined transparency often accorded to the documentary photograph. The pose is brought into view *as pose* precisely when it fails to be seamlessly executed.[24] The discomfort one feels as viewer of these awkward scenes makes one aware of herself in relation to the images, bringing the act of looking itself into view. One is "jar[red] out of a meditative mood," but perhaps provoked into a more critically aware position, encouraged to remember that one is looking at a performance, and a performance of a photograph, a reenactment of an already mediated event.

The foundation of the photographs in performance highlights an embodied relationship to history that was central to Weems's conception of *Constructing History* and to her students' experience of making the work. As Weems has said of this project, "'Through the act of performance, with our own bodies, we are allowed to experience and to connect the historical past to the present—to the now, to the moment. By inhabiting the moment, we live the experience; we stand in the shoes of others and come to know firsthand what is often only imagined, lost, forgotten.'"[25] I reject the idea that performance proffers "firsthand" knowledge of a past. Nevertheless, Weems's work highlights the ways in which performance can bring a past to bear on the present in visible and felt ways, as a *new* experience *now*. As Allison Hersh notes, "When SCAD students acted out the death of Martin Luther King Jr. and re-enacted the student killings at Kent State University, many found themselves moved to tears." "'It was a very powerful experience,' explained Ashley Vieira, a SCAD student who took the class as a senior completing her B. F. A. in photography. 'It definitely made history more real for everybody.'"[26] Performance engages and registers in the body; it is experienced and felt in the present.

As Rebecca Schneider has argued, reenactments suggest that "historical events . . . are never discretely completed, but carry forth in embodied cycles of memory that do not delimit the remembered to the past."[27] Indeed, one might say that the very act of remembering draws a past into the present; one remembers in the time of now. Reenactment amplifies this sense—by performing a historical event, one creates an embodied experience in the present. Because reenactors typically perform events that preceded their lifetimes, one might consider reenactment an embodied form of what Marianne Hirsch has called "postmemory," an inherited memory of the trauma suffered by a previous generation.[28] Weems and her collaborators reenact historical photographs, remediating the image in an attempt to "remember" its past.

Weems's photographic reenactments activate a past in the present through the body. They perform a relationship to the past akin to that which Elizabeth Freeman describes as the queer historical method "erotohistoriography." As Freeman explains,

> Erotohistoriography is distinct from the desire for a fully present past, a restoration of bygone times. Erotohistoriography does not write the lost object into the present so much as encounter it already in the present, by treating the present itself as hybrid. And it uses the body as a tool to effect, figure, or perform that encounter. Erotohistoriography admits that contact with historical materials can be precipitated by particular bodily dispositions, and that these connections may elicit bodily responses, even pleasurable ones, that are themselves a form of understanding. It sees the body as a method, and historical consciousness as something intimately involved with corporeal sensations.[29]

Through performance, Weems and her collaborators use their bodies as vehicles for historical engagement. They encounter a past already in the present in the form of the iconic photograph. By reenacting that image, responding to and reperforming the gestures it documents, they seek to embody a photographic past, to feel its touch in the present.

By conjoining photography and performance in her photographic reenactments, Weems amplifies the disruptive temporality of both. For photography, like reenactment, also accesses a past in the present. In his famous ruminations on photography Barthes deemed the very essence of photography "that-has-been." According to Barthes, the photograph proclaims of its subject, "It has been here, and yet immediately separated; it has been absolutely, irrefutably present, and yet already deferred."[30] Using the present perfect tense "has been," rather than the simple past tense "was," Barthes suggests that the photographic subject's presence in a past extends to the moment of viewing. In the photograph one encounters a past in a future the photograph anticipated. In this way the photograph proffers a hybrid present that conjoins a past, present, and future.

Weems opens the present to a past not only by returning to photographs but also by heightening the melancholic registers of her work. Once again, many of the photographs in *Constructing History* are elegiac in mood (and the video is a "requiem"). In *Mourning*, for example, two African American women, dressed formally in head-to-toe black, sit in wooden chairs on the elevated platform in Weems's constructed classroom (plate 15). A young girl, dressed all in white except for her black Mary Jane shoes, sits at the feet of the veiled woman in the center of the trio, her cheek resting on the woman's knee, her hands held in the woman's lap. All the lines in the image seem to converge on the veiled woman in the middle; she is the apex of a triangle of forms. The circular outline of the clock on the wall behind the woman, partially obscured by her head, looks distinctly like a halo, and a bright white light hovering overhead underscores the religious overtones of the image, which closely recalls the Virgin Mary. Although they press close together, the women and the girl do not look at one another. Each casts her eyes in a different direction, seemingly lost in her own world of contemplation.

The image is a photographic reenactment of Moneta Sleet Jr.'s Pulitzer Prize–winning photograph of Coretta Scott King comforting her daughter Bernice at the Reverend Martin Luther King Jr.'s funeral at Ebenezer Baptist Church in Atlanta, Georgia, on April 9, 1968 (fig. 6.5).[31] As Elizabeth Ware Abston proposes in her reading of Weems's *Mourning*, the tracks for the camera that are visible in many of the images in the series here call attention to "the ubiquitous media presence during the funeral itself." "To emphasize that aspect, the conspicuous tracking camera has been rolled to the far right of the photograph, situated precisely where photographers . . . would have been stationed during the funeral."[32] In this way, Weems's reenactment of Sleet's photograph also calls attention to the mediation of the original event. Indeed, despite the overlapping time lines of her biography and the events she recreates, Weems, like most people alive in the 1960s and 1970s, experienced those events primarily as mediated through images. An "original experience" was an encounter with photographs.

Although Weems's image is titled *Mourning*, it evokes melancholia, the more trenchant sibling of mourning. As outlined in chapter 5, as Freud de-

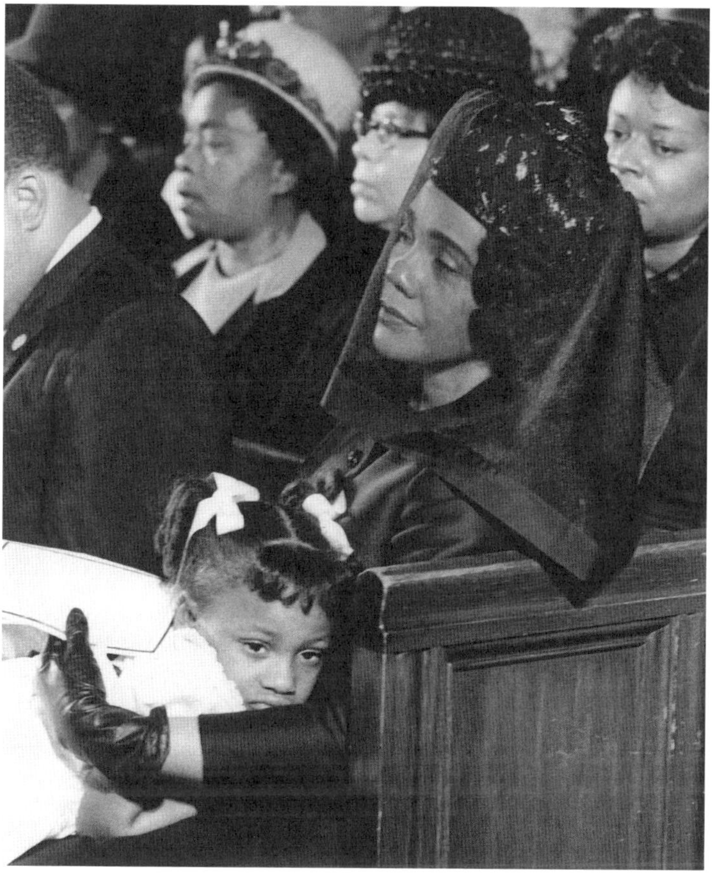

FIGURE 6.5 Moneta Sleet Jr., Coretta Scott King, and daughter Bernice at Martin Luther King Jr.'s funeral, 1968. Courtesy Johnson Publishing Company, LLC.

scribes it, mourning is a process in which the bereaved gradually releases a lost object and learns to live without it. Melancholia, on the other hand, is a state in which the bereaved refuses to relinquish the lost object; melancholia is grief that will not let go. But as Sharon Sliwinski has argued, "Even Freud admitted he had difficulty evaluating whether mourning is ever successful."[33] The border between mourning and melancholia may never be fully delineated, and Weems's *Mourning* registers the unfinished business of melancholia. Once again, as David L. Eng and David Kazanjian have argued, "Melancholia might be said to constitute . . . an ongoing and open relationship with the past."[34] Melancholia, like photography, establishes a relationship to the past that keeps it activated in the present, and Weems's image, performed after Sleet's, and then photographed, amplifies the porous nature of the present.

Weems invites viewers to engage a past and construct a history through a process of witnessing. As she has said, "I've figured out a way of making pictures that suggests that something is being witnessed."[35] In *Constructing History*, as in much of Weems's work, there is a guide, a figure she calls "the muse," who serves as surrogate for both the artist and the audience in the work. As Weems recounts, "The muse made her first appearance in *Kitchen Table* [1990]; this woman can stand in for me and for you; she can stand in for the audience, she leads you into history. She's a witness and a guide." Often played by Weems herself, the witness "is a black woman" who leads the viewer "through the trauma of history": "As a black woman she's engaged with the world around her; she's engaged with history, she's engaged with looking, with *being*."[36] In some work, such as *The Louisiana Project* (2003), *Roaming* (2006), and *Museum Series* (2007–present), Weems-as-muse stands with her back to the camera.[37] Inhabiting every frame, she provides a surrogate for the viewer in the scene, encouraging one to stand with her and observe both past events and the construction of history.

In *Constructing History* Weems figures the witness as a young African American woman dressed in a kimono. In a dreamlike scene she contemplates a cherry tree in blossom as a light snow falls in the fabricated classroom (fig. 6.6). Titled *A Woman Observes* in the series of photographs, this scene also recurs throughout the video, in which the witness is introduced by the narrator as follows: "A Woman stands in the thaw of winter. . . . With one step she could be in the future in an instant or in the past, or in the moment, the now." Weems's muse stands in a place in and out of time. She figures the oscillating temporality of the photograph, which always registers a past moment in a present as it anticipates a future. She inhabits the time of photography.

Scholars have questioned the ability of photodocumentary images, such as the iconic photographs Weems and her students reperform, to inspire ethical witnessing. As Wendy Kozol argues, one cannot assume that viewing such images performs critical work, for it can just as easily reproduce distanced colonial relations. She cautions, "It is vital that we recognize how the witnessing gaze implicates us in larger historical processes of violence, privilege and

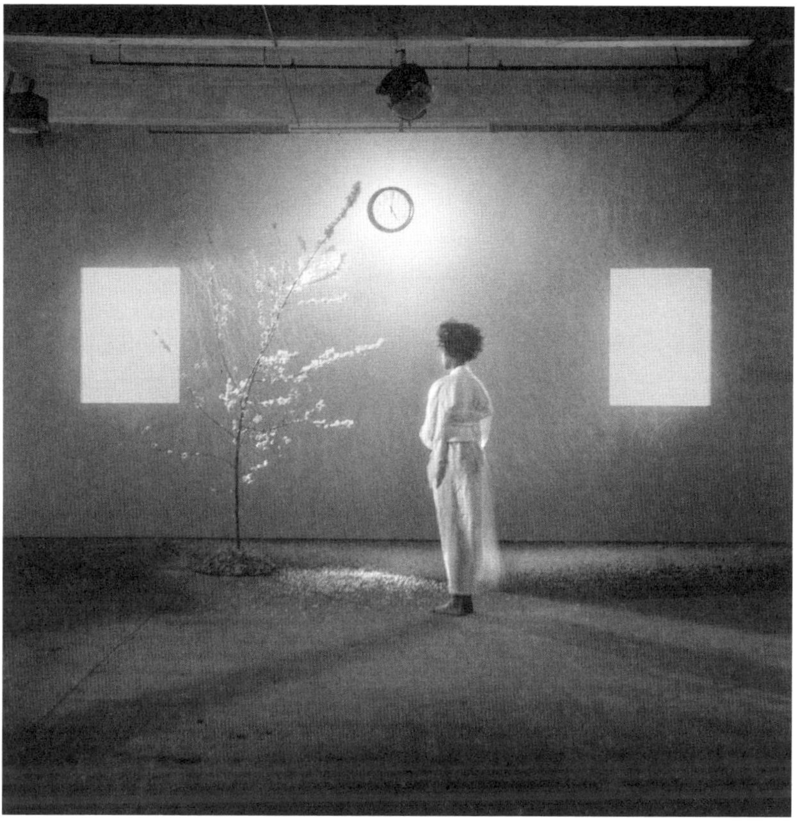

FIGURE 6.6 Carrie Mae Weems, *A Woman Observes*, 2008. Archival pigment print, 61 × 51 inches framed. Copyright Carrie Mae Weems. Courtesy of the artist and Jack Shainman Gallery, New York.

mourning."[38] Heeding Kozol's warning, it is nevertheless important to emphasize that Weems has created her photographic reenactments *after* photo-documentary images, and therefore the circumstances of viewing her images are notably different. The artist prints her photographs in black and white, recalling the conventions of 1960s and 1970s documentary and news photography, but she has literally reframed them. Her square images translate the photographs into the visual language of art and distinguish them from the horizontal images of reportage typically made with 35 millimeter film and 50 millimeter lenses. Weems also evokes multiple viewing contexts with the work—the newspaper, the classroom, the museum—subtly drawing into focus the conventions according to which history is constructed and the circumstances in which witnessing is solicited. Weems highlights the constructedness of her photographs as well as their reiterative nature. One never assumes that she is viewing history, performance, or even photography in an unmediated manner.

And yet, as Weems emphasizes mediation in *Constructing History*, she also underscores immediacy. Indeed, she embraces seemingly incompatible ways of thinking about the photograph: On the one hand, she emphasizes the constructed nature of the image, highlighting its artifice and fabrication (the title of the work is, after all, *Constructing History*), while on the other she emphasizes its indexicality, its indelible link as a tactile trace to a past moment. For Weems, photographs both construct history and offer access to a past moment. She presents the photograph, in Barthes's words, as both "mad and tame": on the one hand tame because "its realism remains relative, tempered by aesthetic . . . habits"; on the other hand mad because its realism is also "absolute and, so to speak, original, obliging the loving and terrified consciousness to return to the very letter of Time."[39] Weems refuses to choose between the two ways of regarding the photograph; instead, she recognizes in the image both "the civilized code of perfect illusions" and "the wakening of intractable reality."[40] Activating the compelling contradictions of the photograph, *Constructing History* presents a past as simultaneously fabricated and immanent. The photograph is a coded message, but its relationship to time is real.

One might say that Weems is struck by Barthes's final conception of the photograph's punctum as an index of time itself. She turns to religious imagery in her distillations of iconic photographs as Barthes turned to the language of religion to describe his ultimate understanding of the punctum. Barthes declares, "I now know that there exists another *punctum* (another 'stigmatum') than the 'detail.' This new *punctum*, which is no longer of form but of intensity, is Time, the lacerating emphasis of the *noeme* (*'that has been'*), its pure representation."[41] Weems's photographs emphasize this temporal rupture, highlighting a present that is punctured by a photographic past. Her pietà photographs recast historical images in a religious iconography of loss that holds out the possibility of redemption.

But *Constructing History* is also uncertain about redemption; it rejects a narrative of historical resolution. Through that ambivalence, Weems also refuses to foreclose on the past, to seal it off from the present. *Constructing His-*

tory invites collaborators and viewers to engage a past in new ways, to remember a past through the embodied experience of photographic reenactment in the present. Weems encourages one to inhabit a melancholic and photographic relation to a past that keeps it present as one constructs a history to face an unknown future.

CHAPTER 7

False Returns

Taryn Simon's *The Innocents*

Taryn Simon's *The Innocents* (2002) is about photography's powerful and problematic relation to criminal identification. The project documents forty-five legal cases of mistaken identification, in which individuals were misrecognized as the perpetrators of violent crimes on the basis of mug shots and other visual aids. The wrongfully convicted are men and one woman who were exonerated on the basis of DNA evidence, but only after they had served major portions of long prison sentences—between seven and eighteen years. Simon photographed individuals in places important to the cases in which they became entangled—"the scene of misidentification, the scene of arrest, the alibi location, or the scene of the crime."[1] Her work questions and redirects photography's institutional role in defining the criminal, highlighting photography's failures—its unreliability and malleability—as she exposes those whom photography itself has helped to victimize.

The photographs are large-scale color portraits (48¼ × 62¼ inches framed) in which subjects for the most part look directly at the camera. Simon has also reproduced the images in a book in which each photograph is paired with a facing page of text that names the subject, the place where the person was photographed, the length of the sentence, and the number of years served. This information is followed by an account of the crime for which the individual was falsely accused and convicted, a description of how the evidence was gathered and utilized, and finally, a statement from the wrongly identified person.

Peter Neufeld and Barry C. Scheck, lawyers who founded the Innocence Project in 1992 at the Benjamin N. Cardozo School of Law in New York City, provided the information about each case for Simon. Their Innocence Project is a nonprofit organization that offers pro bono legal representation to inmates across the country who claim that DNA evidence could prove their innocence.[2] With their colleagues, Neufeld and Scheck have worked to make postconviction DNA testing available to inmates, to secure the proper preservation of evidence, and to reform eyewitness identification processes.[3]

Simon's work, like Deborah Luster's, engages the mug shot and the history of biometric systems used by the carceral state. She troubles the efficacy of the mug shot as a visual tool of identification, showing it to be an unstable register and an unreliable identifier. *The Innocents* demonstrates that the mug shot is susceptible to the malleable memory of eyewitnesses whose vision can be shaped by suggestion and by the racist cultural discourses that enframe men and women of color.[4]

Simon's portraits of exonerated individuals at the scenes of the crimes for which they were convicted are particularly unsettling. They depict double crimes—the crime for which the man or woman was wrongly convicted, and the crime of the wrongful conviction itself. They read like returns, but they are not; instead, they mark first visits to places where a series of events and misidentifications began that radically redirected the life course of Simon's subjects. The photographer brings exonerated people to a *place* that also marks a *time*, namely the beginning of their lives in prison. She draws on the oscillating time of the photograph to teleport her subjects to places that are both before and after their imprisonment. Her false returns fold time around the lacuna of incarceration.

Highlighting the subjects whose lives were dramatically redirected by misidentifications, Simon's project also creates its own lacuna. If *The Innocents* is explicitly about the nature of visual evidence, it is also implicitly about the nature of innocence, and both are laden with complexities here. As the work points to the failure of photography and other visual systems of identification, it also unwittingly points to the failure of policing and the prison industrial complex. As it brings forth and highlights the innocent victims of mistaken identification, *The Innocents* also obscures other victims, leaving those who have suffered violent crime largely in its shadows.

Simon inserts her subjects into a larger cultural repertoire of images, and in viewing them one has the sense that one has seen these images before. She crafts her photographs carefully *as* "scenes": the settings are often ominous, dark, and dramatically lit, as if lifted from film noir, and they include the deserted fields, tangled riverbanks, abandoned lots, and dark alleys often associated with danger. In fabricating such scenes after the faulty facts, and after the consequences of misidentification, Simon reproduces what did not happen but what witnesses might nevertheless have "seen." In this way the photographs subtly suggest how looking and seeing are culturally circumscribed, how one *learns* to identify a criminal.[5]

In one striking image, Charles Irvin Fain stands at the scene of the crime for which he was convicted, on the banks of the Snake River in Melba, Idaho (plate 16).[6] The photograph was taken at night, and Fain looms out of the darkness, a small figure standing just to the left of center. Behind him, the headlights of a car pierce the darkness and cast beams of bright yellow light toward the viewer. Another, unseen light source illuminates Fain and the edges of pine branches that frame the foreground. It is hard to say who is caught in the headlights here, Fain himself, or the viewer.

Many of the subjects are photographed alone, small and isolated in settings that literally and figuratively overwhelm them. A white middle-aged man wearing camouflage stands in the slim dry bed of a stream in a dense thicket. The bushes and trees are bare; they look like wires stretching out to entangle him. An African American man stands in a motel room, number 24, the last in the row; he wears chinos and a Waco Lions T-shirt (plate 17). He is carefully framed in the window, illuminated by light within the room, and stands out conspicuously in the scene.

The photographs announce their staged quality: figures are dramatically lit, even outdoors, and colors are deeply saturated. Simon uses a large-format film camera to make her negatives, which she then scans to produce large-scale color prints. The images participate in a contemporary art aesthetic that muddles the distinction between fact and fiction, unsettling and expanding the category of documentary photography. Like Gregory Crewdson, Jeff Wall, or Philip-Lorca diCorcia, Simon creates scenarios that seem to be extracted from more complete narratives.[7] The photographs are elaborate constructions that gesture toward but do not reveal a larger sequence of events, and they highlight the ways in which "photography's persuasive relationship to realism and documentation is continually in tension with its equally potent capability for fantasy and artificiality."[8] As Simon herself has said, "Photography's ability to blur truth and fiction is one of its most compelling qualities." But as *The Innocents* makes so distressingly clear, "photography's ambiguity, beautiful in one context, can be devastating in another."[9] Simon's aesthetic choices highlight photography's equivocations, making one aware of its capacity to make fiction look like fact.[10] She critiques the penal system's reliance on a malleable medium, but her own photographs amplify the very unreliability they seek to expose. By blurring fiction and fact, Simon's portraits reveal the dynamics that led to the misidentifications and wrongful convictions of her subjects, but they reinstate the exonerated on unsteady photographic ground.

Even when engulfed by their surroundings, Simon's subjects sometimes appear menacing. They are out of place, standing too still, staring. They look directly back at the photographer and viewer, and the sequence of all those direct stares is unnerving. They seem to ask viewers to bear witness to their stories, or perhaps to challenge viewers, confronting them with their own stereotypes and misconceptions. They seem to ask: What do *you* see when you look at me? Do you think you can read my character at a glance? Am I always already guilty in your eyes? Do I look like a criminal type?

Anthony Robinson, released after serving ten years of a twenty-seven-year sentence, dresses formally when he leaves the house, because, as he says, a man "'wearing a shirt, a tie, a pair of slacks, and some hard-soled shoes'" is unlikely to "fit the description" of a man the police are looking for. He records his comings and goings on a daily basis, gathering his own evidence, and securing his own alibis. "I keep records and tables on where I was, what I was doing, and how long I was there. . . . I keep general notations, little scraps of papers. If I go to the store, I'll keep a receipt or I'll make notations on my calendar."[11]

Simon photographed Robinson at the University of Houston, Texas, at the location of the crime for which he was convicted. However, Robinson refused to enter the building and bathroom where the crime took place, because the site was simply too charged. Simon's image of Robinson is a visually complicated one that resembles the cut-back shot in a suspense film. Robinson stands outside a building, looking in; he is unnaturally lit, and his eyes seem to glow. A low horizontal bar in the glass wall visually cuts off his feet, and makes it appear that he is floating outside the window. Despite his somewhat uncanny presence, however, Robinson is also contained within the scene, bound by the beams that divide the glass wall, and small within the frame. He wears pleated khaki pants, a blue short-sleeved shirt and a dark tie. In his words he does not "fit the description" of a man the police would be looking for.

Some of Simon's subjects dress in official attire—military, athletic, or work uniforms—clothing that identifies them as members of groups. Some are photographed with loved ones—partners and children—that link them to larger social networks. These are the fortunate, those who have been able to sustain ties of family and friendship through years of forced absence. As the sister of one of the wrongfully convicted notes, the exonerated are left to re-enter society without any support structures. Those who serve their time and are released on parole have at least some minimal support—a probation officer, job assistance, help finding a place to live, and peer groups. Individuals released after a misidentification are simply let go, left to find their own way in the world.[12]

The subjects consistently remark on the life-changing effects of their misidentification and imprisonment. Some of them remain focused on their cases, on the moment of the arrest; others reflect on their time in prison; and still others comment on the difficulty of returning to life outside. Several are haunted by the idea that it could all happen again. Eric Sarsfield muses, "I can't go out because I really think that someone could recognize me, or someone could say something to somebody else, or something like that—something could happen, something could happen. . . ."[13] He is photographed sitting on a bed in a cluttered bedroom. He slouches and turns droopy eyes toward the camera. A beer can, lighter, and ashtray perch on a small table by the window; another can rests on the tall dresser, and Sarsfield holds another in his hand. The arbitrary and disorienting nature of their arrests and convictions have left these subjects wary and insecure in the ordinary day to day. They are stalled in a present haunted by the past. The consequences of a failed legal system have transformed their lives into constant crime scenes, and the individuals themselves into watchful self-observers. Their lives are constrained and calibrated by the terms of surveillance, evidence, and alibi.

Simon is a sophisticated thinker about photography, its truths and fictions, its role in shaping memory, and its complicated use in eyewitness identification. As she states, "Photography offered the criminal justice system a tool that transformed innocent citizens into criminals, assisted officers in obtaining erroneous eyewitness identifications, and aided prosecutors in securing convictions. The criminal justice system . . . failed to recognize the limitations of relying on photographic images."[14] *The Innocents* troubles the nature of visual identification by showing how malleable visual memory, or memory supported and directed by visual cues, can be. One of Simon's subjects, Jennifer Thompson, a victim of rape and a surviving witness in one of the cases, gives a stunning example of such pliability as she recounts her experience in the police department:

> They asked if I could do a composite sketch. I sat down with a police artist and went through the book. I picked out the nose, the eyes, and the ears that most closely resembled the person who attacked me. It ran in the newspaper the following day. From that composite sketch, a phone call came in that said the sketch resembled someone they knew: Ronald Cotton. Ron's name was then pulled, and he became a key suspect. I was asked to come down and look at the photo array of different men. I picked Ron's photo because in my mind it most closely resembled the man who attacked me. But really what happened was that, because I had made a composite sketch, he actually most closely resembled my sketch as opposed to the actual attacker. By the time we went to do a physical lineup, they asked if I could physically identify the person. I picked out Ronald because in my mind he resembled the photo, which resembled the composite, which resembled the attacker. All the images became enmeshed to one image that became Ron, and Ron became my attacker.[15]

Here, then, the criminal offender emerges through a series of visual images, each supporting a different stage of visual identification. The person ultimately selected is the one who most closely resembles a photograph that resembles a composite sketch that has come to replace a traumatic memory. The photograph helps to identify the sketch, not the perpetrator.

The police sketch is a deeply subjective visual form, made through the collaboration of an eyewitness and a police sketch artist who together attempt to translate a memory into an image using a standardized taxonomy of facial features. Artist Stephen Spretnjak has focused on the instability and variability of the police sketch in his series *Police Composite Drawings* (1992–94) (figs. 7.1–7.2, 7.3–7.4, and 7.5–7.6). Working with a composite artist named Kevin Sampson, of the New Jersey State Police Department, Spretnjak commissioned eighteen people to serve as eyewitnesses, describing Spretnjak to Sampson, who then created composite sketches after their descriptions, replicating the standard police format of pencil on nine-by-twelve-inch paper.[16]

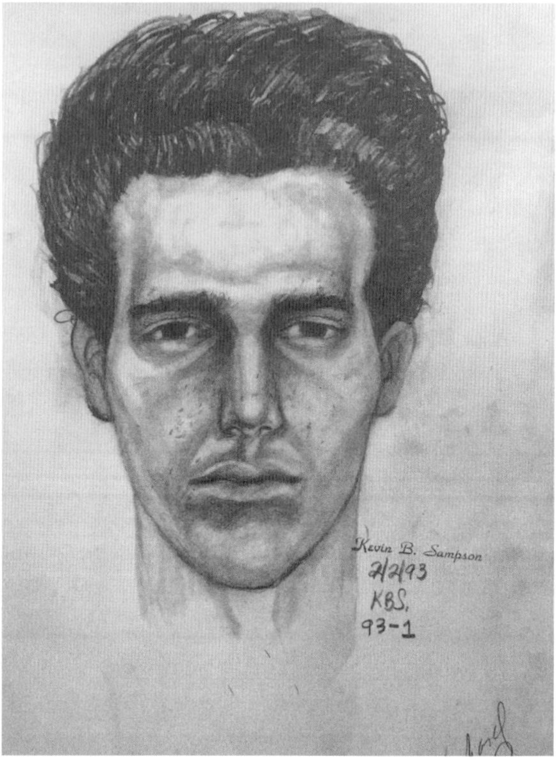

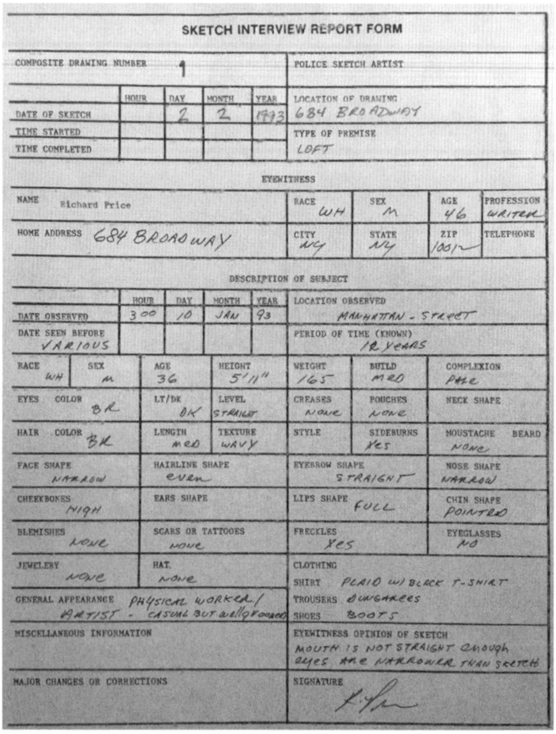

SKETCH INTERVIEW REPORT FORM

COMPOSITE DRAWING NUMBER 1
POLICE SKETCH ARTIST

	HOUR	DAY	MONTH	YEAR
DATE OF SKETCH		2	2	1993
TIME STARTED				
TIME COMPLETED				

LOCATION OF DRAWING 684 BROADWAY
TYPE OF PREMISE LOFT

EYEWITNESS

NAME Richard Price
RACE WH | SEX M | AGE 46 | PROFESSION WRITER
HOME ADDRESS 684 BROADWAY
CITY NY | STATE NY | ZIP 1001[illegible] | TELEPHONE

DESCRIPTION OF SUBJECT

	HOUR	DAY	MONTH	YEAR
DATE OBSERVED	3:00	10	JAN	93
DATE SEEN BEFORE VARIOUS				

LOCATION OBSERVED MANHATTAN - STREET
PERIOD OF TIME (KNOWN) 12 YEARS

RACE WH | SEX M | AGE 36 | HEIGHT 5'11" | WEIGHT 165 | BUILD MED | COMPLEXION PALE
EYES COLOR BR | LT/DK DK | LEVEL STRAIGHT | CREASES NONE | POUCHES NONE | NECK SHAPE
HAIR COLOR BR | LENGTH MED | TEXTURE WAVY | STYLE | SIDEBURNS YES | MOUSTACHE BEARD NONE
FACE SHAPE NARROW | HAIRLINE SHAPE EVEN | EYEBROW SHAPE STRAIGHT | NOSE SHAPE NARROW
CHEEKBONES HIGH | EARS SHAPE | LIPS SHAPE FULL | CHIN SHAPE POINTED
BLEMISHES NONE | SCARS OR TATTOOES NONE | FRECKLES YES | EYEGLASSES NO
JEWELERY NONE | HAT NONE
CLOTHING
SHIRT PLAID W/ BLACK T-SHIRT
TROUSERS DUNGAREES
SHOES BOOTS
GENERAL APPEARANCE PHYSICAL WORKER/ ARTIST - CASUAL BUT wellgroomed
MISCELLANEOUS INFORMATION
EYEWITNESS OPINION OF SKETCH MOUTH IS NOT STRAIGHT enough eyes ARE NARROWER THAN SKETCH
MAJOR CHANGES OR CORRECTIONS
SIGNATURE

FIGURES 7.1, 7.2
Stephen Spretnjak, police composite sketch artist's drawing from memory of eyewitness number 1, *Police Composite Drawings*, 1992–94. Courtesy the artist.

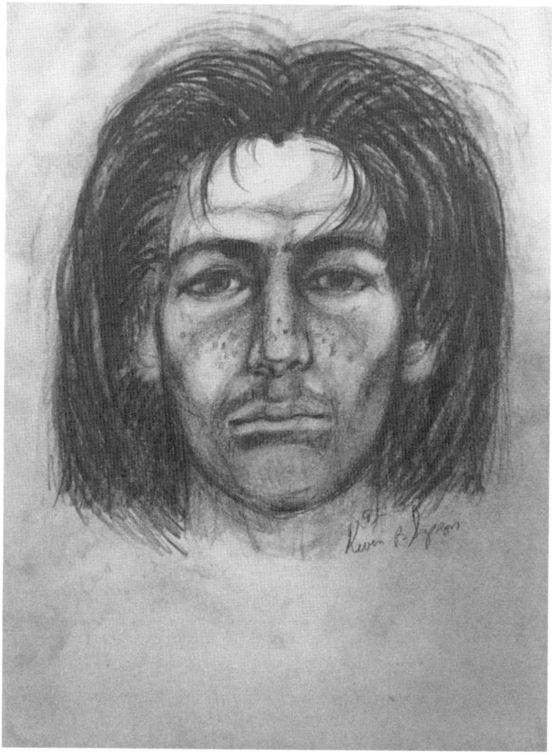

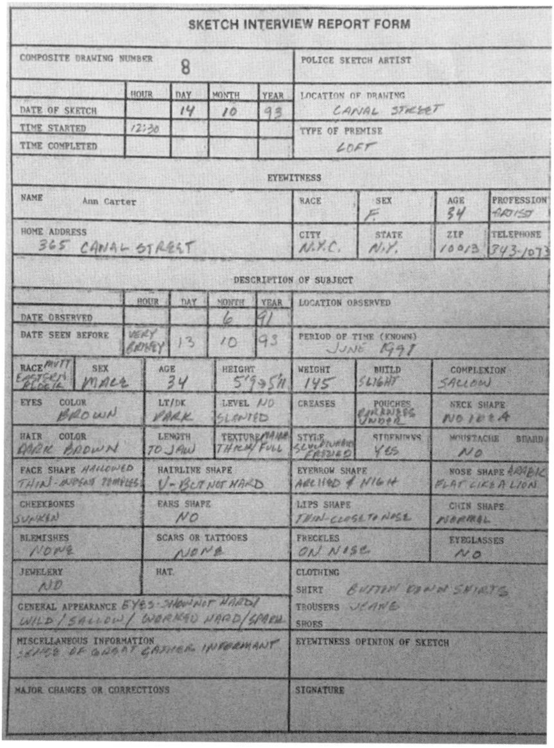

SKETCH INTERVIEW REPORT FORM

COMPOSITE DRAWING NUMBER 8 | POLICE SKETCH ARTIST

	HOUR	DAY	MONTH	YEAR
DATE OF SKETCH		14	10	93
TIME STARTED	12:30			
TIME COMPLETED				

LOCATION OF DRAWING: CANAL STREET
TYPE OF PREMISE: LOFT

EYEWITNESS

NAME: Ann Carter | RACE | SEX: F. | AGE: 34 | PROFESSION: ARTIST
HOME ADDRESS: 365 CANAL STREET | CITY: N.Y.C. | STATE: N.Y. | ZIP: 10013 | TELEPHONE: 343-1073

DESCRIPTION OF SUBJECT

	HOUR	DAY	MONTH	YEAR
DATE OBSERVED			6	91
DATE SEEN BEFORE	VERY [illegible]	13	10	93

LOCATION OBSERVED
PERIOD OF TIME (KNOWN): JUNE 1991

RACE: MUTT EASTERN BLOC[illegible] | SEX: MALE | AGE: 34 | HEIGHT: 5'9→5'11 | WEIGHT: 145 | BUILD: SLIGHT | COMPLEXION: SALLOW
EYES COLOR: BROWN | LT/DK: DARK | LEVEL: NO SLANTED | CREASES | POUCHES: [illegible] UNDER | NECK SHAPE: NO [illegible]
HAIR COLOR: DARK BROWN | LENGTH: TO JAW | TEXTURE: [illegible] THICK/FULL | STYLE: [illegible] FRIZZED | SIDEBURNS: YES | MOUSTACHE: NO | BEARD
FACE SHAPE: HALLOWED THIN-[illegible] TEMPLES | HAIRLINE SHAPE: V-BUT NOT HARD | EYEBROW SHAPE: ARCHED & HIGH | NOSE SHAPE: ARABIC FLAT LIKE A LION
CHEEKBONES: SUNKEN | EARS SHAPE: NO | LIPS SHAPE: THIN-CLOSE TO NOSE | CHIN SHAPE: NORMAL
BLEMISHES: NONE | SCARS OR TATTOOS: NONE | FRECKLES: ON NOSE | EYEGLASSES: NO
JEWELERY: NO | HAT. | CLOTHING — SHIRT: BUTTON DOWN SHIRTS; TROUSERS: JEANS; SHOES
GENERAL APPEARANCE: EYES-[illegible] NOT HARD/ WILD / SALLOW / WORKED HARD/SPARE
MISCELLANEOUS INFORMATION: [illegible] OF GREAT GATHER INFORMANT | EYEWITNESS OPINION OF SKETCH
MAJOR CHANGES OR CORRECTIONS | SIGNATURE

FIGURES 7.3, 7.4
Stephen Spretnjak, police composite sketch artist's drawing from memory of eyewitness number 8, *Police Composite Drawings*, 1992–94. Courtesy the artist.

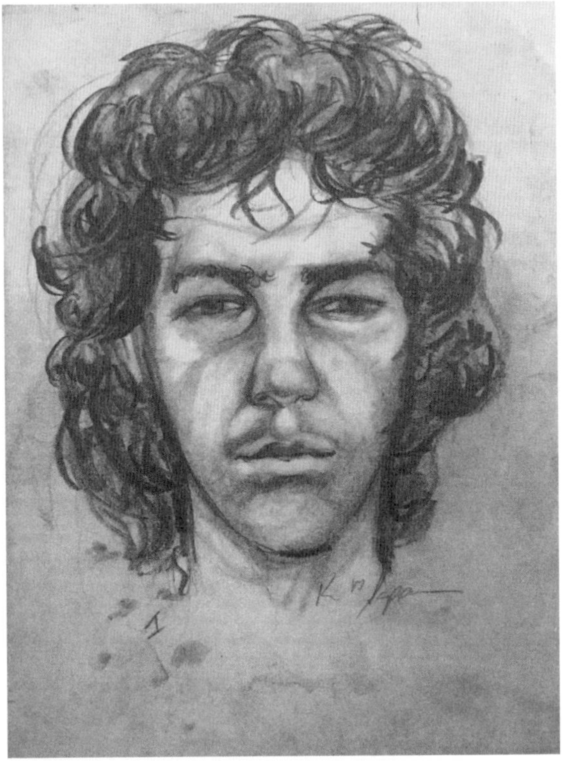

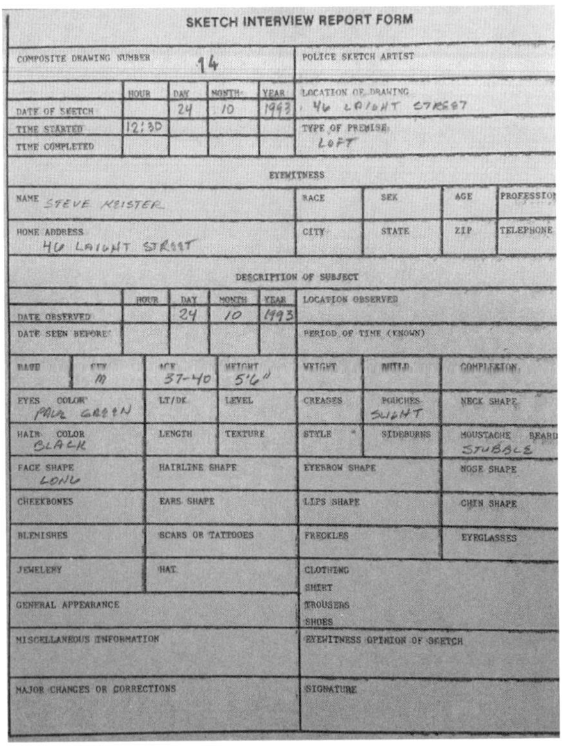

SKETCH INTERVIEW REPORT FORM

COMPOSITE DRAWING NUMBER 14
POLICE SKETCH ARTIST

	HOUR	DAY	MONTH	YEAR
DATE OF SKETCH		24	10	1993
TIME STARTED	12:30			
TIME COMPLETED				

LOCATION OF DRAWING 46 LAIGHT STREET
TYPE OF PREMISE LOFT

EYEWITNESS

NAME STEVE KEISTER
RACE
SEX
AGE
PROFESSION
HOME ADDRESS 46 LAIGHT STREET
CITY
STATE
ZIP
TELEPHONE

DESCRIPTION OF SUBJECT

	HOUR	DAY	MONTH	YEAR
DATE OBSERVED		24	10	1993
DATE SEEN BEFORE				

LOCATION OBSERVED
PERIOD OF TIME (KNOWN)

RACE
SEX M
AGE 37–40
HEIGHT 5'6"
WEIGHT
BUILD
COMPLEXION
EYES COLOR PALE GREEN
LT/DK
LEVEL
CREASES
POUCHES SLIGHT
NECK SHAPE
HAIR COLOR BLACK
LENGTH
TEXTURE
STYLE
SIDEBURNS
MOUSTACHE BEARD STUBBLE
FACE SHAPE LONG
HAIRLINE SHAPE
EYEBROW SHAPE
NOSE SHAPE
CHEEKBONES
EARS SHAPE
LIPS SHAPE
CHIN SHAPE
BLEMISHES
SCARS OR TATTOOES
FRECKLES
EYEGLASSES
JEWELERY
HAT
CLOTHING
SHIRT
TROUSERS
SHOES
GENERAL APPEARANCE
MISCELLANEOUS INFORMATION
EYEWITNESS OPINION OF SKETCH
MAJOR CHANGES OR CORRECTIONS
SIGNATURE

FIGURES 7.5, 7.6
Stephen Spretnjak, police composite sketch artist's drawing from memory of eyewitness number 14, *Police Composite Drawings*, 1992–94. Courtesy the artist.

The divergence among the resulting images of the same "target subject" is fascinating. In some Spretnjak's hair is short and wavy; in others it is long and straight. In some it is dark, in others light. In some he appears to have freckles or spots; in others his skin is clear. In some his hairline is straight; in others it is peaked and heart-shaped. In some his brow and forehead are dramatically contoured; in others they are smooth. The most consistent features across the seventeen sketches are the eyebrows, thick and rather straight, and the thin mustache above his upper lip. Spretnjak's series very clearly demonstrates how people see differently, attending to divergent details of appearance, and consequently how subjects and suspects morph and change according to who is looking, remembering, and describing what they saw. Spretnjak's face changed each time a new person attempted to describe it to the sketch artist.

Spretnjak's project, like Thompson's account, shows how unreliable visual memory, and representations based on that memory, can be. One might imagine that the photograph would provide a more stable image of a suspect than the artist's sketch, but it too is susceptible to misreadings and manipulations. Indeed, from the moment of its advent, and at the height of its popularity, the photographic mug shot was deemed inadequate to identify criminals. Even Alphonse Bertillon, who invented the mug shot and was most responsible for its institutionalization, did not believe photographic evidence alone was sufficient to identify criminals. As discussed in chapter 3, Bertillon augmented his photographic records with a series of nine physical measurements, and his "portrait parle" supplemented mug shots with extensive text. Bertillon's system thus paradoxically underscored the unreliability of visual identification even as it heralded the photographic mug shot.[17] The photograph alone has always been inadequate to the task of identification.

In many ways, Simon's project reproduces the assumptions of Bertillonage. The cases she documents demonstrate how faulty photographic identification can be, and they ultimately rely on another kind of physical mapping—DNA evidence—to determine an individual's innocence or guilt. As the apotheosis of Bertillon's careful physical measurements, DNA typing has been called "nature's perfect identity test,"[18] but it too is an unstable identifier dependent on several levels of mediation, representation, and interpretation. When a match is declared in DNA typing, identity is still *inferred*.[19]

DNA identification is a multistep process that includes sampling, processing, representation, comparison, and probability. First a sample is collected from a crime scene. After the DNA has been extracted, it is cut at base-pair patterns and separated into strands, which are then marked with a radioactive probe. Those radioactive particles are then *exposed to photographic film*, resulting in an image in which DNA fragments appear as bands in an "autoradiograph."[20] DNA typing is therefore ultimately a visual and *photographic* technology.[21]

After the autoradiograph has been produced, it is compared to the autoradiograph of a DNA sample taken from a suspect or suspects (fig. 7.7). If the comparison results in a visible match, that match is evaluated according to the probability of another match within the subject's race-based population group (e.g., Caucasians, African Americans).[22] The potential error involved in determining the subject's "race," as well as the inevitable associations with earlier scientific means of racial typing, such as eugenics, have made this final stage of DNA identification particularly problematic. But there is also room for debate about the method of sampling and the production of the autoradiograph, for as Jonathan Finn has demonstrated, "DNA identification involves the collaboration of a diverse group including police, molecular biologists, population geneticists, and biotechnology corporations."[23] There is much room for error in all of these steps, and even at its best, DNA identification is ultimately based on representation (the autoradiograph) and probability. Unlike the fingerprint, which provides a unique identification, DNA analysis offers only a "probability of identification."[24] It is not, then, "nature's perfect identity test," but instead a highly mediated process based on representation and interpretation.

DNA typing has been widely contested and challenged, even by the lawyers who founded the Innocence Project. In fact, Neufeld and Scheck are best known as prominent members of the O. J. Simpson defense team who challenged the use of DNA evidence in that infamous trial. The televised and widely publicized O. J. Simpson trial of 1995 became a kind of testing ground for DNA typing evidence, and "long portions of the trial were devoted to lessons about DNA."[25]

Practitioners often call DNA typing "DNA *fingerprinting*" in efforts to associate the process with that earlier and today almost uniformly accepted forensic technology. As Simon Cole has argued, "Proponents of genetic identification make no secret of their aspirations to follow in the footsteps of conventional fingerprinting."[26] According to Cole, fingerprinting, like later DNA typing, was first tried in the courts and public opinion in a famous case, *People v. Jennings*, in 1910.[27] Since that time, latent fingerprint examiners (LFPEs) have "successfully managed the image of the fingerprint," maintaining their position as expert viewers at the same time that they have made

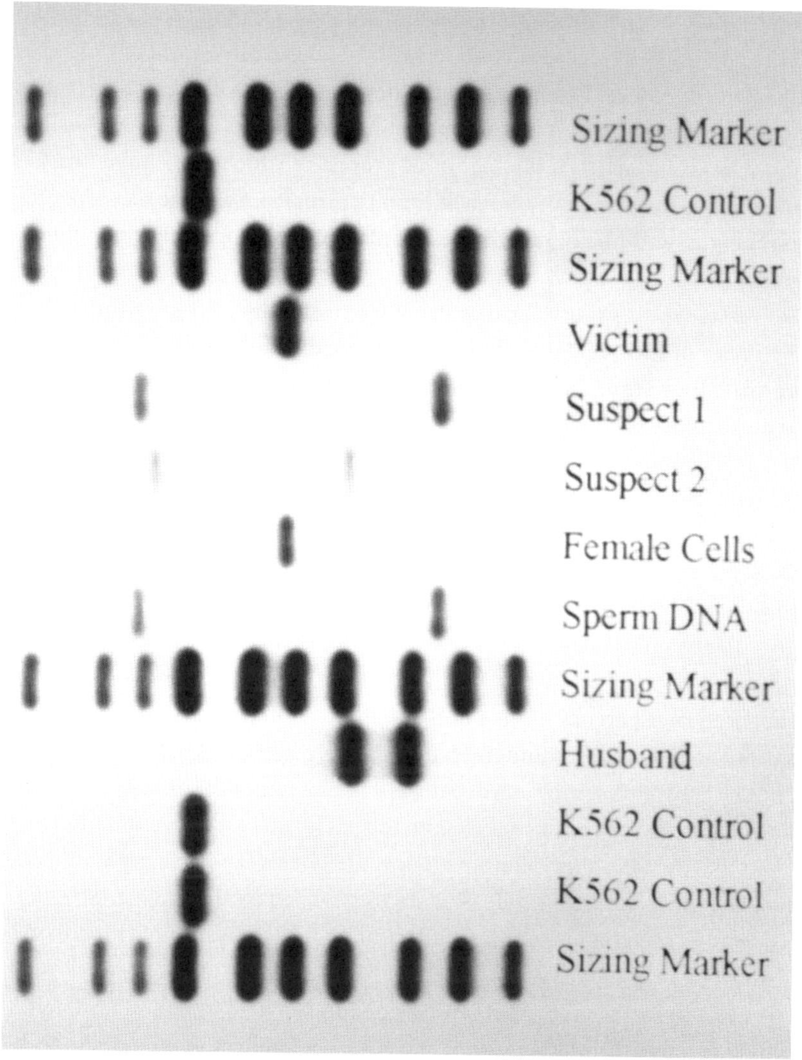

FIGURE 7.7 DNA fingerprint results from rape investigation. Autoradiograph. Martin Shields/Science Source.

jurors and other lay viewers feel that they are seeing for themselves only what is evident. They have also worked to establish unanimity as an LFPE occupational norm (LFPEs do not testify against one another in court).[28] Fingerprint identification is a process in which invisible, latent marks are rendered visible, and it too is ultimately a photographic process in which an examiner makes an image by dusting, developing, or lifting a print from a crime scene, photographing it, and finally reversing and enlarging the fingerprint in a photograph.[29]

DNA typing experts have been less successful than LFPEs in controlling the image of their evidence. It has been more difficult, perhaps, for them to translate the bars of the autoradiograph into definitive identity markers, and to make matches seem transparent to lay viewers. Unlike LFPEs, DNA typing experts have also testified against one another in court, demonstrating the degree of interpretation that is involved in their work. And as Sheila Jasanoff has shown in her study of the O. J. Simpson trial, they have not been granted the same status as expert witnesses; their analysis has been disregarded and superseded by the views of jurors guided by the judge.[30]

In the courts, traces of physical evidence, including fingerprints and DNA, are rendered photographically. As visual technologies, both rely on the supposed transparency of the photograph, and both amplify its indexicality, a characteristic of the photograph that has long been debated by scholars of photography. At issue in such debates is whether or not the photograph functions as a literal trace of its subject (an index), as well as a representation that looks like its subject (an icon). As index, the photograph is thought to function like the fingerprint itself, as an impression left by the subject. DNA typing is not iconographic, nor is it indexical, as it is always a highly mediated, abstract trace of the subject.[31]

Not unlike the mug shots that helped to convict Simon's subjects, DNA typing is liable to interpretation, and it too is finally a photographic technology. And yet, in Simon's project, as well as Neufeld and Scheck's, DNA typing is posed as the corrective to the unreliable photograph. DNA typing rights the picture and exonerates the subject. What, then, do Simon's photographs do? As false returns effected with a fallible medium, they provide an unstable view.

Nearly three-quarters of Simon's subjects are men of color, and most are African American men. (Only twelve of the forty-five "innocents" are apparently white men, and once again, only one is a woman.) The gender ratio is due in part to the nature of the crimes and the means of exoneration—DNA evidence is most readily available in cases of rape. The racial discrepancy underscores the racism that continues to be structurally imbedded in US policing and incarceration, recalling the residues of slavery instituted in the prison industrial complex by the Thirteenth Amendment, as noted in chapter 3. Further, the disproportionate racial numbers demonstrate, as Lisa Marie Cacho has argued, not only how readily African Americans are stereotyped as criminal, but also how criminal activity itself is construed vis-à-vis black bodies.[32] The conflation of blackness with criminality is part of what Maurice O. Wallace has called the "enframement" of black men in US visual culture, and Simon's work taps into and exposes the long history of official and unofficial racial profiling in the United States.[33] *The Innocents* shows how racism continues to inform assumptions about what a criminal looks like, about who is assumed to be guilty, whose life is expendable, who can be deemed "close enough," and who deserves to be locked away.

The fact that rape is at the center of so many of the cases Simon documents also accords with long-standing discourses about the sexualized nature of supposed black male criminality. As many scholars have argued, in the discourses surrounding lynching in the late nineteenth and early twentieth centuries, the torture and murder of black men by white mobs was often "justified" as the retribution of white men unhinged by a black man's purported rape of a white woman. As journalist, editor, and antilynching activist Ida B. Wells documented in the 1890s, the discourse about rape surrounding lynching was so pervasive that people did not bother to consult the facts in particular cases; they just assumed that lynching was a response to rape. Wells discovered that often no woman was involved in the case, and African American men were lynched simply for becoming too prosperous. In other cases, she found that lynching was used to hide and reject an interracial love affair. For suggesting the latter, Wells was run out of town, her newspaper offices were burned, and she herself was threatened with lynching. The discourses Wells identified in the late nineteenth century have persisted throughout the twentieth and twenty-first centuries. As discussed in chapter 5, they could be leveraged as late as 1955 to "justify" the torture and murder of a fourteen-year-old boy.

William Gregory proposes that lingering prohibitions against interracial relationships informed his conviction. Gregory was accused of rape and attempted rape of two white women who lived in his apartment building, where he was the only African American tenant. Describing his trial, he has said,

> The jury's prejudices were in the closet, but the door was cracked. You could tell the door was cracked by the expressions on their faces when my white fiancée said my nails was beautiful and I was handsome. The jury was like, "What is wrong with her?" They cracked the door so to speak. You could see the prejudice on their faces. The spotters in my case looked at the jury, came back and said, "He's convicted." They said that because of what they saw when my fiancée got on the stand—she was a very classy white woman, well kept, came from a rich family. They convicted me with their prejudices, their biases. They basically got rid of their pencils and stopped taking notes.[34]

Gregory's interracial relationship was condemned by the jury and in a telling slippage his "crime" in loving a white woman was transformed into the rape of other white women.

In Simon's photograph, Gregory is tightly framed (plate 18). He sits at the edge of a pool table, his arms wrapped around a woman who burrows her face into his neck. His hands, open and pressed at the woman's waist, display his well-kept fingernails. Gregory looks directly back at the camera, over the woman's shoulder. His embrace is protective perhaps, or possessive. Behind the couple light reflects off a row of pool cues lined up against the wall, and in the upper left corner of the frame, a neon sign for "Miller High Life" suggests a bar. The obfuscation of the woman's face in the photograph is striking. The text identifies her as Gregory's fiancée, Vicki Kidwell, whom he dated prior to his conviction, and who presumably testified for him in court. In the photograph, however, she is not recognizable as an individual, but simply as a light-skinned woman, and as his.

There is no doubt that the lives of the wrongfully convicted were utterly transformed by the failure of a legal system that relies on faulty visual identification, and Simon's work makes these individuals visible, exposing the injustices against them. But her photographs of the innocents also obscure other innocents. For what of the victims of the crimes for which Simon's subjects were wrongfully accused?

The cases recorded in *The Innocents* present a litany of women raped. Almost every single case details an attack on a woman or young girl. And yet, they are not the subjects in this story about the law gone wrong—they are not the "innocent victims." Beyond the gruesome details of the violence recorded in these cases, their plight is not discussed by Simon or Neufeld or Scheck. How does one account for the wrongs committed against them? How does one account for the utter unspoken failure of the law on their behalf? These women are continually marked, but then relegated to invisibility and silence. A short list of attacks detailed in *The Innocents* runs as follows:

> a woman was raped in her home
> she was tied up, raped, and shot in the head
> the assailant dragged her from the road, beat her with a pipe, and raped her
> an eleven-year-old girl
> a young woman was raped
> the naked body of a woman was found
> she was raped and robbed
> a pregnant woman was raped at knifepoint
> a young woman was abducted
> a young mother was raped and repeatedly stabbed
> a young girl was abducted
> a young woman was attacked

If women raped and murdered are not the "innocents" here, are they tacitly deemed guilty? Do survivors bear the burden of these wrongful convictions?

Simon's photograph of Ronald Cotton with Jennifer Thompson is remarkable in this regard. It presents Cotton with the victim of the crime for which he was accused (the very witness who misidentified him). Cotton and Thompson forged a friendship after Cotton served ten and a half years of a life sentence and was exonerated based on DNA testing of a rape kit. Thompson understands the way visual technologies ultimately subverted her eyewitness identification, as outlined earlier, and she has become a public voice against the faults and dangers of the process. Simon's photograph of Cotton and Thompson together, and their combined testimony, help illuminate the depths to which the US legal system fails the victims of violent crime. People were wrongfully convicted for crimes that nevertheless *did occur*.

A photograph included in one of Simon's later projects, *An American Index of the Hidden and Unfamiliar* (2007), further exposes the inadequacies of the legal system. Sexual Assault Kits Awaiting DNA Analysis, Bode Technology Group, Inc., Springfield, Virginia, shows a uniformly beige-colored room, with two tables facing one another, pushed to either side (plate 19).[35] On top of each table is what appears to be a vertical light box or small refrigerator, and below them are plastic shelves holding stacks of white cartons that resemble FedEx boxes, each with a black barcode and a large red sticker. Two high stacks of the white boxes teeter somewhat precariously on the table at the right, and between the two tables, pushed against the back door of the room, sits another set of shelves stacked with boxes. Ziplock plastic bags filled with unidentifiable contents cover all of the remaining surfaces. On the left, large brown UPS cartons, apparently unpacked, are stacked high toward the ceiling, and one imagines that they had contained yet more of the white cartons with red stickers.

Simon's extended caption for the photograph tells the viewer,

> Bode Technologies is the largest private forensic DNA laboratory in the United States. It assists local, state and federal agencies in processing the large number of backlogged sexual assault evidence kits. Nationwide, backlogged sexual assault kits remain in storage, sometimes for years, before being processed for entry into the FBI Laboratory's Combined DNA Index System.
>
> A sexual assault kit, also known as a rape kit, is a sealed white box that contains physical and biological evidence collected from the victim during a medical examination. Sexual assault kits are administered by nurses to assist in identifying and prosecuting the crime's perpetrator. Forensic evidence stored in the kit can include: blood, clothing, fingernail scrapings, hair and semen. Three obstacles have prevented the effective use of rape kits in American law enforcement: the cost of collecting evidence, the cost of having the evidence analyzed, and the capability to process the increasing number of kits.
>
> It was recently estimated that there are as many as half a million sexual assault kits in the U.S. awaiting analysis. In many cases, medical examination and processing costs are the responsibility of the victim. According to RAINN, the Rape, Abuse and Incest National Network, an individual is sexually assaulted every two and a half minutes.

In Simon's photograph, the stacks of white boxes stand in for the victims of rape obscured by the misidentifications and wrongful convictions of *The Innocents*. Here Simon shows the backlog of DNA samples waiting to be processed, highlighting both the insufficiency of a system overwhelmed and the evidence that might help identify actual rapists.[36]

The spectacular crimes visually highlighted by *The Innocents* are not those of rape and murder against women but crimes of misidentification against (mostly) men. The text records the crimes of rape, but rape is demoted to the background against which the wrongfully convicted emerge. In *Sexual Assault Kits Awaiting DNA Analysis* Simon reveals the insignificance accorded to rape, as measured by the lack of resources made available to process the evidence of these crimes. On the other hand, the cases Simon documents in *The Innocents* demonstrate that heavy sentences are brought in rape and murder trials, and that rape is treated as a crime worthy of serious punishment. These cases also suggest, however, that the details don't matter much; for the police, juries, lawyers, judges, and some of the eyewitnesses, any African American man will do.

Simon focuses on dramatic cases of visual misidentification and the law gone wrong, highlighting aberrations in the US penal system. *The Innocents* asks one to query and critique a faulty legal system in which innocent people can be "thrown away" for crimes they have not committed. This is important work. But is one to believe that the US carceral system is otherwise reliable? If the system were working correctly, identifying the "right men," would women be safer? As the social justice movement groups Critical Resistance and Incite! have argued, "Prisons don't work. Despite an exponential increase in the number of men in prisons, women are not any safer and the rates of sexual assault and domestic violence have not decreased."[37] Further, the misidentifications that are central to Simon's *The Innocents* distort the overwhelming fact that victims of rape in the United States most often know their attackers. Finally, by drawing attention to failures in the penal system, *The Innocents* unwittingly upholds the logic of the system itself as otherwise sound. Simon's project does not question the legitimacy of the prison industrial complex, but one might come to such a position by following her false photographic returns.

CODA

A Glimpse Forward

Dawoud Bey's *The Birmingham Project*

How might one imagine a way forward through photographic returns? The oscillating time of the photograph not only infuses the present with a past, it also anticipates the future of another viewer. Although some of the artworks studied here block or deflect the view, such as Sally Mann's obscured battlefields or Lorna Simpson's surrogate props, others solicit viewers with a direct look. They amplify a gaze that seeks to activate viewers who occupy different presents and possible futures. Rashid Johnson, with his hair parted like Frederick Douglass, stares directly out at viewers. Deborah Luster's incarcerated subjects and Taryn Simon's exonerated subjects incite one to see beyond the circumscription of the carceral state and its legacies of racism. Weems's photographic reenactments invite one to imagine the feel of a past in a body that will move forward. The future-facing aspect of these works suggests perseverance and resistance as well as reflection and return.

A brief look at one final work brings photography's temporal fluctuations sharply into view and provides a glimpse forward from a present pervaded by a past. In *The Birmingham Project* (2012–13), Dawoud Bey looks back to the September 15, 1963, white supremacist bombing of the Sixteenth Street Baptist Church in Birmingham, Alabama, that killed four African American girls, and claimed the lives of two African American boys in its aftermath.

Working with Birmingham residents, Bey produced sixteen large-scale black-and-white paired portraits of women and girls, men and boys, staging them in the pews of Bethel Baptist Church, historically an activist congregation, and the Birmingham Museum of Art, historically a segregated institution.[1] The images pair portraits of a girl or boy the age the victim was in 1963 with portraits of a woman or man the age the child would have been if she or he had survived. Bey researched the project for several years before completing it as a commission to commemorate the fiftieth anniversary of the bombing for the Birmingham Museum of Art.

According to Bey, a photograph sent him to Birmingham. It was an image he had seen as a child in 1964, of a young survivor of the bombing, that emblazoned the terrorist attack in his memory.[2] The photograph is indeed haunting. Taken by African American photographer Frank Dandridge, and first published in *LIFE* magazine on September 27, 1963, it shows twelve-year-old Sarah Collins, younger sister of Addie Mae Collins, who was killed in the bombing, lying in a hospital bed.[3] The black-and-white image is framed somewhat askew; Collins seems to cower in the bottom right corner. Her head stands out against an expanse of white bedding. Her face is cut and bloodied, and her forehead appears blistered. She "looks" back at the photographer with eyes completely covered in white bandages, addressing later viewers with a startling, blank white gaze.

Bey's paired portraits vault the past forward and the present back. They perform, in a condensed way, the temporal movement that the other works studied in this book also engage. The doubled portraits provide an imagined before and after—one image represents a violent past and a life cut short, and the other refuses that past with a life that has persisted. In the paired portraits, both subjects look directly out at the photographer and later viewer. They ask one to bear witness to their lives and the lives they temporarily represent as surrogates.[4]

In one of the paired portraits, Mathes Manafee sits sideways in a wooden pew, but turns to look directly at the photographer, projecting an elbow into the foreshortened focal plane, toward the viewer (fig. C.1). Her arched eyebrows give her face an alert look, and her pursed lips suggest that she is on the verge of speech. Next to Manafee, Cassandra Griffin faces squarely forward, resting both elbows on the back of the pew in front of her, as if she is leaning in, toward the photographer. Her eyes are wide and open, and her mouth seems to curve naturally into a smile. Although the two portraits were made

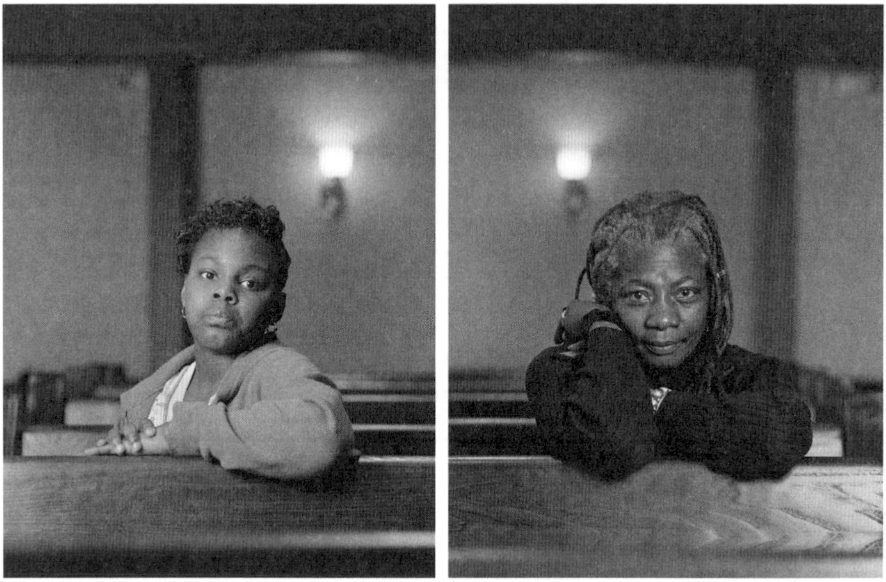

FIGURE C.1 Dawoud Bey, *Mathes Manafee and Cassandra Griffin*, 2012. Two archival pigment prints, each 40 × 32 inches. Copyright Dawoud Bey. Courtesy of Stephen Daiter Gallery, Chicago.

separately, the way they are presented together gives one the sense that Manafee and Griffin are seated next to one another in the pews of Bethel Baptist Church.

The two images refer not only to the martyred child they represent but also to one another. This child and this woman are placed in relation to each other. As Maurice Berger has said, "Despite the half-century that separates them, the paired subjects speak to intermingled histories and shared destinies: adults who helped forge a path of acceptance and stability for African-Americans; the young beneficiaries of their bravery and largess who may well do the same for future generations."[5] Griffin lived through the time of the bombing. Her life was marked by the murder of girls her age, and she had to look forward through that terror to today.

As the two images framed together resonate and rebound off each other, one finds two different modes of photographic time united. The imaginative effect of the portrait of Manafee is to freeze time and catapult a moment, as well as a martyred girl, through her stand-in, forward. The photograph of Manafee becomes a conduit through which a terrible moment on September 15, 1963, accesses the present. The portrait of Griffin marks the persistence of the photograph, symbolically stretching back to 1963 and including all of the moments between then and now. The portraits ask to be read both synchronically and diachronically, and in the dissonance between their temporal movements and effects, one senses the disruption of photography through which a past punctuates the present and also catapults one backward and forward.

In concert with Bey, the artists studied here look back to earlier moments, and importantly, to earlier images that remain in the present. Through photographic returns they activate photography's temporal oscillations. They show how images accrue new meanings as they launch new time lines. Photographs move physically as material objects (or as digital information viewed on physical platforms) as well as imaginatively through reference and deference and association. They relay and ricochet back and forth across time. A past does not stay in the past; a future bursts forward in photographs.

If the photograph is emblematic of the way a past persists in the present, it also foreshadows how fragments of the present will punctuate a future moment. The way forward may be obscured like one of Mann's marred images, but sparks flash in the darkness. The fiery perseverance of Douglass, the fragile aspirations of VanDerZee's subjects, the wary gazes of the exonerated in Simon's photographs—all invite one to consider the future from a past and present moment. They also encourage one to see how the unfinished work of racial justice, including not only the terror and trauma of violence, but also the force of resistance, will continue as well. They incite one to look back and move forward.

NOTES

Introduction

1 Darby English, "Beyond Black Representational Space," in *How to See a Work of Art in Total Darkness* (Cambridge, MA: MIT Press, 2007), 27–70.

2 In *Photographic Returns* I am interested in the way a disparate and diverse group of artists has embraced a dynamic of historical return in the early twenty-first century, a dynamic that specifically engages the temporality of photography to consider multiple moments of racial injustice that range across the nineteenth and twentieth centuries. Other recent studies of race and visual culture that draw on a dynamic of return tend to focus specifically on slavery and its haunting afterimages. Huey Copeland's *Bound to Appear*, for example, focuses on four African American artists—Glenn Ligon, Renée Green, Lorna Simpson, and Fred Wilson—who produced large-scale installation works about slavery between 1991 and 1993. In the work of these artists Copeland identifies a shared practice and politics of rejecting figuration and turning to objects as substitutes for absent bodies in order to give form to "the political-ontological position of black subjectivity" (10). Huey Copeland, *Bound to Appear: Art, Slavery, and the Site of Blackness in Multicultural America* (Chicago, IL: University of Chicago Press, 2013). For another discussion of slavery, visual culture, and "returns," see Huey Copeland and Krista Thompson, "Perpetual Returns: New World Slavery and the Matter of the Visual," *Representations* 113 (winter 2011): 1–15. Kimberly Juanita Brown studies the afterimage of slavery's memory in black women's literary and visual representations, attending to the dynamic of repetition through which slavery is negotiated in the contemporary moment. Kimberly Juanita Brown, *The Repeating Body: Slavery's Visual Resonance in the Contemporary* (Durham, NC: Duke University Press, 2015). Janet Neary shows how contemporary artists adopt the formal strategies of nineteenth-century slave narratives to reveal a strategy of visual resistance that was already present in those narratives. Janet Neary, *Fugitive Testimony: On the Visual Logic of Slave Narratives* (New York: Fordham University Press, 2016). Cheryl Finley traces the afterlife of the slave ship icon in the work of twentieth-century black artists and writers. Cheryl Finley, *Committed to Memory: The Art of the Slave Ship Icon* (Princeton, NJ: Princeton University Press, 2018).

3 See, for example, Penelope Umbrico's *Suns from Sunsets from Flickr* (2006–), penelopeumbrico.net/index.php/project/suns/, accessed February 2, 2017. Kate Palmer Albers discusses this project and others in "Abundant Images and the Collective Sublime," *Exposure* 46, no. 2 (fall 2013): 4–14. In her own discussion of photography and time in the wake of the digital revolution of the last twenty-five years, Sarah Greenough proposes that many artists "have intensely scrutinized photography itself, examining what it is conceptually, ontologically, and physically." Sarah Greenough, "The Memory of Time: Introduction," in *The Memory of Time: Contemporary Photographs at the National Gallery of Art*, Sarah Greenough and Andrea Nelson, with Sarah Kennel, Diane Waggoner, and Leslie J. Ureña (Washington, DC: National Gallery of Art, 2015), 2.

4 John Stauffer, Zoe Trodd, and Celeste-Marie Bernier, *Picturing Frederick Douglass: An Illustrated Biography of the Nineteenth Century's Most Photographed American* (New York: Liveright/W. W. Norton, 2015), ix.

5 Ben Goldberger, Paul Moakley and Kira Pollack, TIME Inc., 100 Photos, The Most Influential Images of All Time, 100photos.time.com, accessed February 3, 2017.

6 Ben Goldberger, Paul Moakley, and Kira Pollack, TIME Inc., 100 Photos, The Most Influential Images of All Time, http://100photos.time.com/about, accessed February 3, 2017.

7 My thinking along these lines is influenced by the critical method Elizabeth Freeman has called "erotohistoriography." For Freeman, erotohistoriography is not about the desire for a past, but about finding a past in a hybrid present. Elizabeth Freeman, *Time Binds: Queer Temporalities, Queer Histories* (Durham, NC: Duke University Press, 2010), 95. In her efforts to narrate "counter-histories of slavery" and to write "a history of the present," Saidiya Hartman also "strives to illuminate the intimacy of our experience with the lives of the dead, to write our now as it is interrupted by this past." Saidiya Hartman, "Venus in Two Acts," *Small Axe* 26 (June 2008): 4. Christina Sharpe's "wake work," which she deems "a method of encountering a past that is not past," is also resonant here. Christina Sharpe, *In the Wake: On Blackness and Being* (Durham, NC: Duke University Press, 2016), 13. I am also indebted to the impulse that informs what Leigh Raiford has described as "critical black memory," which "implies the negotiation, the *use* of history for the present." Leigh Raiford, *Imprisoned in a Luminous Glare: Photography and the African American Freedom Struggle* (Chapel Hill: University of North Carolina Press, 2011), 63.

8 Roland Barthes, *Camera Lucida: Reflections on Photography*, trans. Richard Howard (1980; repr., New York: Hill and Wang, 1981), 115.

9 As Mary Ann Doane has argued, "The concept of the index . . . seems to acknowledge the invasion of semiotic systems by the real." Mary Ann Doane, *The Emergence of Cinematic Time: Modernity, Contingency, the Archive* (Cambridge, MA: Harvard University Press, 2002), 70. For a powerful defense of the photograph as an inadequate but nevertheless necessary form of historical evidence, see Georges

Didi-Huberman, *Images in Spite of All: Four Photographs from Auschwitz*, trans. Shane B. Lillis (Chicago, IL: University of Chicago Press, 2008).

10 Michelle Alexander, *The New Jim Crow: Mass Incarceration in the Age of Colorblindness*, rev. ed. (New York: The New Press, 2011).

11 Elizabeth Edwards, "Photography and the Material Performance of the Past," *History and Theory* 48, no. 4 (December 2009): 150.

12 For an analysis of the transformation of photographic meaning as images move from one discursive location to another, see Rosalind Krauss, "Photography's Discursive Spaces: Landscape/View," *Art Journal* 42, no. 4 (winter 1982): 311–19.

13 The photographic returns studied here have noted precedents. Mark Klett's rephotographic survey project (1977–79) is a salient example in which he and a team of collaborators rephotographed scenes from nineteenth-century survey photography of the American West. Following in the footsteps of Timothy O'Sullivan and William Henry Jackson, they worked to reproduce the views of their predecessors, placing cameras in precise positions and re-creating the same lighting effects over a hundred years later. One might also look to Joel Sternfeld's *On This Site: Landscape in Memorium* (1996) for another kind of return, in this case to sites of violent crime that did not always figure photographically. Some of the places Sternfeld photographs are associated with infamous photographs, such as the Lorraine Motel in Memphis, Tennessee, now the National Civil Rights Museum, where Dr. Martin Luther King Jr. was assassinated, but in many cases his images and text seek to make violence visible in seemingly obscure and innocuous places.

14 Barthes, *Camera Lucida*, 93.

15 Barthes, *Camera Lucida*, 93.

16 Barthes, *Camera Lucida*, 93–94. It is no accident, perhaps, that Barthes's ruminations on photography's disruptive temporality in *Camera Lucida* are permeated by grief at his mother's death. For, as Dana Luciano has argued, grief might be said to resist the time of modern progress. According to Luciano, "The radical reorganization that we understand as the advent of modernity constructed a new vision of time as linear, ordered, progressive, and teleological." Concurrent with the new understandings of time as progressive and linear, however, a culture of grief developed in the United States that resisted the forward momentum of modern time. "The pronounced nineteenth-century attention to grief and mourning . . . responds to anxiety over the new shape of time by insisting that emotional attachment had its own pace—a slower and essentially nonlinear relation to the value of human existence that defended it against the increasingly rapid pace of progress." Dana Luciano, *Arranging Grief: Sacred Time and the Body in Nineteenth-Century America* (New York: New York University Press, 2007), 2.

17 Walter Benjamin, "The Work of Art in the Age of Its Technological Reproducibility," second version, in *Walter Benjamin: Selected Writings*, vol. 3, *1935–1938*,

ed. Howard Eiland and Michael W. Jennings, trans. Edmund Jephcott, Howard Eiland, et al. (Cambridge, MA: Belknap of Harvard University Press, 2002), 117.

18 According to Michael S. Roth, "The dialectical conception of history as embodied duration—the notion that every historical moment contains both layers of the past and seeds of the future—was the field in which photography was inserted in the mid nineteenth century. However, photography's ability to break a 'moment' down into the instantaneous radically disturbs the easy immanence associated with historical narratives that rely on dialectical unfolding." Michael S. Roth, "Photographic Ambivalence and Historical Consciousness," *History and Theory* 48, no. 4 (December 2009): 83.

19 Walter Benjamin, "On the Concept of History," in *Walter Benjamin: Selected Writings*, vol. 4, *1938–1940*, ed. Howard Eiland and Michael W. Jennings, trans. Edmund Jephcott et al. (Cambridge, MA: Belknap of Harvard University Press, 2003), 396.

20 Eduardo Cadava, *Words of Light: Theses on the Photography of History* (Princeton, NJ: Princeton University Press, 1997), 61; emphasis mine.

21 As Cadava has argued, "Benjamin conceives of history in the language of photography." Cadava, *Words of Light*, 3.

22 Benjamin, "On the Concept of History," 390.

23 As Vanessa R. Schwartz proposes, "Benjamin believed that history was a constellation of past and present through which the present would find an image of itself and thus see more clearly." Vanessa R. Schwartz, "Walter Benjamin for Historians," *American Historical Review* 106, no. 5 (December 2001): 1724.

24 Benjamin, "On the Concept of History," 397.

25 See my discussion of the malleability of photographic evidence in "The Evidence of Lynching Photographs," in *Lynching Photographs*, by Dora Apel and Shawn Michelle Smith (Berkeley: University of California Press, 2007), 10–41. In her definition of the "event of photography," Ariella Azoulay includes the potentially "infinite series of encounters" in which, after they are produced (if they are produced), photographs may be seen by distant, unknown viewers at unpredictable future moments. Ariella Azoulay, *Civil Imagination: A Political Ontology of Photography*, trans. Louise Bethlehem (2010; repr., London: Verso, 2015), 23, 26.

26 Walter Benjamin, "Paralipomena to 'On the Concept of History,'" in Eiland and Jennings, ed., *Walter Benjamin: Selected Writings*, vol. 4, 405.

27 Shawn Michelle Smith, *Photography on the Color Line: W. E. B. Du Bois, Race, and Visual Culture* (Durham, NC: Duke University Press, 2004). Ann Cvetkovich and Wendy W. Walters have explored the ways artists and writers challenge official archives that erase, silence, and subordinate the lives of black and lesbian and gay people. Cvetkovich studies alternative archives made by lesbian artists as practices of fantasy made material in *An Archive of Feelings: Trauma, Sexuality, and Lesbian Public Cultures* (Durham, NC: Duke University Press, 2003), and Walters examines how contemporary African diasporic writers revisit the official data of

the archive to propose aspirational imaginings in *Archives of the Black Atlantic: Reading between Literature and History* (New York: Routledge, 2013).

28 Ann Laura Stoler, *Along the Archival Grain: Epistemic Anxieties and Colonial Common Sense* (Princeton, NJ: Princeton University Press, 2010). Elizabeth Edwards, *Raw Histories: Photographs, Anthropology and Museums* (Oxford: Berg, 2001).

29 Edwards, *Raw Histories*, 4.

30 Edwards, *Raw Histories*, 5. As Roland Barthes proclaimed, "The Photograph is pure contingency and can be nothing else." Barthes, *Camera Lucida*, 28.

31 Edwards has more recently studied the ways in which the material practices of the archive seek to contain and control photographic meaning through the directives of the label, the mount, and the archival box. Edwards, "Photography and the Material Performance of the Past," 130–50. For a reading of the latent meanings that reside in the colonial photographic archive, see Gabrielle Moser, "Developing Historical Negatives: The Colonial Photographic Archive as Optical Unconscious," in *Photography and the Optical Unconscious*, ed. Shawn Michelle Smith and Sharon Sliwinski (Durham, NC: Duke University Press, 2017), 229–63.

32 Allan Sekula, "The Body and the Archive," *October* 39 (winter 1986): 3–64; and Allan Sekula, *Photography Against the Grain: Essays and Photo Works, 1973–1983* (Halifax, NS: Nova Scotia College of Art and Design, 1984); Martha Rosler, *Martha Rosler, 3 Works: 1. The Restoration of High Culture in Chile (1972); 2. The Bowery in Two Inadequate Descriptive Systems (1974); 3. in, around, and afterthoughts (on documentary photography) (1981)* (Halifax, NS: Nova Scotia College of Art and Design, 2006); John Tagg, *The Burden of Representation: Essays on Photographies and Histories* (Minneapolis: University of Minnesota Press, 1988).

33 Ulrich Baer, *Spectral Evidence: The Photography of Trauma* (Cambridge, MA: MIT Press, 2002). Margaret Iversen uses the language of "exposure" to draw an analogy between the psychic trace of trauma and the indexical trace of the photograph. Margaret Iversen, "Exposure," in *Photography, Trace, and Trauma* (Chicago, IL: University of Chicago Press, 2017), 1–16.

34 According to Cathy Caruth, trauma is characterized by its "unassimilated nature—the way it was precisely *not known* in the first instance." Cathy Caruth, *Unclaimed Experience: Trauma, Narrative, History* (Baltimore, MD: Johns Hopkins University Press, 1996), 4.

35 For Barthes, the photograph is "a bizarre *medium*," and once again, "a temporal hallucination." Barthes, *Camera Lucida*, 115.

36 Sigmund Freud, "Mourning and Melancholia," in *The Standard Edition of the Complete Psychological Works of Sigmund Freud*, vol. 14, *1914–1916*, trans. James Strachey (1917; repr., London: Hogarth Press, 1957), 243–58. David L. Eng and David Kazanjian, "Introduction: Mourning Remains," in *Loss: The Politics of Mourning*, ed. David L. Eng and David Kazanjian (Berkeley: University of California Press, 2003), 3–4. For other discussions of photography and melancholia, see Sharon Sliwinski, "On Photographic Violence," *Photography and Culture* 2,

no. 3 (November 2009): 303–16, especially 309–10; José Esteban Muñoz, "Photographies of Mourning: Melancholia and Ambivalence in VanDerZee, Mapplethorpe, and *Looking for Langston*," in *Disidentifications: Queers of Color and the Performance of Politics* (Minneapolis: University of Minnesota Press, 1999), 57–74; Shawn Michelle Smith, "Photography between Desire and Grief: Roland Barthes and F. Holland Day," in *Feeling Photography*, ed. Elspeth H. Brown and Thy Phu (Durham, NC: Duke University Press, 2014), 29–46.

37 Walter Benjamin, "Little History of Photography," in *Walter Benjamin: Selected Writings*, vol. 2, part 2, *1931–1934*, trans. Rodney Livingstone, ed. Michael W. Jennings, Howard Eiland, and Gary Smith (Cambridge, MA: Belknap, 1999), 510. Benjamin outlines a radical temporal nonlinearity in his writing on history and the futurity of the photograph's "spark of contingency," and recently scholars have begun to understand such disruptions of linear time as queer. As Elizabeth Freeman proposes, "many queer historiographers . . . take their cue from Walter Benjamin": "Benjamin's 'Theses on the Philosophy of History' powerfully critiques the notion of time as a flat plane on which events march forward in sequence. It suggests a potentially queer vision of how time wrinkles and folds as some minor feature of our own sexually impoverished present suddenly meets up with a richer past, or as the materials of a failed and forgotten project of the past find their uses now, in a future unimaginable in their time." Elizabeth Freeman, "Introduction," *GLQ: A Journal of Lesbian and Gay Studies* 13, nos. 2–3 (2007): 163. Achille Mbembe offers another model of time as multiple and mixed with his theory of "entanglement." According to Mbembe the "time of entanglement" in the postcolony "is not a series but an *interlocking* of presents, pasts, and futures that retain their depths of other presents, pasts, and futures, each age bearing, altering, and maintaining the previous ones." Achille Mbembe, "Introduction: Time on the Move," in *On the Postcolony* (Berkeley: University of California Press, 2001), 16.

38 Baer, *Spectral Evidence*, 181. As Baer has also proposed, "Every photograph is addressed to a beyond that remains undefined" (182).

Chapter 1

1 Roland Barthes, *Camera Lucida: Reflections on Photography*, trans. Richard Howard (1980; repr., New York: Hill and Wang, 1981), 12.

2 Johnson made a series of portraits of homeless men called *Seeing in the Dark* using the Van Dyke process. Amy M. Mooney discusses this work in her entry on Rashid Johnson in *Bulletin of the Detroit Institute of Arts* 86, no. 1/4 (2012): 58–59.

3 Huey Copeland, "Rashid Johnson: Museum of Contemporary Art, Chicago," *Artforum* 50, no. 10 (summer 2012): 303.

4 W. E. B. Du Bois, *The Souls of Black Folk* (1903), intro. by John Edgar Wideman (New York: Vintage/Library of America, 1990), 8.

5 Copeland, "Rashid Johnson," 302.

6 Julie Rodrigues Widholm, "The Moment of Creation," in *Rashid Johnson: Message to Our Folks* (Chicago, IL: Museum of Contemporary Art, Chicago, 2012), 38.

7 As Naomi Beckwith has proposed, Johnson's mixing of images and historical references "expresses the contemporary condition in which multiple possibilities and references make up the self." Naomi Beckwith, "A Post-Black-Power Child: Rashid Johnson's Historical References Enact a Complex Historical Reckoning," *Flash Art* 46, no. 290 (May/June 2013): 131.

8 See Laura Wexler, "'A More Perfect Likeness': Frederick Douglass and the Image of the Nation," 20, 25, and Ginger Hill, "'Rightly Viewed': Theorizations of Self in Frederick Douglass's Lectures on Pictures," 43, in *Pictures and Progress: Early Photography and the Making of African American Identity*, ed. Maurice O. Wallace and Shawn Michelle Smith (Durham, NC: Duke University Press, 2012).

9 Frederick Douglass, "Pictures and Progress: An Address Delivered in Boston, Massachusetts, on 3 December 1861," in *The Frederick Douglass Papers: Series One, Speeches, Debates, and Interviews*, ed. John W. Blassingame (New Haven, CT: Yale University Press, 1985), 3:452–53.

10 Wexler, "'A More Perfect Likeness,'" 21.

11 Frederick Douglass, "Pictures and Progress" (1865), Frederick Douglass Papers at the Library of Congress: Speech, Article, and Book File, ms. pg. 8, American Memory, Library of Congress Manuscript Division, available online at https://www.loc.gov/item/mfd.28009/.

12 Marcy Dinius, "Seeing a Slave as a Man: Frederick Douglass, Racial Progress, and Daguerreian Portraiture," in *The Camera and the Press: American Visual and Print Culture in the Age of the Daguerreotype* (Philadelphia: University of Pennsylvania Press, 2012), 215.

13 Celeste-Marie Bernier, "'The Face of a Fugitive Slave': Representing and Reimagining Frederick Douglass in Popular Illustrations, Fine Art Portraiture and Daguerreotypes," in *Political Memory*, ed. Magnus Brechtken (Göttingen, Germany: Vandenhoeck and Ruprecht, 2012), 27. Bernier is interested in the ways Douglass used photography to contest the conflation of African American individuals into representative types in abolitionist propaganda. See Bernier, "'The Face of a Fugitive Slave,'" especially 12–13; and Celeste-Marie Bernier, "A 'Typical Negro' or a 'Work of Art'? The 'Inner' via the 'Outer Man' in Frederick Douglass's Manuscripts and Daguerreotypes," *Slavery and Abolition* 33, no. 2 (June 2012): 287–303.

14 Celeste-Marie Bernier, "From Fugitive Slave to Fugitive Image: Nineteenth-Century African American Portrait Frontispieces and Interior Illustrations and the Case of Frederick Douglass," unpublished manuscript. I am grateful to Bernier for sharing this manuscript with me.

15 Stephen M. Best, *The Fugitive's Properties: Law and the Poetics of Possession* (Chicago, IL: University of Chicago Press, 2004), 9.

16 Cheryl I. Harris, "Whiteness as Property," *Harvard Law Review* 106, no. 8 (June 1993): 1720.

17 Best, *Fugitive's Properties*, 14; emphasis mine.

18 Best, *Fugitive's Properties*, 14. In his discussion of possessive individualism in seventeenth-century political thought, C. B. Macpherson argues, "Although the individual cannot alienate the whole of his property in his own person, he may alienate his capacity to labour." C. B. Macpherson, *The Political Theory of Possessive Individualism* (Oxford: Oxford University Press, 1962), 264.

19 Douglass, "Pictures and Progress" (1865), Frederick Douglass Papers, ms. pg. 12.

20 Douglass, "Pictures and Progress" (1865), Frederick Douglass Papers, ms. pg. 18.

21 Douglass's model of personhood "hinges," at least in part, "on accepting the codification of personhood as property," in Alexander G. Weheliye's words. Alexander G. Weheliye, *Habeas Viscus: Racializing Assemblages, Biopolitics, and Black Feminist Theories of the Human* (Durham, NC: Duke University Press, 2014), 77.

22 Barthes, *Camera Lucida*, 14, 15.

23 Wexler, "'A More Perfect Likeness,'" 30–31.

24 As Maurice O. Wallace and I have argued, Douglass's thoughts about photography and objectification anticipate W. E. B. Du Bois's conception of double consciousness. However, what is striking about Douglass's take on such visual objectification is his optimism. For Douglass, such objectification and double vision is linked to social progress. Maurice O. Wallace and Shawn Michelle Smith, "Introduction: Pictures and Progress," in *Pictures and Progress: Early Photography and the Making of African American Identity*, ed. Maurice O. Wallace and Shawn Michelle Smith (Durham, NC: Duke University Press, 2012), 8.

25 As Colin L. Westerbeck outlines, Douglass made speaking tours throughout Ohio from 1843 to 1852. In 1847 he traveled with William Lloyd Garrison, but by the end of the year he had begun to part ways with Garrison's strictly nonviolent Abolitionism. Colin L. Westerbeck, "Frederick Douglass Chooses His Moment," *Museum Studies* 24, no. 2 (1999): 155–61.

26 Bernier, "'A Typical Negro,'" 295.

27 Alan Trachtenberg, "Illustrious Americans," in *Reading American Photographs: Images as History, Mathew Brady to Walker Evans* (New York: Hill and Wang, 1989), 21–70.

28 Hill, "'Rightly Viewed,'" 53.

29 Hill, "'Rightly Viewed,'" 46.

30 Matthew Frye Jacobson, *Whiteness of a Different Color: European Immigrants and the Alchemy of Race* (Cambridge, MA: Harvard University Press, 1998), 26. C. B. Macpherson proposes that what makes a man human is "freedom from dependence on the wills of others," and following from that freedom it is understood that "the individual is essentially the proprietor of his own person and capacities, for which he owes nothing to society." Macpherson, *Political Theory of Possessive Individualism*, 263. What Jacobson shows, in conversation with other scholars, is

that such self-possession was racialized by and beyond the institution of slavery. Cheryl Harris demonstrates how self-possession became a status for whites only in light of the dehumanization and commodification of slavery. She argues that whiteness "became a line of protection and demarcation from the potential threat of commodification." "Slavery as a system of property facilitated the merger of white identity and property. Because the system of slavery was contingent on and conflated with racial identity, it became crucial to be 'white,' to be identified as white, to have the property of being white. Whiteness was the characteristic, the attribute, the property of free human beings." Harris, "Whiteness as Property," 1721. As Weheliye has argued, "The tabula rasa of whiteness—which all groups but blacks can access—serves as the prerequisite for the law's magical transubstantiation of a thing to be possessed into a property-owning subject." Weheliye, *Habeas Viscus*, 78.

31 John Stauffer, Zoe Trodd, and Celeste-Marie Bernier, *Picturing Frederick Douglass: An Illustrated Biography of the Nineteenth Century's Most Photographed American* (New York: Liveright/W. W. Norton, 2015). The authors have identified 160 distinct photographs of Douglass ("Introduction," ix).

32 Hill, "'Rightly Viewed,'" 48–49.

33 Wexler, "'A More Perfect Likeness,'" 36.

34 Douglass, "Lecture on Pictures" [title varies], Frederick Douglass Papers at the Library of Congress: Speech, Article, and Book File, ms. pg. 12, American Memory, Library of Congress Manuscript Division, available online at https://www.loc.gov/item/mfd.22004/.

35 Sarah Blackwood, "Fugitive Obscura: Runaway Slave Portraiture and Early Photographic Technology," *American Literature* 81, no. 1 (March 2009): 97.

36 Frederick Douglass, "A Tribute to the Negro," *North Star*, April 7, 1849, 2, quoted in Blackwood, "Fugitive Obscura," 97; Bernier, "'The Face of a Fugitive Slave,'" 11; and Dinius, "Seeing a Slave as a Man," 223.

37 Westerbeck, "Frederick Douglass," 156.

38 Dinius, "Seeing a Slave as a Man," 221–32. I suggest that W. E. B. Du Bois employed a similar visual strategy to undermine the assumptions of eugenicists with his paired portraits of African Americans for the 1900 Paris Exposition. Shawn Michelle Smith, *Photography on the Color Line: W. E. B. Du Bois, Race, and Visual Culture* (Durham, NC: Duke University Press, 2004), especially chapter 2, "The Art of Scientific Propaganda," 43–76.

39 As Henry Louis Gates, Jr., has argued, with his photographic portraits, Douglass was "attempting both to *display and displace*" other representations. Henry Louis Gates, Jr., "Frederick Douglass's Camera Obscura: Representing the Anti-slave 'Clothed and in Their Own Form,'" *Critical Inquiry* 42, no. 1 (autumn 2015): 46. For more on African American uses of portraiture to contest racist representations, see Henry Louis Gates, Jr., "The Face and Voice of Blackness," in *Facing History: The Black Image in American Art, 1710–1940*, by Guy C. McElroy (San

Francisco, CA: Bedford Arts, 1990); Gwendolyn DuBois Shaw, with contributions by Emily K. Shubert, *Portraits of a People: Picturing African Americans in the Nineteenth Century* (Seattle: University of Washington Press, 2006); Deborah Willis, *Let Your Motto Be Resistance* (Washington, DC: Smithsonian Institution, 2007).

40 Douglass, "Pictures and Progress: An Address," 455.

41 Douglass, "Pictures and Progress: An Address," 458.

42 As Orlando Patterson has argued in defining the social death of slavery: "Slaves differed from other human beings in that they were not allowed freely to integrate the experience of their ancestors into their lives, to inform their understanding of social reality with the inherited meanings of their natural forebears, or to anchor the living present in any conscious community or memory." Orlando Patterson, *Slavery and Social Death: A Comparative Study* (Cambridge, MA: Harvard University Press, 1982), 5.

43 Douglass, "Pictures and Progress" (1865), Frederick Douglass Papers, ms. pg. 1.

44 Frederick Douglass, "The Age of Pictures" in Douglass, "Lecture on Pictures" [title varies], Frederick Douglass Papers at the Library of Congress: Speech, Article, and Book File, ms. pg. 35, American Memory, Library of Congress Manuscript Division, available online at https://www.loc.gov/item/mfd.22004/.

45 John Stauffer, "Frederick Douglass and the Aesthetics of Freedom," *Raritan* 25, no. 1 (summer 2005): 126–27.

46 Stauffer, "Frederick Douglass," 127.

47 Stauffer, "Frederick Douglass," 131.

48 Stauffer, "Frederick Douglass," 131.

49 Douglass titled part of his "Lecture on Pictures" "The Age of Pictures," and he began that section by stating, "This may be termed as an age of pictures." Frederick Douglass, "The Age of Pictures" in Douglass, "Lecture on Pictures" [title varies], Frederick Douglass Papers at the Library of Congress: Speech, Article, and Book File, ms. pg. 30, American Memory, Library of Congress Manuscript Division, available online at https://www.loc.gov/item/mfd.22004/.

50 Ulrich Baer, *Spectral Evidence: The Photography of Trauma* (Cambridge: MIT Press, 2002), 24, 181.

51 Walter Benjamin, "Little History of Photography," in *Walter Benjamin: Selected Writings*, vol. 2, part 2, *1931–1934*, ed. Michael W. Jennings, Howard Eiland, and Gary Smith, trans. Rodney Livingstone et al. (Cambridge, MA: Belknap of Harvard University Press, 1999), 510.

52 Repetition with a difference is one of the modes of signifyin(g) outlined by Henry Louis Gates, Jr., in *The Signifying Monkey: A Theory of Afro-American Literary Criticism* (New York: Oxford University Press, 1988). In an interview with Christopher Stackhouse, Johnson notes an intergenerational struggle that I would argue is apparent in works such as *Self Portrait with My Hair Parted Like Frederick Douglass* and *The New Negro Escapist Social and Athletic Club (Emmett).* According to Johnson, "It is not clear how to pay homage to them [those of the

civil rights generation] without sacrificing the freedoms and opportunities that their efforts gave us." Or, as Stackhouse responds, "How are we supposed to culturally address the past, and still move forward?" Christopher Stackhouse, "Rashid Johnson," interview, *Art in America*, April 4, 2012, http://www.artinamericamagazine.com/news-features/magazine/rashid-johnson/. I am especially interested in Johnson's photographic work and the way it draws out the temporal disruption of photography that Douglass anticipated. Jared C. Richardson finds a similar temporal movement in Johnson's sculptural and installation work. According to Richardson, "By invoking the history of black renaissance men, gentleman scholars, and entertainers, Johnson's work plays with various brands of black masculinity and homosociality that simultaneously straddle the past and future. By doing so, his art not only enacts a racialized temporality, but it also chips away at monolithic notions of black masculinity by fabricating contradictory amalgams of race, class, and gender." Jared C. Richardson, "Br(others) Only: Rashid Johnson, Class, and the Fraternal Orders of Afrofuturism" (master's thesis, The University of Texas at Austin, 2012), 6–7.

53 The photograph might be considered both archive and repertoire in Diana Taylor's terms, as it represents both "the *archive* of supposedly enduring materials" and "the so-called ephemeral *repertoire* of embodied practice/knowledge." Diana Taylor, *The Archive and the Repertoire: Performing Cultural Memory in the Americas* (Durham, NC: Duke University Press, 2003), 19.

54 Rebecca Schneider, *Performing Remains: Art and War in Times of Theatrical Reenactment* (London: Routledge, 2011), 141.

Chapter 2

1 For a detailed consideration of Gardner's work, see Kirk Savage, "The Unknowable Dead: The Civil War and the Origins of Modern Commemoration," in *The Civil War in Art and Memory*, ed. Kirk Savage, Studies in the History of Art (Washington, DC: National Gallery of Art, 2016).

2 William A. Frassanito, *Antietam: The Photographic Legacy of America's Bloodiest Day* (New York: Charles Scribner's Sons, 1978), 17.

3 Richard Slotkin, *The Long Road to Antietam: How the Civil War Became a Revolution* (New York: Liveright/Norton, 2012), 395.

4 As Sarah Greenough notes, Massachusetts governor John A. Andrews began to recruit African American soldiers for the 54th Massachusetts Volunteer Regiment almost immediately after President Lincoln signed the Emancipation Proclamation on January 1, 1863. Sarah Greenough, "Seeing What Ought to Be: Photography and the 54th Massachusetts Regiment," in *Tell It with Pride: The 54th Massachusetts Regiment and Augustus Saint-Gaudens' Shaw Memorial*, Sarah Greenough and Nancy K. Anderson, with Lindsay Harris and Renée Ater (Washington, DC: National Gallery of Art, 2013), 3.

5 Slotkin, *Long Road to Antietam*, 395.

6 Slotkin, *Long Road to Antietam*, 364–66.

7 Abraham Lincoln quoted in Slotkin, *Long Road to Antietam*, 364.

8 Anne Wilkes Tucker, "Living Memory," in *Sally Mann: The Flesh and The Spirit*, by John B. Ravenal (Richmond: Virginia Museum of Fine Arts, 2010), 175.

9 Mann went to Antietam asking this question: "Do these fields, upon which unspeakable carnage occurred, where unknowable numbers of bodies are buried, bear witness in some way?" For Mann, they do, or at least she is able to see them in this way. But I am interested in how her photographs point to the impossibility of retrieving that testimony today. Sally Mann, "Bearing Witness," in *Hold Still: A Memoir with Photographs* (New York: Little, Brown and Company, 2015), 411.

10 Ulrich Baer, *Spectral Evidence: The Photography of Trauma* (Cambridge, MA: MIT Press, 2002), 71. Much of my reading of Mann's Antietam photographs is inspired by Baer's interpretation of Dirk Reinartz and Mikael Levin's photographs of Holocaust sites made in the 1990s. See chapter 2, "To Give Memory a Place: Contemporary Holocaust Photography and the Landscape Tradition," in Baer, *Spectral Evidence*, 61–86.

As John Ravenal has written about *Last Measure*, an exhibition of Mann's Civil War battlefield photographs (2001–2), "Here there are no visible figures, but the landscape seems imbued with their presence." See John B. Ravenal, "Sally Mann: The Flesh and The Spirit," in *Sally Mann: The Flesh and The Spirit* (Richmond: Virginia Museum of Fine Arts, 2010), 6.

11 As Mann notes, the collodion wet-plate process bears added symbolic importance for her battlefield photographs because collodion was used to bind wounds during the Civil War. Sally Mann, "Collodion Process," Art 21, November 2001, http://www.art21.org/texts/sally-mann/interview-sally-mann-collodion-process, accessed April 25, 2016.

12 According to Anne Wilkes Tucker, "Mann embraces certain flaws for the way they disrupt a photograph's clear narrative depiction." See Tucker, "Living Memory," 175.

13 For a discussion of the opacity and surface of the photograph, see James Elkins, "Selenite, Ice, Salt," in *What Photography Is* (New York: Routledge, 2012), 16–44, especially 20 and 26.

14 Bob Zeller, *The Blue and the Gray in Black and White: A History of Civil War Photography* (Westport, CT: Praeger, 2005), 71–73.

15 Frassanito, *Antietam*, 17. As Bob Zeller clarifies, "The photographs of the dead of Antietam were the first American images of the carnage of war, but not the first in history" (Zeller, *Blue and the Gray*, 80).

16 Zeller, *Blue and the Gray*, 80.

17 Frassanito, *Antietam*, 17, 286.

18 John M. Harris, "'Truthful as a Record of Heaven': The Battle of Antietam and the Birth of Photojournalism," *Southern Cultures* 19, no. 3 (fall 2013): 89. At the time, Gardner was still working for Mathew Brady, and therefore the engravings after Gardner's photographs that ran in *Harper's* are called "Brady's."

19 Harris, "'Truthful,'" 80.

20 "Brady's Photographs: Pictures of the Dead at Antietam," *New York Times*, October 20, 1862, accessed online December 20, 2013.

21 Frassanito, *Antietam*, 131.

22 Frassanito, *Antietam*, 133.

23 According to William A. Frassanito, this is a "civilian carriage probably belonging to one of the tourists in the throngs who flocked to the battlefield as soon as it was safe enough to witness the site of the fighting" (Frassanito, *Antietam*, 131).

24 Drew Gilpin Faust, *This Republic of Suffering: Death and the American Civil War* (New York: Vintage, 2008), 6–11.

25 Drew Gilpin Faust discusses what were understood to be the dehumanizing aspects of mass burials in chapter 3, "Burying," in Faust, *This Republic of Suffering*, 61–101.

26 Faust, *This Republic of Suffering*, 11.

27 Anthony W. Lee, "The Image of War," in *On Alexander Gardner's* Photographic Sketch Book *of the Civil War*, by Anthony W. Lee and Elizabeth Young (Berkeley: University of California Press, 2007), 37.

28 Lee, "Image of War," 26, 29.

29 Quoted in Lee, "Image of War," 26.

30 After trying for years to obtain permission to photograph at the "Body Farm," in 2001 Mann was invited by Kathy Ryan to photograph the facility on assignment for the *New York Times Magazine*. Mann, *Hold Still*, 420.

31 Sarah Boxer, "Slogging through the Valley of the Shutter of Death," *New York Times*, July 23, 2004, accessed online November 6, 2013.

32 In the United States the legal definition of "privacy" was founded in a problem of photography, as Sarah Parsons has shown. At issue in the article Samuel Warren and Louis Brandeis published in 1890 in the *Harvard Law Review*, titled "The Right to Privacy," were photographs surreptitiously made of singer and actress Marion Manola performing skits cross-dressed and showing her legs in tights. The actress claimed that circulation of the images made without her permission would violate her right to privacy, even though they were taken in her place of public performance, not her home. The court determined for the plaintiff, and newspaper accounts of the case suggested that distribution of the scandalous photographs would be harmful to the performer's young daughter. Sarah Parsons, "Privacy, Photography, and the Art Defense," in *Revealing Privacy: Debating the Understandings of Privacy*, ed. Margherita Carucci (Bern, Switzerland: Peter Lang, 2012), 105–18.

33 Faust, *This Republic of Suffering*, 161, 135.

34 John B. Ravenal, "Matter Lent," in *Sally Mann: The Flesh and The Spirit* (Richmond: Virginia Museum of Fine Arts, 2010), 70.

35 Actually, this liquid-looking effect was produced by "furiously churning maggots" blurred in Mann's six-second exposure. Mann, *Hold Still*, 427.

36 Rebecca Schneider, *Performing Remains: Art and War in Times of Theatrical Reenactment* (London: Routledge, 2011), 100–101.

37 Thomas Keenan and Eyal Weizman, *Mengele's Skull: The Advent of a Forensic Aesthetics* (Berlin: Sternberg Press, 2012), 20.

38 Mary Roach, *Stiff: The Curious Lives of Human Cadavers* (New York: W. W. Norton, 2003), 62.

39 Roach, *Stiff*, 64 and 68.

40 Roach, *Stiff*, 70.

41 Roach, *Stiff*, 64.

42 Roach, *Stiff*, 71.

43 Mark M. Smith, "When Seeing Makes Scents," *American Art* 24, no. 3 (fall 2010): 12–14.

44 On the sound of the photograph, see Fred Moten, *In the Break: The Aesthetics of the Black Radical Tradition* (Minneapolis: University of Minnesota Press, 2003); and Tina M. Campt, *Listening to Images* (Durham, NC: Duke University Press, 2017). On the touch and feel of the photograph, see Carol Mavor, *Pleasures Taken: Performances of Sexuality and Loss in Victorian Photographs* (Durham, NC: Duke University Press, 1995), and *Becoming: The Photographs of Clementina, Viscountess Hawarden* (Durham, NC: Duke University Press, 1999); Margaret Olin, *Touching Photographs* (Chicago, IL: University of Chicago Press, 2012); Tina M. Campt, *Image Matters: Archive, Photography, and the African Diaspora in Europe* (Durham, NC: Duke University Press, 2012); and Elspeth H. Brown and Thy Phu, eds., *Feeling Photography* (Durham, NC: Duke University Press, 2014).

45 See also Carol Mavor, "Odor di Femina: Though You May Not See Her, You Can Certainly Smell Her," *Cultural Studies* 12, no. 1 (1998): 51–81.

46 They invite one to imagine what Jim Drobnick has called their "mise-en-scents." Jim Drobnick, "Volatile Effects: Olfactory Dimensions of Art and Architecture," in *Empire of the Senses: The Sensual Culture Reader*, ed. David Howes (Oxford: Berg, 2005), 272.

47 "Horrors of the Battlefield," *Harper's Weekly*, October 11, 1862, 655.

48 M. M. Smith, "When Seeing Makes Scents," 13.

49 Drobnick, "Volatile Effects," 273.

50 In his discussion of architecture and the "white cube" modernist art gallery, Jim Drobnick has argued that "artists have engaged with aromatic materials to counter, confuse and corrupt assumptions of purely optical experience" (Drobnick, "Volatile Effects," 274). In her fascinating discussion of the masculine gendering of optical primacy in the work of Charcot and Freud, Carol Mavor suggests that the Lacanian gaze is intersensorial; much more than simply vision, it is "a sensate gaze that we can also smell or hear," a gaze that can accommodate rather than exclude an "odor di femina" (Mavor, "Odor di Femina," 72). If smell is gendered for Mavor, it is associated with class distinctions according to Mark Smith. "The odor of class—and the class of odor—started to become especially important in the mid-eighteenth century when Western elites increasingly sought to suppress and deny odor. By some estimations, this amounted to nothing short of an 'olfactive revolution.' An idea championed initially by nobles and

aristocrats but quickly embraced by the emerging middle class in the nineteenth century, olfaction increasingly took on class importance with urbanization and industrialization. Who was deemed smelly and who was considered inodorate—and who got to define the meaning and value of various scents—was critical for class formation which, in turn, was linked to ideas about selfhood. As the nineteenth-century Western bourgeoisie started to stamp the laboring classes especially as reeking, they also paraded themselves as largely inodorate." Mark M. Smith, *Sensing the Past: Seeing, Hearing, Smelling, Tasting, and Touching in History* (Berkeley: University of California Press, 2007), 66.

51 As Diane Ackerman has suggested, "Smell is the most direct of all our senses": "Odor molecules float back into the nasal cavity behind the bridge of the nose, where they are absorbed by the mucosa containing receptor cells bearing microscopic hairs called cilia. Five million of these cells fire impulses to the brain's olfactory bulb or smell center." Diane Ackerman, *A Natural History of the Senses* (1990; repr., New York: Vintage, 1991), 10.

52 Mann, *Hold Still*, 427.

53 Kelly Christian, "'Rather a Grave Subject': The Critical Role of the Nineteenth-Century Postmortem Photograph" (master's thesis, School of the Art Institute of Chicago, 2012).

54 Faust, *This Republic of Suffering*, 147–48.

55 See Geoffrey Batchen, *Forget Me Not: Photography and Remembrance* (New York: Princeton Architectural Press, 2004), for an extensive discussion of these hybrid photo-objects.

56 For further information about Mumler, see Louis Kaplan's edited collection of primary source documents, and his historical and theoretical discussion of those documents in *The Strange Case of William Mumler, Spirit Photographer* (Minneapolis: University of Minnesota Press, 2008).

57 Molly McGarry, *Ghosts of Futures Past: Spiritualism and the Cultural Politics of Nineteenth-Century America* (Berkeley: University of California Press, 2008), 101. See also Tom Gunning, "Phantom Images and Modern Manifestations: Spirit Photography, Magic Theater, Trick Films, and Photography's Uncanny," in *Fugitive Images: From Photography to Video*, ed. Patrice Petro (Bloomington: Indiana University Press, 1995), 51.

58 Crista Cloutier, "Mumler's Ghosts," in *The Perfect Medium: Photography and the Occult*, by Clément Chéroux, Andreas Fischer, Pierre Apraxine, Denis Canguilhem, and Sophie Schmit (New Haven, CT: Yale University Press, 2005), 22–23.

59 Sally Mann, *What Remains* (Boston, MA: Bulfinch Press, 2003).

60 Ravenal, "Sally Mann," 6.

61 Stephen M. Best, *The Fugitive's Properties: Law and the Poetics of Possession* (Chicago, IL: University of Chicago Press, 2004), 9.

62 Lee, "Image of War," 45.

63 John Reekie made the images for Gardner's *Photographic Sketch Book*.

64 As Elizabeth Young has argued, the photograph brings the African American

man's gaze into view. Elizabeth Young, "Verbal Battlefields," in *On Alexander Gardner's* Photographic Sketch Book *of the Civil War*, by Anthony W. Lee and Elizabeth Young (Berkeley: University of California Press, 2007), 87. See also Alan Trachtenberg's reading of this photograph in *Reading American Photographs: Images as History, Mathew Brady to Walker Evans* (New York: Hill and Wang, 1989), 111.

65 Saidiya V. Hartman, *Scenes of Subjection: Terror, Slavery, and Self-Making in Nineteenth-Century America* (New York: Oxford University Press, 1997), 173.

66 Maurice O. Wallace, "Framing the Black Soldier: Image, Uplift, and the Duplicity of Pictures," in *Pictures and Progress: Early Photography and the Making of African American Identity*, ed. Maurice O. Wallace and Shawn Michelle Smith (Durham, NC: Duke University Press, 2012), 251.

67 Orlando Patterson, *Slavery and Social Death: A Comparative Study* (Cambridge, MA: Harvard University Press, 1982).

68 Roland Barthes, *Camera Lucida: Reflections on Photography*, trans. Richard Howard (1980; repr., New York: Hill and Wang, 1981), 96. As Eduardo Cadava elaborates, "It is precisely in death that the power of the photograph is revealed, and revealed to the very extent that it continues to evoke what can no longer be there. . . . In photographing someone, we know that the photograph will survive him, it begins, even during his life, to circulate without him, figuring and anticipating his death each time it is looked at. The photograph is a farewell. It belongs to the afterlife of the photographed." Eduardo Cadava, *Words of Light: Theses on the Photography of History* (Princeton, NJ: Princeton University Press, 1997), 13.

69 For more on Lewis Powell and his afterlife, see Katherine J. Lennard, "Touching Absence: A Reconstruction of Lewis Powell" (master's thesis, School of the Art Institute of Chicago, 2009).

70 My reading of the way Mann marks her presence in her photographs is in concert with Robin Kelsey's reading of nineteenth-century photographer Julia Margaret Cameron's similarly sloppy wet-plate collodion technique: "She left traces of her living presence behind the camera in the fingerprints, streaks, discolored patches, and other blemishes of her prints." Robin Kelsey, "Julia Margaret Cameron Transfigures the Glitch," in *Photography and the Art of Chance* (Cambridge, MA: Belknap Press of Harvard University Press, 2015), 82.

71 Geoffrey Batchen, "Life and Death," in *Suspending Time: Life—Photography—Death* (Shizuoka, Japan: Izo Photo Museum, 2010), 108–29, especially 108 and 126.

72 Barthes, *Camera Lucida*, 80.

Chapter 3

1 Deborah Luster and C. D. Wright, *The Tenth Dorothea Lange-Paul Taylor Prize* (Durham, NC: Center for Documentary Studies, 2001), 7. In the legend to *One Big Self*, the three prisons are identified this way: "ECPPF: East Carroll Parish Prison Farm (Transylvania, Louisiana), minimum security for men; LCIW: Louisiana

Correctional Institute for Women (St. Gabriel, Louisiana), minimum, medium, and maximum security for women; LSP: Louisiana State Penitentiary (Angola, Louisiana), maximum security for men." Deborah Luster and C. D. Wright, *One Big Self: Prisoners of Louisiana* (Santa Fe: Twin Palms, 2003).

2 Deborah Luster, "The Reappearance of Those Who Have Gone" (2002), in *One Big Self: Prisoners of Louisiana*, by Deborah Luster and C. D. Wright (Santa Fe, NM: Twin Palms, 2003), 2. Luster understands their project as a way to make visible "Louisiana's 'invisible' prison population." Luster and Wright, *Tenth Prize*, 9.

3 "Slow violence" is Rob Nixon's term for "attritional catastrophes that overspill clear boundaries in time and space." Rob Nixon, *Slow Violence and the Environmentalism of the Poor* (Cambridge, MA: Harvard University Press, 2011), 7.

4 Bruce Jackson, *Pictures from a Drawer: Prison and the Art of Portraiture* (Philadelphia, PA: Temple University Press, 2009), 10.

5 Nicholas Mirzoeff, *The Right to Look: A Counterhistory of Visuality* (Durham, NC: Duke University Press, 2011). Nicole Fleetwood assesses the more intimate circuits of viewing of "vernacular prison portraits" among family members. According to Fleetwood, "Vernacular prison portraits are produced in makeshift studios and in prison visiting rooms. Incarcerated artists paint backdrops and, in some cases, design sets for their photo shoots. Occasionally, minimal props and accessories are available for staging the photographs. These makeshift studios exist in many prisons across the United States. The photographs capture individual and group portraits commissioned by incarcerated people and document visits from family and friends. Incarcerated people and their visitors purchase these images for typically $2.00–$3.00 per copy, making this a lucrative business for US prisons" (492). As Fleetwood discusses, posing for such photographs affords incarcerated people and their family members a level of intimacy and touch that is otherwise strictly regulated during prison visits (502). Nicole R. Fleetwood, "Posing in Prison: Family Photographs, Emotional Labor, and Carceral Intimacy," *Public Culture* 27, no. 3 (2015): 487–511.

6 Describing her process, she says, "I chose to photograph each person as they presented their very own selves before my camera." Luster, "Reappearance," 3.

7 According to Dennis Childs, "tens of thousands of people converge on Angola during two months of the year to witness untrained prisoner 'rodeo cowboys' perform in events." Childs argues that such spectacles deploy the imprisoned body "as a resource for public amusement, white self-definition, and the normalization of racial capitalist atrocity." Dennis Childs, *Slaves of the State: Black Incarceration from the Chain Gang to the Penitentiary* (Minneapolis: University of Minnesota Press, 2015), 98.

8 As Allan Sekula has described that system, photographs and people were reduced to points in an archive that were at once abstract and also material. According to Sekula, in the "bureaucratic-clerical-statistical system" of documentation privi-

leged by the police in the nineteenth century, it was not the camera that held precedence but the filing cabinet. Allan Sekula, "The Body and the Archive," *October* 39 (winter 1986): 3–64, 16.

9 Library of Congress, Research Guides, 13th Amendment to the U.S. Constitution: Primary Documents in American History, https://www.loc.gov/rr/program/bib/ourdocs/13thamendment.html, accessed November 27, 2017.

10 Childs, *Slaves of the State*, 64. Michelle Alexander, *The New Jim Crow: Mass Incarceration in the Age of Colorblindness*, revised edition (New York: The New Press, 2011), 31.

11 Childs, *Slaves of the State*, 94.

12 According to Jonathan Finn, "As early as 1841, the French police began producing daguerreotypes of prisoners. In the United States, the San Francisco Police Department began daguerreotyping prisoners in 1854, followed by police departments in New York in 1858, Cleveland in the late 1860s, and Chicago in 1870." Jonathan Finn, *Capturing the Criminal Image: From Mug Shot to Surveillance Society* (Minneapolis: University of Minnesota Press, 2009), 6.

13 These images are now housed at the Missouri History Museum. Shayne Davidson, *Captured and Exposed: The First Police Rogues' Gallery in America* (Saint Louis: Missouri History Museum Press, 2017).

14 As instruments of nineteenth-century surveillance, the mug shot and Bertillonage might also be linked to slavery, for as Simone Browne has argued, "The historical formation of surveillance is not outside of the historical formation of slavery." Both visual technologies function as tools of what Browne has called "racializing surveillance," in which "enactments of surveillance reify boundaries, borders, and bodies along racial lines, and where the outcome is often discriminatory treatment of those who are negatively racialized by such surveillance." Simone Browne, *Dark Matters: On the Surveillance of Blackness* (Durham, NC: Duke University Press, 2015), 50, 16.

15 Rachel Hall, *Wanted: The Outlaw in American Visual Culture* (Charlottesville: University of Virginia Press, 2009), 65.

16 Hall, *Wanted*, 66.

17 Finn, *Capturing the Criminal Image*, 6–7.

18 Hall, *Wanted*, 105–6.

19 Hall, *Wanted*, 109–12.

20 Jackson, *Pictures from a Drawer*, 10–11.

21 According to Allan Sekula, photographic portrait practice fluctuates between two poles, one honorific and the other repressive. Sekula, "Body and the Archive," 7.

22 Legend to *One Big Self*.

23 Such practices demonstrate, in Margaret Olin's terms, how "photographs . . . actively participate in building communities and relationships." Margaret Olin, *Touching Photographs* (Chicago, IL: University of Chicago Press, 2012), 17.

24 Interview with the artist, October 4, 1999, New York City.

25 Childs, *Slaves of the State*, 97–101.

26 Ruby C. Tapia, "Profane Illuminations: The Gendered Problematics of Critical Carceral Visualities," PMLA 123, no. 3 (May 2008): 685.
27 Tapia, "Profane Illuminations," 686.
28 Laura Wexler, *Tender Violence: Domestic Visions in an Age of U.S. Imperialism* (Chapel Hill: University of North Carolina Press, 2000).
29 Once again, see Fleetwood, "Posing in Prison."
30 Ta-Nehisi Coates, *Between the World and Me* (New York: Spiegel & Grau, 2015), 98.
31 Artist's talk, Columbia College, Chicago, Illinois, November 10, 2011.
32 Walter Benjamin, "Little History of Photography," in *Walter Benjamin: Selected Writings*, vol. 2, part 2, *1931–1934*, ed. Howard Eiland and Michael W. Jennings, trans. Edmund Jephcott, Howard Eiland, et al. (Cambridge, MA: Belknap of Harvard University Press, 2002), 518.
33 Walter Benjamin, "The Work of Art in the Age of Its Technological Reproducibility," second version (1936), in *Walter Benjamin: Selected Writings*, vol. 3, *1935–1938*, ed. Howard Eiland and Michael W. Jennings, trans. Edmund Jephcott, Howard Eiland, et al. (Cambridge, MA: Belknap of Harvard University Press, 2002), 108.
34 Benjamin, "Work of Art," second version (1936), 108.
35 Luc Sante, *Evidence: NYPD Crime Scene Photographs: 1914–1918* (1992; repr., New York: Barnes and Noble, 2006), xi.
36 The most well-known crime scene photographer of the twentieth century was not a police officer but a freelance photographer for the tabloid press. Weegee, a famous ambulance chaser, photographed crime scenes, tenement fires, Coney Island, and socialite gatherings in New York City in the 1930s and 1940s. Dependent on selling his photographs for his livelihood, he found commercial success with the daily tabloid newspapers, highly visual, sensational papers of a smaller size than the more respectable broadsides such as the *New York Times*, that appealed particularly to subway commuters who could manage them more easily on packed trains. Weegee's photographs for the tabloids, made mostly at night with a flash, are high-contrast images of urban corruption and spectacle. What they lack in tonal range and print quality they make up for in sordid subject matter. In 1938, Weegee was given permission to install a police radio in his car, insuring that he would arrive at the scenes of crime with, and sometimes even before, the police. Anthony W. Lee and Richard Meyer, *Weegee and Naked City* (Berkeley: University of California Press, 2008).
37 Ruth Wilson Gilmore's definition of racism is especially apt here: "Racism is the state-sanctioned and/or extralegal production and exploitation of group-differentiated vulnerability to premature death." Therefore, "economic and environmental justice are central to antiracism." Ruth Wilson Gilmore, *Golden Gulag: Prisons, Surplus, Crisis, and Opposition in Globalizing California* (Berkeley: University of California Press, 2007), 247.
38 Artist's talk, Columbia College, Chicago, Illinois, November 10, 2011.
39 Erika Doss, *Memorial Mania: Public Feeling in America* (Chicago, IL: University of

Chicago Press, 2010), 64. In thinking about Luster's work as a kind of memorial, I am drawing on Erika Doss's discussion of temporary memorials and the cultural work they perform in the United States. To be clear, Luster's photographs are not temporary memorials—they are empty and after the fact. Partly, I think Luster's aim is to draw attention to murders that did not achieve the kind of national response that other horrific events have garnered. See Erika Doss, chapter 2, "Grief: Temporary Memorials and Contemporary Modes of Mourning," in *Memorial Mania*, 61–116.

40 Artist's talk, Columbia College, Chicago, Illinois, November 10, 2011.

41 Henry A. Giroux, "Reading Hurricane Katrina: Race, Class, and the Biopolitics of Disposability," *College Literature* 33, no. 3 (summer 2006): 174.

42 Giroux, "Reading Hurricane Katrina," 184. As George Lipsitz succinctly states, "The organized abandonment of poor and working-class black people in New Orleans prior to the hurricane had left them isolated in high poverty neighborhoods and made them especially vulnerable to the effects of flooding." George Lipsitz, "Learning from New Orleans: The Social Warrant of Hostile Privatism and Competitive Consumer Citizenship," *Cultural Anthropology* 21, no. 3 (August 2006): 464.

43 Luster's text notes that the corpse was found face up.

44 Artist's talk, Columbia College, Chicago, Illinois, November 10, 2011.

45 As Andrea Nelson suggests, "Luster's photographs are circular in format, reminiscent of the earliest Kodak snapshots but on a much larger scale. This format emphasizes a purposeful type of looking, as through a microscope or binoculars. Yet the circular photographs are also unsettling: Like peepholes or views from a gun scope, they make viewers conscious of the act of looking while forcefully disrupting the normal rectangular format of the camera view." Andrea Nelson, entry on Deborah Luster in *The Memory of Time: Contemporary Photographs at the National Gallery of Art*, by Sarah Greenough and Andrea Nelson, with Sarah Kennel, Diane Waggoner, and Leslie J. Ureña (Washington, DC: National Gallery of Art, 2015), 94.

46 Walter Benjamin, "On the Concept of History," in *Walter Benjamin: Selected Writings*, vol. 4, *1938–1940*, trans. Edmund Jephcott et al., ed. Howard Eiland and Michael W. Jennings (Cambridge, MA: Belknap of Harvard University Press, 2003), 392.

Chapter 4

1 Simpson has said that the work is "a kind of homage to various VanDerZee photographs." Maria Christina Villaseñor and Lorna Simpson, "*Nine Props*: An Interview and Art Portfolio," *Paris Review* 138 (spring 1996): 73.

2 Other works in which the figure is removed and replaced by a surrogate include Simpson's installations *Hypothetical* (1992), *Wishbones* (1993), and *Stack of Diaries* (1993). In his reading of Simpson's *Five Rooms* (1991), an installation produced

in collaboration with Alva Rogers, Huey Copeland describes "Simpson's move toward the thing as a figural marker of the body" (86) as a kind of supplement to her "tried-and-true phototextual strategies," a physical addition of objects necessary to "summon the slave past" (78). Huey Copeland, *Bound to Appear: Art, Slavery, and the Site of Blackness in Multicultural America* (Chicago, IL: University of Chicago Press, 2013). For other recent commentary on Simpson's larger body of work, see *Lorna Simpson*, by Joan Simon with contributions by Naomi Beckwith, Marta Gili, Thomas J. Lax, and Elvan Zabunyan (Munich, Germany: Delmonico Books/Prestel, Minneapolis, MN: Foundation for the Exhibition of Photography, Paris: Jeu de Paume, 2013).

3 Lorna Simpson, artist's talk, May 13, 2010, Walker Art Center, https://www.youtube.com/watch?v=cmvEAUfZXHs, accessed January 23, 2016.

4 I viewed the work at the Museum of Contemporary Photography at Columbia College in Chicago.

5 Pierre Bourdieu, *Distinction: A Social Critique of the Judgement of Taste*, trans. Richard Nice (Cambridge, MA: Harvard University Press, 1984).

6 In her reading of Jamaican dancehall culture in the late twentieth and early twenty-first centuries, Krista Thompson examines the ways in which the camera itself can function as a prop in "performances of visibility" (7) that do not necessarily end in the creation of an image. See especially chapter 2, "Video Light: Dancehall and the Aesthetics of Spectacular Un-visibility in Jamaica," in Krista Thompson, *Shine: The Visual Economy of Light in African Diasporic Aesthetic Practice* (Durham, NC: Duke University Press, 2015), 112–68.

7 Rodger C. Birt, "A Life in American Photography," in *VanDerZee: Photographer, 1886–1983*, by Deborah Willis-Braithwaite, with biographical essay by Rodger C. Birt (New York: Harry N. Abrams in association with the National Portrait Gallery, Smithsonian Institution, 1993), 44–45.

8 Birt, "Life in American Photography," 43–44.

9 Leigh Raiford, *Imprisoned in a Luminous Glare: Photography and the African American Freedom Struggle* (Chapel Hill: University of North Carolina Press, 2011), 15. Dawoud Bey calls VanDerZee's portraits "willful acts of self-preservation." Dawoud Bey, "Authoring the Black Image: The Photographs of James VanDerZee," in *The James VanDerZee Studio*, ed. Colin Westerbeck (Chicago, IL: Art Institute of Chicago, 2004), 30.

10 For a recent discussion of this struggle, see Robin Kelsey, "Defining Art against the Mechanical, c. 1860," in *Photography and the Art of Chance* (Cambridge, MA: Belknap of Harvard University Press, 2015), 40–65.

11 As James Elkins has argued, "Photography tends to be conceptualized with the help of brilliant metaphors: people write about perfect windows, lucency, transparency" (20). Instead, Elkins offers "a trinity of failed photographic windows," "selenite, ice, salt" (34), as emblems of the "stunted seeing" (20) and "imperfect visibility" (28) photography proffers. James Elkins, *What Photography Is* (New York: Routledge, 2011).

12 Mary Bergstein, "Lonely Aphrodites: On the Documentary Photography of Sculpture," *Art Bulletin* 74, no. 3 (September 1992): 479.

13 Commenting on Simpson's use of felt in the *Public Sex* series of 1995, Kellie Jones has said, "Simpson's turn to felt was a brilliant one, for it spoke to issues of sensuality on a number of levels. As a fabric it was incredibly tactile, calling out for our touch. Even the process of its creation recalled sexual performance: felt is made by adding moisture to hair and compressing it. Finally, the word itself conjured bodily contact." Kellie Jones, "(Un)Seen and Overheard: Pictures by Lorna Simpson," in Kellie Jones, Thelma Golden, and Chrissie Iles, *Lorna Simpson* (London: Phaidon Press, 2002), 68.

14 Scholars of photography have begun to highlight the haptic in different ways. Elizabeth Edwards and Janice Hart underscore the materiality of the photographic image as object in their coedited book *Photographs/Objects/Histories: On the Materiality of Images* (London: Routledge, 2004); and Elspeth H. Brown and Thy Phu discuss touch in terms of affect in their coedited book *Feeling Photography* (Durham, NC: Duke University Press, 2014). Margaret Olin engages both tactility and feeling in her discussion of photography in *Touching Photographs* (Chicago, IL: University of Chicago Press, 2012), as does Tina M. Campt in *Image Matters: Archive, Photography, and the African Diaspora in Europe* (Durham, NC: Duke University Press, 2012).

15 Eve Kosofsky Sedgwick, *Touching Feeling: Affect, Pedagogy, Performativity* (Durham, NC: Duke University Press, 2003), 15.

16 Thompson, *Shine*, 225.

17 Sedgwick, *Touching Feeling*, 15.

18 According to Brooke Belisle, Simpson's "felt photographs do not emphasize haptic over optic, tactile over visual, surface over depth. Instead, they explore how these categories intersect and suggest how the body and the photograph, as at once visual and visceral experiences, exist at this intersection." Brooke Belisle, "Felt Surface, Visible Image: Lorna Simpson's Photography and the Embodiment of Appearance," *Photography and Culture* 4, no. 2 (July 2011): 166.

19 Olin, *Touching Photographs*, 10.

20 Roland Barthes, *Camera Lucida: Reflections on Photography*, trans. Richard Howard (1980; repr., New York: Hill and Wang, 1981), 80–81.

21 See Olin, *Touching Photographs*, 2.

22 Campt, *Image Matters*, 43.

23 Bergstein, "Lonely Aphrodites," 492. For a further discussion of the photography of sculpture, see Julie Warchol, "'Modeling with Light': Clarence Kennedy's Photographic Sculpture, 1924–1940" (master's thesis, School of the Art Institute of Chicago, 2015).

24 Lorna Simpson, artist's talk, May 13, 2010, Walker Art Center.

25 Willis-Braithwaite and Birt, *VanDerZee*, 115.

26 Villaseñor and Simpson, "*Nine Props*," 75.

27 Siegfried Kracauer, "Photography" (1927), trans. Thomas Y. Levin, *Critical Inquiry* 19, no. 3 (spring 1993): 426.

28 As photographer Lyle Ashton Harris has said, in VanDerZee's work, "the photograph became a document that was suggestive of a larger world, a larger community." *Through a Lens Darkly: Black Photographers and the Emergence of a People*, a film directed by Thomas Allen Harris (2014). Romi Crawford has recently studied photographic communities outside the studio, black photographers and subjects who claimed the street as their setting. Romi Crawford, "Black Photographers Who Take Black Pictures," in *The Wall of Respect: Public Art and Black Liberation in 1960s Chicago*, by Abdul Alkalimat, Romi Crawford, and Rebecca Zorach (Chicago, IL: Northwestern University Press, 2017), 193–212.

29 Sara Blair, *Harlem Crossroads: Black Writers and the Photograph in the Twentieth Century* (Princeton, NJ: Princeton University Press, 2007), 255.

30 Okwui Enwezor, "Repetition and Differentiation—Lorna Simpson's Iconography of the Racial Sublime," in *Lorna Simpson* (New York: Abrams and American Federation of Arts, 2006), 124.

31 This is how Simpson has described the vases in the series. Villaseñor and Simpson, "*Nine Props*," 76.

32 Kristen Eckrich, "Lorna Simpson's *9 Props*: Deconstructing Photographic Portraiture" (master's thesis, American University, Washington, DC, 2014), 23.

33 Enwezor, "Repetition and Differentiation," 121. Huey Copeland, "'Bye, Bye Black Girl': Lorna Simpson's Figurative Retreat," *Art Journal* 64, no. 2 (summer 2005): 63.

34 Nella Larsen rendered the constriction and challenge of such conformity in her novel *Quicksand* (1928). Kevin Gaines and Michele Mitchell have examined the roles of middle-class gender conformity and sexual propriety in African American "uplift" narratives of the early twentieth century. And Monica Miller has examined the black dandy's challenge to such gender norms. Nella Larsen, *Quicksand* (1928), in *Quicksand and Passing*, edited by Deborah McDowell, American Women Writers Series (New Brunswick, NJ: Rutgers University Press, 1986); Kevin K. Gaines, *Uplifting the Race: Black Leadership, Politics, and Culture in the Twentieth Century* (Chapel Hill: University of North Carolina Press, 1996); Michele Mitchell, *Righteous Propagation: African Americans and the Politics of Racial Destiny after Reconstruction* (Chapel Hill: University of North Carolina Press, 2004); Monica L. Miller, *Slaves to Fashion: Black Dandyism and the Styling of Black Diasporic Identity* (Durham, NC: Duke University Press, 2009).

35 Miriam Thaggert, *Images of Black Modernism: Verbal and Visual Strategies of the Harlem Renaissance* (Amherst: University of Massachusetts Press, 2010), 157.

36 Deborah Willis-Braithwaite, "They Knew Their Names," in *VanDerZee*, 10.

37 Willis-Braithwaite, "They Knew Their Names," 13; Mitchell, *Righteous Propagation*, 115.

38 Mitchell, *Righteous Propagation*, 117.

39 The tactics deployed by the authors of conduct literature coincided with Van-

DerZee's visual strategies: "Guidelines within advice literature not only depicted an upright race striving ever upward, but such depictions were, in and of themselves, a form of reproduction not dissimilar to staged studio photographs in which individuals projected desired selves for display and circulation." Mitchell, *Righteous Propagation*, 113.

40 As Jontyle Theresa Robinson has said of Simpson's work, "The props are shrewd, cunning, powerful implements in Simpson's hands and represent the intersection of racial and sexual oppression and power." Jontyle Theresa Robinson, *Bearing Witness: Contemporary Works by African American Women Artists* (New York: Spelman College and Rizzoli International Publications, 1996), 35.

41 For a further discussion of anti-normative gender performance in Simpson's work, see Jones, "(Un)Seen and Overheard," 52–58.

42 The BECC sought greater representation of African American artists in museums, and in 1971, in response to riots at Attica prison, created an Arts Exchange program in correctional facilities. Black Emergency Cultural Coalition Records, Schomburg Center for Research in Black Culture, New York Public Library, available at http://archives.nypl.org/scm/20908, last accessed February 28, 2019.

43 Bridget R. Cooks, "Black Artists and Activism: *Harlem on My Mind* (1969)," *American Studies* 48, no. 1 (spring 2007): 5–39, 27–28. The article has also been republished in Bridget R. Cooks, *Exhibiting Blackness: African Americans and the American Art Museum* (Amherst, MA: University of Massachusetts Press, 2011).

44 Birt, "Life in American Photography," 54.

45 Birt, "Life in American Photography," 53.

46 Birt, "Life in American Photography," 57.

47 Cooks, "Black Artists and Activism," 8 and 5. According to Margaret Olin, the exhibition was organized by "an independent curator, Allon Schoener, who conceived it as a 'communications environment.'" Olin, *Touching Photographs*, 108.

48 Cooks, "Black Artists and Activism," 13. Margaret Olin suggests that the exhibition included "roughly seven hundred images," more than fifty of them by VanDerZee (112). And as Olin confirms, the exhibition included "a fourteen-by-fifty-two-foot mural of VanDerZee's picture of Adam Clayton Powell Sr. with the 1925 Sunday School class of the Abyssinian Baptist Church" (108–9). Olin, *Touching Photographs*.

49 Cooks, "Black Artists and Activism," 25.

50 Birt, "Life in American Photography," 61; and Cooks, "Black Artists and Activism," 24.

51 Coco Fusco, "Uncanny Dissonance: The Work of Lorna Simpson," in *English Is Broken Here: Notes on Cultural Fusion in the Americas* (New York: The New Press, 1995), 97.

52 As Okwui Enwezor has said of *Wigs* (1994), *9 Props* presents its objects "disciplined within the grid of scientific rationality." Enwezor, "Repetition and Differentiation," 118.

53 I discuss the scientific and photographic production of racial types in the nineteenth century in *American Archives: Gender, Race, and Class in Visual Culture* (Princeton, NJ: Princeton University Press, 1999), and *Photography on the Color Line: W. E. B. Du Bois, Race, and Visual Culture* (Durham, NC: Duke University Press, 2004).

54 Carrie Mae Weems appropriates the Agassiz-Zealy images in *From Here I Saw What Happened and I Cried* (1995–96), a work that is contemporary to Simpson's *9 Props*. For extended discussions of Zealy's daguerreotypes for Agassiz, see Brian Wallis, "Black Bodies, White Science: Louis Agassiz's Slave Daguerreotypes," *American Art* 9 (summer 1995): 39–61; Suzanne Schneider, "Louis Agassiz and the American School of Ethnoeroticism: Polygenesis, Pornography, and Other 'Perfidious Influences,'" in *Pictures and Progress: Early Photography and the Making of African American Identity*, ed. Maurice O. Wallace and Shawn Michelle Smith (Durham, NC: Duke University Press, 2012), 211–43; and Molly Rogers, *Delia's Tears: Race, Science, and Photography in Nineteenth-Century America* (New Haven, CT: Yale University Press, 2010). This is another instance of photography used as a tool of "racializing surveillance." Once again, see Simone Browne, *Dark Matters: On the Surveillance of Blackness* (Durham, NC: Duke University Press, 2015), 16.

55 Enwezor has read another series of Simpson's portraits from 2001 in relation to Agassiz's racial typologies. Enwezor, "Repetition and Differentiation," 127–29. Cherise Smith also discusses Simpson's work in relation to Zealy's daguerreotypes for Agassiz. Cherise Smith, "Fragmented Documents: Works by Lorna Simpson, Carrie Mae Weems, and Willie Robert Middlebrook at the Art Institute of Chicago," *Museum Studies* 24, no. 2 (1999): 248–49.

56 Okwui Enwezor, "Social Grace: The Work of Lorna Simpson," *Third Text* 35 (summer 1996): 43–58, 51.

57 As Colin Westerbeck has said, "VanDerZee's portraits are about dreams." Colin Westerbeck, *The James VanDerZee Studio* (Chicago, IL: Art Institute of Chicago, 2004), 16.

58 Darby English, "Beyond Black Representational Space," in *How to See a Work of Art in Total Darkness* (Cambridge, MA: MIT Press, 2007), 34.

Chapter 5

1 Mark Reinhardt, "Picturing Violence: Aesthetics and the Anxiety of Critique," in *Beautiful Suffering: Photography and the Traffic in Pain*, ed. Mark Reinhardt, Holly Edwards, and Erina Duganne (Chicago, IL: University of Chicago Press/Williamstown, MA: Williams College Museum of Art, 2006), 24–25.

2 Monica Davey and Gretchen Ruethling, "After 50 Years, Emmett Till's Body Is Exhumed," *New York Times*, June 2, 2005, nytimes.com, downloaded June 6, 2013.

3 Many scholars and activists repeat the story. For recent retellings, see Jacqueline Goldsby, "The High and Low Tech of It: The Meaning of Lynching and the

Death of Emmett Till," *Yale Journal of Criticism* 9, no. 2 (1996): 245–82; Martin A. Berger, *Seeing through Race: A Reinterpretation of Civil Rights Photography* (Berkeley: University of California Press, 2011); Maurice Berger, *For All the World to See: Visual Culture and the Struggle for Civil Rights* (New Haven, CT: Yale University Press, 2010); Courtney R. Baker, "Emmett Till, Justice, and the Task of Recognition," in *Humane Insight: Looking at Images of African American Suffering and Death* (Urbana-Champaign: University of Illinois Press, 2015), 69–93.

4 Goldsby, "High and Low Tech," 249.

5 Timothy B. Tyson, *The Blood of Emmett Till* (New York: Simon and Schuster, 2017), 202. Returning to Bryant's grocery store, to the scene in which Emmett Till whistled, or flirted with, or simply said, "bye baby," to Carolyn Bryant, Darby English asks one to reconsider Till's gesture as a mark of interracial desire and an optimism about interracial intimacy for which our standard stories about the meaning of Till's death cannot account. Darby English, "Emmett Till Ever After," in *Black Is, Black Ain't*, ed. Hamza Walker and Karen Reimer (Chicago, IL: The Renaissance Society, 2013), 84–99.

6 Carolyn Bryant quoted in Tyson, *Blood of Emmett Till*, 6.

7 Goldsby, "High and Low Tech," 253.

8 According to Courtney R. Baker, Mamie Till taped photographs taken during Emmett's last Christmas to the coffin so that the viewing public at the funeral would have images of Emmett alive to compare to his brutalized corpse. In this way, "The viewing of the body was thus an orchestrated affair, relying in part on the juxtaposition of visual objects to makes its political and affective points." Baker, "Emmett Till," 78.

9 Jacqueline Goldsby, *A Spectacular Secret: Lynching in American Life and Literature* (Chicago, IL: University of Chicago Press, 2006), 295.

10 Brenna Wynn Greer details these events and contextualizes the publication of Jackson's photographs in JET magazine with regard to the broader cultural and marketing ambitions of Johnson Publishing in the postwar period. I am grateful to Greer for sharing with me a portion of her book manuscript, which has now been published. Brenna Wynn Greer, *Represented: The Black Imagemakers Who Reimagined African American Citizenship* (Philadelphia: University of Pennsylvania Press, 2019).

11 Leigh Raiford, *Imprisoned in a Luminous Glare: Photography and the African American Freedom Struggle* (Chapel Hill: University of North Carolina Press, 2011), 88–89.

12 Fred Moten, *In the Break: The Aesthetics of the Black Radical Tradition* (Minneapolis: University of Minnesota Press, 2003), 196.

13 Sharon Sliwinski, *Human Rights in Camera* (Chicago, IL: University of Chicago Press, 2011).

14 Mamie Till-Mobley quoted in Maurice Berger, *For All the World to See*, 104. Mamie Till-Mobley and Christopher Benson, *Death of Innocence: The Story of the Hate Crime That Changed America* (New York: Random House, 2003), 139.

15 Martin A. Berger, *Seeing through Race*, 127–35.
16 Martin A. Berger, *Seeing through Race*, 129.
17 Moten, *In the Break*, 198.
18 Cathy Caruth, *Unclaimed Experience: Trauma, Narrative, and History* (Baltimore, MD: Johns Hopkins University Press, 1996), 4.
19 Caruth, *Unclaimed Experience*, 4–5. As Caruth has argued, trauma operates on survivors; it is defined as much by the shock of survival as by the shock of accident: "Trauma is not simply an effect of destruction but also, fundamentally, an enigma of survival" (*Unclaimed Experience*, 58). As the psyche cannot comprehend the accident it has experienced, it also cannot understand the fact of surviving the ordeal. Till did not survive the ordeal, but his mother did; his death was her trauma.
20 Mamie Till-Mobley quoted in Maurice Berger, *For All the World to See*, 104. Till-Mobley and Benson, *Death of Innocence*, 139.
21 Tyson, *Blood of Emmett Till*, 206.
22 Ulrich Baer, *Spectral Evidence: The Photography of Trauma* (Cambridge, MA: MIT Press, 2002), 7.
23 Goldsby, "High and Low Tech," 263.
24 And as Darby English has argued, they also miss entirely another referent, Till's desire. English, "Emmett Till Ever After."
25 In her reading of a defaced family snapshot recovered from a Serbian-occupied house in the Bosnian War, Sharon Sliwinski argues that the defacement "needs the significance of the family's image to remain at least partially legible." In this case the "before" image is still partially visible as a family snapshot within the "after" image of it defaced. Sharon Sliwinski, "On Photographic Violence," *Photography and Culture* 2, no. 3 (November 2009): 309.
26 Georges Didi-Huberman, *Images in Spite of All: Four Photographs from Auschwitz*, trans. Shane B. Lillis (Chicago, IL: University of Chicago Press, 2008), 33, 39.
27 Davey and Ruethling, "After 50 Years."
28 Thomas Keenan and Eyal Weizman outline the production of a new forensic aesthetics in the exhumation, forensic analysis, and representation of the skeleton of Nazi war criminal Josef Mengele in *Mengele's Skull: The Advent of a Forensic Aesthetics* (Berlin: Sternberg Press, 2012), 20.
29 Keenan and Weizman, *Mengele's Skull*, 25.
30 David L. Eng and David Kazanjian, "Introduction: Mourning Remains," in *Loss: The Politics of Mourning*, ed. David L. Eng and David Kazanjian, 1–25 (Berkeley: University of California Press, 2003), 3–4.
31 Phone conversation with the artist, March 16, 2016.
32 Ann Cvetkovich, *An Archive of Feelings: Trauma, Sexuality, and Lesbian Public Cultures* (Durham, NC: Duke University Press, 2003).
33 Eric Shouse provides a succinct articulation of the differences between feeling, emotion, and affect. Eric Shouse, "Feeling, Emotion, Affect," *M/C Journal* 8, no. 6 (2005), http://journal.media-culture.org.au/0512/03-shouse.php.

34 Lazarus has recently begun to accept digital images and even cellphone camera submissions. In a phone conversation on March 16, 2016, he said that he was unsure about how to display the digital images, thinking that it might make sense to "show" them as they are stored—on hard drives. He noted that *Too Hard to Keep* is becoming an index for the digital turn and its effects on family photography. How will snapshots be passed down as one generation's digital storage devices become obsolete?

35 Conversation with the artist, February 4, 2013, Chicago. The estimate of the number of images was three thousand in 2013. A new estimate of five thousand images was given in a subsequent phone conversation with the artist, March 16, 2016.

36 Conversation with the artist, June 6, 2013, Museum of Contemporary Art, Chicago. Barry Blinderman similarly notes, "Lazarus has curtailed his production of original images, increasingly preferring to collect, archive and install the photographs of others." Barry Blinderman, "Trace and Transience in the Photography of Jason Lazarus," in *Jason Lazarus: Your Time Is Gonna Come* (Normal: University Galleries of Illinois State University, 2013), 68.

37 Margaret Olin, *Touching Photographs* (Chicago, IL: University of Chicago Press, 2012), 17.

38 As Kendra Paitz has said of *Sarasota Photomat*, "The photographers assumed a level of privacy when they dropped off their closed film canisters and received their sealed envelopes of printed photographs, perhaps not thinking of the intermediary whose job it was to physically process the photos." Kendra Paitz, "Come as You Are: Jason Lazarus's Gestures of Inclusion," in *Jason Lazarus: Your Time Is Gonna Come* (Normal: University Galleries of Illinois State University, 2013), 75.

39 *Sarasota Photomat* calls to mind Mark Romanek's film of 2002, *One Hour Photo*, in which Sy, a lonely photo technician, culls his own copies of prints from those he develops. In the film, Sy becomes overly attached to the seemingly perfect Yorkins, and through their photographs creates an elaborate fantasy life. For a reading of the film and "snapshot perversion," see Catherine Zuromskis, *Snapshot Photography: The Lives of Images* (Cambridge, MA: MIT Press, 2013), 66–111.

40 Elspeth Brown and Thy Phu, eds., "Introduction," in *Feeling Photography* (Durham, NC: Duke University Press, 2014), 13.

41 For a discussion of the power dynamics that inform the discourse of "found" photographs, see Tina M. Campt, *Image Matters: Archive, Photography, and the African Diaspora in Europe* (Durham, NC: Duke University Press, 2012), 80–82.

42 Zuromskis, *Snapshot Photography*, 9. Sarah Greenough has studied further how snapshots "show from one time period or generation to the next an evolution of style, subject matter, and function." Sarah Greenough, introduction to *The Art of the American Snapshot, 1888–1978: From the Collection of Robert E. Jackson*, by Sarah Greenough and Diane Waggoner, with Sarah Kennel and Matthew S. Witkovsky (Washington, DC: National Gallery of Art, in association with Princeton University Press, 2007), 5.

43 Conversation with the artist, February 4, 2013, Chicago.

44 Chuck Mobley notes this as well, commenting on "an uneasy and even inevitable paradox that arises" in the work: "not only were these photographs too hard to keep, they were also too hard to destroy." Chuck Mobley, introduction to *thtk (2010–present), Jason Lazarus* (San Francisco, CA: SF Camerawork, 2013), 3.

45 Sliwinski, "On Photographic Violence," 310.

46 Sliwinski, "On Photographic Violence," 310. For Barthes, the photograph "bears the effigy to that crazy point where affect (love, compassion, grief, enthusiasm, desire) is the guarantee of Being. It then approaches, to all intents, madness." Roland Barthes, *Camera Lucida: Reflections on Photography* (1980; repr., New York: Hill and Wang, 1981), 113.

47 According to Lazarus, some young viewers have guessed that the film canisters are batteries. Conversation with the artist, June 6, 2013, Museum of Contemporary Art, Chicago.

48 As Abigail Solomon-Godeau has said of *Too Hard to Keep*, "Its stories withheld and unrevealed . . . acknowledge the fundamental opacity of all photographs." Abigail Solomon-Godeau, "Found Images, Lost Meanings, Invisible Traumas," in *thtk (2010–present), Jason Lazarus* (San Francisco: SF Camerawork, 2013), 57.

49 Paitz, "Come as You Are," 74.

50 As Abigail Solomon-Godeau has commented, the project "is founded on the acknowledgment that the camera image is a material object whose meanings are neither immanent nor fixed but are only an occasion for individual acts of projection and investiture." Solomon-Godeau, "Found Images," 57.

51 Zuromskis, *Snapshot Photography*, 8.

52 Olin, *Touching Photographs*, 17.

53 Ann Cvetkovich, visiting artist program lecture, November 2, 2016, School of the Art Institute of Chicago. See also Cvetkovich, *Archive of Feelings*, and Ann Cvetkovich, "Photographing Objects as Queer Archival Practice," in Brown and Phu, eds., *Feeling Photography*, 273–96. Douglas Nickel has also suggested that "our readings of found images," of anonymous snapshots, are colored by an "affective thrust." Douglas R. Nickel, *Snapshots: The Photography of Everyday Life, 1888 to the Present* (San Francisco, CA: San Francisco Museum of Modern Art, 1998), 14. Marianne Hirsch proposes that family photographs in particular "trigger in their viewers an inclusive, affiliative look" that engenders identifications, sometimes quite deceptively. Marianne Hirsch, "Introduction: Familial Looking," in *The Familial Gaze*, ed. Marianne Hirsch (Hanover, NH: Dartmouth College and University Press of New England, 1999), xi–xxv, xiii. For more on affect and photography, see Brown and Phu, eds., *Feeling Photography*.

54 Conversation with the artist, February 4, 2013, Chicago.

55 Olin, *Touching Photographs*, 129.

56 As Zuromskis reminds one, all snapshots "negotiate both personal desires and the social norms upon which photographic convention has been constructed."

Zuromskis, *Snapshot Photography*, 6. As Marianne Hirsch has argued, "photographs locate themselves precisely in the space of contradiction between the myth of the ideal family and the lived reality of family life." Marianne Hirsch, *Family Frames: Photography, Narrative, and Postmemory* (Cambridge, MA: Harvard University Press, 1997), 8.

57 This is what Bourdieu calls the "family function" of photographic practice. Pierre Bourdieu, *Photography: A Middle-Brow Art* (1965; repr., Stanford: Stanford University Press, 1990), 19.

58 Ariella Azoulay, "Photography," *Mafte'akh* 2e (2011): 65–80, 75.

59 In *Image Matters*, Tina Campt draws one's attention to the overwhelming whiteness of exhibitions of vernacular photography in the past decade. She focuses on the National Gallery of Art's 2007 exhibition *The Art of the American Snapshot, 1888–1978: From the Collection of Robert E. Jackson*, but her insights extend to other exhibitions as well, including *Too Hard to Keep*. See Tina M. Campt, "Interstitial: The Girl and/in the Gaze," in *Image Matters*, 71–82.

60 For more on counterarchives, race, and representation, see Shawn Michelle Smith, *Photography on the Color Line: W. E. B. Du Bois, Race, and Visual Culture* (Durham, NC: Duke University Press, 2004).

61 bell hooks, "In Our Glory: Photography and Black Life," in *Picturing Us: African American Identity in Photography*, ed. Deborah Willis (New York: The New Press, 1994), 48.

62 Raiford, *Imprisoned in a Luminous Glare*, 15.

Chapter 6

1 Paula S. Wallace, foreword, *Carrie Mae Weems: Constructing History: A Requiem to Mark the Moment* (Savannah, GA: Savannah College of Art and Design, 2008), n.p. As Allison Hersh notes, "Students worked as researchers, lighting technicians, prop managers, casting agents and photographers, supervising the production of 'Constructing History.'" Allison Hersh, "A[r]t & Soul: Staging History," *Savannah Morning News*, savannahnow.com, available online at http://savannahnow.com/accent/2008-10-11/soul-staging-history#gsc.tab=0, accessed September 20, 2015.

2 As Leigh Raiford has demonstrated, the Black Panther Party used the media and especially photography to craft an insurgent image. "As photography expanded the Panthers' emergent visibility it also was fundamental to the process of the party's iconization." Leigh Raiford, *Imprisoned in a Luminous Glare: Photography and the African American Freedom Struggle* (Chapel Hill: University of North Carolina Press, 2011), 145.

3 As Laurie Ann Farrell has said, "*Constructing History* illustrates that the past has a profound grip on the future." Laurie Ann Farrell, "An Opus: Carrie Mae Weems," in *Carrie Mae Weems: Constructing History: A Requiem to Mark the Moment* (Savannah, GA: Savannah College of Art and Design, 2008), n.p. In many

ways, it is the photograph that enables a past to grasp a future. Weems returns to the photographs that helped form her understanding of the world in the 1960s. As Deborah Willis has stated, "Photography during the 1950s and 1960s, when Weems was a young observer of the news, shaped her ideas about the human condition." Deborah Willis, "Translating Black Power and Beauty—Carrie Mae Weems," *Callaloo* 35, no. 4 (2012): 994.

4 Keith Jenkins, *Re-thinking History* (1991; repr., London: Routledge Classics, 2003), 14.

5 Jenkins, *Re-thinking History*, 21.

6 Roland Barthes, *Camera Lucida: Reflections on Photography*, trans. Richard Howard (1980; repr., New York: Hill and Wang, 1981), 12.

7 Raiford, *Imprisoned in a Luminous Glare*, 63.

8 Robert Hariman and John Louis Lucaites, *No Caption Needed: Iconic Photographs, Public Culture, and Liberal Democracy* (Chicago, IL: University of Chicago Press, 2007), 144.

9 Hariman and Lucaites, *No Caption Needed*, 145.

10 Hariman and Lucaites, *No Caption Needed*, 156. According to Martin A. Berger, the ambivalence of iconic civil rights photographs is also racialized, for such images contain and constrain a radical critique of racial inequity by reaffirming whites in positions of power. Martin A. Berger, *Seeing through Race: A Reinterpretation of Civil Rights Photography* (Berkeley: University of California Press, 2011).

11 Ruby C. Tapia, *American Pietàs: Visions of Race, Death, and the Maternal* (Minneapolis: University of Minnesota Press, 2011), 18.

12 Siegfried Kracauer, "Photography" (1927), trans. Thomas Y. Levin, *Critical Inquiry* 19, no. 3 (spring 1993): 423.

13 Kracauer, "Photography," 425, 426. Further, for this reason, as Jennifer Tucker has stated, "no photograph can be completely woven into the fabric of any historical narrative." Jennifer Tucker, in collaboration with Tina Campt, "Entwined Practices: Engagements with Photography in Historical Inquiry," special issue "Photography and Historical Interpretation," ed. Jennifer Tucker, *History and Theory, Theme Issue*, 48, no. 4 (December 2009): 8.

14 Siegfried Kracauer, "Time and History" (1963), Beiheft 6: History and the Concept of Time, *History and Theory* 6 (1966): 65–78, 69.

15 Kracauer, "Time and History," 68.

16 Barthes, *Camera Lucida*, 53.

17 Barthes, *Camera Lucida*, 53.

18 Margaret Olin, *Touching Photographs* (Chicago, IL: University of Chicago Press, 2012), 60.

19 Ben Goldberger, Paul Moakley, and Kira Pollack, TIME Inc., 100 Photos, The Most Influential Images of All Time, https://iconicphotos.wordpress.com/2009/05/06/tomoko-uemura-in-her-bath/.

20 Eileen Smith, W. Eugene Smith's widow, will no longer allow *Tomoko Uemura in*

Her Bath to be reproduced. She wishes to protect the privacy of Tomoko Uemura and her family.

21 Cindy Sherman, Gregory Crewdson, Philip-Lorca diCorcia, and Jell Wall, to name only the most prominent artists, are proponents of a photography divorced from a "real world referent." Among them, Sherman is perhaps closest to Weems in that her work has often referred to other images, varying from a general type of image as in *Untitled Film Stills*, to specific paintings as in *History Portraits/Old Masters*.

22 Franklin Sirmans outlines Weems's long-standing dedication to performance in "A World of Her Own: Carrie Mae Weems and Performance," in *Carrie Mae Weems: Three Decades of Photography and Video*, ed. Kathryn E. Delmez (Nashville, TN: Frist Center for the Visual Arts, in association with Yale University Press, 2012), 42–53. As Sirmans notes, in the video *Constructing History: A Requiem to Mark the Moment*, Weems's role as director is much more significant than in her previous work (53).

Robert Storr also calls attention to the performative aspects of Weems's work, noting that in *The Louisiana Project* (2003), *Roaming* (2006), the *Museum Series* (2007–present), and *Constructing History: A Requiem to Mark the Moment* (2008) "the explicit theatricality of her tableaux has only grown." Robert Storr, "Carrie Mae Weems: Anyway I Want It," in *Carrie Mae Weems: Three Decades of Photography and Video*, ed. Kathryn E. Delmez (Nashville, TN: Frist Center for the Visual Arts, in association with Yale University Press, 2012), 28.

23 Philip Auslander, "Carrie Mae Weems," *Artforum International* 47, no. 2 (October 2008): 389–90.

24 My reading here is informed by Robin Kelsey's assessment of Julia Margaret Cameron's work, in which he describes the productive role of "signs of performative failure" in her photographs. Robin Kelsey, *Photography and the Art of Chance* (Cambridge, MA: Belknap of Harvard University Press, 2015), 94.

25 Farrell, "Opus," n.p.

26 Hersh, "A[r]t & Soul."

27 Rebecca Schneider, *Performing Remains: Art and War in Times of Theatrical Reenactment* (London: Routledge, 2011), 32.

28 According to Hirsch, "Postmemory is a powerful and very particular form of memory precisely because its connection to its object or source is mediated not through recollection but through an imaginative investment and creation. This is not to say that memory itself is unmediated, but that it is more directly connected to the past. Postmemory characterizes the experience of those who grow up dominated by narratives that preceded their birth, whose own belated stories are evacuated by the stories of the previous generation shaped by traumatic events that can be neither understood nor recreated." Marianne Hirsch, *Family Frames: Photography, Narrative, and Postmemory* (Cambridge, MA: Harvard University Press, 1997), 22.

29 Elizabeth Freeman, *Time Binds: Queer Temporalities, Queer Histories* (Durham, NC: Duke University Press, 2010), 95–96.

30 Barthes, *Camera Lucida*, 77.

31 Moneta Sleet Jr. was a photographer for *Ebony* magazine and won the Pulitzer Prize for Feature Photography for this photograph in 1969. He was the first African American man and the first African American photographer to win a Pulitzer Prize. Deborah Willis, *Reflections in Black: A History of Black Photographers, 1840 to the Present* (New York: W. W. Norton, 2000), 111, 113.

32 Elizabeth Ware Abston, "Reconstructing the Past: The Power of Visual Culture in Works by Glenn Ligon, Carrie Mae Weems and Michael Ray Charles" (master's thesis, The University of Texas at San Antonio, 2013), 48. As Abston notes, Sleet's photograph was printed in *Ebony* the month following Martin Luther King Jr.'s funeral, and featured on the cover of the magazine in 2006 to mark the death of Coretta Scott King (40).

33 Sharon Sliwinski, "On Photographic Violence," *Photography and Culture* 2, no. 3 (November 2009): 309.

34 David L. Eng and David Kazanjian, "Introduction: Mourning Remains," in *Loss: The Politics of Mourning*, ed. David L. Eng and David Kazanjian, 1–25 (Berkeley: University of California Press, 2003), 3–4.

35 Dawoud Bey and Carrie Mae Weems, "Carrie Mae Weems," interview, *BOMB*, no. 108 (summer 2009): 60–67, 67.

36 Bey and Weems, "Carrie Mae Weems," 66.

37 As Kimberly Juanita Brown has argued, in Carrie Mae Weems's *Roaming* (2006), the artist's body, "placed in the center of a series of buildings meant to connote the hyperpresence of constructed power, provides the linchpin that disturbs the existing narrative." Kimberly Juanita Brown, *The Repeating Body: Slavery's Visual Resonance in the Contemporary* (Durham, NC: Duke University Press, 2015), 177. In Nicole R. Fleetwood's terms, Weems "investigates the productive possibilities" of the ways "the visible black body is always already troubling to the dominant visual field." Nicole R. Fleetwood, *Troubling Vision: Performance, Visuality, and Blackness* (Chicago: University of Chicago Press, 2011), 6. Weems uses her body in the image to effect what Daphne A. Brooks has called an act of "Afro-alienation," "critically defamiliarizing" her body "in order to yield alternative racial and gender epistemologies." Daphne A. Brooks, *Bodies in Dissent: Spectacular Performances of Race and Freedom, 1850–1910* (Durham, NC: Duke University Press, 2006), 5.

38 Wendy Kozol, *Distant Wars Visible: The Ambivalence of Witnessing* (Minneapolis: University of Minnesota Press, 2014), 196.

39 Barthes, *Camera Lucida*, 119.

40 Barthes, *Camera Lucida*, 119.

41 Barthes, *Camera Lucida*, 96.

Chapter 7

1 Taryn Simon, "Photographer's Foreword," in *The Innocents* (New York: Umbrage Editions, 2003), 7.

2 Simon, *Innocents*. This information is noted inside the book cover.

3 Simon collaborated with Neufeld and Scheck to identify her subjects and record their cases. Her project began as an assignment to photograph for a *New York Times Magazine* article on the wrongfully convicted. She then applied for and received a Guggenheim fellowship and pursued the work in 2000 and 2001, and finally completed and exhibited the photographs in 2003.

Sara Rimer, "Life after Death Row," *New York Times Magazine*, December 10, 2000, http://partners.nytimes.com/library/magazine/home/20001210mag-deathrow.html. Sean O'Hagan, "Taryn Simon: The Woman in the Picture," *Observer*, May 21, 2011, http://www.guardian.co.uk/artanddesign/2011/may/22/taryn-simon-tate-modern-interview. Sarah Boxer, "Photography Review; Exonerated, but Locked in Shadow," *New York Times*, June 25, 2003, http://www.nytimes.com/2003/06/25/arts/photography-review-exonerated-but-locked-in-shadow.html.

4 For a discussion of enframement, see Maurice O. Wallace, *Constructing the Black Masculine: Identity and Ideality in African American Men's Literature and Culture, 1775–1995* (Durham, NC: Duke University Press, 2002), especially chapter 1, "On Dangers Seen and Unseen: Identity Politics and the Burden of Black Male Specularity," 19–50.

5 As Katherine Biber has argued, "Simon's photographs invite us—their viewers, law's subjects—to re-enact the errors and violence law has already committed, so that we may not only see the harm that has been done, but also realize how easily it might be repeated. We look at these photographs to learn that the power of vision has seduced us into believing it will enable us to distinguish between innocent and guilty." Katherine Biber, "Photographs and Labels: Against a Criminology of Innocence," *Law/Text/Culture* 10 (2006): 20–21.

6 Simon, *Innocents*, 14.

7 This is how Katherine A. Bussard describes some of Philip-Lorca diCorcia's work. Katherine A. Bussard, *So the Story Goes* (New Haven, CT: Yale University Press and the Art Institute of Chicago, 2006), 39.

8 Bussard, *So the Story Goes*, 39.

9 Simon, *Innocents*, 7.

10 As Geoffrey Batchen has argued, "These are pictures, then, that return us and them [the wrongfully convicted] to the starting points of a brutal reality based on a fiction." Geoffrey Batchen, "Revenant," in *Taryn Simon, A Living Man Declared Dead and Other Chapters I–XVIII*, exhibition catalogue, Tate Modern/Neue Nationalgalerie (Berlin: Nationalgalerie Staatliche Museen; London: MACK, 2011), 1–12, 6.

11 Simon, *Innocents*, 28.

12 Simon, *Innocents*, 38.
13 Simon, *Innocents*, 40.
14 Simon, *Innocents*, 7.
15 Simon, *Innocents*, 42.
16 Stephen Spretnjak, *Police Composite Drawings* (1992–94), http://stephen spretnjak.com/Histories6.html, accessed January 1, 2013.
17 Allan Sekula, "The Body and the Archive," *October* 39 (winter 1986): 3–64.
18 This pronouncement comes from Cellmark Diagnostics, "the private firm that carried out some of the DNA analysis for the LAPD in the Simpson case." Sheila Jasanoff, "The Eye of Everyman: Witnessing DNA in the Simpson Trial," special issue "Contested Identities: Science, Law and Forensic Practice," *Social Studies of Science* 28, no. 5–6 (October–December 1998): 718.
19 Saul Halfon, "Collecting, Testing and Convincing: Forensic DNA Experts in the Courts," special issue "Contested Identities: Science, Law and Forensic Practice," *Social Studies of Science* 28, nos. 5–6 (October–December 1998): 810.
20 Halfon, "Collecting, Testing and Convincing," 807.
21 Jonathan Finn has argued similarly that "the production and interpretation of visual representation is a fundamental component of identification by DNA." Jonathan Finn, *Capturing the Criminal Image: From Mug Shot to Surveillance Society* (Minneapolis: University of Minnesota Press, 2009), 61.
22 Finn, *Capturing the Criminal Image*, 59–61.
23 Finn, *Capturing the Criminal Image*, 62. In an effort to regulate as much of the process as possible, Congress passed the DNA Identification Act, which took effect in 1994, standardizing procedures for collecting and producing DNA evidence according to FBI guidelines. Finn, *Capturing the Criminal Image*, 69–73.
24 Finn, *Capturing the Criminal Image*, 64.
25 Michael Lynch and Sheila Jasanoff, "Introduction: Contested Identities: Science, Law and Forensic Practice," special issue "Contested Identities: Science, Law and Forensic Practice," *Social Studies of Science* 28, no. 5–6 (October–December 1998): 680. Sheila Jasanoff identifies Barry Scheck as "a defense lawyer noted for his successful attacks on DNA-typing evidence," and describes how he challenged LAPD criminalist Denis Fung on violations of DNA sample collecting during the trial. Jasanoff, "Eye of Everyman," 729. Previous to that famous case, Scheck and Neufeld also participated in a lengthy admissibility hearing in *People v. Castro* (1989), helping the defense to successfully deny the presentation of DNA evidence to the jury. Lynch and Jasanoff, "Introduction," 678–79.
26 Simon A. Cole, "Witnessing Identification: Latent Fingerprinting Evidence and Expert Knowledge," special issue "Contested Identities: Science, Law and Forensic Practice," *Social Studies of Science* 28, nos. 5–6 (October–December 1998): 688.
27 Cole, "Witnessing Identification," 687.
28 Cole, "Witnessing Identification," 689, 691, 699 (quotation page 689).
29 Cole, "Witnessing Identification," 690. The photographic representation of the

fingerprint is especially important according to Jonathan Finn because it enables the suspect's body to be studied without the suspect present. Finn, *Capturing the Criminal Image*, 41.

30 Jasanoff, "Eye of Everyman," 734.

31 Although they are not iconic representations, commercial DNA portraits participate in the logics that have animated photographic portraiture since the nineteenth century. As Drew Ayers has argued, popular DNA portraits propose to record and make visible the "interior essence" of their subjects, even if their banded patterns cannot be recognized as representations of specific individuals. Drew Ayers, "Humans without Bodies: DNA Portraiture and Biocybernetic Reproduction," *Configurations* 19 (2011): 307–8. Artist Gary Schneider's *Genetic Self-Portrait* is an interesting work in this vein, as it calls attention to the links between photography and DNA typing, photographic surveillance and genetic mapping, exterior and interior representations of the self, likeness and portrait, body and soul, identification and identity. Gary Schneider, *Gary Schneider: Genetic Self-Portrait* (Syracuse, NY: Light Work, 1999).

32 Lisa Marie Cacho, *Social Death: Racialized Rightlessness and the Criminalization of the Unprotected* (New York: New York University Press, 2012), 2, 11.

33 Wallace, *Constructing the Black Masculine*, 19–50.

34 Simon, *Innocents*, 30.

35 For a consideration of the larger project in which this piece is included, *An American Index of the Hidden and Unfamiliar*, see Jordan Reznick, "Imperceptible Politics: The Photograph and the Aesthetic Experience," *Sightlines* (2012): 278–99.

36 As Jonathan Finn has argued, "The collection of DNA samples within law enforcement proceeds at a rate considerably faster than that of its analysis, producing large backlogs of samples." Finn, *Capturing the Criminal Image*, 75.

37 Critical Resistance and Incite!, "Critical Resistance-Incite! Statement on Gender Violence and the Prison-Industrial Complex," *Social Justice* 30, no. 3 (2003): 142. As Ruth Wilson Gilmore has argued, crime has actually declined more extensively in states that have not invested heavily in prisons: "State by state, those jurisdictions that have not built a lot of prisons and thrown more people into them have enjoyed greater decreases in crime than states where incapacitation became a central government activity." Ruth Wilson Gilmore, *Golden Gulag: Prisons, Surplus, Crisis, and Opposition in Globalizing California* (Berkeley: University of California Press, 2007), 15.

Coda

1 Rebecca Rafferty, "'The Birmingham Project' by Dawoud Bey: Portraits of Stolen Time," *Rochester City Newspaper*, November 12, 2014, https://www.rochestercitynewspaper.com/rochester/the-birmingham-project-by-dawoud-bey/Content?oid=2463191.

2 Bey saw the photograph as it was reproduced in Lorraine Hansberry, *The Movement: Documentary of a Struggle for Equality* (New York: Simon and Schuster, 1964). Dawoud Bey, in conversation with Gaëlle Morel and Karen Irvine, Columbia College, Chicago, April 11, 2019.

3 Liz Ronk, "The Girl Who Lived: Portrait of a Birmingham Church Bombing Survivor, 1963," *TIME* magazine, August 6, 2013, http://time.com/3877750/16th-street-baptist-church-bombing-victim-sarah-collins-1963/.

4 As Leigh Raiford has said, "Bey asked his sitters to look directly at the camera, and by extension to future audiences, with gazes that indict, invite, and challenge us." Leigh Raiford, "Dawoud Bey," special issue "Vision and Justice," *Aperture* 223 (summer 2016): 136.

5 Maurice Berger, "Reimagining a Tragedy, 50 Years Later," Lens blog, *New York Times*, September 13, 2013, https://lens.blogs.nytimes.com/2013/09/13/reimagining-a-tragedy-50-years-later/.

BIBLIOGRAPHY

Abston, Elizabeth Ware. "Reconstructing the Past: The Power of Visual Culture in Works by Glenn Ligon, Carrie Mae Weems and Michael Ray Charles." Master's thesis, The University of Texas at San Antonio, 2013.

Ackerman, Diane. *A Natural History of the Senses*. 1990. Reprint, New York: Vintage, 1991.

Albers, Kate Palmer. "Abundant Images and the Collective Sublime." *Exposure* 46, no. 2 (fall 2013): 4–14.

Alexander, Michelle. *The New Jim Crow: Mass Incarceration in the Age of Colorblindness*. Rev. ed. New York: The New Press, 2011.

Auslander, Philip. "Carrie Mae Weems." *Artforum International* 47, no. 2 (October 2008): 389–90.

Ayers, Drew. "Humans without Bodies: DNA Portraiture and Biocybernetic Reproduction." *Configurations* 19 (2011): 287–321.

Azoulay, Ariella. *Civil Imagination: A Political Ontology of Photography*. Translated by Louise Bethlehem. 2010. Reprint, London: Verso, 2015.

Azoulay, Ariella. "Photography." *Mafte'akh* 2e (2011): 65–80.

Baer, Ulrich. *Spectral Evidence: The Photography of Trauma*. Cambridge, MA: MIT Press, 2002.

Baker, Courtney R. "Emmett Till, Justice, and the Task of Recognition." In *Humane Insight: Looking at Images of African American Suffering and Death*, 69–93. Urbana-Champaign: University of Illinois Press, 2015.

Barthes, Roland. *Camera Lucida: Reflections on Photography*. Translated by Richard Howard. 1980. Reprint, New York: Hill and Wang, 1981.

Batchen, Geoffrey. *Forget Me Not: Photography and Remembrance*. New York: Princeton Architectural Press, 2004.

Batchen, Geoffrey. "Life and Death." In *Suspending Time: Life—Photography—Death*, 108–29. Shizuoka, Japan: Izo Photo Museum, 2010.

Batchen, Geoffrey. "Revenant." In *Taryn Simon, A Living Man Declared Dead and Other Chapters I–XVIII*, 1–12. Exhibition catalogue. Tate Modern/Neue Nationalgalerie and Berlin: Nationalgalerie Staatliche Museen; London: MACK, 2011.

Beckwith, Naomi. "A Post-Black-Power Child: Rashid Johnson's Historical References Enact a Complex Historical Reckoning." *Flash Art* 46, no. 290 (May/June 2013): 128–31.

Belisle, Brooke. "Felt Surface, Visible Image: Lorna Simpson's Photography and the Embodiment of Appearance." *Photography and Culture* 4, no. 2 (July 2011): 157–78.

Benjamin, Walter. "Little History of Photography." In *Walter Benjamin: Selected Writings*, vol. 2, part 2, *1931–1934*, edited by Michael W. Jennings, Howard Eiland, and Gary Smith, translated by Rodney Livingstone et al., 507–30. Cambridge, MA: Belknap of Harvard University Press, 1999.

Benjamin, Walter. "On the Concept of History." In *Walter Benjamin: Selected Writings*, vol. 4, *1938–1940*, edited by Howard Eiland and Michael W. Jennings, translated by Edmund Jephcott et al., 389–400. Cambridge, MA: Belknap of Harvard University Press, 2003.

Benjamin, Walter. "Paralipomena to 'On the Concept of History.'" In *Walter Benjamin: Selected Writings*, vol. 4, *1938–1940*, edited by Howard Eiland and Michael W. Jennings, translated by Edmund Jephcott et al., 401–11. Cambridge, MA: Belknap of Harvard University Press, 2003.

Benjamin, Walter. "The Work of Art in the Age of Its Technological Reproducibility." Second version. In *Walter Benjamin: Selected Writings*, vol. 3, *1935–1938*, edited by Howard Eiland and Michael W. Jennings, translated by Edmund Jephcott, Howard Eiland, et al., 101–33. Cambridge, MA: Belknap of Harvard University Press, 2002.

Berger, Martin A. *Seeing through Race: A Reinterpretation of Civil Rights Photography*. Berkeley: University of California Press, 2011.

Berger, Maurice. *For All the World to See: Visual Culture and the Struggle for Civil Rights*. New Haven, CT: Yale University Press, 2010.

Berger, Maurice. "Reimagining a Tragedy, 50 Years Later." Lens blog. *New York Times*, September 13, 2013. https://lens.blogs.nytimes.com/2013/09/13/reimagining-a-tragedy-50-years-later/.

Bergstein, Mary. "Lonely Aphrodites: On the Documentary Photography of Sculpture." *Art Bulletin* 74, no. 3 (September 1992): 475–98.

Bernier, Celeste-Marie. "'The Face of a Fugitive Slave': Representing and Reimagining Frederick Douglass in Popular Illustrations, Fine Art Portraiture and Daguerreotypes." In *Political Memory*, edited by Magnus Brechtken, 11–33. Göttingen, Germany: Vandenhoeck and Ruprecht, 2012.

Bernier, Celeste-Marie. "From Fugitive Slave to Fugitive Image: Nineteenth-Century African American Portrait Frontispieces and Interior Illustrations and the Case of Frederick Douglass." Unpublished manuscript.

Bernier, Celeste-Marie. "A 'Typical Negro' or a 'Work of Art'? The 'Inner' via the 'Outer Man' in Frederick Douglass's Manuscripts and Daguerreotypes." *Slavery and Abolition* 33, no. 2 (June 2012): 287–303.

Best, Stephen M. *The Fugitive's Properties: Law and the Poetics of Possession*. Chicago, IL: University of Chicago Press, 2004.

Bey, Dawoud. "Authoring the Black Image: The Photographs of James VanDerZee."

In *The James VanDerZee Studio*, edited by Colin Westerbeck. Chicago, IL: Art Institute of Chicago, 2004.

Bey, Dawoud. In conversation with Gaëlle Morel and Karen Irvine, April 11, 2019. Columbia College, Chicago, IL.

Bey, Dawoud, and Carrie Mae Weems. "Carrie Mae Weems." Interview. *BOMB* 108 (summer 2009): 60–67.

Biber, Katherine. "Photographs and Labels: Against a Criminology of Innocence." *Law/Text/Culture* 10 (2006): 19–40.

Birt, Rodger C. "A Life in American Photography." In *VanDerZee: Photographer 1886–1983*, by Deborah Willis-Braithwaite, with biographical essay by Rodger C. Birt, 26–73. New York: Harry N. Abrams in association with the National Portrait Gallery, Smithsonian Institution, 1993.

Black Emergency Cultural Coalition Records. Schomburg Center for Research in Black Culture. New York Public Library.

Blackwood, Sarah. "Fugitive Obscura: Runaway Slave Portraiture and Early Photographic Technology." *American Literature* 81, no. 1 (March 2009): 93–125.

Blair, Sara. *Harlem Crossroads: Black Writers and the Photograph in the Twentieth Century*. Princeton, NJ: Princeton University Press, 2007.

Blinderman, Barry. "Trace and Transience in the Photography of Jason Lazarus." In *Jason Lazarus: Your Time Is Gonna Come*, 68–71. Normal: University Galleries of Illinois State University, 2013.

Bourdieu, Pierre. *Distinction: A Social Critique of the Judgement of Taste*. Translated by Richard Nice. Cambridge, MA: Harvard University Press, 1984.

Bourdieu, Pierre. *Photography: A Middle-Brow Art*. 1965. Reprint, Stanford, CA: Stanford University Press, 1990.

Boxer, Sarah. "Photography Review; Exonerated, but Locked in Shadow." *New York Times*, June 25, 2003.

Boxer, Sarah. "Slogging through the Valley of the Shutter of Death." *New York Times*, July 23, 2004.

"Brady's Photographs: Pictures of the Dead at Antietam." *New York Times*, October 20, 1862.

Brooks, Daphne A. *Bodies in Dissent: Spectacular Performances of Race and Freedom, 1850–1910*. Durham, NC: Duke University Press, 2006.

Brown, Elspeth H., and Thy Phu, eds. *Feeling Photography*. Durham, NC: Duke University Press, 2014.

Brown, Kimberly Juanita. *The Repeating Body: Slavery's Visual Resonance in the Contemporary*. Durham, NC: Duke University Press, 2015.

Browne, Simone. *Dark Matters: On the Surveillance of Blackness*. Durham, NC: Duke University Press, 2015.

Bussard, Katherine A. *So the Story Goes*. New Haven, CT: Yale University Press and the Art Institute of Chicago, 2006.

Cacho, Lisa Marie. *Social Death: Racialized Rightlessness and the Criminalization of the Unprotected*. New York: New York University Press, 2012.

Cadava, Eduardo. *Words of Light: Theses on the Photography of History*. Princeton, NJ: Princeton University Press, 1997.

Campt, Tina M. *Image Matters: Archive, Photography, and the African Diaspora in Europe*. Durham, NC: Duke University Press, 2012.

Campt, Tina M. *Listening to Images*. Durham, NC: Duke University Press, 2017.

Caruth, Cathy. *Unclaimed Experience: Trauma, Narrative, History*. Baltimore, MD: Johns Hopkins University Press, 1996.

Childs, Dennis. *Slaves of the State: Black Incarceration from the Chain Gang to the Penitentiary*. Minneapolis: University of Minnesota Press, 2015.

Christian, Kelly. "'Rather a Grave Subject': The Critical Role of the Nineteenth-Century Postmortem Photograph." Master's thesis, School of the Art Institute of Chicago, 2012.

Cloutier, Crista. "Mumler's Ghosts." In *The Perfect Medium: Photography and the Occult*, by Clément Chéroux, Andreas Fischer, Pierre Apraxine, Denis Canguilhem, and Sophie Schmit, 20–28. New Haven, CT: Yale University Press, 2005.

Coates, Ta-Nehisi. *Between the World and Me*. New York: Spiegel & Grau, 2015.

Cole, Simon A. "Witnessing Identification: Latent Fingerprinting Evidence and Expert Knowledge." Special issue "Contested Identities: Science, Law and Forensic Practice," *Social Studies of Science* 28, nos. 5–6 (October–December 1998): 687–712.

Cooks, Bridget R. "Black Artists and Activism: *Harlem on My Mind* (1969)." *American Studies* 48, no. 1 (spring 2007): 5–39.

Cooks, Bridget R. *Exhibiting Blackness: African Americans and the American Art Museum*. Amherst, MA: University of Massachusetts Press, 2011.

Copeland, Huey. *Bound to Appear: Art, Slavery, and the Site of Blackness in Multicultural America*. Chicago, IL: University of Chicago Press, 2013.

Copeland, Huey. "'Bye, Bye Black Girl': Lorna Simpson's Figurative Retreat." *Art Journal* 64, no. 2 (summer 2005): 62–77.

Copeland, Huey. "Rashid Johnson: Museum of Contemporary Art, Chicago." *Artforum* 50, no. 10 (summer 2012): 302–3.

Copeland, Huey, and Krista Thompson. "Perpetual Returns: New World Slavery and the Matter of the Visual." *Representations* 113 (winter 2011): 1–15.

Crawford, Romi. "Black Photographers Who Take Black Pictures." In *The Wall of Respect: Public Art and Black Liberation in 1960s Chicago*, by Abdul Alkalimat, Romi Crawford, and Rebecca Zorach, 193–212. Chicago, IL: Northwestern University Press, 2017.

Critical Resistance and Incite! "Critical Resistance-Incite! Statement on Gender Violence and the Prison-Industrial Complex." *Social Justice* 30, no. 3 (2003): 141–50.

Cvetkovich, Ann. *An Archive of Feelings: Trauma, Sexuality, and Lesbian Public Cultures*. Durham, NC: Duke University Press, 2003.

Cvetkovich, Ann. "Photographing Objects as Queer Archival Practice." In *Feeling Photography*, edited by Elspeth H. Brown and Thy Phu, 273–96. Durham, NC: Duke University Press, 2014.

Cvetkovich, Ann. Visiting artist program lecture, November 2, 2016. School of the Art Institute of Chicago.

Davey, Monica, and Gretchen Ruethling. "After 50 Years, Emmett Till's Body Is Exhumed." *New York Times*, June 2, 2005.

Davidson, Shayne. *Captured and Exposed: The First Police Rogues' Gallery in America*. Saint Louis: Missouri History Museum Press, 2017.

Didi-Huberman, Georges. *Images in Spite of All: Four Photographs from Auschwitz*. Translated by Shane B. Lillis. Chicago, IL: University of Chicago Press, 2008.

Dinius, Marcy. "Seeing a Slave as a Man: Frederick Douglass, Racial Progress, and Daguerreian Portraiture." In *The Camera and the Press: American Visual and Print Culture in the Age of the Daguerreotype*, 192–232. Philadelphia: University of Pennsylvania Press, 2012.

Doane, Mary Anne. *The Emergence of Cinematic Time: Modernity, Contingency, the Archive*. Cambridge, MA: Harvard University Press, 2002.

Doss, Erika. *Memorial Mania: Public Feeling in America*. Chicago, IL: University of Chicago Press, 2010.

Douglass, Frederick. "The Age of Pictures." In "Lecture on Pictures" [title varies]. Frederick Douglass Papers at the Library of Congress: Speech, Article, and Book File. American Memory, Library of Congress Manuscript Division. https://www.loc.gov/item/mfd.22004/.

Douglass, Frederick. "Lecture on Pictures" [title varies]. Frederick Douglass Papers at the Library of Congress: Speech, Article, and Book File. American Memory, Library of Congress Manuscript Division. https://www.loc.gov/item/mfd.22004/.

Douglass, Frederick. "Pictures and Progress: An Address Delivered in Boston, Massachusetts, on 3 December 1861." In *The Frederick Douglass Papers: Series One, Speeches, Debates, and Interviews*, edited by John W. Blassingame, 3:452–73. New Haven, CT: Yale University Press, 1985.

Douglass, Frederick. "Pictures and Progress." 1865. Frederick Douglass Papers at the Library of Congress: Speech, Article, and Book File. American Memory, Library of Congress Manuscript Division. https://www.loc.gov/item/mfd.28009/.

Douglass, Frederick. "A Tribute to the Negro." *North Star*, April 7, 1849.

Drobnick, Jim. "Volatile Effects: Olfactory Dimensions of Art and Architecture." In *Empire of the Senses: The Sensual Culture Reader*, edited by David Howes, 265–80. Oxford: Berg, 2005.

Du Bois, W. E. B. *The Souls of Black Folk*. Introduction by John Edgar Wideman. 1903. Reprint, New York: Vintage/Library of America, 1990.

Eckrich, Kristen. "Lorna Simpson's *9 Props*: Deconstructing Photographic Portraiture." Master's thesis, American University, Washington, DC, 2014.

Edwards, Elizabeth. "Photography and the Material Performance of the Past." *History and Theory* 48, no. 4 (December 2009): 130–50.

Edwards, Elizabeth. *Raw Histories: Photographs, Anthropology and Museums*. Oxford: Berg, 2001.

Edwards, Elizabeth, and Janice Hart, eds. *Photographs/Objects/Histories: On the Materiality of Images*. London: Routledge, 2004.
Elkins, James. *What Photography Is*. New York: Routledge, 2012.
Eng, David L., and David Kazanjian. "Introduction: Mourning Remains." In *Loss: The Politics of Mourning*, edited by David L. Eng and David Kazanjian, 1–25. Berkeley: University of California Press, 2003.
English, Darby. "Beyond Black Representational Space." In *How to See a Work of Art in Total Darkness*, 27–70. Cambridge, MA: MIT Press, 2007.
English, Darby. "Emmett Till Ever After." In *Black Is, Black Ain't*, edited by Hamza Walker and Karen Reimer, 84–99. Chicago, IL: Renaissance Society, 2013.
Enwezor, Okwui. "Repetition and Differentiation—Lorna Simpson's Iconography of the Racial Sublime." In *Lorna Simpson*, 103–30. New York: Abrams and American Federation of Arts, 2006.
Enwezor, Okwui. "Social Grace: The Work of Lorna Simpson." *Third Text* 35 (summer 1996): 43–58.
Farrell, Laurie Ann. "An Opus: Carrie Mae Weems." In *Carrie Mae Weems: Constructing History: A Requiem to Mark the Moment*. Savannah, GA: Savannah College of Art and Design, 2008.
Faust, Drew Gilpin. *This Republic of Suffering: Death and the American Civil War*. New York: Vintage, 2008.
Finley, Cheryl. *Committed to Memory: The Art of the Slave Ship Icon*. Princeton, NJ: Princeton University Press, 2018.
Finn, Jonathan. *Capturing the Criminal Image: From Mug Shot to Surveillance Society*. Minneapolis: University of Minnesota Press, 2009.
Fleetwood, Nicole R. "Posing in Prison: Family Photographs, Emotional Labor, and Carceral Intimacy." *Public Culture* 27, no. 3 (2015): 487–511.
Fleetwood, Nicole R. *Troubling Vision: Performance, Visuality, and Blackness*. Chicago: University of Chicago Press, 2011.
Frassanito, William A. *Antietam: The Photographic Legacy of America's Bloodiest Day*. New York: Charles Scribner's Sons, 1978.
Freeman, Elizabeth. "Introduction." Special issue "Queer Temporalities," *GLQ: A Journal of Lesbian and Gay Studies* 13, nos. 2–3 (2007): 159–76.
Freeman, Elizabeth. *Time Binds: Queer Temporalities, Queer Histories*. Durham, NC: Duke University Press, 2010.
Freud, Sigmund. "Mourning and Melancholia." 1917. In *The Standard Edition of the Complete Psychological Works of Sigmund Freud*, vol. 14, *1914–1916*, translated by James Strachey, 243–58. London: Hogarth Press, 1957.
Fusco, Coco. "Uncanny Dissonance: The Work of Lorna Simpson." In *English Is Broken Here: Notes on Cultural Fusion in the Americas*, 97–102. New York: The New Press, 1995.
Gaines, Kevin K. *Uplifting the Race: Black Leadership, Politics, and Culture in the Twentieth Century*. Chapel Hill: University of North Carolina Press, 1996.
Gates, Henry Louis, Jr. "The Face and Voice of Blackness." In *Facing History: The*

Black Image in American Art, 1710–1940, by Guy C. McElroy. San Francisco, CA: Bedford Arts, 1990.
Gates, Henry Louis, Jr. "Frederick Douglass's Camera Obscura: Representing the Antislave 'Clothed and in Their Own Form.'" *Critical Inquiry* 42, no. 1 (autumn 2015): 31–60.
Gates, Henry Louis, Jr. *The Signifying Monkey: A Theory of Afro-American Literary Criticism*. New York: Oxford University Press, 1988.
Gilmore, Ruth Wilson. *Golden Gulag: Prisons, Surplus, Crisis, and Opposition in Globalizing California*. Berkeley: University of California Press, 2007.
Giroux, Henry A. "Reading Hurricane Katrina: Race, Class, and the Biopolitics of Disposability." *College Literature* 33, no. 3 (summer 2006): 171–96.
Goldsby, Jacqueline. "The High and Low Tech of It: The Meaning of Lynching and the Death of Emmett Till." *Yale Journal of Criticism* 9, no. 2 (1996): 245–82.
Goldsby, Jacqueline. *A Spectacular Secret: Lynching in American Life and Literature*. Chicago, IL: University of Chicago Press, 2006.
Greenough, Sarah. Introduction to *The Art of the American Snapshot, 1888–1978: From the Collection of Robert E. Jackson*, by Sarah Greenough and Diane Waggoner, with Sarah Kennel and Matthew S. Witkovsky, 1–6. Washington, DC: National Gallery of Art, in association with Princeton University Press, 2007.
Greenough, Sarah. "The Memory of Time: Introduction." In *The Memory of Time: Contemporary Photographs at the National Gallery of Art*, by Sarah Greenough and Andrea Nelson, with Sarah Kennel, Diane Waggoner, and Leslie J. Ureña, 1–15. Washington, DC: National Gallery of Art, 2015.
Greenough, Sarah. "Seeing What Ought to Be: Photography and the 54th Massachusetts Regiment." In *Tell It with Pride: The 54th Massachusetts Regiment and Augustus Saint-Gaudens' Shaw Memorial*, by Sarah Greenough and Nancy K. Anderson, with Lindsay Harris and Renée Ater, 2–19. Washington, DC: National Gallery of Art, 2013.
Greenough, Sarah, and Andrea Nelson, with Sarah Kennel, Diane Waggoner, and Leslie J. Ureña. *The Memory of Time: Contemporary Photographs at the National Gallery of Art*. Washington, DC: National Gallery of Art, 2015.
Greer, Brenna Wynn. *Represented: The Black Imagemakers Who Reimagined African American Citizenship*. Philadelphia: University of Pennsylvania Press, 2019.
Gunning, Tom. "Phantom Images and Modern Manifestations: Spirit Photography, Magic Theater, Trick Films, and Photography's Uncanny." In *Fugitive Images: From Photography to Video*, edited by Patrice Petro, 42–71. Bloomington: Indiana University Press, 1995.
Halfon, Saul. "Collecting, Testing and Convincing: Forensic DNA Experts in the Courts." Special issue "Contested Identities: Science, Law and Forensic Practice," *Social Studies of Science* 28, nos. 5–6 (October–December 1998): 801–28.
Hall, Rachel. *Wanted: The Outlaw in American Visual Culture*. Charlottesville: University of Virginia Press, 2009.

Hansberry, Lorraine. *The Movement: Documentary of a Struggle for Equality*. New York: Simon and Schuster, 1964.

Hariman, Robert, and John Louis Lucaites. *No Caption Needed: Iconic Photographs, Public Culture, and Liberal Democracy*. Chicago, IL: University of Chicago Press, 2007.

Harris, Cheryl I. "Whiteness as Property." *Harvard Law Review* 106, no. 8 (June 1993): 1707–91.

Harris, John M. "'Truthful as a Record of Heaven': The Battle of Antietam and the Birth of Photojournalism." *Southern Cultures* 19, no. 3 (fall 2013): 79–94.

Harris, Thomas Allen, dir. *Through a Lens Darkly: Black Photographers and the Emergence of a People*. 2014.

Hartman, Saidiya V. *Scenes of Subjection: Terror, Slavery, and Self-Making in Nineteenth-Century America*. New York: Oxford University Press, 1997.

Hartman, Saidiya V. "Venus in Two Acts." *Small Axe* 26 (June 2008): 1–14.

Hersh, Allison. "A[r]t and Soul: Staging History." *Savannah Morning News*, October 11, 2008. http://savannahnow.com/accent/2008-10-11/soul-staging-history.

Hill, Ginger. "'Rightly Viewed': Theorizations of Self in Frederick Douglass's Lectures on Pictures." In *Pictures and Progress: Early Photography and the Making of African American Identity*, edited by Maurice O. Wallace and Shawn Michelle Smith, 41–82. Durham, NC: Duke University Press, 2012.

Hirsch, Marianne. *Family Frames: Photography, Narrative, and Postmemory*. Cambridge, MA: Harvard University Press, 1997.

Hirsch, Marianne. "Introduction: Familial Looking." In *The Familial Gaze*, edited by Marianne Hirsch, xi–xxv. Hanover, NH: Dartmouth College and University Press of New England, 1999.

hooks, bell. "In Our Glory: Photography and Black Life." In *Picturing Us: African American Identity in Photography*, edited by Deborah Willis, 42–53. New York: The New Press, 1994.

"Horrors of the Battlefield." *Harper's Weekly*, October 11, 1862.

Iversen, Margaret. "Exposure." In *Photography, Trace, and Trauma*, 1–16. Chicago, IL: University of Chicago Press, 2017.

Jackson, Bruce. *Pictures from a Drawer: Prison and the Art of Portraiture*. Philadelphia, PA: Temple University Press, 2009.

Jacobson, Matthew Frye. *Whiteness of a Different Color: European Immigrants and the Alchemy of Race*. Cambridge, MA: Harvard University Press, 1998.

Jasanoff, Sheila. "The Eye of Everyman: Witnessing DNA in the Simpson Trial." Special issue "Contested Identities: Science, Law and Forensic Practice," *Social Studies of Science* 28, nos. 5–6 (October–December 1998): 713–40.

Jenkins, Keith. *Re-thinking History*. 1991. Reprint, London: Routledge Classics, 2003.

Jones, Kellie. "(Un)Seen and Overheard: Pictures by Lorna Simpson." In *Lorna Simpson*, by Kellie Jones, Thelma Golden, and Chrissie Iles, 26–103. London: Phaidon Press, 2002.

Kaplan, Louis. *The Strange Case of William Mumler, Spirit Photographer.* Minneapolis: University of Minnesota Press, 2008.

Keenan, Thomas, and Eyal Weizman. *Mengele's Skull: The Advent of a Forensic Aesthetics*. Berlin: Sternberg Press, 2012.

Kelsey, Robin. *Photography and the Art of Chance*. Cambridge, MA: Belknap Press of Harvard University Press, 2015.

Kozol, Wendy. *Distant Wars Visible: The Ambivalence of Witnessing.* Minneapolis: University of Minnesota Press, 2014.

Kracauer, Siegfried. "Photography." 1927. Translated by Thomas Y. Levin. *Critical Inquiry* 19, no. 3 (spring 1993): 421–36.

Kracauer, Siegfried. "Time and History." 1963. Beiheft 6: History and the Concept of Time, *History and Theory* 6 (1966): 65–78.

Krauss, Rosalind. "Photography's Discursive Spaces: Landscape/View." *Art Journal* 42, no. 4 (winter 1982): 311–19.

Larsen, Nella. *Quicksand*. In *Quicksand and Passing*, edited by Deborah McDowell, 1–142. American Women Writers Series. 1928. Reprint, New Brunswick, NJ: Rutgers University Press, 1986.

Lee, Anthony W. "The Image of War." In *On Alexander Gardner's* Photographic Sketch Book *of the Civil War*, by Anthony W. Lee and Elizabeth Young, 8–51. Berkeley: University of California Press, 2007.

Lee, Anthony W. Introduction to *Weegee and Naked City*, by Anthony W. Lee and Richard Meyer, 1–11. Berkeley: University of California Press, 2008.

Lee, Anthony W., and Richard Meyer. *Weegee and Naked City*. Berkeley: University of California Press, 2008.

Lennard, Katherine J. "Touching Absence: A Reconstruction of Lewis Powell." Master's thesis, School of the Art Institute of Chicago, 2009.

Lipsitz, George. "Learning from New Orleans: The Social Warrant of Hostile Privatism and Competitive Consumer Citizenship." *Cultural Anthropology* 21, no. 3 (August 2006): 451–68.

Luciano, Dana. *Arranging Grief: Sacred Time and the Body in Nineteenth-Century America*. New York: New York University Press, 2007.

Luster, Deborah. Artist's talk, November 10, 2011. Columbia College, Chicago, IL.

Luster, Deborah. "The Reappearance of Those Who Have Gone." 2002. In *One Big Self: Prisoners of Louisiana*, by Deborah Luster and C. D. Wright, 1–4. Santa Fe, NM: Twin Palms, 2003.

Luster, Deborah, and C. D. Wright. *One Big Self: Prisoners of Louisiana*. Santa Fe, NM: Twin Palms, 2003.

Luster, Deborah, and C. D. Wright. *The Tenth Dorothea Lange-Paul Taylor Prize.* Durham, NC: Center for Documentary Studies, 2001.

Lynch, Michael, and Sheila Jasanoff. "Introduction: Contested Identities: Science, Law and Forensic Practice." Special issue "Contested Identities: Science, Law and Forensic Practice," *Social Studies of Science* 28, nos. 5–6 (October–December 1998): 675–86.

Macpherson, C. B. *The Political Theory of Possessive Individualism*. Oxford: Oxford University Press, 1962.

Mann, Sally. "Collodion Process." Art 21. November 2001. https://art21.org/read/sally-mann-collodion-process/.

Mann, Sally. *Hold Still: A Memoir with Photographs*. New York: Little, Brown and Company, 2015.

Mann, Sally. *What Remains*. Boston, MA: Bulfinch Press, 2003.

Mavor, Carol. *Becoming: The Photographs of Clementina, Viscountess Hawarden*. Durham, NC: Duke University Press, 1999.

Mavor, Carol. "Odor di Femina: Though You May Not See Her, You Can Certainly Smell Her." *Cultural Studies* 12, no. 1 (1998): 51–81.

Mavor, Carol. *Pleasures Taken: Performances of Sexuality and Loss in Victorian Photographs*. Durham, NC: Duke University Press, 1995.

Mbembe, Achille. "Introduction: Time on the Move." In *On the Postcolony*, 1–23. Berkeley: University of California Press, 2001.

McGarry, Molly. *Ghosts of Futures Past: Spiritualism and the Cultural Politics of Nineteenth-Century America*. Berkeley: University of California Press, 2008.

Meyer, Richard. "Learning from Low Culture." In *Weegee and Naked City*, by Anthony W. Lee and Richard Meyer, 13–61. Berkeley: University of California Press, 2008.

Miller, Monica L. *Slaves to Fashion: Black Dandyism and the Styling of Black Diasporic Identity*. Durham, NC: Duke University Press, 2009.

Mirzoeff, Nicholas. *The Right to Look: A Counterhistory of Visuality*. Durham, NC: Duke University Press, 2011.

Mitchell, Michele. *Righteous Propagation: African Americans and the Politics of Racial Destiny after Reconstruction*. Chapel Hill: University of North Carolina Press, 2004.

Mobley, Chuck. Introduction to *thtk (2010–present), Jason Lazarus*, 2–3. San Francisco, CA: SF Camerawork, 2013.

Mooney, Amy M. "Rashid Johnson." In *Bulletin of the Detroit Institute of Arts* 86, no. 1/4 (2012): 58–59.

Moser, Gabrielle. "Developing Historical Negatives: The Colonial Photographic Archive as Optical Unconscious." In *Photography and the Optical Unconscious*, edited by Shawn Michelle Smith and Sharon Sliwinski, 229–63. Durham, NC: Duke University Press, 2017.

Moten, Fred. *In the Break: The Aesthetics of the Black Radical Tradition*. Minneapolis: University of Minnesota Press, 2003.

Muñoz, José Esteban. "Photographies of Mourning: Melancholia and Ambivalence in VanDerZee, Mapplethorpe, and *Looking for Langston*." In *Disidentifications: Queers of Color and the Performance of Politics*, 57–74. Minneapolis: University of Minnesota Press, 1999.

Neary, Janet. *Fugitive Testimony: On the Visual Logic of Slave Narratives*. New York: Fordham University Press, 2016.

Nickel, Douglas R. *Snapshots: The Photography of Everyday Life, 1888 to the Present.* San Francisco, CA: San Francisco Museum of Modern Art, 1998.

Nixon, Rob. *Slow Violence and the Environmentalism of the Poor.* Cambridge, MA: Harvard University Press, 2011.

O'Hagan, Sean. "Taryn Simon: The Woman in the Picture." *Observer*, May 21, 2011.

Olin, Margaret. *Touching Photographs.* Chicago, IL: University of Chicago Press, 2012.

Paitz, Kendra. "Come as You Are: Jason Lazarus's Gestures of Inclusion." In *Jason Lazarus: Your Time Is Gonna Come*, 72–77. Normal: University Galleries of Illinois State University, 2013.

Parsons, Sarah. "Privacy, Photography, and the Art Defense." In *Revealing Privacy: Debating the Understandings of Privacy*, edited by Margherita Carucci, 105–18. Bern, Switzerland: Peter Lang, 2012.

Patterson, Orlando. *Slavery and Social Death: A Comparative Study.* Cambridge, MA: Harvard University Press, 1982.

Rafferty, Rebecca. "'The Birmingham Project' by Dawoud Bey: Portraits of Stolen Time." *Rochester City Newspaper*, November 12, 2014. https://www.rochestercitynewspaper.com/rochester/the-birmingham-project-by-dawoud-bey/Content?oid=2463191.

Raiford, Leigh. "Dawoud Bey." Special issue "Vision and Justice," *Aperture* 223 (summer 2016): 136.

Raiford, Leigh. *Imprisoned in a Luminous Glare: Photography and the African American Freedom Struggle.* Chapel Hill: University of North Carolina Press, 2011.

Ravenal, John B. "Matter Lent." In *Sally Mann: The Flesh and the Spirit*, 70–72. Richmond: Virginia Museum of Fine Arts, 2010.

Ravenal, John B. "Sally Mann: The Flesh and the Spirit." In *Sally Mann: The Flesh and the Spirit*, 1–8. Richmond: Virginia Museum of Fine Arts, 2010.

Reinhardt, Mark. "Picturing Violence: Aesthetics and the Anxiety of Critique." In *Beautiful Suffering: Photography and the Traffic in Pain*, edited by Mark Reinhardt, Holly Edwards, and Erina Duganne, 13–36. Chicago, IL: University of Chicago Press/Williamstown, MA: Williams College Museum of Art, 2006.

Reznick, Jordan. "Imperceptible Politics: The Photograph and the Aesthetic Experience." *Sightlines* (2012): 278–99.

Richardson, Jared C. "Br(others) Only: Rashid Johnson, Class, and the Fraternal Orders of Afrofuturism." Master's thesis, The University of Texas at Austin, 2012.

Rimer, Sara. "Life after Death Row." *New York Times Magazine*, December 10, 2000.

Roach, Mary. *Stiff: The Curious Lives of Human Cadavers.* New York: W. W. Norton, 2003.

Robinson, Jontyle Theresa. *Bearing Witness: Contemporary Works by African American Women Artists.* New York: Spelman College and Rizzoli International Publications, 1996.

Rogers, Molly. *Delia's Tears: Race, Science, and Photography in Nineteenth-Century America.* New Haven, CT: Yale University Press, 2010.

Ronk, Liz. "The Girl Who Lived: Portrait of a Birmingham Church Bombing Survivor, 1963." *TIME* magazine, August 6, 2013. http://time.com/3877750/16th-street-baptist-church-bombing-victim-sarah-collins-1963/.

Rosler, Martha. *Martha Rosler, 3 Works: 1. The Restoration of High Culture in Chile (1972); 2. The Bowery in Two Inadequate Descriptive Systems (1974); 3. in, around, and afterthoughts (on documentary photography) (1981).* Halifax, NS: Nova Scotia College of Art and Design, 2006.

Roth, Michael S. "Photographic Ambivalence and Historical Consciousness." *History and Theory* 48, no. 4 (December 2009): 82–94.

Sante, Luc. *Evidence: NYPD Crime Scene Photographs: 1914–1918.* 1992. Reprint, New York: Barnes and Noble, 2006.

Savage, Kirk. "The Unknowable Dead: The Civil War and the Origins of Modern Commemoration." In *The Civil War in Art and Memory*, edited by Kirk Savage, 81–102. Studies in the History of Art. Washington, DC: National Gallery of Art, 2016.

Schneider, Gary. *Gary Schneider: Genetic Self-Portrait.* Syracuse, NY: Light Work, 1999.

Schneider, Rebecca. *Performing Remains: Art and War in Times of Theatrical Reenactment.* London: Routledge, 2011.

Schneider, Suzanne. "Louis Agassiz and the American School of Ethnoeroticism: Polygenesis, Pornography, and Other 'Perfidious Influences.'" In *Pictures and Progress: Early Photography and the Making of African American Identity*, edited by Maurice O. Wallace and Shawn Michelle Smith, 211–43. Durham, NC: Duke University Press, 2012.

Schwartz, Vanessa R. "Walter Benjamin for Historians." *American Historical Review* 106, no. 5 (December 2001): 1721–43.

Sedgwick, Eve Kosofsky. *Touching Feeling: Affect, Pedagogy, Performativity.* Durham, NC: Duke University Press, 2003.

Sekula, Allan. "The Body and the Archive." *October* 39 (winter 1986): 3–64.

Sekula, Allan. *Photography Against the Grain: Essays and Photo Works, 1973–1983.* Halifax, NS: Nova Scotia College of Art and Design, 1984.

Sharpe, Christina. *In the Wake: On Blackness and Being.* Durham, NC: Duke University Press, 2016.

Shaw, Gwendolyn DuBois, with contributions by Emily K. Shubert. *Portraits of a People: Picturing African Americans in the Nineteenth Century.* Seattle: University of Washington Press, 2006.

Shouse, Eric. "Feeling, Emotion, Affect." *M/C Journal* 8, no. 6 (2005). http://journal.media-culture.org.au/0512/03-shouse.php.

Simon, Joan, with contributions by Naomi Beckwith, Marta Gili, Thomas J. Lax, and Elvan Zabunyan. *Lorna Simpson.* Munich, Germany: Delmonico Books/Prestel/Minneapolis, MN: Foundation for the Exhibition of Photography/Paris: Jeu de Paume, 2013.

Simon, Taryn. *The Innocents.* New York: Umbrage Editions, 2003.

Simpson, Lorna. Artist's talk, May 13, 2010. Walker Art Center, Minneapolis, Minnesota. https://www.youtube.com/watch?v=cmvEAUfZXHs.

Sirmans, Frank. "A World of Her Own: Carrie Mae Weems and Performance." In *Carrie Mae Weems: Three Decades of Photography and Video*, edited by Kathryn E. Delmez, 42–53. Nashville, TN: Frist Center for the Visual Arts, in association with Yale University Press, 2012.

Sliwinski, Sharon. *Human Rights in Camera*. Chicago, IL: University of Chicago Press, 2011.

Sliwinski, Sharon. "On Photographic Violence." *Photography and Culture* 2, no. 3 (November 2009): 303–16.

Slotkin, Richard. *The Long Road to Antietam: How the Civil War Became a Revolution*. New York: Liveright/Norton, 2012.

Smith, Cherise. "Fragmented Documents: Works by Lorna Simpson, Carrie Mae Weems, and Willie Robert Middlebrook at the Art Institute of Chicago." *Museum Studies* 24, no. 2 (1999): 244–59, 271–72.

Smith, Mark M. *Sensing the Past: Seeing, Hearing, Smelling, Tasting, and Touching in History*. Berkeley: University of California Press, 2007.

Smith, Mark M. "When Seeing Makes Scents." *American Art* 24, no. 3 (fall 2010): 12–14.

Smith, Shawn Michelle. *American Archives: Gender, Race, and Class in Visual Culture*. Princeton, NJ: Princeton University Press, 1999.

Smith, Shawn Michelle. "The Evidence of Lynching Photographs." In *Lynching Photographs*, by Dora Apel and Shawn Michelle Smith, 10–41. Berkeley: University of California Press, 2007.

Smith, Shawn Michelle. *Photography on the Color Line: W. E. B. Du Bois, Race, and Visual Culture*. Durham, NC: Duke University Press, 2004.

Smith, Shawn Michelle. "Photography between Desire and Grief: Roland Barthes and F. Holland Day." In *Feeling Photography*, edited by Elspeth H. Brown and Thy Phu, 29–46. Durham, NC: Duke University Press, 2014.

Solomon-Godeau, Abigail. "Found Images, Lost Meanings, Invisible Traumas." In *thtk (2010–present), Jason Lazarus*, 50–58. San Francisco, CA: SF Camerawork, 2013.

Spretnjak, Stephen. *Police Composite Drawings* (1992–94). http://stephenspretnjak.com/Histories6.html, accessed March 27, 2019.

Stackhouse, Christopher. "Rashid Johnson." Interview. *Art in America*, April 4, 2012.

Stauffer, John. "Frederick Douglass and the Aesthetics of Freedom." *Raritan* 25, no. 1 (summer 2005): 114–36.

Stauffer, John, Zoe Trodd, and Celeste-Marie Bernier. *Picturing Frederick Douglass: An Illustrated Biography of the Nineteenth Century's Most Photographed American*. New York: Liveright/Norton, 2015.

Stoler, Ann Laura. *Along the Archival Grain: Epistemic Anxieties and Colonial Common Sense*. Princeton, NJ: Princeton University Press, 2010.

Storr, Robert. "Carrie Mae Weems: Anyway I Want It." In *Carrie Mae Weems: Three*

Decades of Photography and Video, edited by Kathryn E. Delmez, 20–31. Nashville, TN: Frist Center for the Visual Arts, in association with Yale University Press, 2012.

Tagg, John. *The Burden of Representation: Essays on Photographies and Histories.* Minneapolis: University of Minnesota Press, 1988.

Tapia, Ruby C. *American Pietàs: Visions of Race, Death, and the Maternal.* Minneapolis: University of Minnesota Press, 2011.

Tapia, Ruby C. "Profane Illuminations: The Gendered Problematics of Critical Carceral Visualities." *PMLA* 123, no. 3 (May 2008): 684–87.

Taylor, Diana. *The Archive and the Repertoire: Performing Cultural Memory in the Americas.* Durham, NC: Duke University Press, 2003.

Thaggert, Miriam. *Images of Black Modernism: Verbal and Visual Strategies of the Harlem Renaissance.* Amherst: University of Massachusetts Press, 2010.

Thirteenth Amendment to the Constitution. Primary Documents in American History. https://www.loc.gov/rr/program/bib/ourdocs/13thamendment.html, accessed September 18, 2018.

Thompson, Krista. *Shine: The Visual Economy of Light in African Diasporic Aesthetic Practice.* Durham, NC: Duke University Press, 2015.

Till-Mobley, Mamie, and Christopher Benson. *Death of Innocence: The Story of the Hate Crime That Changed America.* New York: Random House, 2003.

Trachtenberg, Alan. *Reading American Photographs: Images as History, Mathew Brady to Walker Evans.* New York: Hill and Wang, 1989.

Tucker, Anne Wilkes. "Living Memory." In *Sally Mann: The Flesh and the Spirit*, by John B. Ravenal, 171–77. Richmond: Virginia Museum of Fine Arts, 2010.

Tucker, Jennifer, in collaboration with Tina Campt. "Entwined Practices: Engagements with Photography in Historical Inquiry." Special issue "Photography and Historical Interpretation," *History and Theory* 48, no. 4 (December 2009): 1–8.

Tyson, Timothy B. *The Blood of Emmett Till.* New York: Simon and Schuster, 2017.

Villaseñor, Maria Christina, and Lorna Simpson. "*Nine Props*: An Interview and Art Portfolio." *Paris Review* 138 (spring 1996): 72–86.

Wallace, Maurice O. *Constructing the Black Masculine: Identity and Ideality in African American Men's Literature and Culture, 1775–1995.* Durham, NC: Duke University Press, 2002.

Wallace, Maurice O. "Framing the Black Soldier: Image, Uplift, and the Duplicity of Pictures." In *Pictures and Progress: Early Photography and the Making of African American Identity*, edited by Maurice O. Wallace and Shawn Michelle Smith, 244–66. Durham, NC: Duke University Press, 2012.

Wallace, Maurice O., and Shawn Michelle Smith. "Introduction: Pictures and Progress." In *Pictures and Progress: Early Photography and the Making of African American Identity*, edited by Maurice O. Wallace and Shawn Michelle Smith, 1–17. Durham, NC: Duke University Press, 2012.

Wallace, Paula S. Foreword. In *Carrie Mae Weems: Constructing History: A Requiem to Mark the Moment.* Savannah, GA: Savannah College of Art and Design, 2008.

Wallis, Brian. "Black Bodies, White Science: Louis Agassiz's Slave Daguerreotypes." *American Art* 9 (summer 1995): 39–61.

Walters, Wendy W. *Archives of the Black Atlantic: Reading between Literature and History.* New York: Routledge, 2013.

Warchol, Julie. "'Modeling with Light': Clarence Kennedy's Photographic Sculpture, 1924–1940." Master's thesis, School of the Art Institute of Chicago, 2015.

Weheliye, Alexander G. *Habeas Viscus: Racializing Assemblages, Biopolitics, and Black Feminist Theories of the Human.* Durham, NC: Duke University Press, 2014.

Westerbeck, Colin L. "Frederick Douglass Chooses His Moment." *Museum Studies* 24, no. 2 (1999): 144–61.

Westerbeck, Colin L. *The James VanDerZee Studio.* Chicago, IL: Art Institute of Chicago, 2004.

Wexler, Laura. "'A More Perfect Likeness': Frederick Douglass and the Image of the Nation." In *Pictures and Progress: Early Photography and the Making of African American Identity,* edited by Maurice O. Wallace and Shawn Michelle Smith, 18–40. Durham, NC: Duke University Press, 2012.

Wexler, Laura. *Tender Violence: Domestic Visions in an Age of U.S. Imperialism.* Chapel Hill: University of North Carolina Press, 2000.

Widholm, Julie Rodrigues. "The Moment of Creation." In *Rashid Johnson: Message to Our Folks,* 26–43. Chicago, IL: Museum of Contemporary Art, Chicago, 2012.

Willis, Deborah. *Let Your Motto Be Resistance.* Washington, DC: Smithsonian Institution, 2007.

Willis, Deborah. *Reflections in Black: A History of Black Photographers, 1840 to the Present.* New York: W. W. Norton, 2000.

Willis, Deborah. "Translating Black Power and Beauty—Carrie Mae Weems." *Callaloo* 35, no. 4 (2012): 993–95.

Willis-Braithwaite, Deborah. "They Knew Their Names." In *VanDerZee: Photographer, 1886–1983,* by Deborah Willis-Braithwaite, with biographical essay by Rodger C. Birt, 8–25. New York: Harry N. Abrams in association with the National Portrait Gallery, Smithsonian Institution, 1993.

Young, Elizabeth. "Verbal Battlefields." In *On Alexander Gardner's* Photographic Sketch Book *of the Civil War,* by Anthony W. Lee and Elizabeth Young, 52–94. Berkeley: University of California Press, 2007.

Zeller, Bob. *The Blue and the Gray in Black and White: A History of Civil War Photography.* Westport, CT: Praeger, 2005.

Zuromskis, Catherine. *Snapshot Photography: The Lives of Images.* Cambridge, MA: MIT Press, 2013.

INDEX